WITHDRAWN
UTSA LIBRARIES

THE STATUE OF AMERICUS VESPUCIUS IN THE PORTICO OF THE
UFFIZI PALACE IN FLORENCE.

THE CONTINENT OF AMERICA

ITS DISCOVERY AND
ITS BAPTISM

AN ESSAY ON THE NOMENCLATURE OF THE OLD CONTINENTS

A CRITICAL AND BIBLIOGRAPHICAL INQUIRY INTO THE NAMING OF AMERICA AND INTO THE GROWTH OF THE COSMOGRAPHY OF THE NEW WORLD; TOGETHER WITH AN ATTEMPT TO ESTABLISH THE LANDFALL OF COLUMBUS ON WATLING ISLAND, AND THE SUBSEQUENT DISCOVERIES AND EXPLORATIONS ON THE MAIN LAND BY AMERICUS VESPUCIUS

BY

JOHN BOYD THACHER

AMSTERDAM
MERIDIAN PUBLISHING CO
1971

Unabridged reprint of the edition
New York 1896

ISBN 90 6041 061 0

LIBRARY
University of Texas
At San Antonio

TO MY OWN
WIFE
WHOSE CHEERFUL COURAGE
KEPT THE PRESENT WORK IN HAND
FINDING FOR ME ODD MINUTES AND HOURS
OUT OF DAYS GIVEN TO THE EXACTIONS
OF TRYING PUBLIC SERVICE
THIS BOOK IS
DEDICATED

PREFACE

The chief purpose of this book is to establish the time and place of the naming of America. Baptism suggests birth, and the naming of America leads us back to its discovery. To speak of Vespucius is to tell of Columbus, and we have thus been persuaded by the association and sequence of important events to follow the first voyage of Columbus, the discoverer, and the first voyage of Vespucius, the explorer, and to determine with some degree of certainty the landfall of each.

It is no part of this inquiry to accompany the parent stock of the peoples of the Western Hemisphere across some ice-bridge in Bering Straits or over the stepping-stones of the Aleutian islands. We have no concern with the adventures of the Papæ of Ireland or with the followers of St. Brandon. The possible discoveries of Biarni Heriulsson and of Eric and of Leif and of Thorvald cannot interest us now. Nor can we listen to the story told the Zeni brothers by a shipwrecked sailor, of a country away to the south of Greenland where there were strange cities and great temples. The Columbian discovery, the opening of the New World, the bestowal of a name to distinguish it among the continental divisions of the earth, the explorations which revealed its contours —these are the subjects which invite us.

The greater portion of this book was prepared in the year 1893. Its publication has been delayed because, as it made its way through the press, certain subjects appealed for further elucidation, and thus both the text and the illustrations have been extended. We have reproduced in this book for the first time, in chronological order and in full size, all the important early American maps which appeared in printed and dated form.

The space consumed in the bibliographical discussion of the Vespucian letters is justified by the importance of the subject. Upon those letters hang the truth of the narrative and the right of Americus to be known as the discoverer of the continent and its *primus hospes*. The details employed in the description of maps and books may not be appreciated by the ordinary reader, but the student and the librarian will be reconciled to the introduction of information which will enable them to identify the genuine and to detect the false. Unless especially stated to the contrary, original examples of the books mentioned in the course of this work are in the library of the author, and thus the reader may have some assurance of the opportunity afforded for study and examination.

The water-mark which appeared in the paper used in the first edition of the *Cosmographiæ Introductio*, printed at St.-Dié in April 25 (old style), 1507, is reproduced in the hand-made paper specially prepared for this book.

Foot-notes have been discarded. If a statement is pertinent there is room for it in the home of the text, and care has been taken not to draw the reader's attention far from the subject.

We acknowledge the aid and advice of Professor J. Howard Gore in the preparation of our Part VII, treating of Scientific Geography; we owe to Captain Frank H. Mason the happy phrase we have used as a heading to Part V, and we are in debt of courtesy to the trustees of the Lenox Library, New York City, for permission to photograph some pages of the Eyriès copy of the *Cosmographiæ Introductio* and the Mercator map of 1538.

J. B. T.

ALBANY, October 21, 1895.

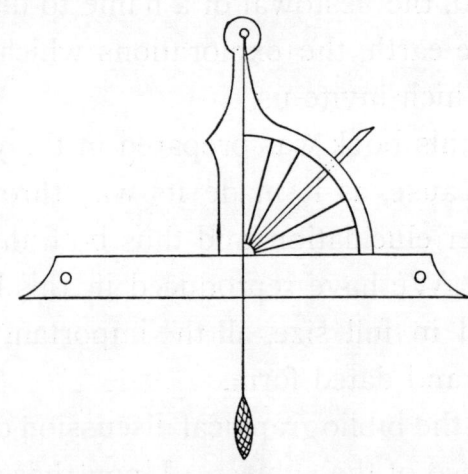

CONTENTS

Part I. Cosmography
Its Gradual Growth, with an Inquiry into the Nomenclature of the Old Continents

	PAGE
CHAPTER I. INTRODUCTORY	3
CHAPTER II. CHARTOGRAPHY OF THE OLD WORLD	8
CHAPTER III. NOMENCLATURE OF THE OLD CONTINENTS	16

Part II. The Discovery of the New World
The Landfall of Columbus, and the Establishment of Watling Island as Guanahani

	PAGE
CHAPTER I. GUANAHANI AND THE FIVE CLAIMANTS	23
CHAPTER II. THE TWO LETTERS AND THE "HISTORIE."	27
CHAPTER III. LAS CASAS' ABRIDGEMENT OF THE JOURNAL	31
CHAPTER IV. TRANSLATION OF LAS CASAS' ABRIDGEMENT	41
CHAPTER V. METHODS OF IDENTIFYING GUANAHANI	51
CHAPTER VI. WATLING ISLAND THE TRUE GUANAHANI	56

CONTENTS

Part III. The Life of Vespucius

With an Account of his Voyages, and an Attempt to Establish the Landfall on the Continent of North America

	PAGE
CHAPTER I.	
THE EARLY DAYS OF VESPUCIUS	61
CHAPTER II.	
THE ROYAL DECREES AND THE FIRST VOYAGE	65
CHAPTER III.	
THE LANDFALL ON THE CONTINENT	70
CHAPTER IV.	
DISCUSSION OF THE NARRATIVE	75
CHAPTER V.	
THE SECOND, THIRD, AND FOURTH VOYAGES	79

Part IV. The First Voyage of Vespucius

Its published Narration, with the Italian, Latin, and English Texts of the First Part of the Famous Letter

CHAPTER I.	
THE FIRST VOYAGE OF AMERICUS VESPUCIUS WITH THE ITALIAN, LATIN, AND ENGLISH TEXTS	87

Part V. The Baptismal Font of America

St.-Dié, the little Town in the Vosges Mountains where the New World was Christened

CHAPTER I.	
ST.-DIÉ IN LORRAINE	115
CHAPTER II.	
THE COTERIE OF THREE	117
CHAPTER III.	
THE PRESS OF ST.-DIÉ	119

CONTENTS

Part VI. The "Cosmographiæ Introductio"

The Book which Conferred the Name America; with a Review of the Four Alleged Editions Printed at St.-Dié in 1507

	PAGE
CHAPTER I.	
THE INCEPTION OF THE WORK	125
CHAPTER II.	
THE ALLEGED FOUR EDITIONS	129
CHAPTER III.	
THE ROMANCE OF THE UNIQUE EDITION	132
CHAPTER IV.	
THE REAL PRIORITY OF THE ALLEGED SECOND EDITION	140
CHAPTER V.	
THE BAPTISMAL WORDS	145
CHAPTER VI.	
THE LOST MAP	149
CHAPTER VII.	
THE LOST MAP, CONCLUDED	154
CHAPTER VIII.	
THE END OF THE LITTLE TREATISE ON GEOGRAPHY	159
CHAPTER IX.	
THE SECOND TRACT ON THE FOUR VOYAGES OF AMERICUS VESPUCIUS	162

Part VII. Scientific Geography

CHAPTER I.

THE SCIENCE AMONG THE ANCIENTS—THE COMPUTATIONS OF ERATOSTHENES . . . 169

CHAPTER II.

CLAUDIUS PTOLEMY, AND HIS CONTRIBUTIONS TO THE SCIENCE . 174

CONTENTS

CHAPTER III.
THE UNIT OF MEASURE EMPLOYED BY THE ANCIENTS 178

CHAPTER IV.
MODERN GEOGRAPHY: ITS UNIT OF MEASURE AND THE LENGTH OF A DEGREE 181

CHAPTER V.
GEOGRAPHICAL INSTRUMENTS IN USE IN THE TIME OF COLUMBUS . 186

CHAPTER VI.
MERCATOR'S PROJECTIONS. 189

Part VIII. The Chartography of the New World
The Contour of the Continent as it was developed on the Early Maps

CHAPTER I.
THE FIRST MAP OF THE OLD AND NEW WORLDS 195

CHAPTER II.
THE FIRST MAP — CONTINUED 199

CHAPTER III.
THE CANTINO AND CANERIO MANUSCRIPT MAPS 205

CHAPTER IV.
THE RUYSCH MAP 209

CHAPTER V.
LEGENDS ON THE RUYSCH MAP 212

CHAPTER VI.
NOMENCLATURE OF THE RUYSCH MAP 216

CHAPTER VII.
THE PTOLEMY AND PETER MARTYR MAPS OF 1511 220

CHAPTER VIII.
THE STOBNICZA PTOLEMY OF 1512 226

CONTENTS

CHAPTER IX.
THE WALDSEEMÜLLER PTOLEMY OF 1513 229

CHAPTER X.
THE FIRST MAP WITH THE NAME OF AMERICA 239

CHAPTER XI.
FATA VIAM INVENIENT 244

CHAPTER XII.
THE BACKWARD STEP REGAINED 250

CHAPTER XIII.
THE STATUE OF AMERICA 253

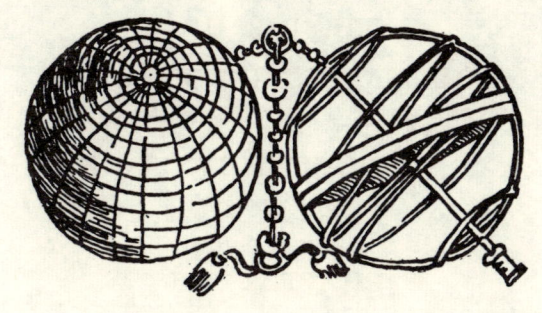

LIST OF ILLUSTRATIONS

THE STATUE OF AMERICUS VESPUCIUS IN THE PORTICO OF THE UFFIZI
PALACE IN FLORENCE . . . . Frontispiece

Part I. Cosmography

	PAGE
THE WORLD OF HOMER (B. C. 962–927)	9
THE WORLD OF HECATÆUS (B. C. 550–480)	10
THE WORLD OF HERODOTUS (B. C. 484–406)	11
THE WORLD OF ERATOSTHENES (B. C. 276–194)	12
THE WORLD OF STRABO (B. C. 54–A. D. 24)	13
THE WORLD OF POMPONIUS MELA (A. D. 50)	14
THE WORLD OF DIONYSIUS PERIEGETES (B. C. 30 [?]–A. D. 150 [?])	15

Part II. The Discovery of the New World

MAP FROM CAPTAIN BECHER'S "THE LANDFALL OF COLUMBUS" facing 26
FACSIMILE OF THE TITLE-PAGE OF THE "HISTORIE" OF COLUMBUS, 1571, 28
WATLING ISLAND, SHOWING THE LANDING PLACE OF COLUMBUS, facing 56

Part III. The Life of Vespucius

FACSIMILE AUTOGRAPH OF VESPUCIUS 61
FACSIMILE LETTER OF VESPUCIUS TO HIS FATHER 62
FACSIMILE AUTOGRAPH LETTER OF PIER SODERINI
FACSIMILE AUTOGRAPH OF GEORG ANTONIUS VESPUCIUS } facing 62
FACSIMILE AUTOGRAPH OF RENÉ, DUKE OF LORRAINE
CHART OF THE VOYAGES OF VESPUCIUS ADAPTED FROM VARNHAGEN, facing 78

Part IV. The First Voyage of Vespucius

FACSIMILE TITLE-PAGE OF THE FIRST (ITALIAN) EDITION OF THE
LETTER OF VESPUCIUS DESCRIBING HIS VOYAGES . . . facing 87

Part V. The Baptismal Font of America

VIEWS OF THE BAPTISMAL FONT OF AMERICA . . . . facing 115

THE TOWN OF ST.-DIÉ, IN LORRAINE. FROM AN ORIGINAL DRAWING OF THE SIXTEENTH CENTURY . . . . . . facing 119

Part VI. The "Cosmographiæ Introductio"

COLLATIONS OF THE VARIOUS ST.-DIÉ EDITIONS OF THE "COSMOGRAPHIÆ INTRODUCTIO" . . . . facing 125

FACSIMILE PAGES OF TEXT OF THE "COSMOGRAPHIÆ INTRODUCTIO" 134–137

FACSIMILE WOODCUT IN THE "COSMOGRAPHIÆ INTRODUCTIO" . . 147

FACSIMILE OF ADVERTISEMENT IN THE "COSMOGRAPHIÆ INTRODUCTIO" 148

FACSIMILE OF THE PAGES IN "COSMOGRAPHIÆ INTRODUCTIO" WHICH NAMED AMERICA 158

FACSIMILE PAGES OF THE SECOND TRACT ON THE FOUR VOYAGES OF VESPUCIUS 164

Part VII. Scientific Geography

PORTRAIT OF PTOLEMY, FROM THE "MARGARITA PHILOSOPHICA," 1504 . 175

MAP OF THE WORLD, SHOWING LOCATIONS AT WHICH DEGREES OF LATITUDE HAVE BEEN MEASURED TO DETERMINE THE CIRCUMFERENCE OF THE EARTH . . . . facing 181

FACSIMILE LETTER OF MERCATOR 191

Part VIII. The Chartography of the New World

THE MAP OF JUAN DE LA COSA, DRAWN ABOUT 1500 ON OX-HIDE, THE FIRST MAP SHOWING THE NEW DISCOVERIES . . . facing 195

TITLE PAGE OF THE ORTELIUS OF 1570, IN WHICH FOR THE FIRST TIME THE CONTINENT OF AMERICA WAS SYMBOLIZED BY A HUMAN FIGURE . . . . facing 254

LIST OF MAPS

Facsimile Reproductions, Exact Size of Original Maps

(CHRONOLOGICALLY ARRANGED AT END OF THIS VOLUME)

THE FIRST ENGRAVED MAP OF THE WORLD, FROM THE PTOLEMY GEOGRAPHY OF 1478.

PORTION OF A MAP FROM THE PTOLEMY GEOGRAPHY OF 1482, SHOWING GREENLAND FOR THE FIRST TIME.

RUYSCH MAP, 1507–8. THE FIRST ENGRAVED MAP SHOWING THE NEW WORLD.

MAP OF THE NEW WORLD. FROM THE SYLVANUS PTOLEMY OF 1511.

MAP OF THE NEW WORLD, FROM PETER MARTYR'S "FIRST DECADE," SEVILLE, 1511, SHOWING THE COAST OF FLORIDA BEFORE THE PONCE DE LEON DISCOVERY.

MAP OF THE WORLD FROM THE PTOLEMY GEOGRAPHY PRINTED IN CRACOW ABOUT 1512.

MAP FROM THE PTOLEMY GEOGRAPHY PRINTED AT STRASBURG IN 1513. MADE BY WALDSEEMÜLLER ABOUT 1507, SHOWING THE DISCOVERIES OF VESPUCIUS.

MAP OF THE WORLD, BY APIANUS. FROM SOLINUS POLYHISTORIA, 1520. THE FIRST MAP CONTAINING THE NAME AMERICA.

PORTION OF A MAP FROM THE PTOLEMY GEOGRAPHY OF 1522.

MAP OF ORONTIUS FINE. MADE IN 1531, AND PUBLISHED IN THE PARIS GRYNAEUS OF 1532.

THE MERCATOR MAP OF 1538, THE FIRST TO APPLY THE NAME AMERICA TO THE ENTIRE WESTERN CONTINENT.

MAP FROM THE MUNSTER EDITION OF PTOLEMY'S GEOGRAPHY, PRINTED AT BASLE IN 1540.

MAP OF THE NEW WORLD, BY GASTALDI. FROM THE FIRST ITALIAN EDITION OF PTOLEMY'S GEOGRAPHY OF 1548.

WESTERN HALF OF WORLD—MAP FROM THE ATLAS OF ORTELIUS, 1570.

The Continent of America

A Series of Fourteen Maps
from 1478 to 1570
showing the gradual growth of the geographical
knowledge of the New World,
and the development of its contour lines
as depicted by contemporary scholars.

PART I

Cosmography

Its gradual Growth, with an Inquiry into the Nomenclature of the Old Continents

PART 1

THE CONTINENT OF AMERICA

CHAPTER I

Introductory

AMERICA — *quarta orbis pars* — alone of the divisions of the earth can show the record of its birth and the certificate of its baptism. The twenty-first day of October (New Style) is the anniversary of the discovery of the New World, and the fifth day of May (New Style) is the anniversary of its christening.

The propriety of the name given to the New World has been questioned for nearly four centuries. The time and place and circumstances of its baptism have been understood only within the last fifty years. For generations Americus Vespucius was regarded as an unjust man reaping where another had sown, and by fraud bestowing his name upon a land discovered by another. In 1837 Alexander von Humboldt published in Paris the fourth volume of his "Examen Critique de l'Histoire et de la Géographie du Nouveau Continent." This author unearthed a book printed in 1507 at St.-Dié, Lorraine, which bore witness to the innocence of Americus Vespucius in fastening his name on the New World. This book was the "Cosmographiæ Introductio," or "Rudiments of Geography," and is to-day, as it always will be, one of the most interesting books connected with American history. Besides the little work on the rudiments of geography, this book contains the four voyages of Vespucius translated from French into Latin, the former being itself a translation from an Italian original. In discussing the history of the naming of our continent, we must discuss the propriety of the name, and in discussing the propriety of the name we are forced to consider the credibility of these voyages. There are those who will interpret the agitation of these questions as intended to take from Christopher Columbus something of his honor, and to remove his statue to a less conspicuous niche in the temple of fame. No one can take the wreath from the brow of the true hero. Heroes differ from each other as the stars differ one from another. The glory of the first discoverer is one glory, and the glory of the subsequent explorer is another glory. The shadow of the latter never hides the bright light which falls on the discoverer. And so, placing Americus Vespucius the Florentine in his right place in history will not obscure the glorified figure of Christopher Columbus the Genoese. Between Columbus with his mighty purpose, his unyielding faith supported by the instinct of a cloistered priest and a sympathetic woman, sailing out into unknown seas which the imagination filled with horrible monsters and countless dangers—between this man and any subsequent navigator there is a gulf which neither leagues nor years can ever cross. Napoleon is none the less the first soldier of history because Ney had a will of iron, or because Murat could ride fast on horseback.

Columbus himself had no jealousy of Americus, although he must have known of his voyages. The original of the following letter from Columbus to his son Diego is still in the possession of the Duke of Veragua:

Muy caro fijo: Diego Mendez partió de aquí lunes tres de este mes. Despues de partido fablé con Amerigo Vespuchi, portador desta, el cual va allá llamado sobre cosas de navegacion.— El siempre tuvo deseo de me hacer placer: es mucho hombre de bien: la fortuna le ha sido contraria como á otros muchos: sus trabajos no le han aprovechado tanto como la razon requiere. El va por mio y en mucho deseo de hacer cosa que redonde á mi bien, si á sus manos está. Yo non sé de acá en que yo le emponga que á mi aproveche, porque non sé que sea lo que allá le quieren. El va determinado de hacer por mí todo lo á él que fuere posible. Ved allá en que puede aprovechar, y trabajad por ello, que el lo hará todo y fablará, y lo porná en obra; y sea todo secretamente porque non se haya dél sospecha. Yo, todo lo que se haya podido decir que toque á esto, se lo he dicho, y enformado de la paga que á mí se ha fecho y se haz. . . .
Fecha en Sevilla á cinco de Febrero.
Tu padre que te ama mas que á sí,
S.
S. A. S.
X M Y
XPO FERENS.—

Henry Harrisse, in his "Notes on Columbus," a privately printed edition of only ninety-nine copies (New York, 1861), translated this letter as follows:

My very dear Son: Diego Mendez left this place on Monday the 3d instant. Since his departure I have spoken with Amerigo Vespuchi, the bearer of this, who has been summoned to the court for business relating to navigation. He has always shown himself anxious to be useful to me; he is a very honest man; he has been unlucky, like many others, and his labors have not profited him, as he had a right to expect. He leaves this place, entertaining the best dispositions towards me, and with a strong desire to do something in my behalf if he possibly can. I do not know what commission to give him that might be useful to me, for I am not aware of the purpose for which he has been called to the court. He leaves, determined to do for me all he can. See how he may be made useful to me, for he will do everything; he will do and resort to all things; and let all this be done secretly, that he may not be suspected. So far as I am concerned, I have told him as regards my business everything, and informed him how I have been and how I am rewarded for my labors. . . .

Seville, February 5th [1505].

Thy father, who loves thee more than he loves himself,

S.
S. A. S.
X M Y
XPO FERENS.

In No. CXXVI of the "Documentos Diplomaticos" as given by Navarrete, Vol. II, page 229, we discover the following passage governing the entail:

D. Diego, mi hijo, ó cualquier otro que heredare este mayorazgo, despues de haber heredado y estado en posesion de ello, firme de mi firma, la cual agora acostumbro, que es una X con una S encima, y una M con una A romana encima, y encima della una S y despues una Y griega con una S encima con sus rayas y virgulas.

Don Diego, my son, or any other who shall inherit this entail, after inheriting and coming into possession of the same, shall sign with my signature which I now make use of, which is an X with an S over it, and an M with a Roman A over it, and over that an S, and then a Greek Y, with an S over it, with its lines and commas.

The ingenuity of four centuries has been occupied with the interpretation of the mysterious characters of this signature. Ferdinand Columbus tells us that his father had the habit of always trying his pen before writing, and generally first penned the words, *Jesus cum Maria sit nobis in via.* In a will executed on the 22d of February in the year 1498, he signs the document with the following characters:

·S·
S· A· S·
X M Y
El Almirante.

Some have read these characters as follows: *Servidor sus Altezas sacras, Cristo, Maria, Isabel.*

Others have read them, *Servus supplex Altissimi salvatoris, Christus, Maria, Josephus.*

In "Notes and Queries," a writer suggested the letters as the initials of these words: *Salve sancta alma sanctissimi Christi Mater* υἱῷ Χρίξῳ *ferens el Almirante.*

The cipher is generally read by taking the third line first and reading the "X" as the initial Greek letter of *Christus*, the last letter of *Christus* being "s," the first letter of the second line—and so on, reading from below upwards:

```
S       A       S
 o              u
  t      i       h
   s             p
    i    r       e
     p           s
                  o
X       M       Y
```
Christopher.

It will be shown further on that the four voyages of Vespucius were printed in the Italian language several months before this letter was written, and from the many editions we have—although most of them are undated—it is impossible that their publication should not have been known to Columbus; and yet he forms an inner circle of friendship to which he admits himself, his son Diego, and the honest, faithful, tried Americus Vespucius.

Ferdinand Columbus was the Admiral's son by Beatrix Enriquez, a lady with whom the discoverer fell in love when in his fifty-second year. The son had two virtues: one was his pride in his father's achievements; the other was his love for books. He collected a library of twenty thousand volumes, many of which had been the property of the Admiral himself. This magnificent library was presented by Ferdinand Columbus to the cathedral of Seville; and, although many books and manuscripts have been lost, it is still a valuable collection, and forms to-day what is known as the Columbian Library of Seville. He was an indefatigable annotator, as was his father before him, and many of his books are filled with his manuscript notes. Among the books in this library over which Ferdinand Columbus had pored, and the leaves of which he had filled with marginal notes, was a copy of the "Cosmographiæ Introductio," printed at Strasburg in 1509, identical in all essential points with the St.-Dié editions of 1507. There, staring him in the face, was the twice-uttered suggestion that the *quarta orbis pars* should be called America after its discoverer Americus; and there, confronting him, was the plain distinct narrative of the first Vespucian voyage, undertaken in May, 1497. Yet there is no word of dissent. This son was so sensitive of his father's good name that, stung with the allusion to his lowly birth (*vilibus ortus parentibus*) in the note by Giustiniani accompanying the XIXth psalm in the Polyglot Psalter printed in Genoa in 1516, he wrote and prepared the "Historie," to do justice to the Admiral's lineage and virtues. Would such a son tacitly admit the claim of Americus that he had put his foot on continental land a full year before his father if it had not been true? and, being true, was not the finder entitled to have his own name given it? His father was none the less the great first discoverer; indeed, Americus himself in the account of his second voyage — a fact greatly overlooked — gives the credit for the discovery of the *islands* to Columbus. To be tenderly solicitous for the memory of those who have done great things in the world is the pleasant duty of succeeding generations. To resent every critical inquiry into the surroundings of a hero or the exploits of his followers is to cast reflection on the stability and self-sustaining character of that hero's glory. Columbus is one of the few giant figures of the world. We may stand before him and praise him and his works. We need not be troubled to place his statue in position, or shift it for the morning and the evening light. It stands to-day, as it has stood these four hundred years, and as it will stand forever, great, grand, colossal.

CHAPTER II

Chartography of the Old World

IF the origin and distribution of the human race are ever correctly traced, it will be by means of language, by the identity or similarity of names of peoples, places, and things. The soil does not produce its people, as the ancient Greeks believed. We have been taught that the earth has been peopled by movements from the mountain-sides of Ararat. Speculation travels in circles, but, as each round in the speculation on the origin and diffusion of the human race is completed, it has failed to substitute a more believable account than the history of mankind as written by Moses, in which we are told that the sons of Noah are the three roots from which have come the countless children of men. The movements were westward to the Mediterranean, eastward to beyond the Caspian Sea, and southward to the Persian Gulf. New homes, new conditions, new employments, modified and changed the speech and language of the settlers, creating new dialects until now only a few words remain to tell the story of a common origin. These words are mostly names of places, and are monuments marking the roads over which the tribes passed to new homes and distant countries.

The beginning of geography is in these early journeyings. The peoples who scattered over the Asiatic and European continents gave to countries and seas names which had a common source in the Aryan language. It is apparent that, if we are to trace the names of the great divisions of the earth given by the ancients and retained by us, we must look for their origin in some language close to the parent-speech. Before inquiring into the nomenclature of the continents it will be well to look at the development of these geographical divisions in the form of maps.

The Homeric poems furnish us with materials for the first map of the world. The earth is a flat disk, with an outer periphery of water called the river Oceanus. There are two unnamed divisions, with a boundary line running from the northeast to the southwest. (See Plate 1.)

The exact science of geography tells us how large a part of these Homeric writings are imaginative. The voyages of Ulysses and his companions would not be considered in our day very extensive or daring. No adventurer at the time of the Trojan war had gone out into the river Oceanus, the broad Atlantic. The two divisions are not designated by names, although probably they had been called for generations by the same titles we give them now.

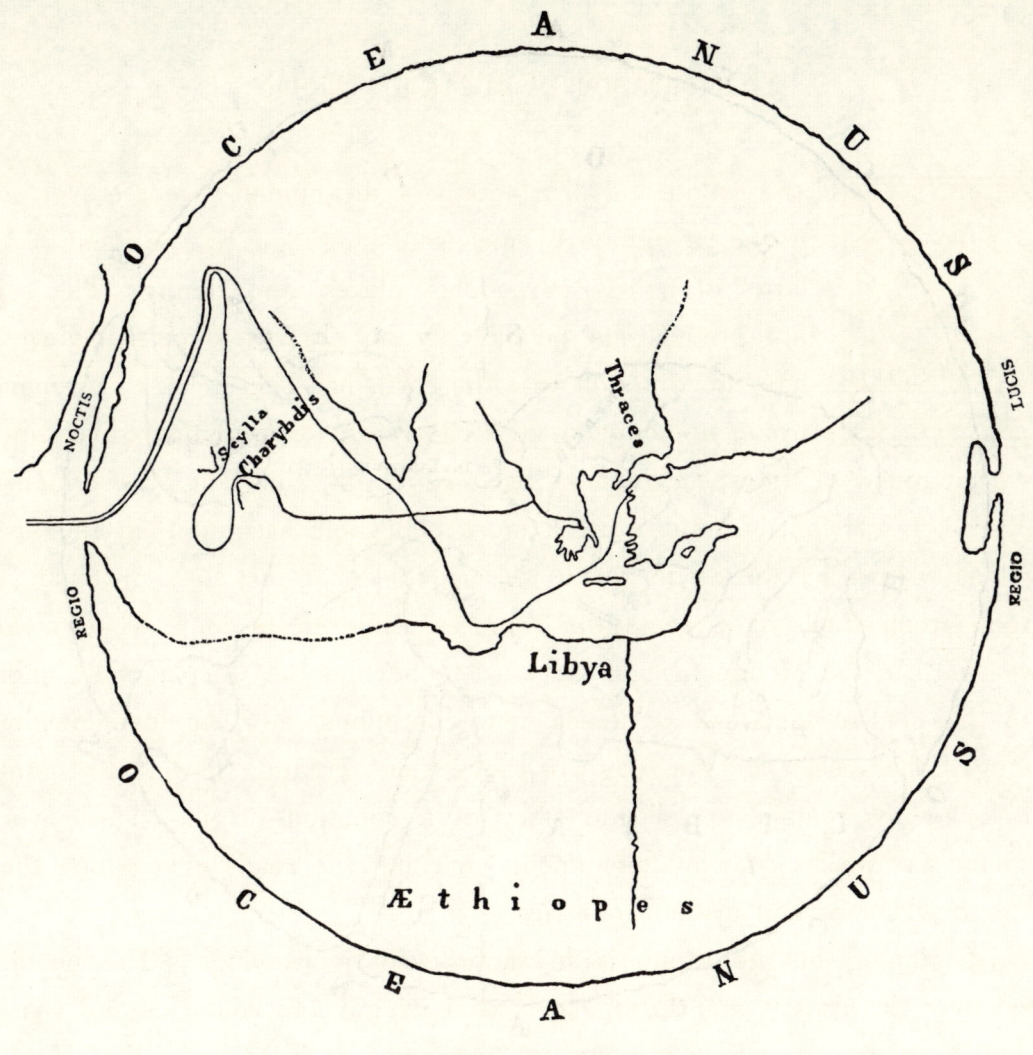

1. HOMER (B. C. 962–927).

Homer, in the second book of the Iliad, speaks of Ἀσίῳ ἐν λειμῶνι, but he refers evidently to the meadow-lands of Asias, the King of Lydia. On this map we see antipodal designations which we believe we shall be able to show further on were the real and natural geographical terms afterward, and from a primitive language, applied to the divisions of the earth. The East is *Regio lucis*, and the West *Regio noctis*. Libya appears as a district, not as a continent. Homer's allusion to the "Isles of the Blessed," in the fourth book of the Odyssey, is, of course, purely imaginative. The West, unknown and mysterious, was the home of the departed, the restful Elysium. The "Fortunate Isles," out in the West Atlantic, were unknown to Homer.

Hecatæus the Milesian, who flourished between 550 and 480 B. C., has left us fragments of a work on geography from which a map can be constructed showing the world in two divisions—Europe being all that portion north and west of the *Nostrum*

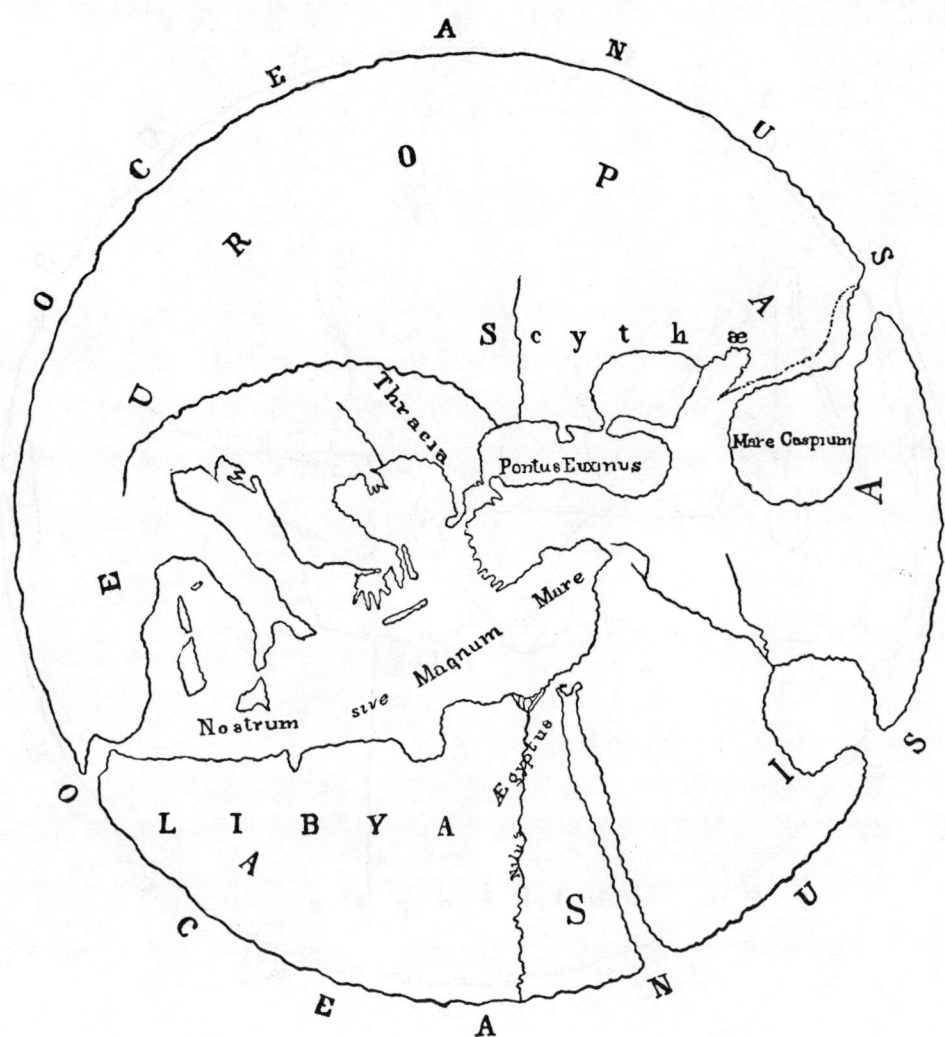

2. HECATÆUS (B. C. 550–480).

Mare (Mediterranean Sea), the *Pontus Euxinus* (Black Sea), and the *Mare Caspium* (Caspian Sea), and Asia all that portion south and east of these seas, including Libya. (See Plate 2.)

Some writers have reported that the map made by Hecatæus was engraved upon metal. Herodotus, book v, describing the interview which Aristagoras of Miletus had at Sparta with Cleomenes, says: "He brought with him a brazen tablet, on which was engraved the entire circuit of the earth, with all its seas and rivers." If so, it is the only map on metal of which we have record until the Ptolemaic maps were printed on copper by Arnold Buckinck at Rome in 1478. A copy of this 1478 edition was in the possession of Christopher Columbus, and is still preserved, enriched with the autographic annotations of that great man. It has been said that Hecatæus did not devise but simply improved a map sketched by Anaximander, a citizen of Miletus and a disciple of Thales. Diogenes Laertius says of Anaximander: "He was the first person who made a map of the earth and sea, and also a globe, and showed the solstices and equinoxes."

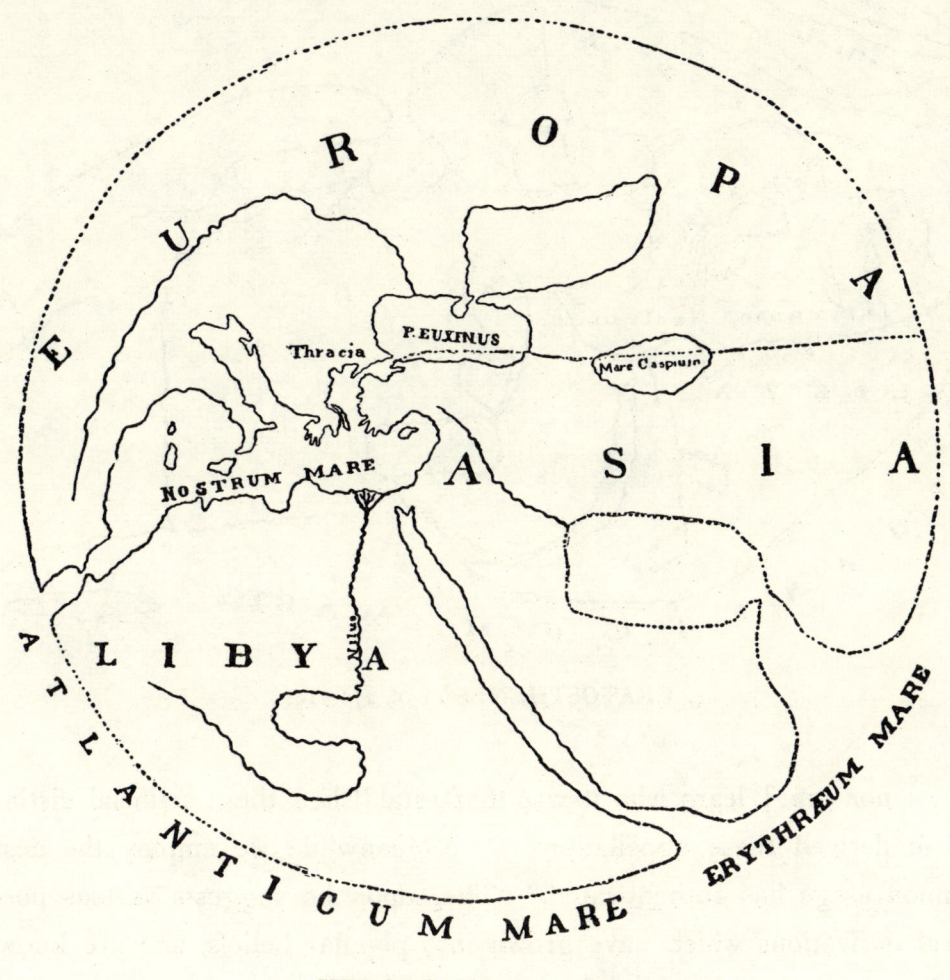

3. HERODOTUS (B. C. 484–406).

Herodotus, who lived 484–406 B. C., the most learned of Greeks and the most delightful of the early prose-writers, gives us a map of the world with the three continents designated thereon, Asia, Europe, and Libya (Africa), the latter being divided from Asia by the Arabian Sea. (See Plate 3.)

The Pillars of Hercules are here seen for the first time, Ximiera in Africa and Gibraltar in Europe, forming the Straits of Gades of the time of Columbus. The ancients believed that Hercules opened these rocks to let in the Atlantic, and that here his labors ended. Herodotus denies that there is a sea on the farther side of Europe, and declares it the invention of a poet. He says (book IV, 45): "But as to Europe, no one hitherto has discovered whether on the north and on the east it is surrounded by the sea. In extent it is known to reach as far as both Asia and Libya. Nor can I conjecture why, as the earth is one, it has received three names — the names of

4. ERATOSTHENES (B. C. 276-194).

women; ... nor can I learn who it was that established these artificial distinctions, or whence were derived these appellations. ... Meanwhile we employ the designations which common usage has authenticated." Thereupon he suggests various poetical and mythological derivations which have grown into popular beliefs, and are known to the school-children of to-day.

Chronological order suggests our noting here what Plato, the philosopher, said of the sphericity of the earth, because it was his theory, fortified by Strabo four hundred years later, and then for more than one thousand years almost forgotten, that led Toscanelli to write his letter to Columbus — which in turn led to the discovery of the New World. In the third section of his treatise on Timæus the Locrian, Plato says: "The world, too, is in a good state, as regards its shape and movement; as regards the former, in being a sphere, so that it is similar to itself on all sides and is able to contain all the rest of shapes of the same kind as itself; as regards the latter, in exhibiting forever the changes dependent on a circle." It is interesting to note here that the first printed edition of Plato translated out of Greek into Latin by Marsilius Ficinus was edited by Georgius Antonius Vespucius, the uncle of our Americus, and under whom Americus studied at Florence.

Eratosthenes, a native of Cyrene, flourished between 276 and 194 B. C. He may be called the first real cosmographer. He first attempted to measure the extent and circumference of the earth. The Alexandrian library was in his charge, and his knowledge and industry increased its munificent equipment. His map marks an advance in discoveries and voyaging. The river Nilus divides Asia from Libya. Some bold navigator had visited Britain, and even beyond, for we see Thule situated, as Pliny afterward said, a six days' sail beyond and to the northeast of Britain. (See Plate 4.)

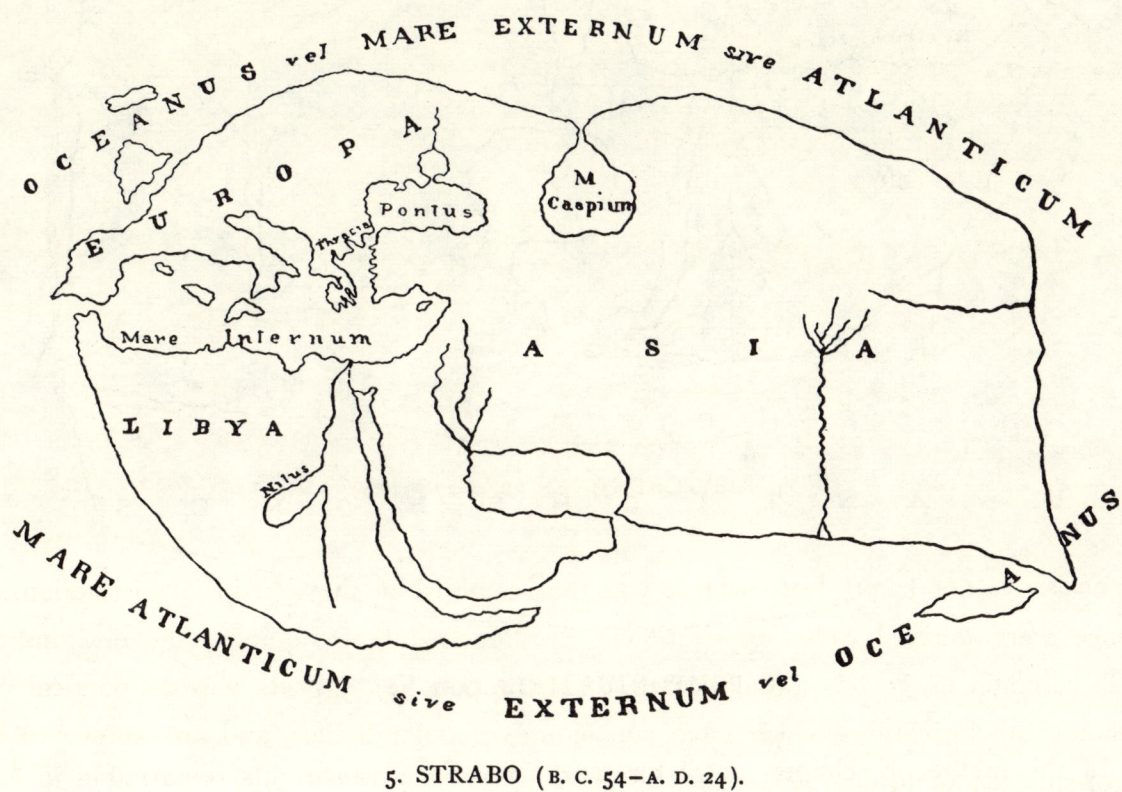

5. STRABO (B. C. 54–A. D. 24).

Pliny, book IV, says that the most remote northern land is Thule, "in which there is no night at the summer solstice, when the sun is passing through the sign of Cancer, while on the other hand at the winter solstice there is no day." Some writers made this Thule of Pliny's identical with Thylemark in Norway. The general opinion is that the Thule laid down by Eratosthenes is Iceland, to which our Columbus made his first long sea-voyage in 1477, if the account in the "History of Columbus" by his son Ferdinand, printed in 1571, may be believed.

Strabo, the celebrated Greek geographer, lived from 54 B. C. to the twenty-fourth year of our era. His is the most pretentious and valuable geographical work of the ancients. In his map Libya is separted from Asia by the *Sinus Arabicus;* but there is no mention of Africa either as a province or the larger continental designation. (See Plate 5.)

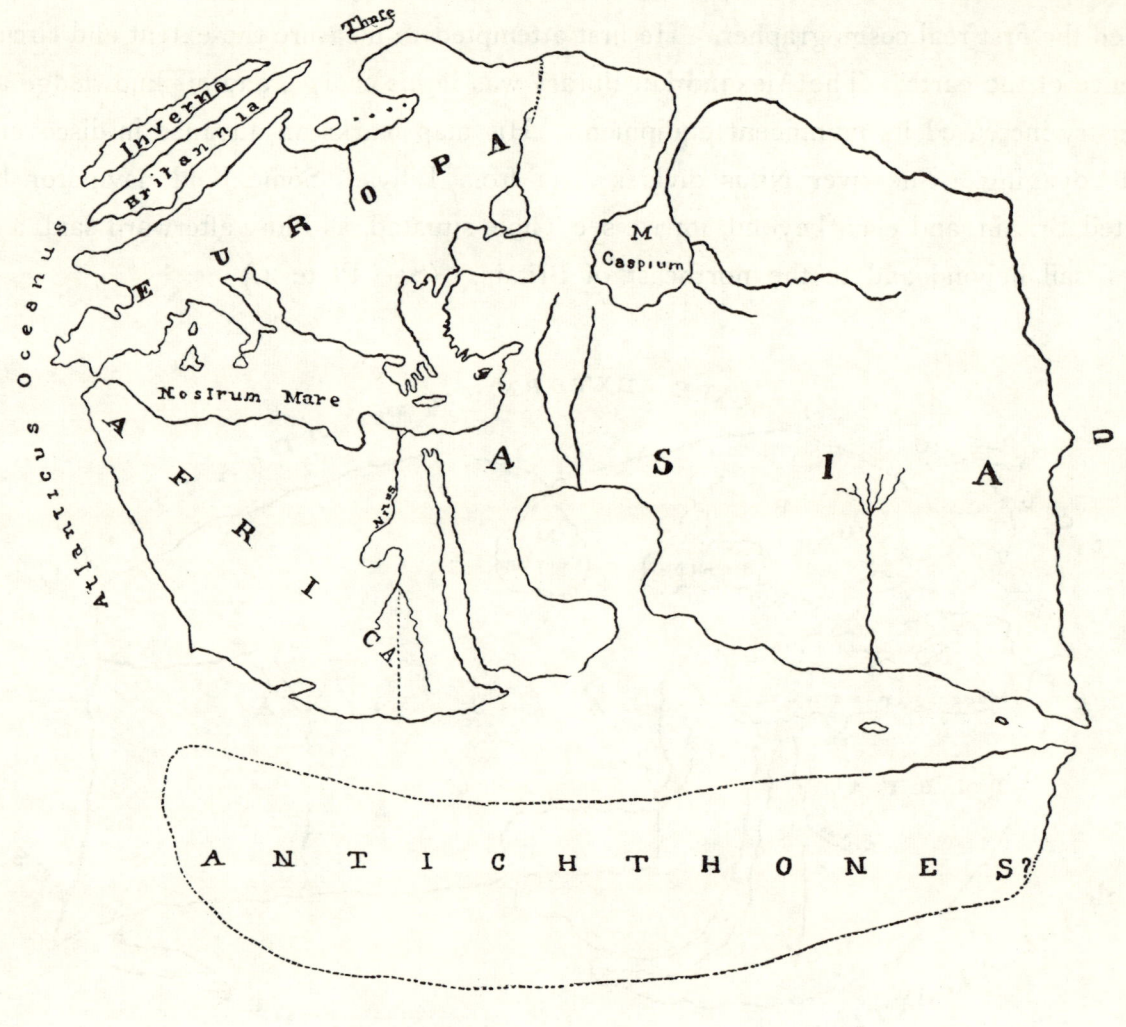

6. POMPONIUS MELA (A. D. 50).

In the first book, chapter 4, of his work, Strabo advances his remarkable idea — remarkable because, as suggested above, it was the direct but long-delayed *motif* which led to the discovery of America, and which gave to the Bahama Islands, Haiti, and Cuba the name of the West Indies. Strabo says: "The temperate zone, which we have already designated as the longest zone, is that which the mathematicians denominated a continuous circle returning upon itself. So that, if the extent of the Atlantic Ocean were not an obstacle, we might easily pass by sea from Iberia to India, still keeping in the same parallel." It is peculiarly appropriate that the new era should have produced this great man, who first of all pointed the way around the globe. Nearly fifteen centuries passed before there was born a soul great enough to try the unknown but certain path. Some day, when we have reached the statue-building age, we will raise a monument to Strabo of Amasia.

Pomponius Mela, the earliest Roman geographer, is the first to distinguish on a map the three continents by the names they now bear. Libya gives place to Africa both in designating the Roman province of Africa, including the territory about Carthage, and its larger application to the continent. Following the plan of Eratosthenes, the Nile separates Africa from Asia. (See Plate 6.)

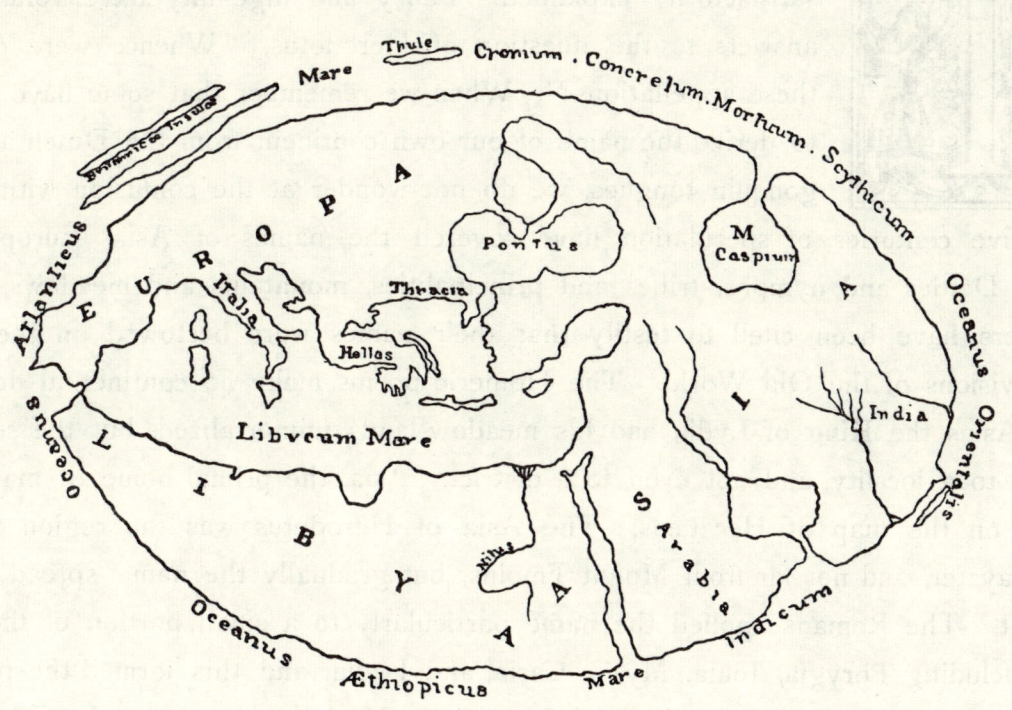

7. DIONYSIUS PERIEGETES (B. C. 30 [?]–A. D. 150 [?]).

Dionysius Periegetes, the geographer, a native of Arabia Felix, lived about 150 A. D., as Scaliger says. Upon his map the Nile still bounds Asia on the west, but the third continent is called Libya, and not Africa, nor is the Roman province so designated. (See Plate 7.)

Claudius Ptolemæus, the founder of modern geography, was an Egyptian by birth, and lived in Alexandria about the middle of the second century. His geographical writings, in eight books, were the authority until the beginning of the sixteenth century, and we will see in another chapter that it was while contemplating and preparing a new edition of Ptolemy, in 1507, that the little band of students in the Vosgian Gymnase conceived the idea of calling the New World after the Florentine navigator Americus Vespucius.

CHAPTER III

Nomenclature of the Old Continents

HE nomenclature of the continents of the Old World will never be satisfactorily explained. Fancy and ingenuity have volunteered answers to the question of Herodotus, "Whence were derived these appellations?" When we remember that some have sought to derive the name of our own continent from the Dutch and Algonquin tongues, we do not wonder at the confusion with which twenty-five centuries of speculation have covered the names of Asia, Europe, and Africa. Deities and nymphs, tribes and principalities, mountains and meadows, winds and rivers have been cited to testify that their names were bestowed on the three great divisions of the Old World. The Homeric poems make no continental designations. Asias the King of Lydia had his meadow-lands immortalized, but the sense is confined to a locality, and not even to a district. Asia, the primal home of man, first appears on the map of Hecatæus. The Asia of Herodotus was the region around about Cayster, and not far from Mount Tmolus, but gradually the name spread to the continent. The Romans applied the name particularly to a small portion of the peninsula including Phrygia, Ionia, Mysia, Caria, and Lydia, and this formed the proconsular province of Asia in the time of Augustus. Mythologists trace the derivation to the nymph of whom Marcus Terentius Varro, in his "De Lingua Latina," says: "Asia dicta ab nympha, ex qua et Japeto trahitur Prometheus." Others have declared this nymph to be a daughter of Oceanus and Tethys. There was another of this name, Asia Perfecta, the wife of Pharaoh, who cared for Moses, and whom Mahomet placed in that quartet of perfect women, Asia, Mary, Khadyah, and Fatima. Smith, in his "Dictionary of Greek and Roman Geography," calls attention to the fact that in this mythical genealogy Asia is of the Titanic race, while Europa is of the race of Zeus. This Titan, Japetus, was the young man with shepherd staff who came down the mountain-side of Ararat with his brothers Ham and Shem to people anew the earth. The name of Asia is by others derived from Ash-Kenaz, from the location on the shores of the Euxine and its situation in Asia Minor. Malte-Brun illustrates the

natural extension of a geographical appellation from a part to the whole by the duchy of Allemagne, which was made to stand for the whole of Germany, and by the district of Italia in a far-off corner of Calabria, which gave its name to the great peninsula. D'Anville says that Europe and Africa, as well as Asia, have had the names of districts extended to cover their entire continents. The Phœnicians derived the name from a root signifying "of the sun," and hence, as we may say, the East. Some have sought to derive the name from the Etesian winds which blew steadily from the north and northwest for forty days during the season of the dog-days. Pliny says Phrygia in the western part of Asia was the first part of the Asiatic continent which received the name of Asia; this district was bounded on the east by Lycaonia, on the west by the Ægean Sea, on the south by the Egyptian Sea, and on the north by Paphlagonia. Bochart derives the name of Asia from a Hebrew or Phœnician word signifying "the middle," meaning that Europe was on one side and Africa on the other. The river Orontes in Syria was sometimes called *El Asi*, or "the reversed,"—"the obstinate," as some etymologists have it,—alluding to its course, which is the opposite to that of the Euphrates and Tigris.

The popular derivation of Europe is from *Europa*, the daughter of Agenor, King of Phœnicia, and of Telephassa. Jupiter, disguised as a bull, carried her to the island of Crete. One can see no connection between this fable and the continent, for Europa was carried from Syria to Crete and thence, as some say, to Africa; in any event there is no reference to her having set foot in the land called Europe. Diodorus tells the story, with a brave ship-captain called Taurus—bull—for the hero, and others say she was carried off by a Cretan merchant-ship whose prow bore the figure of a bull's head. Hesiod, in the "Theogony," mentions both Europa and Asia as the daughters of Oceanus and Tethys. Pomponius Mela and the early writers declare the continent to be named after her. Some have derived the name from the worship of *Eur-op*, "the serpent of the sun." The Greek words εὐρός, "broad," and ὠπή, "view," have been suggested by some as the origin of the name, referring to the broad view afforded the inhabitant of Asia as he looked upon the coast-line of the opposite continent. In the Scriptures Europe is the land of the Gentiles. Εὖρος, the southeast wind, has also, been thought the possible derivation of the word. In the Homeric Hymn to Apollo there is allusion to the land of Europe, suggesting a possible continental signification. The passage occurs where the god, after declaring his purpose to build a temple which shall be an oracle to men, says:

Ἠμὲν ὅσοι Πελοπόννησον πίειραν ἔχουσιν
Ἠδ' ὅσοι Εὐρώπην τε καὶ ἀμφιρύτας κατὰ νήσους:

Both those men who live in rich Peloponnesus and those
who live in Europe and the islands encircled by the sea.

In any event, even allowing these Homeric minor poems to have been of later period, this is probably the earliest mention of a European country. Many have derived the continental appellation from the Thracian province of that name of which Heraclea was the metropolitan city. Others, and this we take to be its true derivation as applied first to any land or district, have found the name in the Phœnician root *oreb*, meaning "the west or setting sun," the *Regio noctis* of Homer.

Africa, which in the Homeric map is a part of Asia, is perhaps better able to tell us its baptismal name and whence it came. Josephus, the historian, quoting from Alexander Polyhistor, the Greek historian,—who in turn quotes from Cleodemus Malchus,—says that Ophren, a grandson of Abraham and of Keturah his second wife, made war against Libya and took it, and that his grandchildren, when they inhabited the country, called it, from his name, Africa. But mythology has much to say of this matter of names even for Africa, and derives the name from *Afer*, the companion of Hercules. Some have thought it came from a Hebrew word *aphar*, meaning "dust," well describing the sandy earth of much of the country. Others have sought it in φρίχη, "cold," and α privative,—"without cold,"—an admirable description of the climate. It has also been derived from the Latin *aprica*, "sunny"—another happy expression. Bochart takes it from a Phœnician word meaning "a head of grain," alluding to the plentiful Egyptian *dhoura*. It has already been said that the country around Carthage was first called Africa, and that the term was extended to cover the whole of Libya, the most southern of the continents. Leo suggests two possible derivations: one from the Arabic word *furak*, to "break off," or "separate"; and the other from a certain Arabian king, Iphric or Iphricus, who was driven out of Asia by the Assyrians. Ham and his descendants, when they moved southward, settled in that region which was called Egypt, or the land of Ham. We read in the Psalms of David, "And smote all the firstborn in Egypt; the chief of their strength in the tabernacles of Ham." And again we read, "Israel also came into Egypt; and Jacob sojourned in the land of Ham."

It was apparently in the peninsula of the lesser Asia that occurred those first distinctions of places which gradually but naturally spread to continental appellations. If the earliest distributions were as we suppose, they were due to that natural divider the river Halys. This river from its source in the east flowed through Cappadocia toward the west; then, entering the Phrygian district, it was reinforced by its southern branch, and, forming a great bend, continued from the south to the north until it entered the Euxine. The second son of Noah, Japheth, established himself on the west side of this natural dividing line, while Shem, the founder of the Semitic races, remained on the east side. Within that comparatively small region was room for the relative terms "the people of the East," or the men of Asia, and the "people of the West," or the men of Europe. Many groups of villages in our own country are to-day locally known as the east village and the west village; and it requires no exercise of fancy to attribute to those early settlers of the two great continents the same natural distinctions.

The theories of the monogenists and of the polygenists both admit of a Noah and of Noachic dispersions. In the one case, however, the whole race of mankind has its spring in the loins of the old patriarch, while in the other the Mosaic history treats only of a single race, physiologically intended for certain geographical distribution and for certain climatic conditions, leaving other races each to its own creation by a common creator and working out its own development for a common end. The three streams take their origin from our Noah under either theory. Under the first theory, the streams flow along undisturbed, each to the extremity of its own continent; under the other theory, the streams have met and mingled with other streams from other sources. Fortunately for the even tenor of our way, and for the readers who accompany us, we are not much concerned with the various ethnical streams: the one which alone interests us is easy to follow.

If we have been able to show the great confusion which attends any attempt to discover the origin of the names of the three continents of the Old World and the uncertainty as to the time of their baptisms or the identity of their sponsors, we have accomplished our purpose, and, we hope, prepared the way for self-congratulation in the hearts of Americans, since not only do they know for whom their world is called, but the very day and hour of its baptismal ceremony.

PART II

The Discovery of the New World

The Landfall of Columbus, and the Establishment of Watling Island as Guanahani

CHAPTER I

Guanahani and the Five Claimants

THE exact spot in the New World on which Columbus first set foot will always possess peculiar interest. One might expect this spot would have been marked and identified beyond chance of doubt or dispute within a short time after the discovery, and yet each of at least five of the smaller Bahama islands is to-day pointed out as the site of the true landfall. Cuba and Santo Domingo early became the scene of attraction, and the true Guanahani was not visited for many years until the time when its simple people were carried off and made to wear away their lives in the gold-mines of New Spain. Modern writers who have tried to fix the identity of the true Guanahani have followed one of three plans:

First. Applying to the different islands the physical descriptions given by Ferdinand Columbus in his "Historie," and by Las Casas in his abridgment of the journal of the great Admiral.

Second. Tracing the course of the fleet backward from the island of Juan or Cuba, by means of the sailing memoranda in the journal.

Third. Following the course sailed from the island of Gomera in the Canaries to Guanahani, and from there to Cuba, by the same recorded sailings.

Juan Bautista Muñoz published his "Historia del Nuevo Mundo" at Madrid in 1793, after a labor of nineteen years. This writer says of Guanahani: "In my opinion, it is the same island that is now called Watling." His judgment was good, and his conclusions are ours also; but it would have gratified us if he had stated the reasons for his opinion.

Washington Irving, to whom we can grant a plenary indulgence for not halting long in a search for facts, lest his delightful pen corrode, said of the landfall in the 1828 London edition of his "Life of Columbus":

> The island where Columbus had thus, for the first time, set his foot upon the New World, is one of the Lucayos, or the Bahama Islands, and was called by the natives Guanahanè: it still retains the name of San Salvador, which he gave it, though called by the English Cat Island. The light which he had seen the evening previous to his making land may have been on Watling Island, which lies a few leagues to the east.

It is plain that, finding on the maps an island of the Bahama group called San Salvador, Irving was content to accept it as the true Guanahani. It was also an easy way to account for the mysterious light which Columbus and Pedro Gutierrez saw from the castle of the deck of the *Santa Maria* at ten o'clock on the evening of October 11; but the distance from Watling Island to Cat Island was not considered by the distinguished author. The nautical knowledge which fixed him in his determination to call Cat Island the true Guanahani, in the appendix to the third volume of his "Life and Voyages of Columbus" (New York, 1848), is said to have been furnished by Commander Alexander Slidell Mackenzie, United States Navy.

However, a greater than Irving in the field of investigation was soon to take up the subject. Alexander von Humboldt, in the third volume of his "Examen Critique de l'Histoire de la Géographie du Nouveau Continent" (Paris, 1837), accepts Cat Island as San Salvador, and summons two classes of witnesses to prove its identity: *first*, the modern maps and common tradition; and *second*, the old map of Juan de la Cosa and the journal of Ponce de Leon, as well as some of the early charts. The map of La Cosa was discovered by Von Humboldt in the library of his friend Baron Walckenaer in Paris, in the year 1832. It is now in the Naval Museum at Madrid. A reduced facsimile is shown at the end of this book, and from it the student can exercise his fancy in determining the true San Salvador with the same certainty as was assured to Von Humboldt. La Cosa accompanied Columbus on one or more of his voyages to the Indies, and might have heard from the very lips of the Admiral the location of the landfall. Navarrete, Vol. III, page 586, is authority for a strong professional relationship existing between Columbus and the famous pilot Juan de la Cosa; and Henry Harrisse, in his "Discovery of North America" (London, 1892), calls attention to the fact that La Cosa was not only a companion of Columbus on his memorable first voyage, but that he was a part owner of the flag-ship *Santa Maria*, which was wrecked on the coast of Hispaniola, December 25, 1492, and that he received an indemnity for his loss.

There is not sufficient detail in La Cosa's map to warrant any one in ascribing to Cat Island the honor of being San Salvador. The standard of Leon and Castile is seen in the map, planted on an island to which La Cosa gives the name Yumey, and this is easily identified in later maps as Long Island, or our Ferdinand Island. Guanahani is seen to the eastward, with the island of Santa Maria de la Concepcion lying between it and Yumey. Von Humboldt cites the journal of Juan Ponce de Leon upon his expedition in 1512 to the Lucayos Islands and to Florida in search of his fountain of youth. The expedition started from Porto Rico, and its course was N. W. by N. "In the course of five days they arrived at an island called El Viejo, in latitude 22° 30′ north. The next day they arrived at one of the Lucayos called Caycos.

On the eighth day they anchored at another island called Yaguna in 24°. Thence they passed to the island of Manuega in 24° 30', and on the eleventh day they reached Guanahani, which is in 25° 40' north. The island of Guanahani was the first discovered by Columbus on his first voyage and which he called San Salvador." This description is taken from Herrera. Von Humboldt says that El Viejo may have been Turk's Island, the Guanahani of Navarrete. Certainly Antonio de Alaminos, the famous pilot of the expedition, knew that El Viejo was not one of the Lucayos. Captain G. V. Fox, United States Navy, has identified Yaguna, the stopping-place on the eighth day, with Little Inagua. If Ponce de Leon made 287 miles, the distance from Porto Rico to Grand Turk Island, in five days, he was traveling at the rate of 57.4 miles per day. If he was at Little Inagua on the eighth day out, and at Guanahani on the eleventh, it would represent a distance, if traveled at above the average speed before made, of 172.2 miles. The distance from Little Inagua to Watling Island is 176 miles, while to Cat Island it is 213. We are still confronted with the 25° 40' of latitude applied to the Guanahani of Ponce de Leon, but we may avail ourselves of the criticism passed upon Antonio de Alaminos by Von Humboldt himself, who says that he made all his positions about one degree too far north.

We need not stop to consider the claim of Navarrete that Grand Turk is San Salvador. Neither in its physical characteristics nor in the subsequent sailings does it at all answer the requirements of the landfall. The claim of Francisco Adolpho de Varnhagen, the Brazilian writer, for the island of Mariguana is equally worthless. One never could find an island to the southwest of this to play the part of Santa Maria, or the second island. Mariguana has no large lake in the center, and lacking that, no Bahama island shall be our Guanahani.

Captain Fox has written the most elaborate disquisition yet contributed to this subject. It forms part of the report for 1880 made by the United States Coast and Geodetic Survey, and is entitled "Methods and Results," and was printed at the Government Printing Office. Although we do not accept his conclusions, we regard it as the most valuable contribution toward solving the problem of the first landing-place of Columbus in the New World which has been made, particularly from the method pursued in presenting the different theories. He has his own theory, and pursues it with eagerness. Samana or Atwood Cay, the Guanahani of Captain Fox, is a small island containing little more than eight square miles. Its east end is 23° 05' north latitude and 73° 37' longitude west of Greenwich. He made a personal inspection of the Bahama group, and certainly, with the same resources and with the books, maps, and manuscripts possessed by other writers, he should have reached a result commensurate with his *methods*. He did not attain this result. The island fails in every physical test applied to it from the journal of the Admiral, and from the biography by Ferdinand Columbus. Cat Island contains 160 square miles, Watling has 60, Mariguana has 96, Turk has only 6.87 square miles. It will be remembered that on the day following his landing, after having had time to examine the island, Columbus said of it: "This island is very large and very flat, and has very green trees and much water, and a very large lake in the middle, but without any mountains. It is all so green that it is a pleasure to look at it." It must have been well peopled, because of the crowds which came to the shore, and because of their canoes, fitted, some of them, to carry forty at a time.

In 1856 Captain A. B. Becher of the Royal Navy published in London a valuable work, entitled "The Landfall of Columbus." It includes a translation, by the author, of Navarrete's first volume containing the journal of Columbus. There is a very happy arrangement of a running commentary under the journal and on the same page, putting the reader into immediate possession of the author's own impressions and interpretations of the journal. Captain Becher had the best aid which the Hydrographic Office of the English Admiralty could afford, the plan of Watling Island having been sketched by Captain E. Barnett of the Royal Navy, an officer who has contributed by his surveys to the improvement of the charts of the West Indies. The true Guanahani or San Salvador is fully identified by Captain Becher with Watling Island, but the subsequent course marked on the chart to the second, third, and fourth islands is not naturally derived from the journal nor the relative positions of the several islands. This attempt by Captain Becher to solve the problem is important in view of the settled belief that tradition having given the name San Salvador to Cat Island, and such eminent writers as Washington Irving and Alexander Von Humboldt having there located the landfall, there could be no room for controversy or even question. When professional sailors and navigators like Captain Becher and Captain Barnett boldly denied that Columbus could have landed so far to the westward and made a journey to Cuba on any such lines as laid down by the journal, the public attention was arrested, and men listened with something of respect to the calm and dignified assertions of experts. The expedition sent out by the Chicago "Herald," and subsequent researches carried on by government authority, have strengthened the belief in Watling Island as the landfall of the discoverer four hundred years ago.

CHAPTER II

The Two Letters and the "Historie"

COLUMBUS wrote two letters, practically of the same contents, giving a general account of his voyage. The one was addressed to Luis de Santangel, chancellor of the house of Aragon, and dated on the caravel (the *Niña*) off the Canaries, February 15, 1493. The other was addressed to Gabriel Sanchez, the treasurer of Aragon, and dated off the Azores, February 18, 1493. The error of location in the first letter is obvious. In neither of these letters is there a clue to the landfall. These letters were written in the Spanish language, and published probably in the summer of 1493. There is in the Lenox Library in New York a unique copy of a folio Spanish edition of the letter addressed to the "Escribano de Racion" Luis de Santangel. This edition is distinguished by the introduction into the text of many Catalonian words, and is regarded as the first printed copy of the letter. In the Ambrosian Library in Milan there is a unique copy of a quarto Spanish edition addressed also to the Escribano de Racion. Of the second letter, addressed to Gabriel Sanchez, there has come down to us no printed copy of an original Spanish text, although it was translated into Latin and several editions were issued in 1493 and the years immediately following. These letters are the only contemporaneous printed accounts we have of the discovery. Columbus is known to have kept a journal in which he entered the daily events occurring on his first voyage, doubtless giving such a minute statement of his landing in the New World and his course among the islands afterward as would enable the geographer and student to identify the imprint of his foot on Guanahani and the wanderings of his fleet among the Bahama group. This journal is lost, but it was preserved for many years after the death of Columbus, and certain authors have quoted largely and apparently literally from its manuscript pages. In the life of Columbus by his son Ferdinand, of which an account will soon be given, toward the close of the fifteenth chapter and speaking of the departure upon the memorable

journey from Palos on Friday, August 3, 1492, it is said: "He began then to record in his journal the minutest details which occurred, mentioning the winds and telling how much progress he made upon his way with each; he wrote also the names of birds and fishes; that was his method in the four voyages he made to the Indies." But in addition Columbus was a skilled chartographer. In Chapter IV of the biography we find part of a letter written to the King of Castile, in which he says: "I gave myself to Astrology as much as was necessary, and in like manner to Geometry and to Arithmetic. The soul gave ingenuity and the hands acquired aptitude in drawing the sphere and on it the cities, the mountains, the rivers, the islands and the ports, all in their proper places." In the letter to the King and Queen which begins the manuscript journal of Columbus as transcribed by Bartolomé de las Casas, there is the following passage: "Moreover, Sovereign Princes, besides describing every night the occurrences of the day, and every day those of the preceding night, I intend to draw up a nautical chart which shall contain the several parts of the ocean and land in their proper situations; and also to compose a book to represent the whole by picture with latitudes and longitudes." We know that for years he and his brother Bartholomew supported themselves by drawing maps and charts. An accomplished sailor, thus equipped by education and practice, must have carefully mapped every land he saw in the New World, and above all that important and blessed first land to which he gave the sacred name of San Salvador.

There were two writers who had personal knowledge of Columbus, and who gave detailed accounts of the Admiral and his first voyage. The first of these was his son Ferdinand, who was four years of age when the memorable voyage was made, and but eighteen years of age when his father died. He wrote a biography of the discoverer, but it was not published until 1571, after passing through several hands, and thirty-two years after Ferdinand's death. The "Historie," as many bibliographers call this book, the title-page of which is herewith given, was written in Spanish; but there is no evidence

MAP FROM CAPTAIN BECHER'S "THE LANDFALL OF COLUMBUS," SHOWING A NEW INTERPRETATION OF THE COURSE OF THE FIRST VOYAGE OF COLUMBUS.

that it was ever printed until, being translated into the Italian, it issued from the press in Venice in 1571. The first Italian edition was translated into French and printed at Paris in 1681, and not 1680, as Brunet has it. We have both these editions before us, and if the original Spanish suffered as much by translation into Italian as the latter has by turning into French, students may well grieve. It must be remembered that Ferdinand Columbus had in his possession the manuscript papers, books, and maps belonging to his father, some of which are still preserved at Seville. Ferdinand died in 1539.

We give below a literal translation from the first edition of that portion of the "Historie" which recounts the landing on Guanahani and the course of the fleet until the island of Juan or Cuba was reached.

[Recto folio 51.] When it was day they saw that it was an island fifteen leagues in length, level, without mountains, full of very green trees and beautiful water, and with a large lagoon in the center. . . .

The Admiral rose from his knees and gave to this island the name of San Salvador. . . .

[Recto folio 53.] Jewels and metals were not seen among them [the natives], except some gold leaves which they wore attached to holes in their noses; upon being asked whence they had that gold, they replied by their signs, from that part of the South where there was a King who had many pieces and vases of gold. Pointing their fingers, they showed that towards that part of the South and to the Southwest were many other islands and great lands. . . .

[Verso folio 53.] The Sunday following, which was the 14th of October, the Admiral coasted with his boats along the shores of this island toward the northwest in order to see something of it, and in that part where he went, he found a large harbor or port, capable of holding all the ships of Christendom. . . .

The Admiral gave [Recto of folio 54] to all strings of glass beads, glad to see in the people so much simplicity. Finally he arrived at a peninsula which with pains in three days he might have circumnavigated, habitable, and where one could make a good fortress. Here he saw six houses of the same Indians, with many gardens around about, as beautiful as they usually are in the month of May, in Castile. But because the people that day were tired with so much rowing, and perceiving clearly that so far as he had seen this was not the land that he sought, nor of enough utility to warrant him in remaining there longer, he took seven of these Indians that they might serve as interpreters, and returning to the ships departed for other islands which they saw from the peninsula, and these also appeared level, green and well populated, as these same Indians affirmed. *He arrived at one of these islands which was seven leagues distant, the next day, Monday, the 15th of October, and gave it the name "Santa Maria de la Concepcion." The side of this island towards San Salvador extended north and south for a length of five leagues of coast. But the Admiral sailed along the coast east and west, which is in length more than ten leagues.* And when they reached towards the west, descended to the land to do that which they had done in the past. Here the people of the island ran quickly to see the Christians, showing the same [Verso of folio 54] astonishment as the others had exhibited. The Admiral seeing that all the islands were much alike, *on the following day, which was Tuesday, sailed towards the west for eight leagues to another island much larger, with a coast running along northeast and southwest more than twenty-eight leagues.* This island was very level and with a beautiful beach and he took pleasure in giving it the name La Fernandina. But before they arrived at this island and the island of La Concepcion, they found a man in a small canoe who had a piece of bread and a calabash of water and a little earth similar to vermilion with which these people painted their bodies, as we have said above, and some dry leaves which they esteemed very much as being odorous and healthful, and in a little basket he carried a string of green glass beads and two *bagattini* [a small coin] by which they judged that this man came from San Salvador, having passed La Concepcion and thence to Fernandina, bearing news of the Christians to these countries. But because the passage had been long and he was already tired, as soon as he came up to the ships with his canoe and was taken on board and treated courteously by the Admiral, who had in mind as soon as he might land to send him as messenger, which he did, giving him some little things in order that he might distribute them among the others. . . .

[Recto of folio 55.] In order to know the island better, he sailed from there towards the northwest to the mouth of a beautiful port, which had a little island in the entrance, but one would not be able to enter there [Verso of folio 55] for the slight depth it had; nor did they care about entering, so as not to go farther away from an inhabited island and which was in sight and not far distant. This was the largest island they had seen to that time, but it had not more than twelve or fifteen houses, made after the fashion of a pavilion. . . .

Because in the said island of Fernandina they found nothing of any importance, on Friday the 19th of October, they went to another isle called Saometto, to which the Admiral gave the name Isabella, in order to proceed with order in his names; since, the first, by the Indians called Guanahani, for the glory of God, who had revealed it to him and saved him from so many perils, he called San Salvador; and the second because of his reverence for the Conception of the Madonna, and because her favor is the principal thing the Christians [Recto of folio 56] desire, he called Santa Maria de la Concepcion; and the third that the Indians called [blank in the original], in memory of the Catholic King, Don Fernando, he called Fernandina; and the fourth, Isabella, out of respect to her royal Highness, Queen Donna Isabella. And the first one found after that, that is to say Cuba he called Juan, in memory of the Prince Don Juan, heir of Castile, trusting that with these names he might satisfy himself, having remembered the spiritual and the temporal. The truth is that as to goodness, size and beauty the island of Fernandina was a great way in advance of the other islands, because, besides being copiously supplied with water, beautiful fields and trees, among which were many aloes, one could see here certain eminences and hills that the other islands did not possess, as they were very level. The Admiral being greatly enamoured of its beauty and in order to perform the ceremony of taking possession, descended into some fields, as remarkable for amenity and beauty as are those of Castile in the month of April. Here one heard the song of the nightingale and so gentle were these birds that they hardly knew enough to fly from man; they not only flitted among the trees but soared in the air in such flocks that they obscured the light of the sun.

CHAPTER III

Las Casas' Abridgment of the Journal

N the year 1825 there was begun at Madrid, by royal command, a publication entitled "Coleccion de los Viages y Descubrimientos," by Don Martin Fernandez de Navarrete. There were five quarto volumes, the first two dated 1825, the third dated 1829, and the fourth and fifth volumes dated 1837. In 1828 so much of this work as related to Columbus was translated into French by Chalumeau de Verneuil and his colleague De la Roquette, and printed at Paris in three octavo volumes under the title "Relations des Quatre Voyages entrepris par Christophe Columb." It is scarcely more than a very poor translation from the first volume of Navarrete, but is much more frequently met with in public libraries than the original Spanish edition. The second writer referred to before as having personal knowledge of Columbus and as having given an account of his voyages from the Admiral's relations, is Bartolomé de las Casas. He was a native of Seville, where he was born in 1474, and received his education in the University of Salamanca. His father Francisco had been with Columbus on his first voyage, and he himself is said to have been with the Admiral on his third voyage in 1498. It is certain that he knew personally and intimately the great discoverer, and enjoyed the rich opportunity of learning from his lips the circumstances attending the discovery of the New World. It is known that Columbus wrote with his own hand a daily journal recording minutely what happened upon his first voyage, the course pursued, the islands visited, and such other information as a navigator, a traveler, and an investigator would be likely to note. This original journal was in the possession of Las Casas and before him when he wrote concerning the four voyages of Columbus. He says that the journal has been abridged by him, but that in many places he has quoted from it the very words and at length. Las Casas was much in America, having been made a priest at a somewhat mature age, and created Bishop of Chiapa, in Mexico, in 1544, devoting much of his time to promoting the interests or, more properly, endeavoring to ameliorate the hard condition of the Indians. Soon

after his appointment to the bishopric he retired to the monastery of San Gregorio in Valladolid, and engaged in literary labors, composing his "Historia de las Indias." When by royal command Navarrete undertook to write his great work, he had placed at his disposal all the documents the public and private archives of Spain could furnish. Among the rest was the original manuscript of Las Casas. Thus we have the account of Columbus's first voyage taken from the original manuscript of one who knew Columbus, whose father had been with him on his voyage of discovery, and who had, at the time of his writing, the original manuscript journal of Columbus reciting the events as they occurred. There is no English translation of Navarrete's work, although in 1827 Samuel Kettell published in Boston a very poor translation of that portion of the first volume which relates to the first voyage of Columbus. We give the original Spanish of Navarrete's "Journal of Columbus" (beginning with the entry for October 10, 1492) which is interesting because of its presenting the entire ground upon which the famous mutiny legend rests. Our extract from the "Journal" ends on October 28 with his landing on the island of Cuba.

Miercoles 10 *de Octubre:* Navegó al Ouesudueste, anduvieron á diez millas por hora y á ratos doce y algun rato á siete, y entre dia y noche cincuenta y nueve leguas: contó á la gente cuarenta y cuatro leguas no mas. Aquí la gente ya no lo podia sufrir: quejabase del largo viage; pero el Almirante los esforzó lo mejor que pudo dándoles buena esperanza de los provechos que podrian haber. Y añadia que por demas era quejarse, pues que él había venido á las Indias, y que así lo había de proseguir hasta hallarlas con el ayuda de nuestro Señor.

Jueves 11 *de Octubre:* Navegó al Ouesudueste, tuvieron mucha mar mas que en todo el viage habian tenido. Vieron pardelas y un junco verde junto á la nao. Vieron los de la carabela Pinta una caña y un palo, y tomaron otro palillo labrado á lo que parecia con hierro, y un pedazo de caña y otra yerba que nace en tierra, y una tablilla. Los de la carabela Niña tambien vieron otras señales de tierra y un palillo cargado descaramojos. Con estas señales respiraron y alegráronse todos. Anduvieron en este dia hasta puesto el sol viente y siete leguas.

Despues del sol puesto navegó á su primer camino al Oueste: andarian doce millas cada hora, y hasta dos horas despues de media noche andarian noventa millas, que son veinte y dos leguas y media. Y porque la carabela Pinta era mas velera é iba delante del Almirante halló tierra y hizo las señas quel Almirante habia mandado. Esta tierra vido primero un marinero que se decia Rodrigo de Triana; puesto que el Almirante á las diez de la noche, estando en el castillo de popa, vido lumbre, aunque fue cosa tan cerrada que no quiso afirmar que fuese tierra; pero llamó á Pero Gutierrez, repostero destrados del Rey, é díjole, que parecia lumbre, que mirase él, y asi lo hizo y vídola: díjolo tambien á Rodrigo Sanchez de Segovia quél Rey y la Reina enviaban en el armada por veedor, el cual no vido nada porque no estaba en lugar dó la pudiese ver. Despues quel Almirante lo dijo se vido una vez ó dos, y era como una candelilla de cera que se alzaba y levantaba, lo cual á pocos pareciera ser indicio de tierra. Pero el Almirante tuvo por cierto estar junto á la tierra. Por lo cual cuando dijeron la *Salve*, que la acostumbran decir é cantar á su manera todos los marineros y se hallan todos, rogó y amonestólos el Almirante que hiciesen buena guarda al castillo de proa, y mirasen bien por la tierra, y que al que le dijese primero que via tierra le daria luego un jubon de seda, sin las otras mercedes que los Reyes habian prometido, que eran diez mil maravedis de juro á quien primero la viese. A las dos horas despues de media noche pareció la tierra, de la qual estarian dos leguas. Amañaron todas las velas, y quedaron con el treo que es la vela grande sin bonetas, y pusiéronse á la corda temporizando hasta el dia Viernes que llegaron á una isleta de los Lucayos, que se llamaba en lengua de indios *Guanahani.* Luego vieron gente desnuda, y el Almirante salió á tierra en la barca armada, y Martin Alonso Pinzon y Vicente Anes, su hermano, que era capitan de la Niña. Sacó el Almirante la bandera Real y los capitanes con dos banderas de la Cruz Verde, que llevaba el Almirante en todos los navios por seña con una F y una Y: encima de cada letra su corona, una de un cabo de la ✠ y otra de otro. Puestos en tierra vieron árboles muy verdes y aguas muchas y frutas de diversas maneras. El Almirante llamó á los dos capitanes y á los demas que saltaron en tierra, y á Rodrigo Descovedo, Escribano de toda el armada, y á Rodrigo Sanchez de Segovia, y dijo que le diesen por fe y testimonio como él por ante todos tomaba, como de hecho tomó, posesion de la dicha isla por el Rey é por la Reina sus señores, haciendo las protestaciones que se requirian, como mas largo se contiene en los testimonios que allí se hicieron por escripto. Luego se ayuntó allí mucha gente de la isla. Esto que se sigue son palabras formales del Almirante, en su libro de su primera navegacion y descumbrimiento de estas Indias. "Yo (dice él) porque nos tuviesen mucha amistad, porque conoscí que era gente que mejor se libraria y convertiria á nuestra Santa Fé con amor que no por fuerza; les dí á algunos de ellos unos bonetes colorados y unas cuentas de vidrio que se ponian al pescuezo, y otras cosas muchas de poco valor con que hobieron mucho placer y quedaron tanto nuestros que era maravilla. Los cuales despues venian á las barcas de los navíos adonde nós estabamos, nadando y nos traían papagayos y hilo de algodon en ovillos y azagayas, y otras cosas muchas, y nos las trocaban por otras cosas que nós les dabamos, como cuentecillas de vidrio y cascabeles. En fin todo tomaban y daban de aquello que tenian de buena voluntad. Mas me pareció que era gente muy pobre de todo. Ellos andan todos desnudos como su madre los parió, y tambien las mugeres, aunque no vide mas de una farto moza, y todos los que yo ví eran todos mancebos, que ninguno vide de edad de mas de treinta años: muy bien hechos, de muy fermosos cuerpos, y muy buenas caras: los cabellos gruesos cuasi como sedas de cola de caballos, é cortos: los cabellos traen por encima de las cejas, salvo unos pocos de tras que traen largos, que jamas cortan: dellos se pintan de prieto, y ellos son de la color de los canarios, ni negros ni blancos, y dellos se pintan de blanco, y dellos de colorado, y dellos de lo que fallan, y dellos se pintan las caras, y dellos todo el cuerpo, y dellos solos los ojos, y dellos solo el nariz. Ellos no traen armas ni las cognocen, porque les amostré espadas y las tomaban por el filo, y se cortaban con ignorancia. No tienen algun fierro: sus azagayas son unas varas sin fierro, y algunas de ellas tienen al cabo un diente de pece, y otras de otras cosas. Ellos todos á una mano son de buena estatura de grandeza, y buenos gestos, bien hechos; yo vide algunos que tenian señales de feridas en sus cuerpos, y les hice señas que era aquello, y ellos me amostraron como allí venian gente de otras islas que estaban acerca y les querian tomar, y se defendian; y yo creí, é creo, que aquí vienen de tierra firme á tomarlos por captivos. Ellos deben ser buenos servidores y de buen ingenio, que veo que muy presto dicen todo lo que les decia, y creo que ligeramente se harian cristianos, que me pareció que ninguna secta tenian. Yo, placiendo á nuestro Señor, levaré de aquí al tiempo de mi partida seis á V. A. para que deprendan fablar. Ninguna bestia de ninguna manera vide, salvo papagayos en esta isla." Todas son palabras del Almirante.

Sabado 13 *de Octubre:* "Luego que amaneció vinieron á la playa muchos destos hombres, todos mancebos, como dicho tengo, y todos de buena estatura, gente muy fermosa: los cabellos no crespos, salvo corredios y gruesos, como sedas de caballo, y todos de la frente y cabeza muy ancha mas que otra generacion que fasta aquí haya visto, y los ojos muy fermosos y no pequeños, y ellos ninguno prieto, salvo de la color de los canarios, ni se debe esperar otra cosa, pues está Lesteoueste con la isla del Hierro en Canaria so una línea. Las piernas muy derechas, todos á una mano, y no barriga, salvo muy bien hecha. Ellos vinieron á la nao con almadias, que son hechas del pie de un árbol, como un barco luengo, y todo de un pedazo, y labrado muy á maravilla segun la tierra, y grandes en que en algunas venian cuarenta ó cuarenta y cinco hombres, y otras mas pequeñas, fasta haber dellas en que venia un solo hombre. Remaban con una pala como de fornero, y anda á maravilla; y si se le trastorna luego se echan todos á nadar, y la enderezan y vacian con calabazas que traen ellos. Traían ovillos de algodon filado y papagayos, y azagayas, y otras cositas que seria tedio de escrebir, y todo daban por cualquiera cosa que se los diese. Y yo estaba atento y trabajaba de saber si habia oro, y vide que algunos dellos traían un pedazuelo colgado en un agujero que tienen á la nariz, y por señas pude entender que yendo al Sur ó volviendo la isla por el Sur, que estaba allí un Rey que tenia grandes vasos dello, y tenia muy mucho. Trabajé que fuesen allá, y despues vide que no entendian en la ida. Determiné de aguardar fasta mañana en la tarde, y despues partir para el Sudueste, que segun muchos dellos me enseñaron decian que habia tierra al Sur y al Sudueste y al Norueste, y questas del Norueste les venian á combatir muchas veces, y así ir al Sudueste á buscar el oro y piedras preciosas. Esta isla es bien grande y muy llana y de arboles muy verdes, y muchas aguas, y una laguna en medio muy grande, sin ninguna montaña, y toda ella verde, ques placer de mirarla; y esta gente farto mansa, y por la gana de haber de nuestras cosas, y teniendo que no se les ha de dar sin que den algo y no lo tienen, toman lo que pueden y se echan luego á nadar; mas todo lo que tienen lo dan por cualquiera cosa que les den; que fasta los pedazos de las escudillas, y de las tazas de vidrio rotas rescataban, fasta que ví dar diez y seis ovillos de algodon por tres ceotis de Portugal, que es una blanca de Castilla, y en ellos habria mas de una arroba de algodon filado. Esto defendiera y no dejára tomar á nadie, salvo que yo lo mandára tomar todo para V. A. si hobiera en cantidad. Aquí nace en esta isla, mas por el poco tiempo no pude dar asi del todo fé, y tambien aquí nace el oro que traen colgado á la nariz; mas por no perder tiempo quiero ir á ver si puedo topar á la isla de Cipango. Agora como fue noche todos se fueron á tierra con sus almadias."

Domingo 14 *de Octubre:* "En amaneciendo mandé aderezar el batel de la nao y las barcas de las carabelas, y fue al luengo de la isla, en el camino del Nornordeste, para ver la otra parte, que era de la otra parte del Leste que habia, y tambien para ver las poblaciones, y vide luego dos ó tres y la gente, que venian todos á la playa llamándonos y dando gracias á Dios; los unos nos traían agua, otros otras cosas de comer; otros, cuando veían que yo no curaba de ir á tierra, se echaban á la mar nadando y venian, y entendiamos que nos preguntaban si eramos venidos del cielo; y vino uno viejo en el batel dentro, y otros á voces grandes llamaban todos hombres y mugeres: venid á ver los hombres que vinieron del cielo: traedles de comer y de beber. Vinieron muchos y muchas mugeres, cada uno con algo, dando gracias á Dios, echándose al suelo, y levantaban las manos al cielo, y despues á voces nos llamaban que fuesemos á tierra: mas yo temia de ver una grande restinga de piedras que cerca toda aquella isla al rededor, y entre medias queda hondo y puerto para cuantas naos hay en toda la cristiandad, y la entrada dello muy angosta. Es verdad que dentro desta cinta hay algunas bajas, mas la mar no se mueve mas que dentro en un pozo. Y para ver todo esto me moví esta mañana, porque supiese dar de todo relacion á vuestras Altezas, y tambien á donde pudiera hacer fortaleza, y vide un pedazo de tierra que se hace como isla, aunque no lo es, en que habia seis casas, el cual se pudiera atajar en dos dias por isla; aunque yo no veo ser necessario, porque esta gente es muy simplice en armas, como verán vuestras Altezas de siete que yo hice tomar para le llevar y deprender nuestra fabla y volvellos, salvo que vuestras Altezas cuando mandaren puedenlos todos llevar á Castilla, ó tenellos en la misma isla captivos, porque con cincuenta hombres los terná todos sojuzgados, y les hará hacer todo lo que quisiere; y despues junto con la dicha isleta estan huertas de árboles las mas hermosas que yo ví, é tan verdes y con sus hojas como las de Castilla en el mes de Abril y de Mayo, y mucha agua. Yo miré todo aquel puerto, y despues me volví á la nao y dí la vela, y vide tantas islas que yo no sabia determinarme á cual iria primero, y aquellos hombres que yo tenia tomado me decian por señas que eran tantas y tantas que no habia número, y anombraron por su nombre mas de ciento. Por ende yo miré por la mas grande, y aquella determiné andar, y así hago y será lejos desta de San Salvador, cinco leguas y las otras dellas mas, dellas menos: todas son muy llanas, sin montañas y muy fértiles, y todas pobladas, y se hacen guerra la una á la otra, aunque estos son muy simplices y muy lindos cuerpos de hombres."

Lunes 15 *de Octubre:* "Habia temporejado esta noche con temor de no llegar á tierra á sorgir antes de la mañana por no saber si la costa era limpia de bajas, y en amaneciendo cargar velas. Y como la isla fuese mas lejos de cinco leguas, antes será siete, y la marea me detusvo, seria medio dia cuando llegué á la dicha isla, y fallé que aquella haz, ques de la parte de la isla de San Salvador, se corre Norte Sur, y hay en ella cinco leguas, y la otra que yo seguí se corria Leste Oueste, y hay en ella mas de diez leguas. Y como desta isla vide otra mayor al Oueste, cargué las velas por andar todo aquel dia fasta la noche, porque aun no pudiera haber andado al cabo del Oueste, á la cual puse nombre la isla de Santa María de la Concepcion, y cuasi al poner del sol sorgí acerca del dicho cabo por saber si habia allí oro, porque estos que yo habia hecho tomar en la isla de S. Salvador me decian que ahí traian manillas de oro muy grandes á las piernas y á los brazos. Yo bien creí que todo lo que decian era burla para se fugir. Con todo, mi voluntad era de no pasar por ninguna isla de que no tomase posesion, puesto que tomado de una se puede decir de todas; y sorgí é estuve hasta hoy Martes que en amaneciendo fuí á tierra con las barcas armadas, y salí, y ellos que eran muchos así desnudos, y de la misma condicion de la otra isla de San Salvador, nos dejaron ir por la isla y nos daban lo que les pedia. Y porque el viento cargaba á la traviesa Sueste no me quise detener y partí para la nao, y una almadia grande estaba abordo de la carabela Niña, y uno de los hombres de la isla de San Salvador, que en ella era, se echó á la mar y se fue en ella, y la noche de antes á medio echado el otro [á nado (?)] y fue atrás la almadia, la cual fugió que jamas fue barca que le pudiese alcanzar, puesto que le teniamos grande avante. Con todo dió en tierra, y dejaron la almadia, y alguno de los de mi compañía salieron en tierra tras ellos, y todos fugeron como gallinas, y la almadia que habian dejado la llevamos abordo de la carabela Niña, adonde ya de otro cabo venia otra almadia pequeña con un hombre que venia á rescatar un ovillo de algodon, y se echaron algunos marineros á la mar porque él no queria entrar en la carabela, y le tomaron; y yo que estaba á la popa de la nao, que vide todo, envié por él, y le dí bonete colorado y unas cuentas de vidrio verdes pequeñas que le puse al brazo, y dos cascabeles que le puse á las orejas, y le mandé volver su almadia que tambien tenia en la barca, y le envié á tierra; y dí luego la vela para ir á la otra isla grande que yo via al Oueste, y mandé largar tambien la otra almadia que traia la carabela Niña por popa, y vide despues en tierra al tiempo de la llegada del otro á quien yo habia dado las cosas susodichas, y no le habia querido tomar el ovillo de algodon puesto quel me lo queria dar; y todos los otros se llegaron á él, y tenia á gran maravilla é bien le pareció que eramos buena gente, y que el otro que se habia fugido nos habia hecho algun daño y que por esto lo llevábamos, y á esta razon usé esto con él de le mandar alargar, y le dí las dichas cosas porque nos tuviesen en esta estima, porque otra vez cuando vuestras Altezas aquí tornen á enviar no hagan mala compañía; y todo lo que le dí no valia cuatro maravedis. Y así partí, que serian las diez horas, con el viento Sueste y tocaba de Sur para pasar á estotra isla, la cual es grandísima, y adonde todos estos hombres que yo traigo de la de San Salvador hacen señas que hay muy mucho oro, y que lo traen en los brazos en manillas, y á las piernas, y á las orejas, y al nariz, y al pescuenzo. Y habia de esta isla de Santa María á esta otra nueve leguas Leste Oueste, y se corre toda esta parte de la isla Norueste Sueste, y se parece que bien habria en esta costa mas de veinte y ocho leguas en esta faz, y es muy llana sin montaña ninguna, así como aquellas de San Salvador y de Santa María, y todas playas sin roquedos, salvo que á todas hay algunas peñas acerca de tierra debajo del agua, por donde es menester abrir el ojo cuando se quiere surgir é no surgir mucho acerca de tierra, aunque las aguas son siempre muy claras y se ve el fondo. Y desviado de tierra dos tiros de lombarda hay en todas estas Islas tanto fondo que no se puede llegar á él. Son estas Islas muy verdes y fértiles, y de aires muy dulces, y puede haber muchas cosas que yo se, porque no me quiero detener por calar y andar muchas Islas para fallar oro. Y pues estas dan así estas señas que lo traen á los brazos y a las piernas, y es oro porque les amostré algunos pedazos del que yo tengo, no puedo errar con el ayuda de nuestro Señor que yo no le falle adonde nace. Y estando á medio golfo destas dos Islas es de saber de aquella de Santa María y de esta grande, á la cual pongo nombre la Fernandina, fallé un hombre solo en una almadia que se pasaba de la isla de Santa María á la Fernandina, y traia un poco de su pan, que seria tanto como el puño, y una calabaza de agua, y un pedazo de tierra bermeja hecha en polvo y despues amasada, y unas hojas secas que debe ser cosa muy apreciada entre ellos, porque ya me trujeron en San Salvador dellas en presente, y traia un cestillo á su guisa en que tenia un ramalejo de cuentecillas de vidrio y dos blancas, por las cuales conoscí quel venia de la isla de San Salvador, y habia pasado á aquella de Santa Maria, y se pasaba á la Fernandina, el cual se llegó á la nao; yo le hice entrar, que así lo demandaba él, y le hice poner su almadia en la nao, y guardar todo lo que él traia; y le mandé dar de comer pan y miel, y de beber; y así le pasaré á la Fernandina, y le daré todo lo suyo, porque dé buenas nuevas de nos para á nuestro Señor aplaciendo, cuando vuestras Altezas envien acá, que aquellos que vinieren resciban honra, y nos den de todo lo que hobiere."

Martes 16 *de Octubre:* "Partí de las islas de Santa María de la Concepcion, que seria ya cerca del medio dia, para la isla Fernandina, la cual amuestra ser grandísima al Oueste, y navegué todo aquel dia con calmeria; no pude llegar á tiempo de poder ver el fondo para surgir en limpio, porque es en esto mucho de haber gran diligencia por no perder las anclas; y así temporicé toda esta noche hasta el dia que vine á una poblacion, adonde yo surgí, é adonde habia venido aquel hombre que yo hallé ayer en aquella almadia á medio golfo, el cual habia dado tantas buenas nuevas de nos que toda esta noche no faltó almadias aborado de la nao, que nos traian agua y de lo que tenian. Yo á cada uno le mandaba dar algo, es á saber algunas contecillas, diez ó doce dellas de vidrio en un filo, y algunas sonajas de laton destas que valen en Castilla un maravedi cada una, y algunas agujetas, de que todo tenian en grandísima excelencia, y tambien los mandaba dar para que comiesen cuando venian en la nao miel de azúcar; y despues á horas de tercia envié el batel de la nao en tierra por agua, y ellos de muy buena gana le enseñaban á mi gente adonde estaba el agua, y ellos mismos traian los barriles llenos al batel, y se folgaban mucho de nos hacer placer. Esta isla es grandísima y tengo determinado de la rodear, porque segun puedo entender en ella, ó cerca della, hay mina de oro. Esta isla está desviada de la de Santa María ocho leguas cuasi Leste Oueste; y este cabo adonde yo vine, y toda esta costa se corre Nornorueste y Sursueste, y vide bien veinte leguas de ella, mas ahí no acababa. Agora escribiendo esto dí la vela con el viento Sur para pujar á rodear toda la isla, y trabajar hasta que halle Samaot, que es la isla ó ciudad adonde es el oro, que así lo dicen todos estos que aquí vienen en la nao, y nos lo decian los de la isla de San Salvador y de Santa María. Esta gente es semejante á aquella de las dichas islas, y una fabla y unas costumbres, salvo questos ya me parecen algun tanto mas doméstica gente, y de tracto, y mas sotiles, porque veo que han traido algodon aquí á la nao y otras cositas que saben mejor refetar el pagamento que no hacian los otros; y aun en esta isla vide paños de algodón fechos como mantillos, y la gente mas dispuesta, y las mugeres traen por delante su cuerpo una cosita de algodon que escasamente les cobija su natura. Ella es isla muy verde y llana y fertilísima, y no pongo duda que todo el año siembran panizo y cogen, y así todas otras cosas; y vide muchos árboles muy disformes de los nuestros, y dellos muchos que tenian los ramos de muchas maneras y todo en un pie, y un ramito es de una manera y otro de otra, y tan disforme que es la mayor maravilla del mundo cuanta es la diversidad de la una manera á la otra, verbi gracia, un ramo tenia las fojas á manera de cañas y otro de manera de lentisco; y así en un solo árbol de cinco ó seis de estas maneras; y todos tan diversos: ni estos son enjeridos, porque se pueda decir que el enjerto lo hace, antes son por los montes, ni cura dellos esta gente. No le conozco secta ninguna, y creo que muy presto se tornarian cristianos, porque ellos son de muy buen entender. Aquí son los peces tan disformes de los nuestros ques maravilla. Hay algunos hechos como gallos de las mas finas colores del mundo azules, amarillos, colorados y de todas colores, y otros pintados de mil maneras; y las colores son tan finas que no hay hombre que no se maraville y no tome gran descanso á verlos. Tambien hay ballenas: bestias en tierra no vide ninguna manera, salvo papagayos y lagatos; un mozo me dijo que vido una grande culebra. Ovejas ni cabras ni otra ninguna bestia vide; aunque yo he estado aquí muy poco, que es medio dia, mas si las hobiese no pudiera errar de ver alguna. El cerco desta isla escribiré despues que yo la hobiere rodeado."

Miercoles 17 de Octubre: "A medio dia partí de la poblacion adonde yo estaba surgido, y adonde tomé agua para ir rodear esta isla Fernandina, y el viento era Sudueste y Sur; y como mi voluntad fuese de seguir esta costa desta isla adonde yo estaba al Sueste, porque así se corre toda Nornorueste y Sursueste, y queria llevar el dicho camino de Sur y Sueste, porque aquella parte todos estos indios que traigo y otro de quien hobe señas en esta parte del Sur á la isla á que ellos llaman *Samoet*, adonde es el oro; y Martin Alonso Pinzon, capitan de la carabela Pinta, en la cual yo mandé á tres de estos indios, vino á mí y me dijo que uno dellos muy certificadamente le habia dado á entender que por la parte del Nornorueste muy mas presto arrodearia la isla. Yo vide que el viento no me ayudaba por el camino que yo queria llevar, y era bueno por el otro: dí la vela al Nornorueste, y cuando fue acerca del cabo de la isla, á dos leguas, hallé un muy maravilloso puerto con una boca, aunque dos bocas se le puede decir, porque tiene un isleo en medio, y son ambas muy angostas, y dentro muy ancho para cien navíos si fuera fondo y limpio, y fondo al entrada: parecióme razon del ver bien y sondear, y así surgí fuera dél, y fuí en él con todas las barcas de los navíos, y vimos que no habia fondo. Y porque pensé cuando yo le ví que era boca de algun rio habia mandado llevar barriles para tomar agua, y en tierra hallé unos ocho ó diez hombres que luego vinieron á nos, y nos amostraron ahí cerca la poblacion, adonde yo envié la gente por agua, una parte con armas otros con barriles, y así la tomaron; y porque era lejuelos me detuve por espacio de dos horas. En este tiempo anduve así por aquellos árboles, que era la cosa mas fermosa de ver que otra que se haya visto; veyendo tanta verdura en tanto grado como en el mes de Mayo en el Andalucía, y los árboles todos estan tan disformes de los nuestros como el dia de la noche; y así las frutas, y así las yerbas y las piedras y todas las cosas. Verdad es que algunos árboles eran de la naturaleza de otros que hay en Castilla, por ende habia muy gran diferencia, y los otros árboles de otras maneras eran tantos que no hay persona que lo pueda decir ni asemejar á otros de Castilla. La gente toda era una con los otros ya dichos, de las mismas condiciones, y así desnudos y de la misma estatura, y daban de lo que tenian por cualquiera cosa que les diesen; y aquí vide que unos mozos de los navíos les trocaron azagayas por unos pedazuelos de escudillas rotas y de vidrio, y los otros que fueron por el agua me dijeron como habian estado en sus casas, y que eran de dentro muy barridas y limpias, y sus camas y paramentos de cosas que son como redes de algodon: ellas las casas son todas á manera de alfaneques, y muy altas y buenas chimeneas; mas no vide entre muchas poblaciones que yo vide ninguna que pasase de doce hasta quince casas. Aquí fallaron que las mugeres casadas traian bragas de algodon, las mozas no, sino salvo algunas que eran ya de edad de diez y ocho años. Y ahí habia perros mastines y branchetes, y ahí fallaron uno que habia al nariz un pedazo de oro que seria como la mitad de un castellano, en el cual vieron letras: reñí yo con ellos porque no se lo resgataron y dieron cuanto pedia, por ver que era y cuya esta moneda era; y ellos me respondieron que nunca se lo osó resgatar. Despues de tomada la agua volví á la nao, y dí la vela, y salí al Norueste tanto que yo descubrí toda aquella parte de la isla hasta la costa que se corre Leste Oueste, y despues todos estos indios tornaron á decir que esta isla era mas pequeña que no la isla Samoet, y que seria bien volver atras por ser en ella mas presto. El viento allí luego mas calmó y comenzó á ventar Ouesnorueste, el cual era contrario para donde habiamos venido, y así tomé la vuelta y navegué toda esta noche pasada al Lestesueste, y cuando al Leste todo y cuando al Sueste; y esto para apartarme de la tierra porque hacia muy gran cerrazon y el tiempo muy cargado: el era poco y no me dejó llegar á tierra á surgir. Así que esta noche llovió muy fuerte despues de media noche hasta cuasi el dia, y aun está nublado para llover; y nos al cabo de la isla de la parte del Sueste adonde espero surgir fasta que aclarezca para ver las otras islas adonde tengo de ir; y así todos estos dias despues que en estas Indias estoy ha llovido poco ó mucho. Crean vuestras Altezas que es esta tierra la mejor é mas fertil, y temperada, y llana, y buena que haya en el mundo."

Jueves 18 *de Octubre:* "Despues que aclaresció seguí el viento, y fuí en derredor de la isla cuanto pude, y surgí al tiempo que ya no era de navegar; mas no fuí en tierra, y en amaneciendo dí la vela."

Viernes 19 *de Octubre:* "En amaneciendo levanté las anclas y envié la carabela Pinta al Leste y Sueste y la carabela Niña al Sursueste, y yo con la nao fuí al Sueste, y dado orden que llevasen aquella vuelta fasta medio dia, y despues que ambas se mudasen las derrotas y se recogieran para mí; y luego antes que andásemos tres horas vimos una isla al Leste, sobre la cual descargamos, y llegamos á ella todos tres navíos antes de medio dia á la punta del Norte, adonde hace un isleo y una restinga de piedra fuera de él al Norte, y otro entre él y la isla grande; la cual anombraron estos hombres de San Salvador, que yo traigo, la isla Saomete, á la cual puse nombre la Isabela. El viento era Norte, y quedaba el dicho isleo en derrota de la isla Fernandina, de adonde yo habia partido Leste oueste, y se corria despues la costa desde el isleo al Oueste, y habia en ella doce leguas fasta un cabo, á quien yo llamé el Cabo Hermoso, que es de la parte del Oueste; y así es fermoso, redondo y muy fondo, sin bajas fuera de él, y al comienzo es de piedra y bajo, y mas adentro es playa de arena como cuasi la dicha costa es, y ahí surgí esta noche Viernes hasta la mañana. Esta costa toda, y la parte de la isla que yo ví, es toda cuasi playa, y la isla mas fermosa cosa que yo ví; que si las otras son muy hermosas, esta es mas: es de muchos árboles y muy verdes, y muy grandes; y esta tierra es mas alta que las otras islas falladas, y en ella algun altillo, no que se le pueda llamar montaña, mas cosa que afermosea lo otro, y parece de muchas aguas allá al medio de la isla; de esta parte al Nordeste hace una grande angla, y ha muchos arboledos, y muy espesos y muy grandes. Yo quise ir á surgir en ella para salir á tierra, y ver tanta fermosura; mas era el fondo bajo y no podia surgir salvo largo de tierra, y el viento era muy bueno para venir á este cabo, adonde yo surgí agora, al cual puse nombre Cabo Fermoso, porque así lo es; y así no surgí en aquella angla, y aun porque vide este cabo de allá tan verde y tan fermoso, así como todas las otras cosas y tierras destas islas que yo no sé adonde me vaya primero, ne me sé cansar los ojos de ver tan fermosas verduras y tan diversas de las nuestras, y aun creo que ha en ellas muchas yerbas y muchos árboles, que valen mucho en España para tinturas y para medicinas de especería, mas yo no los cognozco, de que llevo grande pena. Y llegando yo aquí á este cabo vino el olor tan bueno y suave de flores ó árboles de la tierra que era la cosa mas dulce del mundo. De mañana antes que yo de aquí vaya iré en tierra á ver que es aquí en el cabo; no es la poblacion salvo allá mas adentro adonde dicen estos hombres que yo traigo, que está el Rey y que trae mucho oro; y yo de mañana quiero ir tanto avante que halle la poblacion, y vea ó haya lengua con este Rey, que segun estos dan las señas él señorea todas estas islas comarcanas, y va vestido, y trae sobre sí mucho oro; aunque no doy mucha fé á sus decires, así por no los entender yo bien, como en cognoscer quellos son tan pobres de oro que cualquiera poco que este Rey traiga les parece á ellos mucho. Este á quien yo digo Cabo Fermoso creo que es isla apartada de Saometo, y aun hay ya otra entremedias pequeña: yo no curo así de ver tanto por menudo, porque no lo podia facer en cincuenta años, porque quiero ver y descubrir lo mas que yo pudiere para volver á vuestras Altezas, á nuestro Señor aplaciendo, en Abril. Verdad es que fallando adonde haya oro ó especería en cantidad me deterné fasta que yo haya dello cuanto pudiere; y por esto no fago sino andar para ver de topar en ello."

Sabado 20 *de Octubre:* "Hoy al sol salido levanté las anclas de donde yo estaba con la nao surgido en esta isla de *Saometo* al cabo del Sudueste, adonde yo puse nombre el Cabo de la Laguna y á la isla la Isabela, para navegar al Nordeste y al Leste de la parte del Sueste y Sur, adonde entendí de estos hombres que yo traigo que era la poblacion y el Rey de ella; y fallé todo tan bajo el fondo que no pude entrar ni navegar á ello, y vide que siguiendo el camino del Sudueste era muy gran rodeo, y por esto determiné de me volver por el camino que yo habia traido del Nornordeste de la parte del Oueste, y rodear esta isla para [conocerla(?)] el viento me fue tan escaso que yo no nunca pude haber la tierra al longo de la costa salvo en la noche; y por ques peligro surgir en estas islas, salvo en el dia que se vea con el ojo adonde se echa el ancla, porque es todo manchas, una de limpio y otra de non, yo me puse á temporejar á la vela toda esta noche del Domingo. Las carabelas surgieron porque se hallaron en tierra temprano, y pensaron que á sus señas, que eran costumbradas de hacer, iria á surgir; mas no quise."

Domingo 21 *de Octubre:* "A las diez horas llegué aquí á este cabo del isleo, y surgí y asímismo las carabelas; y despues de haber comido fuí en tierra, adonde aquí no habia otra poblacion que una casa, en la cual no fallé á nadie que creo que con temor se habian fugido porque en ella estaban todos sus aderezos de casa. Yo no les dejé tocar nada, salvo que me salí con estos capitanes y gente á ver la isla; que si las otras ya vistas son muy fermosas y verdes y fértiles, esta es mucho mas y de grandes arboledos y muy verdes. Aquí es unas grandes lagunas, y sobre ellas y á la rueda es el arboledo en maravilla, y aquí y en toda la isla son todos verdes y las yerbas como en el Abril en el Andalucía; y el cantar de los pajaritos que parece que el hombre nunca se querria partir de aquí, y las manadas de los papagayos que ascurecen el sol; y aves y pajaritos de tantas maneras y tan diversas de las nuestras que es maravilla; y despues ha árboles de mil maneras, y todos de su manera fruto, y todos huelen que es maravilla, que yo estoy el mas penado del mundo de no los cognoscer, porque soy bien cierto que todos son cosa de valía, y de ellos traigo la demuestra, y asimismo de las yerbas. Andando así en cerco de una destas lagunas vide una sierpe, la cual matamos y traigo el cuero á vuestras Altezas. Ella como nos vido se echó en la laguna, y nos le seguimos dentro, porque no era muy fonda, fasta que con lanzas la matamos; es de siete palmos en largo; creo que destas semejantes hay aquí en esta laguna muchas. Aquí cognoscí del liñaloe, y mañana he determinado de hacer traer á la nao diez quintales, porque me dicen que vale mucho. Tambien andando en busca de muy buena agua fuimos á una poblacion aquí cerca, adonde estoy surto media legua; y la gente della como nos sintieron dieron todos á fugir, y dejaron las casas, y escondieron su ropa y lo que tenian por el monte; y no dejé tomar nada ni la valia de un alfiler. Despues se llegaron á nos unos hombres dellos, y uno se llegó del todo aquí: yo dí unos cascabeles y unas cuentecillas de vidrio, y quedó muy contento y muy alegre, y porque la amistad creciese mas y los requiriese algo le hice pedir agua, y ellos despues que fuí en la nao vinieron luego á la playa con sus calabazas llenas y folgaron mucho de dárnosla, y yo les mandé dar otro ramalejo de cuentecillas de vidrio, y dijeron que de mañana vernian acá. Yo queria hinchir aquí toda la vasija de los navios de agua; por ende si el tiempo me da lugar luego me partiré á rodear esta isla fasta que yo haya lengua con este Rey, y ver si puedo haber dél el oro que oyo que trae, y despues partir para otra isla grande mucho, que creo que debe ser Cipango, segun las señas que me dan estos indios que yo traigo, á la cual ellos llaman Colba, en la cual dicen que ha naos y mareantes muchos y muy grandes, y de esta isla otra que llaman Bosio que tambien dicen qués muy grande, y á las otras que son entremedio veré así de pasada, y segun yo fallare recaudo de oro ó especería determinaré lo que he de facer. Mas todavía tengo determinado de ir á la tierra firme y á la ciudad de Guisay, y dar las cartas de vuestras Altezas al Gran Can, y pedir respuesta y venir con ella."

Lunes 22 de Octubre: "Toda esta noche y hoy estuve aquí aguardando si el Rey de aquí ó otras personas traerian oro o otra cosa de sustancia, y vinieron muchos de esta gente, semejantes á los otros de las otras islas, así desnudos, y asi pintados dellos de blanco, dellos de colorado, dellos de prieto, y asi de muchas maneras. Traían azagayas y algunos ovillos de algodon á resgatar, el cual trocaban aquí con algunos marineros por pedazos de vidrio, de tazas quebradas, y por pedazos de escudillas de barro. Algunos dellos traían algunos pedazos de oro colgado al nariz, el cual de buena gana daban por un cascabel destos de pie de gavilano y por cuentecillas de vidrio: mas es tan poco, que no es nada: que es verdad que cualquiera poca cosa que se les dé ellos tambien tenian á gran maravilla nuestra venida, y creian que eramos venidos del cielo. Tomamos agua para los navíos en una laguna que aquí está acerca del *cabo del isleo*, que así la nombré; y en la dicha laguna Martin Alonso Pinzon, capitan de la Pinta, mató otra sierpe tal como la otra de ayer de siete palmos, y fice tomar aquí del linaloe cuanto se falló."

Martes 23 de Octubre: "Quisiera hoy partir para la isla de Cuba, que creo que debe ser Cipango segun las señas que dan esta gente de la grandeza della y riqueza, y no me deterné mas aquí ni [blank in the original] esta isla al rededor para ir á la poblacion, como tenia determinado, para haber lengua con este Rey ó Señor, que es por no me detener mucho, pues veo que aquí no hay mina de oro, y al rodear de estas islas ha menester muchas maneras de viento, y no vienta así como los hombres querrian. Y pues es de andar adonde haya trato grande, digo que no es razon de se detener salvo ir á camino, y calar mucha tierra fasta topar en tierra muy proprovechosa, aunque mi entender es questa sea muy provechosa de especería; mas que yo no la cognosco que llevo la mayor pena del mundo, que veo mil maneras de árboles que tienen cada uno su manera de fruta, y verde agora como en España en el mes de Mayo y Junio, y mil maneras de yerbas, eso mesmo con flores, y de todo no se cognosció salvo este linaloe de que hoy mandé tambien traer á la nao mucho para llevar á vuestras Altezas. Y no he dado ni doy la vela para Cuba, porque no hay viento, salvo calma muerta y llueve mucho; y llovió ayer mucho sin hacer ningun frio, antes el dia hace calor, y las noches temperadas como en Mayo en España en el Andalucía."

Miercoles 24 de Octubre: " Esta noche á media noche levanté las anclas de la isla Isabela del Cabo del isleo, ques de la parte del Norte á donde yo estaba posado para ir á la isla de Cuba, á donde oí desta gente que era muy grande y de gran trato, y habia en ella oro y especerías y naos grandes y mercaderes; y me amostró que al Ouesudueste iria á ella, y yo asi lo tengo, porque creo que si es así como por señas que me hicieron todos los indios de estas islas y aquellos que llevo yo en los navíos, porque por lengua no los entiendo, es la isla de Cipango de que se cuentan cosas maravillosas, y en las esperas que yo ví y en las pinturas de mapamundos es ella en esta comarca, y así navegué fasta el dia al Ouesudueste, y amaneciendo calmó el viento y llovió, y asi casi toda la noche; y estuve así con poco viento fasta que pasaba de medio dia y entonces tornó á ventar muy amoroso, y llevaba todas mis velas de la nao, maestra, y dos bonetas, y trinquete, y cebadera, y mezana, y vela de gavia, y el batel por popa; así anduve al camino fasta que anocheció y entonces me quedaba el Cabo Verde de la isla Fernandina, el cual es de la parte de Sur á la parte de Oueste, me quedaba al Norueste, y hacía de mí á él siete leguas. Y porque ventaba ya recio y no sabia yo cuanto camino hobiese fasta la dicha isla de Cuba, y por no la ir á demandar de noche, porque todas estas islas son muy fondas á no hallar fondo todo en derredor, salvo á tiro de dos lombardas, y esto es todo manchado un pedazo de roquedo y otro de arena, y por esto no se puede seguramente surgir salvo á vista de ojo, y por tanto acordé de amainar las velas todas, salvo el trinquete, y andar con él, y de á un rato crecia mucho el viento y hacía mucho camino de que dudaba, y era muy gran cerrazon, y llovía: mandé amainar el trinquete y no anduvimos esta noche dos leguas, &c."

Jueves 25 de Octubre: Navegó despues del sol salido al Oueste Sudueste hasta las nueve horas, andarian cinco leguas: despues mudó el camino al Oueste: andaban ocho millas por hora hasta la una despues de medio dia, y de allí hasta las tres, y andarian cuarenta y cuatro millas. Entonces vieron tierra, y eran siete á ocho islas, en luengo todas de Norte á Sur: distaban de ellas cinco leguas, &c.

Viernes 26 de Octubre: Estuvo de las dichas islas de la parte del Sur, era todo bajo cinco ó seis leguas, surgió por allí. Dijeron los indios que llevaba que habia dellas á Cuba andadura de dia y medio con sus almadias, que son navetas de un madero adonde no llevan vela. Estas son las canoas. Partió de allí para Cuba, porque por las señas que los indios le daban de la grandeza y del oro y perlas della pensaba que era ella, conviene á saber Cipango.

Sabado 27 de Octubre: Levantó las anclas salido el sol de aquellas islas, que llamó las islas de Arena por el poco fondo que tenian de la parte del Sur hasta seis leguas. Anduvo ocho millas por hora hasta la una del dia al Sursudueste, y habrian andado cuarenta millas, y hasta la noche andarian veinte y ocho millas al mesmo camino, y antes de noche vieron tierra. Estuvieron la noche al reparo con mucha lluvia que llovió. Anduvieron el Sabado fasta el poner del sol diez y siete leguas al Sursudueste.

Domingo 28 de Octubre: Fue de allí en demanda de la isla de Cuba al Sursudueste, á la tierra della mas cercana, y entró en un rio muy hermoso y muy sin peligro de bajas ni otros inconvenientes, y toda la costa que anduvo por allí era muy hondo y muy limpio fasta tierra: tenia la boca del rio doce brazas, y es bien ancha para barloventear; surgió dentro, diz que á tiro de lombarda. Dice el Almirante que nunca tan hermosa cosa vido, lleno de árboles todo cercado el rio, fermosos y verdes y diversos de las nuestras, con flores y con su fruto, cada uno de su manera. Aves muchas y pajaritos que cantaban muy dulcemente: habia gran cantidad de palmas de otra manera que las de Guinea y de las nuestras; de una estatura mediana y los pies sin aquella camisa, y las hojas muy grandes, con las cuales cobijan las casas; la tierra muy llana: saltó el Almirante en la barca y fue á tierra, y llegó á dos casas que creyó ser de pescadores y que con temor se huyeron, en una de las cuales halló un perro que nunca ladró, y en ambas casas halló redes de hilo de palma y cordeles, y anzuelo de cuerno, y fisgas de hueso y otros aparejos de pescar, y muchos huegos dentro, y creyó que en cada una casa se juntan muchas personas: mandó que no se tocase en cosa de todo ello, y así se hizo. La yerba era grande como en el Andalucía por Abril y Mayo. Halló verdolagas muchas y bledos. Tornóse á la barca y anduvo por el rio arriba un buen rato, y diz que era gran placer ver aquellas verduras y arboledas, y de las aves que no podia dejallas para se volver. Dice que es aquella isla la mas hermosa que ojos hayan visto, llena de muy buenos puertos y rios hondos, y la mar que parecia que nunca se debia de alzar porque la yerba de la playa llegaba hasta cuasi el agua, la cual no suele llegar donde la mar es brava: hasta entonces no habia experimentado en todas aquellas islas que la mar fuese brava. La isla, dice, ques llena de montañas muy hermosas, aunque no son muy grandes en longura salvo altas, y toda la otra tierra es alta de la manera de Sicilia: llena es de muchas aguas, segun pudo entender de los indios que consigo lleva, que tomó en la isla de Guanahani, los cuales le dicen por señas que hay diez rios grandes, y que con sus canoas no la pueden cercar en veinte dias. Cuando iba á tierra con los navíos salieron dos almadias ó canoas, y como vieron que los marineros entraban en la barca y remaban para ir á ver el fondo del rio para saber donde habian de surgir, huyeron las canoas. Decian los indios que en aquella isla habia minas de oro y perlas, y vido el Almirante lugar apto para ellas y almejas, ques señal dellas, y entendia el Almirante que allí venian naos del Gran Can, y grandes, y que de allí á tierra firme habia jornada de diez dias. Llamó el Almirante aquel rio y puerto de San Salvador.

CHAPTER IV

Translation of Las Casas' Abridgment

THE following translation into English is almost literal, and nearly as possible preserves the ruggedness of the original:

Wednesday, October 10: He sailed toward the west-southwest, going at the rate of ten miles an hour, or sometimes twelve, and for a short space at seven miles an hour. During the day and night together, he sailed fifty-nine leagues, but reported to the crew only forty-four. Here the crew could stand it no longer, and complained of the long voyage; but the Admiral encouraged them as best he could, holding out hopes of the profits which they might gain. And he added that it was useless for them to complain, for he had come to find the Indies, and he would continue until he found them, with the help of God.

Thursday, October 11: He sailed toward the west-southwest, encountering a much heavier sea than at any previous time during the voyage. They saw *pardelas* [a grayish bird] and a green reed near the ship. Those on board the Pinta saw a stalk of cane and a pole, and took on board another little pole which had the appearance of having been worked with an iron tool, and a piece of cane and another plant which grows on land, and a little slab of wood. Those on board the Niña also saw other signs of land, one of which was a little branch loaded with rose-hips. With these signs, all breathed more freely and rejoiced. During that day before sunset they sailed twenty-seven leagues.

After sunset he sailed on his first course, toward the west, going at the rate of twelve miles an hour, and by two o'clock in the morning they had gone ninety miles, which are equal to twenty-two leagues and a half. Because the Pinta was the better sailer and went in advance of the Admiral's caravel, those on board discovered land, and made the signals which the Admiral had ordered. Land was first seen by a sailor named Rodrigo de Triana, although at ten o'clock the night before, the Admiral, standing on the castle of the poop, saw a light, but it was so indistinct that he could not be sure that it was land, so called Pedro Gutierrez, a gentleman of the king's bedchamber, and he told him there seemed to be a light and told him to look. He did so, and saw it. He also told Rodrigo Sanchez of Segovia, whom the king and queen had sent with the fleet as inspector; but he saw nothing, not being in a position where he could see it. After the Admiral called their attention to it, they saw the light once or twice, and it was like that of a little wax candle which was being lifted and raised. This did not seem to many to be an indication of it, but the Admiral was certain that they were close to land. Consequently, when the crew came together to chant and sing in their own way the Salve, as was their custom, all being present, the Admiral requested and admonished them particularly to keep a good lookout from the forecastle and to look sharp for land, and he said that to him who first discovered it he would give a silken doublet in addition to the other reward which the king and queen had promised, which was a pension of ten thousand maravedis to him who first saw land. At two o'clock in the morning land was seen, about two leagues off. They shortened sail, leaving only a storm square sail, which is the mainsail without bonnet-sails, and lay to until Friday morning, on which they arrived at one of the small islands of the Lucayos which the Indians called Guanahani. They soon saw naked people on the shore, and the Admiral, Martin Alonzo Pinzon, and Vicente Anes, his brother, who was captain of the Niña, set off for the shore, in the armed boat. The Admiral unfurled the royal standard, and each of the captains one of the flags of the Green Cross which the Admiral carried on board all of the ships as a distinguishing flag, having on one side of the cross the letter F and on the other the letter Y, with a crown above each letter. As soon as they had landed, they saw bright green trees, much fresh water, and fruits of many kinds. The Admiral called the two captains and all the rest who had leaped ashore, and Rodrigo Escovedo, secretary of the whole fleet, and Rodrigo Sanchez of Segovia, and asked them all to witness that he, in their presence, was taking, as he in fact took, possession of that island for the king and the queen, their masters, making all the declarations required, as are contained more fully in the documents there executed in writing. In a short time a great crowd of the natives had gathered. The following are the exact words of the Admiral which he wrote in the journal of his first voyage, in which he discovered these Indies: "I," said he, "because they were very friendly to us, and because I recognized that it would be better to convert them to our Holy Faith by love than by force, gave to some of them colored caps and some strings of beads, which they put around their necks, and many other things of little value, which gave them much pleasure and made them wonderfully friendly toward us. Afterward, when we were in the ship's boats, they came swimming to us and brought us parrots, and balls of cotton thread, and spears, and many other things, which they exchanged with us for other things which we gave them, such as strings of beads and little bells. In fact they would take anything and give whatever they had most willingly. But they appeared to me to be a very poor people. They walk about naked as their mothers bore them, the women as well as the men; although I saw only one girl, and she was quite young. But all that I saw were young—not one of them older than thirty years. They were well formed, with handsome bodies and attractive faces, and their hair was as coarse, almost, as that of a horse's tail, and short. They wear their hair falling down to their eyebrows, except a few locks behind, which they wear long and never cut. Some of them paint themselves in dark colors, for they are the color of the Canary Islanders, neither black nor white; and others paint themselves in white, and others in red, and others in whatever color they happen to find. Some of them paint their faces, and some their whole bodies, and some only around their eyes, and others the nose only. They do not carry arms, nor do they know what they mean; for I showed them swords, and they took hold of them by the blade and cut themselves through ignorance. They have no iron; their spears are slender rods without iron, though some of them are tipped with fishes' teeth, and others with other things. As a class they are all of good height, graceful in their movements, and well built. I saw some who had scars on their bodies, and I asked them by signs what these meant, and they told me by signs how people from other islands close by came and tried to take them captive and how they defended themselves; and I believed, and still believe, that those who came to take them captive came from the mainland. They ought to be good servants and intelligent, for I see that they quickly repeat everything that I said to them; and I believe it will be easy to make them Christians, because it seemed to me that they had no religion. If it please God, when I leave here I will take six of them to Your Highnesses in order that they may be taught to speak. The only animals of any kind that I saw in this island were parrots." All these are the words of the Admiral.

Saturday, October 13: "As soon as it was light, many of these men came to the shore. They were all young, as I have said, and of good height, a very handsome people. Their hair is not curled, but stiff and coarse like horse-hair, and they all have very broad foreheads and heads, broader than I ever saw in any other race. Their eyes are very pretty, and not small, and they are never very dark-colored, being like the Canary Islanders; and nothing else could be expected, for this island is directly west, on the same line with the island of Hierro, one of the Canaries. The legs of all of them are very straight, their stomachs do not protrude, and on the whole they are very well built. They came to the ship in canoes, which are made of the trunk of a single tree, like a long boat, and all of a single piece, wonderfully built, considering the country. Some were large enough to accommodate forty or forty-five men, and others smaller: some so small that they held only one man. They rowed with a paddle like a baker's oven-spade, and moved with wonderful quickness. If the boat capsizes, they all swim about and turn over the boat and bail out the water with calabashes which they carry with them. They brought balls of spun cotton, and parrots, and spears, and other little things which it would be tiresome to describe, and they would give them all for anything that was offered to them. I was watchful, and endeavored to find out if they had gold. I noticed that several wore a little piece hanging in a hole in their nose, and by signs I was able to learn that by going toward the south, or rounding the island toward the south, there would be found a king who had great vessels full of gold, and who had an abundance of it. I tried to persuade them to go there, but afterward saw that they did not wish to go. I determined to wait until to-morrow afternoon and then set out for the southwest,—for many of them had told me by signs that there was land to the south and to the southwest and to the northwest, and that the people from the northwest came frequently to fight them,—and then continue on to the southwest in search of gold and precious stones. This island is very large and very flat, and has very green trees and much water and a very large lake in the middle, but without any mountains. It is all so green that it is a pleasure to look at it. The people are extremely gentle, and are so anxious to have our things that, thinking that we will not give them anything unless they give us something in exchange, and having nothing, they take whatever they can lay hands on and throw themselves into the water and swim ashore. But they will give everything they have for whatever is offered to them. They will buy even the pieces of crockery and broken glasses. I even saw them give sixteen balls of spun cotton for three *ceotis* [a small coin] of Portugal, which is one *blanca* [one half maravedi] of Castile; and these sixteen balls would weigh more than twenty-five pounds. This I prohibited, and allowed no one to take any unless I had ordered it taken for Your Highnesses, had there been a quantity. Cotton grows in this island, but for want of time I was unable to see for myself. The gold also is found here which they wear hanging in their noses. But I did not wish to lose time, preferring to set out to try and find the island of Japan. Now as night had come, they all have gone ashore in their canoes."

Sunday, October 14: "As soon as it was light, I ordered the boat of the ship and those of the caravels to be made ready, and set out along the coast of the island toward the north-northeast to see the other part of it,— which was on the other side of the east,—and also to see the towns. I soon saw two or three, the people of which all came down to the beach calling out and giving thanks to God. Some brought us water and others things to eat. When they saw that I did not wish to land, some of them threw themselves into the sea and came swimming to us, and we understood them to ask us if we had come from heaven. One old man climbed into the boat, and others called out with loud voices to all the men and women to come and see the men who had come from heaven, and to bring them food and drink. Many men and women came, every one bringing something, giving thanks to God, throwing themselves on the ground, lifting their hands toward heaven, and then calling loudly that we come ashore. But I was afraid, because I saw a great reef of rocks which surrounds the island, within which is space and depth for as many ships as there are in all Christendom, but the entrance is very narrow. It is true that inside this reef are some sunken rocks, but the sea does not move any more than the water in a well. And in order to see all this I set out this morning, that I might be able to give a full account to your Highnesses, and also that I might know where a fort could be built. I saw a piece of land which is like an island, although it is not one, upon which were six houses. This peninsula could in two days be made into an island, though I do not believe that would be necessary, for these people are so inexpert in the use of arms, as Your Highnesses can see by the seven which I have had captured in order to take them and teach them our language and then return them, or if your Highnesses order, they can all be taken to Castile or kept captive in this same island, because with fifty men the whole could be kept in subjection and made to do whatever might be desired. Also close to that peninsula are the most beautiful groves of trees which I ever saw, whose leaves are as green as those of Castile in the months of April and May, and plenty of fresh water. I examined that whole harbor, and afterward returned to the ship and set sail. I saw so many islands that I could not decide to which I would first go, and those men whom I had taken with me told me by signs that there were more and more past counting, and named more than a hundred. At last I looked for the largest, and determined to go to that. I did so, and it will be about five leagues from San Salvador; and of the others, some are more and some less than this distance. All are very flat, without mountains, and very fertile, and all inhabited. The people of the different islands make war with each other, although they are very simple-minded and have very beautiful bodies."

Monday, October 15: "I had been standing off and on last night, being afraid to get near enough to the shore to anchor before morning, because I did not know whether the shore was free from shoals, intending at dawn to clew up. As the island was more than five leagues distant,—perhaps as much as seven,—and as the tide detained me, it was noon when I arrived at the island and found that that coast which is toward San Salvador runs north and south and was five leagues in length. The other coast, which I followed, ran from east to west, and was more than ten leagues in length. As from this island I saw a larger one toward the west, I clewed up the sails, for I had gone all that day until night because I could not yet have reached the western extremity, to which I gave the name of island of Santa Maria de la Concepcion, and about sunset anchored near the aforesaid cape in order to learn if there were gold there; for those whom I had ordered taken captive in the island of San Salvador told me that in this island the natives wore large rings of gold on their arms and legs. I rightly believed that all they told me was in order to deceive me and escape. Nevertheless my desire was not to pass by any island without taking possession of it; although possession taken of one, the same might be said of all. I anchored and waited until to-day, Tuesday, when at daybreak I went ashore with the boats, well armed, and stepped on land. The inhabitants, who were very numerous and naked and in similar condition to those of the island of San Salvador, allowed us to go about the island, and gave us whatever I asked of them. And because the wind was increasing against the coast, southeast, I did not want to wait, but set out for the ship. One of their large canoes was alongside the caravel Niña, and one of the men from San Salvador who was on board of her threw himself into the sea and escaped in the canoe. And in the middle of the preceding night the other [blank in original] and he went after the canoe, which moved so rapidly that there never was a boat which could have overtaken it, as they had a long start of us. Nevertheless it reached the land and they left the canoe, and when some of my company went ashore after them, they all scattered like chickens. The canoe which they had left we brought alongside the Niña. Just then, at the other end of the caravel, there was seen another small canoe containing a man who had come to barter a ball of yarn. Some sailors threw themselves into the sea and took him prisoner because he did not want to come on board. I, who was on the poop of my ship, saw it all, and sent for the Indian and gave him a red cap and some strings of small green glass beads which I put on his arms, and two little bells which I put in his ears, and I ordered his canoe, which I had on board, returned to him, and sent him ashore. Immediately after, we set sail for the other large island which I saw toward the west. I ordered also that the other large canoe which the Niña was towing at her stern should be set adrift. I afterward saw that when the man to whom I had given the things already mentioned, and from whom I had not accepted the ball of yarn which he wished to give me, reached the shore, the others gathered around him and he thought it wonderful; and surely it seemed to him that we were good people, and that the other man who had fled had done us some harm and for that reason we had taken him prisoner. For this reason I had ordered him set free, and had given him the before mentioned things in order that they might think well of us, and so that another time when Your Highnesses send future expeditions here they will not encounter enmity; for all that I gave him was not worth four maravedis. I then set out (it was about ten o'clock), with the wind from the southeast inclining to the south, in order to go to that other island, which is very large, and where those whom I had brought with me from San Salvador told me, by signs, there is a great deal of gold, and where the inhabitants wear it on their arms like bracelets, and on the legs and in the ears, and in the nose and around the neck. From the island of Santa Maria to this other island it is nine leagues east to west, and all that part of the island ran from the northwest toward the southwest, and it seemed as if there might be on this side of the coast more than twenty-eight leagues. It is very level, without any mountains, the same as San Salvador and Santa Maria, and all being beach without rocks except that all these islands have a few rocks near land but below the water, making it necessary to keep a sharp lookout, and when one wishes to anchor not to do so near the shore, although the water is always very clear and the bottom is readily seen. And in all these islands, at two lombard-shots from shore, there is such a depth that no one can fathom it. These islands are very green and fertile and have a balmy atmosphere, and there may be many things of which I do not know, because I do not care to delay, for I wish to reconnoiter and visit many islands in order to find gold: because these men tell me by signs that they wear gold on their arms and legs, and it is gold, for I showed them some pieces which I have, and I cannot fail, with the help of God, to find where it is. When we were in the middle of the channel between the two islands,—that is to say, Santa Maria and the other large one, to which I gave the name of Fernandina,—I found a man alone in a canoe who was going from the island of Santa Maria to that of Fernandina. He had with him a piece of their bread the size of a man's fist, a calabash of water, and a lump of red earth which had been powdered and then molded, and some dry leaves which seem to be highly prized by them, for they brought them to me in San Salvador as a present. He also had a little basket in their manner, in which was a collection of strings of glass beads, and two *blancas*, and by these I recognized that he had come from San Salvador and had gone from there to Santa Maria and from there was going to Fernandina. When he arrived at the ship, I took him aboard, as he asked me to do, and put his canoe on board also, and gave orders to guard well what he was carrying, and that he be given bread and syrup and something to drink; and thus I will take him to Fernandina, and will give him all his things in order that he may speak well of us, so that it may please God, when Your Highnesses send here, that those who come may be received with honor, and that they may give us of all that they have."

Tuesday, October 16: "I set out from the island of Santa Maria de la Concepcion at about midday for the island of Fernandina, which showed very large toward the west. I sailed all day, with little wind, and could not arrive in time to see the bottom in order to get a clear anchorage; for in this it is necessary to exercise great care not to lose the anchors. And so I stood off and on all night, and in the morning came to a village where I anchored. The man whom I had found yesterday in his canoe in the middle of the bay had come from this town, and had given such a good report of us that all night there was no lack of canoes around the ship, which brought us water and whatever other things they had. I ordered something given to each one of them,—that is to say, some little strings of beads, ten or twelve glass ones on a thread, and some little brass bells such as are worth a maravedi each in Castile, and some straps—all of which they thought wondrously fine. I also ordered that there be given them syrup to eat when they came on board. About nine o'clock in the morning I sent the ship's boat on shore for water, and they very good-naturedly pointed out to my men where the water was, and they themselves brought the full barrels to the boat, and it pleased them much to thus oblige us."

"This island is very large, and I have determined to sail around it, because, as I understand it, it is on it or near it that there is a mine of gold. This island is almost eight leagues east and west of Santa Maria, and the point to which I have come and all this coast runs north-northwest and south-southeast, and I saw fully twenty leagues of it, and it did not end there. Now, while I am writing, I have set sail with the wind from the south, in order to strive to sail around the island and work until I find Saomete, which is the island or city where the gold is; for all of those who are on board say that, and those of San Salvador and Santa Maria all told us the same. These people are similar to those on the other islands, with the same speech and same habits except that they seem to be a little more gentle and more tractable, and more intelligent; for I have noticed that those who have brought cotton and other things here to the ship understand better how to bargain about the payment—something the others have never done. In this island I have even seen cotton cloth made into capes, and the people are more obliging, and the women wear in front of their bodies a little piece of cloth, which scarcely covers them at all. It is an island very green and level and exceedingly fertile, and I do not doubt but that all the year round they sow and gather corn, and the same with everything else. I saw many trees very different in appearance from ours, and many of them had branches of many kinds all from one trunk, and one little branch is of one kind and another of another, and so different in appearance that it is the most marvelous thing in the world how wide is the difference between one kind and the other. For example, one branch will have leaves like canes and another leaves like those of the mastic-tree, and thus on one tree there will be five or six different kinds, and all so very different. Nor are they grafted, because it might be said that they were, but they grow wild in the woods, nor do these people care for them. I know of no religion among them, and I believe that they will quickly become Christians, for they are very intelligent. Here the fishes are so different from ours that it is wonderful. There are some looking like cocks, with the brightest colors in the world,—blue, yellow, red and every color, and others colored in a thousand ways; their different hues being so exquisite that no man can look at them without being astonished and delighted. There are also whales. I saw no animals on land except parrots and lizards, but one boy told me that he had seen a big snake. Neither sheep, goats, nor any other animal did I see; but I have been here but a short time,—that is, a half a day,—but if there had been any, I could not have failed to see some of them. I shall describe the trip around the island after I have finished it."

Wednesday, October 17: "At noon I set out from the village off which I had anchored and where I had taken on board water, in order to sail around this island of Fernandina. The wind was southwest and south, and I wished to follow the coast of this island from where I was toward the southeast, for the whole coast runs from the north-northwest to the south-southeast, and I wished to follow that same direction toward the south and southeast, because all those Indians which I had brought with me, and another, made signs that the island which they call Saomete, where the gold is, is in that part toward the south. Martin Alonzo Pinzon, the captain of the caravel Pinta, with whom I had sent three of these Indians, came to me and told me that one of them had very positively given him to understand that by sailing north-northwest it would be much quicker to get around the island. I saw that the wind would not help me on the route which I wished to take, and was fair for the other route, so set sail for the north-northwest. When I had nearly reached the end of the island, or about two leagues of it, I found a marvelous harbor with a mouth—or it even might be said with two mouths, because there is an island in the middle, and both are very narrow. Within, it is broad enough for a hundred ships if it were deep and with a clear bottom, and were deep at the entrance. It seemed to me right to examine and sound it, and so I anchored outside and entered with all the ships' boats, and we found that it had insufficient depth. Because I had thought when I saw it that it was the mouth of some river, I had ordered barrels taken in order to get water. On shore we found eight or ten men, who soon came to us and pointed out to us not far off a village where I sent the men for water, part of them with arms and the rest with the barrels, and so they got it. As it was quite far, I was detained two hours, and meanwhile I walked about among the trees, which are the most beautiful things that were ever seen, as I saw them as green and as bright as in the month of May in Andalucia; and all the trees are as different from ours as the day is from the night, and the same is true of the fruits and the herbs and the stones and everything. It is true that some trees were of a similar nature to those of Castile; but, after all, there were great differences, and other trees of other kinds were so many that there is no person who can say that they have any resemblance to any tree in Castile. The people are just the same as those already described, of the same conditions, equally naked, and of the same height. They gave whatever they had for whatever was offered to them. Here I saw some of the sailors getting darts for bits of broken crockery and glass. The others who went for the water told me that they had been in their houses, which are well swept and clean inside. Their beds and bags for holding things are like nets made of cotton. Their houses are all like tents, and very high and with good chimneys. Among the many villages I saw, none possessed more than twelve or fifteen houses. Here they saw that the married women wear breeches made of cotton, but the girls do not, except some which had reached the age of eighteen years. There were there mastiffs and hounds, and they found there one man who had a piece of gold in his nose the size of half a *castellano* [a gold coin], upon which they saw letters. I berated them because they did not buy it and pay whatever he asked, in order to see what money and whose money it was; but they replied that he did not dare to barter it. After taking water, I returned to the ship and set sail, going toward the northwest far enough for me to see all of that coast until it runs east and west. After this all the Indians repeated that this island was smaller than Saomete, and that it would be best to turn around in order to get there sooner. The wind then ceased, and shortly began to blow west-northwest, which was the opposite from whence we had come, and so I turned around and sailed all that night to the east-southeast, sometimes wholly east, sometimes to the southeast, and this to keep away from the land, for it was very dark and the weather threatening. The wind was light, and did not let me get near enough to land to cast anchor. To-night it has rained very hard from after midnight until almost daylight, and it is still cloudy and threatening rain. We are at the end of the island toward the southeast, where I hope to anchor until it is clear enough to see the other islands where I want to go. And thus every day that I have been in the Indies it has rained more or less. I beg Your Highnesses to believe that this land is the best, and most fertile, and most temperate, and level, and good which there is in the world."

Thursday, October 18: "As soon as it had cleared, I followed with the wind and went around the island as much as I could, and anchored when I could no longer sail. I did not go ashore again, but at daybreak set sail."

Friday, October 19: "At daybreak I weighed anchor and sent the caravel Pinta to the east and southeast, and the caravel Niña to the south-southeast, and I with the ship went to the southeast, and gave orders that they follow those routes until noon, after which both should change their courses and rejoin me. Before we had gone three hours, we saw to the east an island to which we directed our course, and all three ships came together there before noon at the point toward the north where there is an islet and a reef outside it toward the north, and another between it and the large island, which latter the men I had brought from San Salvador called Saomete, and to which I gave the name of Isabella. The wind was from the north, and this islet lay on the way from the island of Fernandina, whence I had come east-west, and afterward the coast ran from the islet to the west, and it was twelve leagues to a cape which I called Cape Beautiful, which is the point toward the west; and it is beautiful, round, and with water very deep, without shoals outside of it. At first it is low and stony, but farther in there is a sandy beach the same as almost all the coast is, and there I anchored to-night (Friday) until morning. All of this coast and the part of the island which I saw is almost all beach, and the island is the handsomest thing I have seen; for if the others are very beautiful, this one is more so, for there are many trees, and they are very green and very large, and this land is higher than the other islands we have found, and there is on it a little hill—for it can hardly be called a mountain—which makes it more handsome than the others. It seems as if there were plenty of water there in the middle of the island. From this part toward the northeast, the coast makes a great angle, and there are forests very thick and very large. I wished to anchor off it in order to go ashore and see so much beauty, but the water was shallow, and I could not anchor except a long way from shore, and the wind was fair to come to this cape where I am now anchored and to which I have given the name of Cape Beautiful, for such it is; and so I did not anchor at that angle, for I saw from there this cape, so green and so beautiful, just like all the other things of these lands and islands, so that I do not know to which to go first, nor can my eyes ever tire of seeing so much beautiful verdure and so different from ours, and I believe that there are among them many herbs and trees which would have great value in Spain for dyes or for medicines; but I do not know them, which I greatly regret. When I arrived at this cape, there came an odor so beautiful and soft from the flowers or trees of the land that it was the sweetest thing in the world. In the morning, before I go away, I will go ashore and see what there is on this cape. There is no village here, except one farther in where the men whom I have brought say that there is a king who has a great deal of gold; and in the morning I want to go far enough to find that village and see or have speech with this king, who, as they tell me by signs, rules all of the neighboring islands and is clothed and wears upon his person much gold: however, I do not give much faith to what they say, both because I do not understand them well, and because I see they are so poor that no matter how little gold this king wears, it will seem to them to be much. This to which I have given the name of Cape Beautiful is, I believe, on an island separate from Saomete, and that there is even another small one between. I do not wish to examine very minutely, for I could not do that in fifty years, because I want to see and discover all that I can in order to return to Your Highnesses, if God is willing, in April. The truth is, that when I find where there is gold or spices in quantity, I will stop there until I get all of them that I can, and for this reason I do nothing but keep going until I find them."

Saturday, October 20: "To-day at sunrise I weighed anchor from where the ship was anchored at this island of Saomete, at the cape toward the southwest (to which I gave the name of Cape of the Lake, and to the island the name of Isabella), in order to sail to the northeast and to the east from the southern and southeastern part, where I understood from those men whom I had brought that the village and the king of it are. I found the water so shallow that I could neither enter nor sail to it, and I saw that following the route to the southwest would be a long way around, so for this reason I determined to return by the route I had followed from the north-northeast of the western part, and sail around the island to [explore it]. The wind was so slight that I never could get near shore except at night, and as it is dangerous to anchor in these islands except during the day, when it can be seen where to drop the anchor, for it is all in patches, one spot being free from rocks and another not, I stood off and on all this Sunday night. The caravels anchored because they found themselves near land early, and they thought that on account of the signals they made, as was the custom, I would go to anchor, but I did not wish to."

Sunday, October 21: "At ten o'clock I arrived here at this end of the island and anchored, as also did the caravels, and after having breakfast I went ashore. Here I found no village—only one house, in which we found no one; but I think that they had run away through fright, because all their household goods were there. I did not let my men touch anything, but set out with the captains and the men to see the island, which, if the others we have so far seen are very beautiful and green and fertile, this is much more so, and there are large groves which are very green. Here are some large lakes, and the growth around them is perfectly wonderful; and here, as in all the island, everything is green, and the grass is as it is in April in Andalucia. And the singing of the birds! It would seem as if a man would never want to leave here. And the flocks of parrots darken the sun, and there are birds of so many different kinds and so different from ours that it is marvelous. And after them are the trees, of a thousand kinds and each with its fruit, and all odoriferous, which is wonderful. And I am the sorriest man in the world because I do not know them, because I feel certain that they are all things of value; and of them I bring samples, and also of the herbs. While walking around one of these lakes, I saw a snake which we killed, and I am bringing the skin to Your Highnesses. When it saw us it threw itself into the lake, and we followed it—for the water was not deep—until we had killed it with our lances. It is seven palms long. I believe that there are many like this in these lakes. Here I recognized the aloe, and to-morrow I have determined to have ten hundredweight of it brought to the ship, for they tell me it is very valuable. Also, while walking in search of good water we went to a village near here — perhaps half a league—the people of which, as soon as they saw us, all ran away, leaving their houses and hiding their clothing and the other things they had in the woods. I did not let any of my people take anything, not even of the value of a pin. Afterward a few of their men came to us, and one came clear to the camp, to whom I gave some bells and some little strings of beads, and it made him very happy and contented. In order to have our friendship increase, and as something was needed from them, I made him ask for water. After I had gone on board the ship, they came to the beach with calabashes full and took great pleasure in giving it to us; so I ordered that they be given another bunch of strings of beads, and they said that they would come again in the morning. I wished to fill here all the casks in the ships with water. Consequently, if the weather be favorable I will leave here, to sail around this island until I have an interview with that king and see if I can get that gold from him which I hear he wears, and after that set out for another very large island, which I believe must be Japan according to the signs which these Indians I have brought make, and which they call Colba, and where they say they have large ships and many great merchants, and from there to another island which they call Bosio, which they say is also very large, and to the other intermediate ones which I will see in passing; and finding indication of gold or spices, I will decide what to do. I have already made up my mind to go to the mainland and to the city of Guisay, and give Your Highnesses' letters to the Grand Kahn, and ask an answer, and come home with it."

Monday, October 22: "All last night and to-day I have been waiting here for the king of this country, or other persons, to bring gold or other things of value. Many people have come, similar to those of the other islands, likewise naked and likewise painted—some white, some red, some almost black, and so on in many ways. They bring spears and some balls of cotton to trade, which articles some of the sailors have bought with pieces of glass, of broken cups, and for pieces of earthen pots. Some few of them have pieces of gold suspended in their nose, which they give with good grace for a bell — the kind they attach to the foot of a hawk—and for strings of glass beads: but so very little that it is nothing; and it is the truth that it makes no difference how insignificant the thing is which is given to them. They think our coming wonderful, and believe that we have come from heaven. We are taking water for the ships from a lake which is near to the Cape of the Islet — for so I have named it; and in the same lake Martin Alonzo Pinzon, the captain of the Pinta, killed another snake seven palms long, the same kind as the one of yesterday. Here I had taken on board all the aloes which could be found."

Tuesday, October 23: "I would like to set out to-day for the island of Cuba, which I believe must be Japan according to what these people say by signs about its great size and wealth; and I shall not remain here any longer, neither [to sail] around the island to go to the village, as I had decided, in order to have an interview with this king or lord. I do this not to lose time, for I can see that there is no gold-mine here; and in order to sail around these islands it would be necessary to have many kinds of wind, and the wind does not blow as men desire. The thing is, then, to go where there is big trade; and I say that there is no reason for waiting longer, but to continue the voyage and examine much land until we find a profitable country, although it is plain to me that this island is well supplied with spices, although I do not know them, which gives me the greatest sorrow in the world; for I see a thousand kinds of trees each of which has its own kind of fruit and as green now as in Spain in the months of May and June, and a thousand kinds of herbs, and as many of flowers, and of them all I do not know any except this aloe, of which I have ordered to-day also a great quantity brought to the ship to take to Your Highnesses. I have not set sail, nor am I about to set sail, for Cuba; for there is no wind, but a dead calm, and it rains a great deal. Yesterday it rained very much, but it did not grow cold; but the days are hot and the nights mild, as in May in Spain and Andalucia."

Wednesday, October 24: "To-night at midnight I weighed anchor from the island of Isabella at the Cape of the Islet—which is the part toward the north, where I had been settled—in order to go to the island of Cuba, which I hear from these people is very large and has a great trade, and that there are there gold and spices and large ships and merchants, and they point toward the west-southwest and say I should go that way to it. And so I think, for I believe that, by the signs which they have made, these Indians of these islands and those whom I have aboard, because we cannot understand their language, it is the island of Japan of which they tell such wonderful things; for on all the globes which I saw, and the drawings of maps of the world, it is in these regions. And so I sailed until daybreak toward the west-southwest, when the wind went down, and it was raining as it had been almost all night, and I was thus with little wind until afternoon, when the weather changed and the wind blew fresh; so I carried all sail on the ship,—the mainsail, the two bonnet-sails, the foresail, the spritsail, the mizzensail, the maintopsail, and the boat astern,—and so I sailed until night fell, and then Green Cape on the island Fernandina, of which it is the southern point of the western part, was to the northwest of me, and I was about seven leagues from it. As it was now blowing hard, and as I did not know how far it was to that island of Cuba, and as I did not want to approach it in the night,—for around all these islands the water is very deep and one cannot find bottom except at two lombard-shots from shore, and this space is all spotted, here sand, there rock, so that it is not safe to anchor except when one can see,—for this reason I decided to lower the sails—all except the foresail, and sail with it. But after a little the wind increased greatly, and we were going so fast that I was afraid, as it was very dark and raining; so I ordered the foresail lowered, and this night we have not made two leagues," etc.

Thursday, October 25: He sailed after the sun was up to the west-southwest until nine o'clock, having gone five leagues; afterward, changing the route to the west, going at the rate of eight miles an hour until one o'clock in the afternoon; and after that until three o'clock, having gone forty-four miles. They then saw land,—some seven or eight islands, all extending from north and south and about five leagues off, etc.

Friday, October 26: He was to the south of those islands, and all was shallow for five or six leagues, and he anchored there. The Indians whom he had with him stated that they could go from those islands to Cuba in a day and a half in their canoes, which are boats of a single piece of wood and without sails. They call them canoes. He set out from there for Cuba, for, from the signs made by the Indians of its size and the gold and pearls there, he thought that it was the one—that is, Japan.

Saturday, October 27: He raised the anchors at sunrise from those islands which he called the Sandy Isles for the very shallow water there is for six leagues to the south. He sailed at the rate of eight miles an hour toward the south-southwest until one o'clock, having gone forty miles, and before night went twenty-eight miles more in the same direction. Before night he saw land. They lay to that night, on account of the great quantity of rain which fell. Saturday they sailed, up to the time of sunset, seventeen leagues toward the south-southwest.

Sunday, October 28: He went from there in search of the island of Cuba to the south-southwest, to the nearest land, and entered into a beautiful river without danger of running aground or any other inconveniences; and all the coast which he traversed had deep water and was free from rocks. The mouth of the river was twelve fathoms broad—wide enough to tack in. He anchored within it, he says, at lombard-shot distance. The Admiral says that he never saw anything so beautiful. The river was bordered with trees, beautiful and green, and different from ours, each with its flowers and fruits after its kind, and with many birds, large and small, who sang sweetly. There were many kinds of palms, different from those of Guinea and our own. They are of medium height, without that fabric around the base, and with large leaves with which they roof their houses. The land is very level. The Admiral jumped into the boat and went ashore, and arrived at two houses which he thought were those of fishermen who fled in fright. In one of them they found a dog of a kind which never barks, and in both houses they found nets made of palm fiber, and fish-lines, and a hook made of horn, and bone harpoons, and other implements for fishing. There were many fires in the houses, and he thought that many persons lived together in one house. He ordered that not a thing be touched, and the order was obeyed. The grass was tall like it is in Andalucia in April and May. He found much purslane and amaranths. He returned to the boat, and went up the river for quite a distance; and he says that it was great pleasure to see such greenness and such groves and the birds, so that he could hardly leave it to return. He says that that island is the most beautiful that eyes have ever seen, full of beautiful harbors and deep rivers; and it seems as if the sea never ran high, for grass on the beach grew almost to the edge of the water, which could not happen if the sea were rough. Up to that time he had not experienced in all those islands a heavy sea. He says that the island is full of beautiful mountains, which, though of no great length, are high, as all the land is, like that of Sicily. He says there is plenty of water in the interior, as he understood from the Indians he had with him and who he had taken in the island of Guanahani, for they told him by signs that there were ten large rivers, and that in their canoes they could not sail around it in twenty days. When he was going to the island with the ships, two boats or canoes were coming out; but when they saw that the sailors were entering the boat and rowing in order to look at the bottom of the river to find out where they ought to anchor, they fled in their canoes. The Indians say that in those islands are mines of gold and pearls, and the Admiral saw a likely place where there were mussels, which are a sign of pearls. The Admiral understood from them that large ships of the Grand Kahn come there, and that from there to the mainland was ten days' journey. The Admiral called that bay and harbor San Salvador.

CHAPTER V

Methods of Identifying Guanahani

ITH the above extracts from the "Historie" by Ferdinand Columbus and from the journal of Columbus, the reader is ready to apply to the problem the first two methods spoken of at the beginning of this part. The third method must ever be unsatisfactory. From September 8, 1492, when he departed from Gomera in the Canaries, until October 12, when he landed at Guanahani,—33½ days,—he had sailed 1178⅓ nautical leagues, or 3535 nautical miles. The leagues used by Columbus were equal to four Italian miles, and the Italian mile is 4842 English feet. Thus the number of leagues run by his log from Gomera to Guanahani was 1111 leagues, equal to 1178⅓ nautical leagues, or 3535 nautical miles,— about 3458 miles on a straight course. At whichever island in the Bahama group we attempt to land him by this reckoning, we find his log has overrun it by many miles. The following table will show the relative difference between the logged course and the real course:

Distance from Gomera to Grand Turk, 2834 miles.	Distance overrun, 624 miles.
" " " " Mariguana, 3032 "	" " 426 "
" " " " Samana, 3071 "	" " 387 "
" " " " Watling, 3105 "	" " 353 "
" " " " Cat, 3141 "	" " 317 "

The current in that part of the Atlantic is very strong. Columbus arrived at the speed of his vessel by his eye, the log-line not having been used until the sixteenth century. He had no aid from those accurate chronometers and fine nautical instruments which the ship-captain of to-day possesses. His time he got from a sand hour-glass. The variation of the compass and its changed relationship to the North Star were a surprise to Columbus, and on two occasions in the journal, under date of September 13 and September 17, 1492, he mentions the alarm of his pilots and sailors at noticing the erratic needle. Therefore it must be apparent that conclusions fixed on such doubtful courses and disturbed distances must be uncertain and unsatisfactory.

There remain, however, two more hopeful methods. With the chart of the Bahama

Islands before us, we may mark out the route of the discoverer backward from Cuba to San Salvador. The point on the Cuban shore where Columbus landed on Sunday, October 28, 1492, is fixed at Puerto del Padre, and is the only port which has the necessary depth of water and which is far enough to the westward to answer the requirements of the south-southwest course sailed by Columbus from the Sandy Islands. Emptying into that bay there was a river which had twelve fathoms of water at its mouth. On the afternoon of October 25 Columbus arrived off some small islands which he called Las Islas de Arena. Captain Fox points to the resemblances which these islands bear to the description so correctly given in the journal. They are eight in number, are 60 miles north-northeast of the northeast coast of Cuba, extending north-northwest ½ west and south-southeast ½ east for 21 miles. Such a group of islands can be found nowhere else in the Bahamas. From these islands the Indians told him Cuba was distant only a day and a half. He left these islands at sunrise of Saturday, October 27, sailing south-southwest eight miles an hour, until at night they had accomplished sixty-eight miles. Early on the morning of Wednesday, October 24, Columbus had sailed from the rocky islet of Isabella, following a west-southwesterly course. It rained, with little wind, at intervals all day, until, as it came toward night, Columbus marked the southwest cape of Fernandina, or his third island, and which later we shall identify as Long Island, as bearing northwest from where he was, distant seven leagues, or twenty-two nautical miles. He took in all sail that night, and estimated in the morning that he had not gone more than two leagues. At sunrise of Thursday, October 25, he sailed west-southwest; but at 9 A. M. he turned more toward the west, and at three o'clock in the afternoon he saw the land of Las Islas de Arena. These islands are now called the Ragged Islands, and form the southeasterly edge of the Great Bahama Bank. Columbus remained at anchor off the southern part of these islands from three o'clock on Thursday until sunrise of Saturday, October 27.

Cape Verde of the island of Fernandina is thus fixed with precision. It was on the southwestern end of the third island discovered and visited by Columbus, to which he gave the name of Fernandina. Its location not only forms the point of departure for the fourth island, or Isabella, but it demonstrates that Columbus never set foot on Grand Exuma, which Washington Irving calls the third island of Columbus. The southwestern part of the island of Exuma is simply an impossible place for Columbus to have been, or from which to have taken his reckoning in going to Cuba. If Columbus had sailed from the northwest side of Long Island on his journey southward to Cuba, he must have crossed the Banks nearly entire, and his journal would have described the incessant soundings. There is no spot or place on this route which can possibly be taken for Las Islas de Arena.

The fourth island of Columbus, called by him Isabella and by the Indians Saomete, really consists of two islands,—the northern identified by us as Crooked Island, and the southern as Fortune Island. There is between these a small island. The first land for which Columbus made on this fourth island was an isolated rock to which he gave the name of Cabo del Isleo, or Cape of the Islet. It has been known of late years as Bird Rock. The northwest end of Fortune Island we identify as Cape Hermosa, so called by Columbus because of its great beauty. The southwest cape of the island he called Cape Laguna. He decided to circumnavigate the island to the northeast and the east by the southeast and south in his search for the settlement and the king. The singular space of water inclosed between the rocky islet and the within island is sufficiently described by Columbus to enable a navigator positively to identify it with the physical peculiarities alone found in the Crooked Island or, as they are called on some charts, the Fragrant Isle group.

The course from the rocky islet of the fourth island, or Isabella, back to the third island, or Fernandina, is almost due west with the least bit of north in it. When Columbus sailed from Fernandina at daybreak of Friday, October 19, it will be recalled that the three caravels took a course to the eastward and southeastward for three hours, when an island was discovered *in the east*. This is the island the Indians who had come with Columbus from San Salvador called Saomete, to which he gave the name of Isabella, and which we have identified with Crooked or Fortune Island.

We have now traced Columbus to his anchorage off the southwest end of an island from which he departed at daybreak on Friday, October 19. This island was his Fernandina, off which he arrived on the night of Tuesday, October 16, but on which he did not land until daylight the next morning.

Ferdinand Columbus describes this island of Fernandina as very large, with a coast running northwest and southeast more than twenty-eight leagues. To learn the trend of the shore and the extent of the island, the Admiral sailed along toward the northwest to the mouth of a beautiful port which had a little island in the entrance. Navarrete quotes from the journal of Columbus the following description of the island of Fernandina: "This island is very large, and I have determined to sail around it; because, as I understand it, it is on it or near it that there is a mine of gold. This island is almost eight leagues east and west of Santa Maria, and the point to which I have come and all this coast runs north-northwest to south-southeast, and I saw fully twenty leagues of it, and it did not end there." This well describes the Long Island of our map and the Fernandina of the Admiral's journal. Columbus continues: "At noon [of Wednesday] I set out from the village off which I had anchored and where I had taken on board water, in order to sail around this island of Fernandina. The wind was southwest and south, and I wished to follow the coast of this island from where I was toward the southeast, for the whole coast runs from the north-northwest to the south-southeast." Columbus remarked that it was his wish to sail south, but that he was persuaded to sail north-northwest by Martin Alonso Pinzon. Before, however, he had reached a point two leagues from the end, he came to a very remarkable port with a rocky islet at the entrance, within which port was room for a hundred vessels. From here the Admiral sailed to the northwest until he came to the end of the island and where the coast turned westward. Here, the wind changing and the Indians advising him to go to the south, he turned around and sailed east-southeast all night, until he came to anchor at the southeast end of the island, and which we recognize as Cape Verde. Clarence Harbor, which answers the description of a beautiful port with a rocky islet at its entrance, was probably the site of his first anchorage at this island. His assertion at the beginning of this day's account that the coast trends north-northwest, and that he has seen twenty leagues of it already, conveys an erroneous impression. The journal was written up the next day, when he truthfully could have said he had seen twenty leagues of it. There is nothing to show that Columbus sailed due east and west from the second island, Santa Maria. He says that he made for a large island which was westward of Santa Maria, but he may have, and probably did, run a trifle south of west. From where he landed he sailed north-northwest on again starting out. He found this beautiful port at two leagues' distance from the end of the island, and then went northwest until he reached the end of the island. He left the settlement where he had anchored at noon of the 17th of October, and consumed the time up to sunset in examining the coast and the harbor, with frequent haltings, and in consultations with the Pinzons and the Indians. But when there came a change of wind he turned about, and was all night going southeasterly to the end of the island we call Cape Verde. It is plain that if this was any part of Exuma from which he was trying to steer, he must have gone due east, and not south. It is also plain that, having the wind with him both times, he could not have made as long a journey, in point of time, going north-northwest, as after turning around he made in going southeast by south. Therefore he must have touched this island for the first time somewhere between the middle and the north end, probably about eight or ten leagues from the north end of the island.

And now, how did the Admiral arrive at Fernandina? He came from an island which lay to the eastward, and which he himself had named Santa Maria de la Concepcion. If Long Island be the third island or the Fernandina of Columbus, then it follows that Rum Cay is Santa Maria, or the second island, for it is the only island to the eastward, and eight or nine leagues away from Long Island. A single glance at the map will show this. This island of Santa Maria on its east coast ran north to south about five leagues, and looked *toward San Salvador*, distant to the north about seven leagues. It ran east and west more than ten leagues. He traveled along the east-and-west coast, and at sunset came to anchor at a cape which terminates the island toward the west. This was the southwest end of the island; for Columbus speaks of going ashore in the armed boats to inquire for gold, and says that after a time, the wind blowing southeast upon the shore where the vessels lay, he determined not to remain, and set out for the ship, after which he set sail for the other large island to the west.

The language employed in the original Spanish would certainly indicate that under date of Monday, October 15, the Admiral is describing a journey from off the south coast of this first island to the second island, and that the entire day was occupied in this passage to its western extremity; and while the language of the journal is somewhat obscure, the description of the size of the second island is sufficiently correct to identify it with Rum Cay. It is twice as long from east to west along the side Columbus followed as it is wide from north to south. Some writers, through careless reading, have made Columbus pass by this second island without either landing or giving it a name. Again, some have sought to identify the second island with the little island put down on the maps as Concepcion, and on which the British ship *Southampton* was wrecked in 1812. It is a double cay, and this fact and the presence of a large hill called "Booby Cay" have led some to call it the true second island, the double cay accounting for the expression in the Admiral's journal that on the morning of Tuesday, October 16, he left "the *Islands* of Santa Maria," speaking of more than one, and the high hill accounting for a longer object of vision from the masthead of the Admiral's ship. There are three objections to the selection of this double cay as the second island:

First, the direction of the second and third islands in respect to each other was east and west, whereas the double cay is north of the third island;

Second, the direction of the second island should be southwest of San Salvador, whereas the double cay is due west of Watling Island;

Third, the double cay is much smaller than Rum Cay, and Columbus passed by no island without, as he says, taking possession thereof.

If Rum Cay be the Santa Maria, or the second island of Columbus, and he reached it by sailing six or seven leagues in a southerly direction from San Salvador, the first island, whence could he have come but from Watling Island? There is none other possible as a point of departure.

CHAPTER VI

Watling Island the true Guanahani

HE first method—that of applying to the different islands the physical descriptions given by Ferdinand Columbus and taken from the journal of the Admiral—is the most satisfactory and convincing. The large lagoon in the middle of the island is a feature sufficient of itself to identify Watling Island as San Salvador, since no other large island of the Bahama group possesses such a distinguishing topographical mark. Its belt of coral, while common to many islands, by its presence is another witness to certify to its claim. The fertility of the island is such as to warrant the name given it to-day — the Garden of the Bahamas.

Watling Island is situated in latitude 23° 55' north, longitude 74° 28' west, from Greenwich. It is twelve miles in length, north and south, and nearly seven miles in breadth, containing about sixty square miles. It owes its name, tradition says, to a Captain George Watling, an old privateer in command of a ship in the time of the bucaneers. In the map drawn by Diego Ribero, the celebrated cosmographer of the Emperor Charles V., and which he finished in 1529, Guanahani is put down as opposite to the eastern extremity of Cuba, in the same meridian as the point of the coast called Baracoa. Baracoa is only a few leagues to the westward of that extreme eastern point of Cuba made interesting by its quaint name of Cape Alpha and Omega, given it by Columbus on his first voyage in December, 1492. While this name does not appear in the account of the first voyage, in speaking of his second voyage, when he went from Hispaniola across to the east end of Cuba, Columbus says he named that point when he reached it first Cape Alpha and Omega. Ferdinand Columbus, Las Casas, and Peter Martyr all say this. The significance in this name lies in the belief of the Admiral that Cuba made part of the Asiatic continent, and that this cape was the Alpha or beginning of the Indies to all those coming from the east, and the Omega or end to all those coming from the west. As will be seen by referring to the map, we fix the first anchorage and the exact site of the landfall on the west side of the island, off Riding Rocks, near Cockburn Town, the main settlement on the island. From

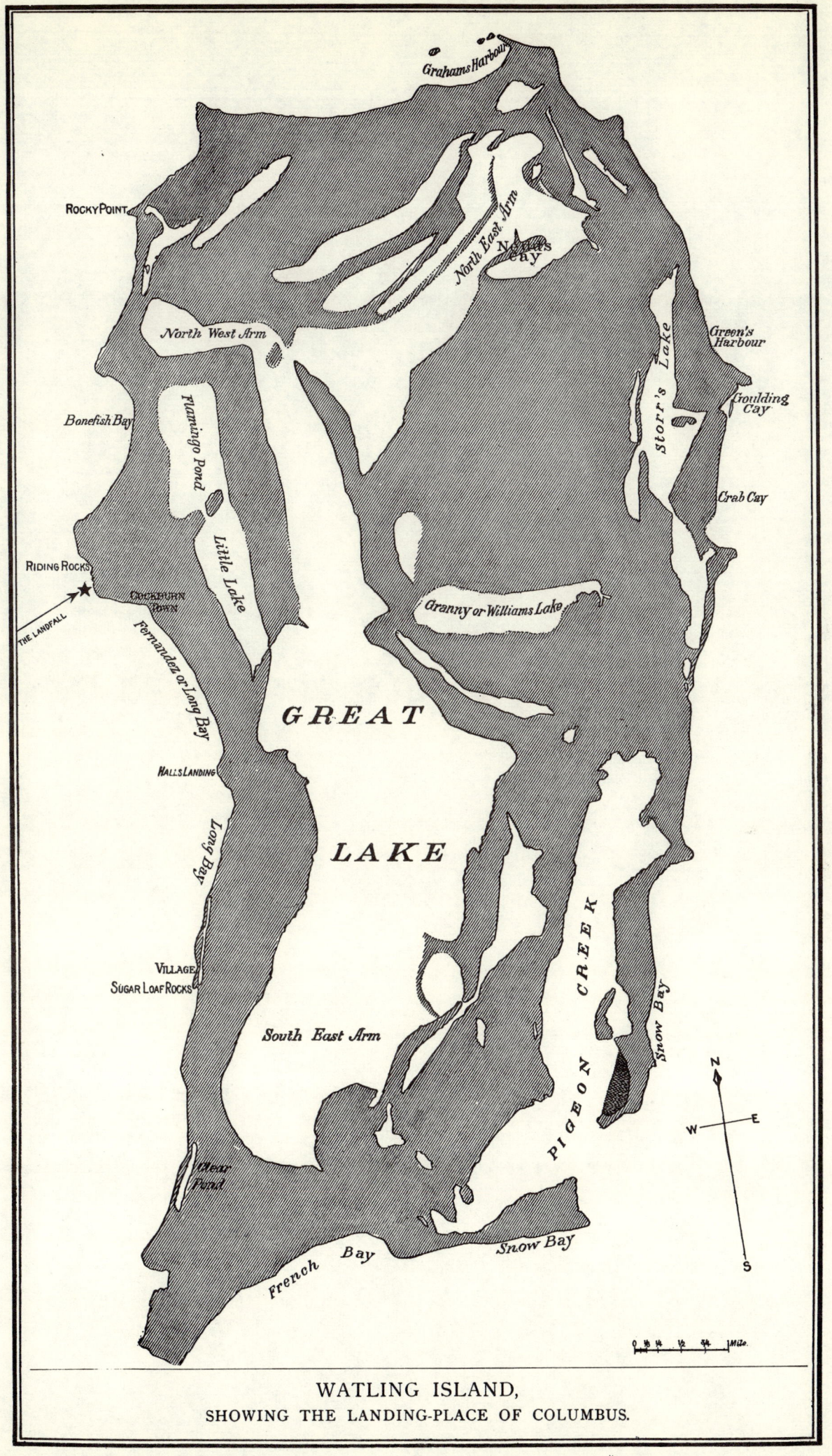

WATLING ISLAND,
SHOWING THE LANDING-PLACE OF COLUMBUS.

the time that the ships of Columbus anchored in the early morning of Friday, October 12, until they set sail on the evening of Sunday, October 14, there is nothing to indicate that they were moved. The prevailing winds are from the east, and no ship would or could anchor on the windward side. The journal tells us that the sea on October 11, 1492, was "much heavier than at any previous time during the voyage." He was sailing due west at the hour of the discovery, presumably with an east wind. That it was strong is seen from the statement that they were sailing twelve miles an hour. There is no port or anchorage possible on the east side. The course sailed on Wednesday was west-southwest, at occasionally twelve miles an hour, and on Thursday, October 11, it was almost due west at the same rate of speed. It is possible that the land which was sighted at two o'clock on the following morning was the north end of Watling Island. Sailors acquainted with that locality tell us that a ship such as Columbus had, with its sails taken in as he states his were, with the wind strong from the east, would drift to the southwest, and it is probable that he was not far from the spot indicated in the map to the south and on the west side of the island when the morning broke. Here is the only proper landing-place on the entire island. His sailor instinct must have pointed it out to the Admiral. It is to-day the only safe and natural anchorage on the island.

We may arrive at the probable landfall by the following process of reasoning. It will be recalled that in the journal for Saturday, October 13, he says: "Y por señas pude entender que yendo al Sur ó volviendo la isla por el Sur . . ." ("I by signs was able to learn that by going toward the south or *rounding the island to the south*, . . .")

This phrase eliminates the south side of the island, and the natural conditions eliminate the east side, from our search after the location of the site of the landfall. On the morning of Sunday, October 14, the Admiral gets out his boats and leaves the ship, rowing in a north-northeasterly direction. This certainly eliminates the north end of the island from our consideration, or else we must behold the Admiral rowing in a direction which will take him out to sea. Moreover, he says he went "to see the other part of it, which was on the other side of the east." He describes a part of the island so accurately that it is easily identified to-day as the north part. The Admiral says, in speaking of the invitation of the natives for him to land as he approached this part:

But I was afraid because I saw a great reef of rocks which surrounds the island, within which is space and depth for as many ships as there are in all Christendom, but the entrance is very narrow. It is true that inside this reef are some sunken rocks, but the sea does not move any more than water in a well. And in order to see all this I set out this morning that I might be able to give a full account to Your Highnesses, and also that I might know where a fort could be built. I saw a piece of land that is like an island, although it is not one, upon which were six houses. This peninsula could in two days be made into an island.

There is just such a natural harbor with its entrance at the northwest end of the island. To the east is a tongue of land, and in "two days," or in a short time, and with but little engineering labor, there could be excavated a canal, thus cutting off the north end and making it an island. Here in after times some one else saw its strategic advantage, and to-day there lies on the ground an old cannon which once pointed to the west and commanded the harbor entrance. The water within this harbor is quiet as the waters of a well, and there are depth and room enough for many navies.

Watling Island has a political existence. Its population of 675 souls unite with the 367 inhabitants of Rum Cay to form a constituency which sends one member to the House of Assembly for the Bahama Islands. The seat of local government is in the island of New Providence. It is said that at one time the island was celebrated for its live stock, and in particular horses, cargoes of these being sent annually to Jamaica. The principal settlement on the island is Cockburn Town, at the point where we find the landfall. It has a sea approach with a good and easy anchorage. On Dixon Hill, on the northeast end, is a lighthouse with the most powerful light in the Bahamas. It is situated in latitude 24° 06' and in longitude 74° 26'.

Most students who have been readers rather than investigators of the first voyage of Columbus, have been content with the charming story of Washington Irving, or with the authoritative voice of Alexander von Humboldt. To-day the careful student reads the original Spanish of Navarrete, and verifies its statements concerning the landfall by what competent sailors who have visited the locality have to tell of the Bahama group.

The route sailed by Columbus from his landfall on the morning of October 12, 1492, until he touched the shore of Cuba, is here outlined with probable accuracy. If ever mortal hand shall hold the original journal of the Admiral, many new and clearer readings may be found. But, until then, availing ourselves of the three methods of investigation above noticed, we may declare that the Watling Island of to-day is the true Guanahani which first knew the foot of the European discoverer, and thus pointed the way to a new stage and new scenes on which were to be old plays and the reappearance of ancient history.

PART III

The Life of Vespucius

With an Account of his Voyages and an Attempt to Establish the Landfall on the Continent of North America

CHAPTER I

The Early Days of Vespucius

IN the olden days, when honor and arms were a profession, the portrait of an English knight was hung in his castle hall to commemorate a noble life; after a time some documents were falsely interpreted to his disloyalty, and the portrait was turned to the wall: it remained there in dishonor until for another generation time yielded up the truth, and then the portrait was given again to the light, its features softened, its color deepened, richness and glory added with its patient years. Something like this has taken place with the remembrance of Vespucius. In his life he was not without honor, although Columbus, in his letter to his son Diego, dated February 5, 1505, enrolls him among the unfortunate ones who have not attained their desires. During the latter part of his life, and for many years after his death, he was recognized as the chief explorer and the real discoverer of the new continental lands. Then a few blundering types and a scolding historian turned his portrait in dishonor to the wall, and it has remained for our age to place it where it belongs, in full light, not to the disparagement of Columbus, but to the exoneration of a great historical character.

Americus Vespucius was the third son of Anastasio Vespucius and of Lisabetta Mini, his wife. The father was a notary of Florence, where the son was born on March 9, 1451. The name was written, as will be seen from the accompanying facsimile, Amerigo Vespucci; and the Christian name was pronounced Amerígo, not Amérigo.

We learn from Bandini, "Vita" (1745), page xxiv, and other writers, that our Vespucius studied under the direction of his uncle Fra Giorgio Antonio Vespucius, a father of the Dominican order and a warm personal friend of Savonarola. This uncle was a great scholar, both in Greek and Latin, and many of the classics printed in Italy during the fifteenth century were edited by his care and knowledge. Toward the close of 1476 Americus, on account of the plague which ravaged Florence, went to Mugello in Trebbio, where he wrote his father in Latin, frankly acknowledging his weakness in that tongue, since he had not at his side his learned uncle to correct his grammar and his rhetoric. The following is the letter:

TRANSLATION.

HONORED FATHER: I beg you not to wonder that I have not written to you of late, inasmuch as I have been thinking that my uncle on his arrival would give you a full account of me. I have, besides, been busy with writing out the rules of accidence and putting them into Latin,—if I dare call it so,—in order that I might be able on my return to show you the little book in which I have brought together said rules, as you desired me to do. As regards my doings and pursuits, I suppose you have already been informed of them by my uncle, for whose return I am ardently longing, in order that I may be able to continue more readily my studies under your and under his guidance. Three or four days ago Georgius Antonius handed over several letters for you to Mr. Nerotto, an ecclesiastic who, I believe, is a very worthy and studious person, which letters he wishes you to answer. As for the rest, there is nothing here in the way of news, except that everybody wishes to leave this place and to return to the city; but no certain day has yet been decided on, although we hope it will be in the near future, if the terror of the plague does not increase, which God avert!

There is one I desire to recommend to your favor, and that one is my poor and unhappy neighbor, whose hopes and means all rest in his own and our house, and respecting whom I have spoken at length with you. I beg you to take care of all his concerns and attend to them diligently and accurately, so that, you being present, his own absence may not give rise to any anxiety. Jointly with him, or shortly after his departure, I shall hasten to you. I wish you all prosperity and health, and beg you to present my greetings to the family and recommend me to my mother and other relations. Mugello in Trebbio, the 19 October, 1476.   Your Son,

AMERICUS VESPUCIUS.

It was at his uncle's school that Americus formed the acquaintance of Pier Soderini, afterward (from 1502 to 1512) the gonfalonier of the Florentine Republic,

AUTOGRAPH LETTER OF PIER SODERINI,
SCHOOLFELLOW OF AMERICUS VESPUCIUS, AND GONFALONIER OF FLORENCE.

AUTOGRAPH OF GEORG ANTONIUS VESPUCIUS,
UNCLE AND TEACHER OF VESPUCIUS.

AUTOGRAPH OF RENÉ, DUKE OF LORRAINE,
PATRON OF THE ST. DIÉ COTERIE.

and to whom he dedicated the account of his four voyages. The eldest brother of Americus, Antonio, took a university course at Pisa, but the second son, Jerome, and our Americus preferred a commercial career. Jerome, about 1480, went to Palestine to engage in the Eastern trade; and in a letter written to his brother Americus, dated July 24, 1489, and confided to the care of Father Carnesecchi, who was returning to Italy from Palestine, he relates the losses he has suffered after nine years of labor. Americus remained at Florence, and was admitted as a clerk to the great commercial house of the Medici. This house did a considerable business with Spain and other Mediterranean countries, and had its agents in almost every important center. It is not easy to fix the exact date of his departure from Florence to establish himself as the agent for the house at Cadiz. Some notarial writings prove that he was still in Florence in 1490. These documents also disclose the fact that Americus was complaining to the courts that his mother — his father presumably being dead — was trying to deprive him of his rights. It is probable that, soon after, he left for Spain with a fellow-employee named Donato Niccolini. Bandini in 1745 printed a portion of a letter placed in his hands by the Abbé Scarlatti, and which was written by Vespucius January 30, 1492, from Cadiz. In this letter he says that either he or Niccolini will soon return to Florence, thus indicating that they had been some time located in this agency. However, this letter is not admitted as genuine by scholars. A paleographical examination discloses its fraudulent character. The paper is much more modern than that in use in the fifteenth century, and the ink was evidently prepared for the occasion. Moreover, neither the writing in the body of the letter nor the signature is like that of Vespucius, and the style of composition does not suggest the Florentine sailor. In 1497 Vespucius declared he had gone into Spain to occupy himself with commercial affairs, and that he already had been following this business for more than four years. Juanoto Berardi, a Florentine, had established himself in business in Seville about the year 1486. He was a friend of Columbus, and on many occasions had equipped vessels for expeditions to the Antilles and for other voyages. On April 9, 1495, he signed with the king and queen a contract, by which he bound himself to loan to the crown twelve vessels of nine hundred tons, or an average of seventy-five tons each. The vessels were evidently to be gotten ready in fleets of four, and the first four were equipped the same month, the command being given to Juan Aguado. This date (April 9, 1495) is important, for it was on the following day that the sovereigns issued the decree which took from Columbus the monopoly of voyaging in the Indies, and made it possible for any native Spaniard within certain easy limitations to fit out an expedition. Gómara, in his "Historia General de las Indias," printed at Saragossa in 1553, declares that some of these expeditions sailed as private speculations of the king; and it will be noticed that Vespucius distinctly states that it was on the command of the king, Ferdinand, and not in the joint names of the king and queen, that his first voyage was undertaken. This declaration is twice made in the same letter describing his first voyage. Gómara further says: "There is no record of those expeditions which pushed their discoveries toward the north to the Baccalaos and to Labrador, nor of those which from 1495 to 1500 were made toward the coast of Paria." Humboldt, in the fourth volume of his "Examen Critique," page 267, has asserted that Vespucius is proved, by documentary evidence (discovered by Juan Bautista Muñoz and preserved in the archives of La Casa de Contratacion de Seville), to have been engaged in equipping the third expedition of Columbus. If this were true, if there were in existence an official paper connecting Vespucius with this third voyage of the Admiral, then his own first voyage never took place, and he must be written down a monumental deceiver. All the ground for the above assertion is found in an item for a large sum of money paid Vespucius, as will be seen below. In June, 1495, four more ships were ready, and the last in September of the same year. In December, 1495, Berardi died. The contract had been fulfilled, but the last four ships were wrecked on the coasts of Andalucia soon after sailing. Berardi had not received the full amount he was entitled to under the contract, and he was himself in arrears in paying his sailors. At this juncture Americus Vespucius undertook to pay these claims, and on the 12th of January, 1496, he received from the treasurer Pinelo 10,000 maravedis for this purpose.

CHAPTER II

The Royal Decrees and the First Voyage

EARLY in the year 1497, King Ferdinand determined upon an expedition to the New World on his own account. The open door through which adventurers sailed to the Indies was particularly aggravating to Columbus, and weakened the concession to which he believed himself entitled by reason of his discovery. This door was opened on April 10, 1495, and numerous were the parties which availed themselves of the right to pass unrestricted to the new regions. But the soul of Columbus was in arms against the injustice done him by these free privileges, and already the king saw the necessity for yielding. Harrisse, in his "Discovery of North America," makes Columbus seem to recommend and encourage the fitting out of these expeditions. He quotes Bernaldez, "Cronica de los Reyes Catolicos," but the passage itself makes it plain that every concession was the result of negotiations, and negotiations mean mutual advantages.

The following is the famous royal decree of April 10, 1495, translated from the Spanish of Navarrete, Vol. II, p. 165:

Royal decree determining what is to be observed with regard to those who wish to go and establish themselves in the Indies, and relating also to those who desire to go and discover new lands. [Original in the archives of the Duke of Veraguas. Registered in the court seal document room in Simancas, and authenticated copies in that of the Indies in Seville.]

Don Fernando and Doña Isabel, by the Grace of God, King and Queen of Castile, etc. Inasmuch as we are informed that several persons, citizens and inhabitants of certain cities, villages, towns and ports of our kingdoms and realms, our subjects and native-born citizens, might desire to go to discover other isles and continents composing the Indies in the Ocean Sea, in addition to the isles and continents which by our mandate have already been discovered in said part of the Ocean Sea, and to barter in them and to seek gold, metals, and other merchandise; likewise that others might wish to live in and inhabit the island of Hispaniola that has been discovered and found by our order, if they were given license by us to do so, and if they were aided in their maintenance for a certain time, and that they do not do so on account of the prohibition that by our mandate was imposed (to wit: that no person should go to the Indies without our license and command, under certain penalties); and as we have seen that the discovery of the said islands and continents and bartering in them, and the further settling of the said island of Hispaniola which has been discovered, is a service to God our Lord, because their conversation with the natives might draw these latter inhabitants of the said land to a knowledge of God our Lord and convert them to our Holy Catholic faith; and moreover, as it is a service to us and to the common well-being and profit of our kingdoms and realms and of our subjects and native-born citizens,— we therefore agree to give permission, and by these presents do give and concede license, to the aforesaid our subjects and native-born citizens, that they may go to the said isles and continents to discover them and barter in them, upon the following conditions and after the manner as hereinafter contained in this our letter, and declared in this form.

Firstly, That all ships that may go to the region of the said isles, in whichsoever of the ways hereinafter in this our letter contained, must depart from the city of Cadiz, and not from any other port, and that before they set sail, they shall present themselves before the officials that will be by us assigned, or before whomsoever may have our authority, in order that those who go to the said Indies may be known, and in order that they may execute and observe, each one according to his particular case, those orders which hereinafter in this letter will be contained; that whatsoever persons may wish to go to live in and inhabit the aforesaid island of Hispaniola, without pay, may go, and go without impediment, and that there they shall be free and untaxed, and that they need not pay any impost whatsoever, and may have for themselves, for their own use, and for their heirs, or for whomsoever may have legal jurisdiction, the houses they may have made, the lands they may have cultivated, the gardens they may have planted, according as lands and employment will be assigned to them in said isles, by the persons that by us have or will have charge; and that such persons who so live in and inhabit the said island of Hispaniola and who have no pay from us, as aforesaid, shall have maintenance given them for one year; and we further wish, and it is our pleasure and will, that going with license from those who may have authority from us, to the said island of Hispaniola, they may have for themselves the third part of the gold that they may find and collect in the said isle, provided that it has not been obtained by barter, and the other two thirds shall be for us, which two thirds they shall deliver to the receiver who will be placed in the said isle by us; and furthermore, the persons going with license may have for themselves all the merchandise and whatsoever things they find in said isle, giving the tenth part to us, or to whomsoever has authority from us to receive it, except the gold, of which two thirds is to be given to us as aforesaid, all of which merchandise must have been bartered for in the said island of Hispaniola, and which is to be brought before our officials, and the two thirds part of the gold paid to the receiver whom we shall appoint, and the tenth part of all the other things as before stated.

Item: Furthermore, that whatsoever persons, our subjects and native-born citizens, may wish to do so, may go from this time forth, as it were, for our pleasure and by our will, to discover islands and continents in the said part of the said Indies, and likewise to those that are discovered up to the present, as well as any others whatsoever, and barter in them (provided that it be not in the said island of Hispaniola; but they may buy of the Christians that are there or will be there, all things or merchandise whatsoever, providing that it be not gold), all of which they can do in whatsoever ships they may desire, provided that at the time they leave our kingdoms they shall sail from the city of Cadiz, and that they there present themselves before our officials in order that they shall convey from that place in each one of such ships one or two persons who will be appointed by our officials before whom they will present themselves, and furthermore, so that they may carry our freight to the extent of one tenth of the ship's tonnage capacity without freight charges, and this freight of ours which they convey they will discharge in the said island of Hispaniola and will deliver it to the person or persons that there will have authority to receive it for our account, having been sent by our command, taking his or their receipt to show how they may have received it; and we wish it, and it is our pleasure, that of all things which the said persons shall find in the said islands and continents they shall have nine parts, and the other tenth shall be for us, which latter they must pay us at the time they return to our kingdom and to the said city of Cadiz, where they have to return first in order to pay to the person who may have authority from us to receive it, after which they may go to their houses, or wherever they wish, with whatever they may have brought with them, and at the time they sail from the said city of Cadiz they will have to give security that they will so do.

Item: Furthermore, that whosoever may wish to convey supplies of whatsoever kind to the said island of Hispaniola, or whatever other isles that by our command will be populated, from these said islands, they may convey them and there sell them freely and for the prices which will be arranged between them and their customers, and for which they will then be paid in merchandise or in the gold which may have been found there; and if all or part of said supplies shall be sold to our officials who will be there for the maintenance of the people who there serve us, they must pay them and pay them there as aforesaid, or they may give them orders by which they may be paid here, by which orders we guarantee that they will receive payment, provided that at the time the said ships, in which were the said supplies, sailed, they sailed from the said city of Cadiz; to the end that they should there present themselves before our aforesaid officials, and carry, without freight charges, to the tenth part of the capacity of such ships, such cargo as we shall order for the said island, as above specified, and that they may obligate themselves to pay the tenth part of that which they may bring back and for which they have there bartered according to as is contained in the above chapter, and on the return they shall be obliged to come to the said city of Cadiz to pay it as aforesaid.

Finally, inasmuch as we have granted to Don Cristobal Colon, our Admiral of the said Indies, the right to load with freight each one of the said ships that might go to the Indies to the extent of the eighth part of their tonnage capacity, it is our pleasure that of every seven ships that will go to the said Indies the said Admiral, or whomsoever may have his authority, may load one entire ship in order to make the said trade.

All of the aforesaid, and each and every part of it, we command that it may be observed and executed in all and for all, according to the above which our letter contains; and in order that the above contents may be brought to the notice of all, we order that it be proclaimed in all the squares and markets and other places customarily used for this purpose, by all the cities and villages and towns and ports of Andalucia and other parts of our kingdom where it shall be suitable, and that a copy of it be given to whatsoever person may desire it. To which mandate we give this our letter subscribed by our names and sealed with our seal.

Given in the city of Madrid, 10th day of the month of April, year of the birth of our Saviour Jesus Christ, one thousand four hundred and ninety-five.

I, the King. I, the Queen.

I, Fernando Alvarez de Toledo, Secretary of the King and of the Queen our Lords: written by their order. Certified: Doctor Rodericus. Registered: Doctor Francisco Diaz (Chancellor).

The following is the royal decree dated June 2, 1497, twenty-three days after the king's expedition had sailed away from the city of Cadiz. The original decree was in the archives of the Duke of Veraguas, and is registered in the Archives de Indias in Seville:

Don Ferdinand and Doña Isabella, by the grace of God, King and Queen of Castile, etc.: Whereas when Don Cristobal Colon, our Admiral of the Ocean Sea, went to discover land in the said Ocean Sea, he took with him by our order a certain contract, and afterward when on the first voyage he found and discovered, by the grace and with the help of God our Lord, the said Indies and continent, we confirmed and approved said treaty and contract, taken by him upon our command, and we gave him anew and ordered to be given certain privileges and grants, agreeing with the contents of the said contract, letters, and privileges; and now the said Don Cristobal Colon, our Admiral of the Ocean Sea, has made complaint to us, ever since the issuance of our ordinance and decree, embodied in certain chapters, the contents of which are as follows:

[A literal copy of the preceding royal decree is here inserted.]

The Admiral Don Cristobal Colon says of our said ordinance and decree and its tenor, that it was given to the prejudice of the grants which he holds from us and of the powers they conferred upon him; he prays and requests that we shall give orders to provide a remedy or otherwise as our pleasure may be; and as it was not nor is it our intention or wish to injure the said Don Cristobal Colon, our Admiral of the

Ocean Sea, in any way, nor to go or allow anything to happen contrary to said contract, privileges, and grants, which we have formerly given him for the services done for us, therefore we intend to grant him other privileges; by this ordinance, if necessary, we confirm and approve said contracts, privileges, and grants made by us to our Admiral, and it is our wish and will that they shall be complied with and guarded in every respect according to what is contained in them, and we strictly forbid that any person or persons shall dare go contrary to them or any part of them at any time or in any manner under the penalties therein contained; and if their tenor or their form or any part of them in any way prejudices the said decree, which we hereby order to be issued and embodied as above, we revoke it for the present, and it is our wish and will that it shall have no power or effect whatever, at any time or in any way, to the prejudice of the Admiral; and of what we have now granted and confirmed we order to give this present (copy) signed with our names and sealed with our seals. Given at the city of Medina del Campo, on the 2d day of June, in the year of the birth of our Saviour Jesus Christ the 1497th. I, the King — I, the Queen — I, Fernando Alvarez de Toledo, Secretary of the King and Queen, our Lords: written by their order. Certified — Rodericus, Doctor. Registered — Alonzo Perez. Francisco Diaz, Chancellor. No fees.

Before issuing a decree withdrawing the permission for free voyages, Ferdinand resolved to give himself an opportunity to put some money in his private purse. He called to his aid four most skilled and competent men. At the head of the expedition was, most probably, Vicente Yañez Pinzon, the youngest of the three Pinzon brothers of Palos, and who had been in command of the little caravel *Niña* on the first Columbian voyage. The Pinzons were the most important family of Palos, and it is said the family is still in existence in that town and within the present generation had an admiral of Spain within its ranks. The eldest brother, Martin Alonso, was in command of the *Pinta* on the memorable first Columbian voyage, and his treachery to the Admiral is generally admitted. He is said by some to have died from chagrin on discovering that Columbus, whom he had abandoned, had survived and had reached Spain in safety. In another account he is made to die in the convent of La Rábida, where he was carried mortally ailing from his ship. There is evidence of the attachment the Pinzons had for their home, seafaring men though they were; for on Vicente Yañez's voyage to the coast of Brazil, in 1499–1500, he named one of the points of land *Santa María de la Rábida*, as may be seen on the map in the Ptolemy of 1513.

Another member of this expedition was Juan de la Cosa, a native of the province of Santander, where he was born about the year 1460. This man makes an interesting figure in the early American voyages. He owned the caravel *Santa María*, the flag-ship of Columbus, which was wrecked on Christmas eve, 1492, off the northern shore of Hispaniola, a sacrifice to the gods of discovery. The *Santa María* was a ship built in Cantabria for trading with Flanders, and while not fast, was of strong sea-going quality, decked over, and peculiarly attractive in the eyes of Columbus as the leading vessel for this bold enterprise. Writers are not agreed as to the relations between Columbus and La Cosa. A seaman, Bernardo de Ibarra, declared he had heard the Admiral complain that La Cosa was going about saying he knew more than Columbus, although the latter had taught him all he knew of navigation. As La Cosa had graduated from the rough school of the Bay of Biscay, and was captain as well as owner of the largest available ship in the port of Palos when the expedition was fitting, it is not likely that Columbus was at pains to teach him much in the rudiments of his art. On the other hand, the *Santa María*, according to Navarrete, was lost when the sea was as calm as a basin of water, and the vessel touched the fatal rock so softly that no man save him at the helm was for the instant conscious of the accident. Some one was to blame, but it does not appear that the momentary annoyance of Columbus ever led to any formal charge of incompetence or cowardice against La Cosa. It is known that the latter returned with the Admiral on the *Niña*, when he might by the latter's orders have been left on the island of Hispaniola to perish like the unfortunate forty who remained at La Navidad; and it is also a matter of record that he formed one of the important staff surrounding Columbus on the occasion of his second voyage the following year. But effectually to clear the skirts of the Biscayan pilot from all blame, we find record that their most Catholic Majesties did order him to be reimbursed and satisfied for the value of his ship. He was rewarded, and not punished. La Cosa is important to us in our study of the chartography of the New World, and we must not lose sight of him.

The exact function of Vespucius on this expedition and in the midst of such skilled navigators is not determined. According to his own statement, he was solicited to go by the king.

The King Don Fernando of Castile being about to despatch four ships to discover new lands towards the west, I was chosen by his Highness to go in that fleet to aid in making discovery.

This is not the language of presumption or usurpation. He does not anywhere claim that it was his ship, his fleet, his expedition. He certainly possessed two qualifications which made his services desirable—the one to the fleet; the other to the king. He understood astronomy and the use of the quadrant's predecessor, the astrolabe. But doubtless his chief recommendation in the speculative eyes of the king was his acquaintance with commercial methods; and therefore it is more than probable that he went as a sort of supercargo, to weigh out the food and to weigh in the gold and to keep accurate tally of the royal share. Years spent in the counting-house of the Medici fitted him beyond other followers of the sea for this particular service. Actors in great events for the most part dread the pen. We owe to the ledger-books and the methodical files of the Florentine business house not only the first satisfactory account of the new lands and of the customs of the people, but the very truthfulness of figures themselves which went into the plain, straightforward narrative as told by Vespucius.

CHAPTER III

The Landfall on the Continent

IT was on the 10th day of May, in the year 1497, that the little fleet sailed out of the port of Cadiz. The reader, by comparing the Italian and Latin texts of this first voyage, will observe among the many discrepancies the difference in the date of departure. If the voyage of John Cabot, alleged to have been made in the spring of 1497, to what is now the coast of the United States, was worthy of credence, the ten days between May 10, as given in the primitive text, and May 20, as in the Latin translation of the St.-Dié edition, would be of the first importance in order to land our Americus on the continent in advance of the Genoese-Bristol sailor. Henry Harrisse has so effectually disposed of the claims of the Cabots that no scholar to-day seriously contends for English priority in continental discoveries. However, constant recurrence to the primitive text must be had as we proceed. We may therefore, as we pass along, briefly recite the bibliographical marks which distinguish these editions. Our author states that the fleet took a direct course for the Canary Islands, situated in the Ocean Sea (Atlantic), set in the third climate, over which the north pole has an elevation of 27½ degrees beyond the horizon. The Latin edition makes this 27⅔ degrees north latitude. At the Canaries, which were reached in about ten days' sailing from Cadiz, the fleet tarried for eight days, getting provisions of wood and water. Setting sail again, and beginning their course by west and a quarter southwest, they went on for thirty-seven days—the Latin says twenty-seven days—until they reached a land which they believed to be a continent, distant westerly from the Canaries 1000 leagues, with the north pole elevated 16 degrees above the horizon, and the instruments showing a longitude of 75 degrees westward from the Canaries. Making an allowance of an error of a single degree in his latitude and about eight degrees in his longitude,—not a great allowance considering the instruments he used,—the landfall would be on the coast of Honduras, not far from Cape

Gracias á Dios. It is natural to inquire how it came about that none of the islands in the Caribbean Sea were first sighted. We know that the country to the north, along which the fleet afterward traveled, is picketed by monstrous volcanic mountains, and yet no mention is made of these gigantic signal-stations. The answer is the same to both inquiries. Dense fogs prevail at certain seasons, curtaining land from sea, and a hundred vessels might creep near to the coast without sighting the outlying islands.

From Cape Gracias á Dios the course was northwest for two days, where they found a harbor sufficiently secure for their ships. This was perhaps a port near Cape Cameron. Vespucius, in speaking of the coast between the point first touched and the safe port, employs the word *spiaggia*, indicating a level coast devoid of hills; and this term exactly describes the coast-line between Cape Gracias á Dios and Cape Cameron. The description of the people and their habits is long and detailed, and one can see how interesting and popular such an account would be to European readers at the beginning of the sixteenth century. In the letter written toward the end of the year 1502 or the beginning of 1503 and addressed to Lorenzo di Pier Francesco de' Medici, while composed particularly as the result of his third voyage, he seems to have given some details of his first and eventful expedition. This went through twelve editions in Latin, testifying to the public interest in the recital. The Paris edition of Jehan Lambert, by reason of its carrying the complete name of the member of the Medici family to whom it was dedicated, is regarded by bibliographers as the first edition. Only one German edition quotes correctly the name, inserting "Francesco" as in Lambert's edition.

Traveling on again, still along the coast, they came to a country where they beheld a village of forty-four houses, built, like Venice, upon the water. Many locate this in Campeche Bay, to the north of Tabasco. The St.-Dié Latin edition speaks of twenty houses instead of forty-four. Here occurred a vigorous engagement between the Europeans and the natives, fifteen or twenty of the latter being killed. Leaving this place, the fleet skirted the coast for eighty leagues (320 Italian miles), when they came across a new people, different in speech and customs. This was in the province of Lariab, probably near Tampico in Mexico. And now we come to a typographical error which is alone guilty of bringing the good name of our Americus into disrepute. When this was translated into the St.-Dié Latin edition the word "Lariab" became "Parias." Columbus, on the occasion of his third voyage in 1498, discovered the Gulf of Paria. In 1499 Americus Vespucius sailed on his second voyage with Alonso de Ojeda, and on that expedition they visited the coast of Paria, on the north coast of South America, as far as the Gulf of Maracaybo. Suddenly in the year 1507 a little book is printed in the Vosgian Mountains, suggesting in its first part that the New World should be called America because it was discovered by Americus, and containing in the latter part the assertion that he was the first to discover the province of Paria. When attention was called to this, one half the world said Americus had tried to despoil Columbus of his honor, and the other half of the world—the cheerful, blundering half, always ready with forced explanations—said that Americus simply mixed his dates, and was describing, after all, the Ojeda expedition of 1499, and therefore was not a discoverer, but a follower of the Genoese Admiral to the coast of Paria.

Gómara, whose "Historia General de las Indias" we have frequently cited, says that the coast of Honduras was visited by the pilots Pinzon and Solís several years before it was seen by Columbus. Oviedo, in his work bearing the same title, says that the Gulf of Honduras (Higueras) was discovered by the pilots Vicente Yañez Pinzon and Juan Diaz de Solís and Pedro de Ledesma, with three caravels, before Vicente Yañez discovered the river Amazon (Marañon). But before these writers we have the authority of Peter Martyr, who in the seventh book of his second decade, printed in 1516, says: "Vincentius Annez cognito jam experimento patenti Cubam esse insulam, processit ulterius, et terras alias ad occidentem Cubae offendit: sed tactas prius ab almiranto." These last five words are not quoted by modern writers when they refer to Peter Martyr's testimony. They certainly weaken the case, but they certainly exist.

The reader will notice that on the Solinus map, made by Petrus Apianus and printed in 1520 (see facsimile at end of the book), the location of Lariab is correctly given as the coast of Mexico, but the province is named "Parias," as taken from the St.-Dié Latin edition. It is a singular coincidence that it is on this very map that the name of "America" appears for the first time upon an engraved *mappamundi*, but applied to the southern part of the New World instead of to North America. This was the result, so far as the name was concerned, of reading the numberless editions of "Mundus Novus" describing the third voyage of Americus. But the maker of the map knew also of the famous first voyage.

The description given by Americus of the country of Lariab in North America does not correspond with the description which Columbus gave of Paria in South America, more than two thousand miles away. The people of Paria struck Columbus and his companions as of unusual size. The people of Lariab were only of medium size in the eyes of Americus. But the description of the inhabitants of the country near Cape Cameron which Columbus gave in the account of his voyage in 1502 does agree strikingly with the description of the same people given by Americus in 1497.

The three native words for foods used by Vespucius—"Iuca," "Cazabi," and "Ignami"—are common to the West Indian Islands and the adjacent shores of the mainland.

The first is the starchy root of a shrubby plant (*Manihot utilissima*), and is still known as "yuca" in Spanish-American countries, where it forms the staple food of many of the inhabitants. Cazabi, or cassave, denotes the flat cakes made from the flour formed by grating, washing, and drying the yuca-root. Ignami, or ñami (*Dioscorea*), known in English-speaking countries as the yam, is the sweetish, starchy root of an herbaceous vine. Iuca and Cazabi appear in print for the first time in the "Lettera." The third word, under the form of "inhame," appears earlier in the manuscript of Pedro Vaz de Caminha, written in 1500.

The practice of depilation, as applied to the eyebrows and the lashes, was common as late as 1870 among the Apaches and Indian tribes roaming over Texas and New Mexico. Their want of ceremony in most of the affairs of life, their rites of sepulture, their peculiar and effective use of cold water as a febrifuge, their constant resort to phlebotomy, their dieting in sickness, identify this people with the natives living on the coast of Mexico. It might have been expected of the narrative of Vespucius that it would have borne us some tidings of that wonderful people the Aztecs, and their interesting life on the plateau of Mexico; but the Indians of the coast were at enmity with them, and only once did Vespucius and his companions go back from the coast. The arrows described by Vespucius as in use among the natives in 1497, were made by the Apaches as late as 1886. The use of women as burden-bearers is still characteristic of American Indians. All that Vespucius said of their making war, their government, their treatment of the children and the aged, their habits of body, the employment of implements of war and peace, the manufacture of pottery, their hammocks of cotton or vegetable fiber, their valuation of green stones as great riches, the union in them of simplicity and cunning, of gentleness and barbarity,—all describe with more or less accuracy the native tribes and their descendants of Mexico in North America.

The word *Lariab* itself is probably a compound or, rather, a phrased native word, and it is thought that the Quiche natives — the termination *-ab* belonging to that speech — misunderstood the inquiry of the Spaniards as to the name of their province, and replied, "Lar Yab,"—that is to say, "There are many." Varnhagen thinks this word is pure Huaxtèque, and mentions the names of three ancient Huaxtèque villages— Tanlajab, Tancuayalab, Tancuallalab—all ending in *-ab*. That the country visited by Vespucius could not have been in South America is manifest from what he says of its location: "This land is within the torrid zone, close to or just under the parallel described by the Tropic of Cancer: where the pole of the horizon has an elevation of 23 degrees, at the extremity of the second climate." When the sun in its annual journey is in its most northern declination, the parallel is called the Tropic of Cancer, and 23° 28' of north latitude mark this climatic zone. If Americus knew anything of the heavens, he knew when the extremity of this "second climate" was reached, and no writer could have more carefully located the scene of his story. Has the Genoese Admiral so carefully located his own landfalls either on the Bahama island or on the coast of Cuba as to fix them beyond the question of the student? The descriptions of the land and rivers, of the birds and animals, of the forests and of the fruits of the trees, the minute accounts of the people and of their customs, make it more than probable that at Tampico, near the mouth of the river Panuco, just under the Tropic of Cancer, is to be found the spot where Americus Vespucius halted so long in the province of Lariab.

The fleet then left this province of Lariab and navigated along the coast, always in sight of land, until it had accomplished 870 leagues, still going in the direction of the "Maestrale." This passage has enraged many a reader. If the course described as *maestrale* be to the northwest, then Americus must have traveled overland nearly to the coast of California. But Harrisse calmly ignores the westerly trend of this course, and takes note only of its northerly meaning, and we find comfort in following his lead.

CHAPTER IV

Discussion of the Narrative

THERE are two weak points in the narrative of Vespucius, which stand therein like great interrogation points, between the landing-place in Honduras and the province of Lariab. The first is the failure to identify *little Venice*, or Veneziola. Vespucius says: "We landed in a harbor, where we found a village built like Venice, upon the water: there were about forty-four large dwellings in the form of huts erected upon very thick piles, and they had their doors or entrances in the style of drawbridges, and from each house one could pass through all by means of the drawbridges which stretched from house to house; and when the people thereof had seen us, they appeared to be afraid of us, and immediately drew up all the bridges; and while we were looking at this strange action we saw coming across the sea about twenty-two canoes, which are a kind of boats constructed from a single tree." This description of a little Venice has given some foundation for the statement that this pile-built village was not on the coast of North America at all, but near Lake Maracaybo in Venezuela. Certainly, so far as we know, there were no people on the coast of Mexico or Central America who lived habitually in this way. That the lowlands to the west of Yucatan, near the Gulf of Mexico, abounded in lakes and lagoons and were frequently inundated is well established. Two rivers— the Tabasco and the Usumasinta—with many mouths make of the shore a low, marshy plain. Beginning with June, for a long rainy season, the country is full of sloughs, and there is no traveling by land. As late as 1750 Padre Zepeda, a Jesuit missionary, in speaking of the tribes in Costa Rica, says they built their huts in the trees to escape from the floods. Bancroft says on many parts of the coast of Darien and on the Gulf of Urabá the villages are built on the water. The people told Vespucius that they were at the sea for the purpose of fishing, and so had built temporary homes over the water to be convenient in this business. We know that these Indians frequently changed their abodes, and thus may we account for not finding remains of these strange villages, as would be the case if they had been substantially built, or if it had been the customary form of dwelling among this people. Again it is barely possible that Vespucius mixed his notes on two different voyages, and that the memorandum concerning little Venice, seen on the occasion of his second voyage along the coast of Venezuela, became incorporated in the narration of the events occurring on his first voyage. It must be remembered that this account of his four voyages was not written until September 4, 1504 — more than seven years after the eventful first expedition of 1497. We have already remarked on the strange omission in the narrative of any volcano or the sight of any snow-capped mountain, such as Tuxtla or Orizaba; and the frequent fogs which cover these eternal hills might well account for the failure to see them, and consequently to tell of their wonders. But there is another weak point which we cannot satisfactorily explain.

The little fleet must have touched the southern coast of the ancient Mexican empire, and when it halted so long at Panuco it must have been close to its other frontier on the northeast. Within these border-lands, on the high plateau, at that very time, were powers and principalities, priests and pantheons, provinces and palaces. While Giotto was designing the Campanile in Florence, some Aztec architect was building Tenochtitlan, the capital of Anahuac. A century and a half had passed since the building of the city, and in that time there had been developed a civilization which may have been as great as it certainly was mysterious. There was an influential government, there were laws, an enlightened jurisprudence, schooled diplomacy, disciplined armies. Astronomy and architecture flourished and were honored. Music, sculpture, and mural painting exalted the people. Five thousand priests in the great temple administered to the spiritual aspirations of the nation, and prayed for the return of Quetzalcohuatl, that mysterious white-bearded divinity or man whose second coming was to bring peace and joy. All these things, in kind or degree, were moving to and fro in a world not many leagues from where the little fleet lay anchored; and yet in the narration of his journey, written in one paper to instruct and amuse the friend of his youth, and in another paper to a patron and the representative of the greatest family of Florence, he speaks never a word of a civilization in the midst of barbarism. Can this omission be satisfactorily explained? Shall we say that Vespucius saw or at least heard something of this Mexican civilization, and simply failed to include an account of it in his narration, either by accident or under the design of placing it in his more pretentious work which he tells us over and over again he proposed writing under the title of "Le Quattro Giornate." This book was a diary written during the course of his four voyages. While still talking of the province of Lariab in his account of his first voyage, he says:

> Amongst that people and in their land, I knew and beheld so many of their customs and ways of living, that I do not care to enlarge upon them; for your Magnificence must know that in each of my voyages I have noted the most wonderful things, and I have indited it all in a volume after the manner of a geography, and I entitle it "The Four Journeys," in which work the things are comprised in detail, and as yet there is no copy of it given out, as it is necessary for me to revise it.

This book never was given out,—at least no copy of such a book has ever been known,—and thus have we been deprived of the history and records made by the first formal chronicler of the New World and its marvels. The natives, as will soon be seen, told Vespucius all about their anthropophagous enemies on the islands out at sea, but do not appear to have spoken of their civilized neighbors or enemies a little way back in the interior. We may admit that Vespucius did not hear of these neighbors, but it is difficult for us to believe that the natives themselves had no knowledge of them. The ancient Mexicans, however, were not a maritime people. The lake, on an island of which their city had been founded, they might well call *nostrum mare*, and they went not down to the sea in ships. This city was on a table-land, the last of three great terraces stretching back from the Atlantic Ocean, and which are respectively 3000, 6000, and 8000 feet above the level of the sea. These terraces are the *tierra caliente*, or hot coast-land; the *tierra templada*, or temperate land; and the *tierra fria*, or cold land of the elevated regions. They constituted natural barriers between the natives of the coast and the progressive occupants of the high plateau. That a few years later there were hostilities between them we know, from the aid Cortés and the conquerors received when they went up against the great city and broke the heart of Montezuma. Some day we may find the lost "Quattro Giornate," or the archæologist may clear up the mystery by showing the roving character of the native tribes near Tampico at the end of the fifteenth century, and the fact that they themselves did not know of the Aztec warriors on the hills above them.

It must have been about the 1st of November that the fleet left this province of Lariab, which is believed to have been Tampico in Mexico, and coasted the shore for 870 leagues. Here again is a stumbling-block in the course described as *maestrale*, or toward the northwest. The words are *tutta via verso el maestrale*, "still following a northwest course." Certainly the fleet could not literally have traveled 870 leagues to the northwest, but in starting away from the mouth of the Panuco, or from the cape just north of the river, the course at starting would be west of north, and Vespucius, not always exact in his writings, may have had that in mind; or he may have been mindful of the general direction from the Canaries, and desirous of making pronounced the great distance he had traveled along a common circle westward from his own shores, and of definitely declaring his arrival at a point 82 degrees westward from the Grand Canary, or about 92½ degrees from Cadiz, thus traversing a fourth part of our globe.

With this thought in mind, he may have employed a term of navigation which has ever since perplexed the commentators of the Vespucian voyages.

Mapping out these 870 leagues on a marine chart, and making allowances for the windings of the coast, the mouths of the Mississippi, and the long course around the southerly point of Florida, it brings our fleet to about Cape Hatteras, in latitude 35° 14′ north, the easternmost point of North Carolina, and which stretches far out into the broad Atlantic. Vespucius says that after coasting these 870 leagues, and having been already thirteen months on the voyage, and the vessels being much damaged, it was determined by a general council to haul the ships on land for the purpose of calking the leaky sides. "And when we came to this determination," he says, "we were close to a harbor the best in the world." Cape Hatteras is separated from the mainland by a magnificent bay, Pamlico Sound, not unworthy of being called the "best harbor in the world," since it is 80 miles in length by 30 miles in width.

In the "Premier Voyage de Amerigo Vespucci," printed in Vienna in 1869, Varnhagen seeks to establish the northern limit of this voyage at Cape Cañaveral, about 28° 30′ north latitude. In his "Amerígo Vespucci," printed in Lima, 1865, he makes this northern limit at Cape Hatteras, and is strongly tempted to let it reach even to Chesapeake Bay. The course which the fleet took on leaving land, and which brought them to the hostile isles, if we admit that the latter were the Bermudas, would indicate that the point of departure was Hatteras.

The boats having been repaired after a lapse of thirty-seven days, and the fleet being ready to start homeward, the natives desired that Americus and his companions should revenge them on some cruel enemies who dwelt far out to sea on some islands, and who made periodic excursions to the mainland to enslave the inhabitants, and even ate their prisoners. As the islands were on their way, the Europeans resolved to revenge the wrongs perpetrated against a people who had shown them kindness and friendliness. Taking only seven of the natives with them, on the condition that they should return alone in their canoes, they departed from the shores of the newly found continent and sailed seven days out to sea between east and northeast. At the end of this time they came upon many islands, some inhabited and some deserted, and finally fought a battle with the natives of one, frightening many with the noise of their guns and killing not a few. The natives called this island Iti. Two hundred and twenty-two prisoners were carried into captivity, and bidding adieu to the seven Indians from the mainland, the fleet set sail for Spain, reaching Cadiz on the 15th of October, 1498, where they were well received, and where, as Vespucius incidentally remarks, they sold their slaves.

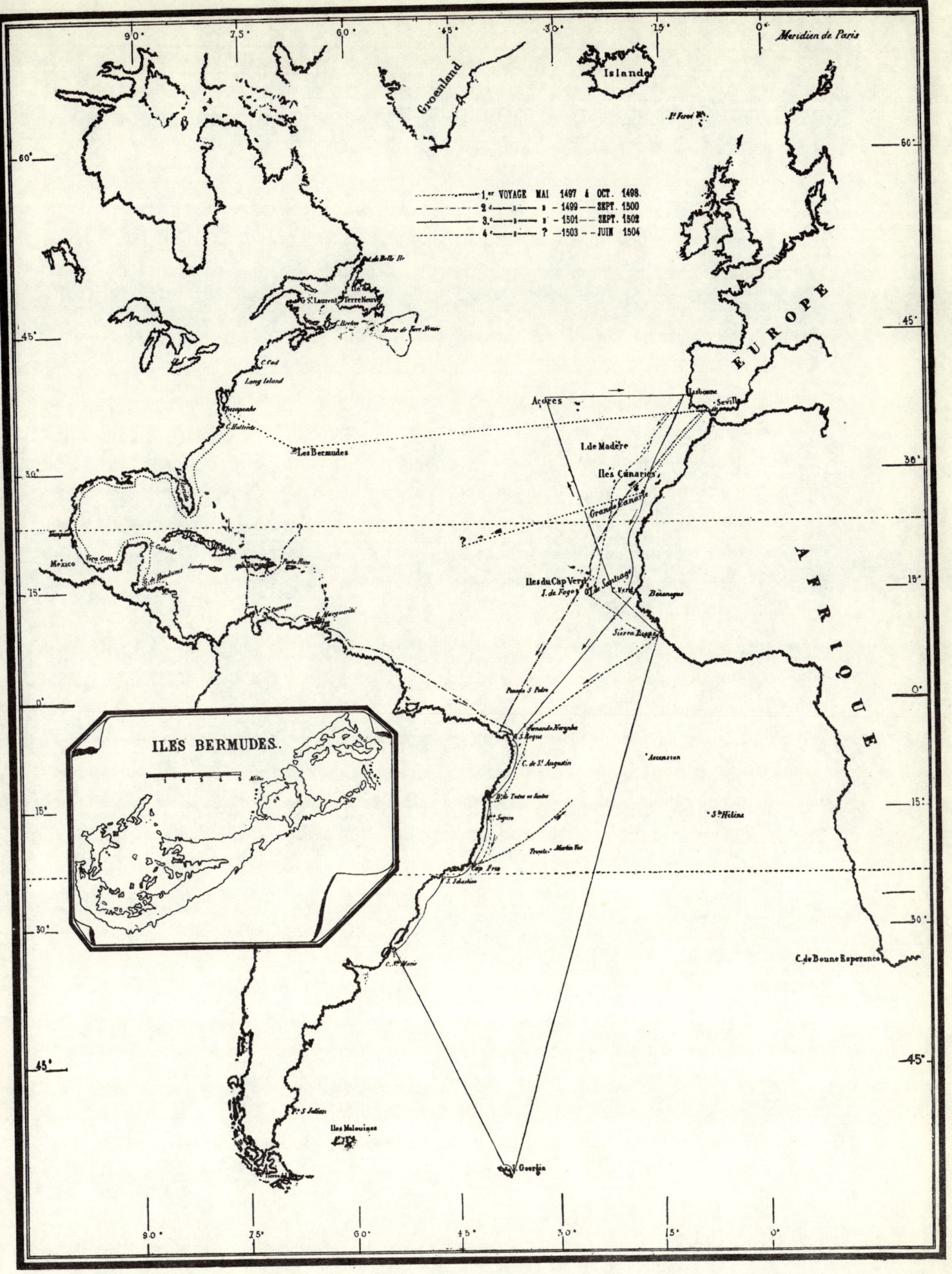

CHART OF THE VOYAGES OF VESPUCIUS. ADAPTED FROM VARNHAGEN.

CHAPTER V

The Second, Third, and Fourth Voyages

ETWEEN October 15, 1498, and May 16, 1499, there are no records of the employment of Vespucius. On the latter date, however, we find him again upon the Ocean Sea with a fleet of three vessels under the Spanish flag, and with Alonso de Ojeda as commander. Juan de la Cosa was likewise of the company, and shared with Vespucius the responsibility of pilot duty. The course of the fleet was southwest from Cadiz, and, passing in sight of the Great Canary, the first halt was made at the Cape Verd Islands. After journeying for four and forty days, they touched upon a land which they deemed a part of the continent, and continuous with that land discovered on the first voyage. "The which [*new land*] is situated within the torrid zone, and southwardly beyond the equinoctial line, above which the southern pole rises to the elevation of five degrees beyond every climate," which, being interpreted, means that they believed themselves in five degrees of south latitude. Here they found the land inundated so that they were unable to land. They steered east-southeast, and had made their way with difficulty, probably as far as Cape San Roque, when the strong currents compelled them to turn about and go to the northwest, where they found a bay or port with a fine large island in its mouth. This was either the Amazon, holding in its mouth the island Marajo, or the Gulf of Paria with the beautiful Trinidad for its island setting. The Waldseemüller map seems to identify the former as the fine port with the large island. It was here they had a fight with a people called *Caniballi*, "who ate human flesh," and the word *Canibales* appears on the Waldseemüller map at this very spot. Except for the application of the word Caniballi to the harbor and its island lying on the coast of Brazil and southeast of the Gulf of Paria, the text would clearly describe the latter with the fleet entering the gulf on the south side of the island, passing around it, and issuing from the harbor on its north side, thereafter pursuing a westward course till it reached the island of Margarita, fifteen leagues out to sea, which is called on the map *Delarapossa*. Here they found a people the most brutish

they had yet seen, but who treated them kindly. On the island was little if any water, and the people continually chewed leaves which had become moist by the dew of the night. From this island they went westward to another which is down on the map as *Insula Gigantum*, the modern Curaçoa, and on which they not only found traces of a people of great size, but saw some young girls of a stature so tall that they marveled and thought of carrying them away into Castile as prodigies. Nine of the men were soon put in jeopardy of their lives by the sudden appearance of thirty-six male giants carrying large bows and arrows and knobbed clubs. Vespucius himself gave the name of the Isle of Giants to this island. By reason of having been a year at sea, and their stock of provisions getting perilously short owing to the warm latitudes in which they were, having twice crossed the equinoctial line, they concluded to repair their ships and start for home. While seeking a safe harbor for this purpose, they fell in with a people who had fine pearls. With such valuable merchandise as glass balls and beads, and looking-glasses and sheets of tin, not worth in all the sum of forty ducats, they secured 952 ounces of rich pearls. Having calked their vessels, they made for the island of Antiglia or Hispaniola. As this is the passage in which Americus acknowledges that Columbus preceded him as discoverer, we quote it:

> We departed, and through the necessity of our victualing we made for the island of Antiglia, which is the same that Christophal Colombo discovered several years ago; where we took in much store of provision and remained two months and seventeen days; where we underwent many perils and troubles with the very Christians who were in this island along with Colombo — I believe through envy, but, in order not to be prolix, I refrain from narrating them. We departed from the said island on the 22d day of July; and we navigated during a month and a half, and entered into the port of Cadiz, which was on the 8th day of September, by daylight, ending my second voyage.

There is good reason for believing that Alonso de Ojeda and the pilot Juan de la Cosa on the flag-ship separated from the other two vessels of the fleet some time during the latter part of August, 1499, and that the flag-ship was wrecked, Ojeda arriving at San Domingo in a small boat on the 5th of September, 1499. It is also well established that the fleet discovered on this voyage the Gulf of Maracaybo. At the mouth of the Orinoco River, past which the fleet must have gone, the water in the Gulf of Paria is fresh and sweet, and in the Waldseemüller map of 1513 we find the words *Hoc mare est de dulci aqua*. When Vespucius with the two remaining ships of the fleet reached Hispaniola, a revolt had taken place against the Admiral and his brother, which, although it was suppressed before Bobadilla and aid arrived from Spain, was still a serious and historic insurrection. Nevertheless we find no account in the narrative of Vespucius of the wreck of the flag-ship, the discovery of the gulf, the mysterious appearance of fresh water in the open sea, or the first American rebellion

Therefore the failure of Vespucius, in speaking of his first voyage, to remark upon the Aztec civilization or to repeat some wild traveler's tale concerning the mysterious people of the high plateau, assuming that their existence had been brought to his knowledge, need not surprise us. Americus takes pains to tell us over and over again that he has set down here only a few of the wonderful things he saw.

While resting at Seville after his long voyage, a countryman of his, Giuliano di Bartholomeo de Giocondo, brought to Vespucius from the king Don Manuel of Portugal a proposition to repair to Lisbon and enter his service. The Portuguese, whose maritime discoveries were somewhat clouded in the greater glory of Columbus and Spanish expeditions, had a sudden and accidental return to glory through the voyage of Pedro Alvarez de Cabral, who, starting for the East Indies, found himself eventually on the coast of Brazil, a discoverer against his will. The voyage fired the Portuguese king with a renewed desire for discovery, and the royal needs demanded no less an agent than our Vespucius. Accordingly the latter set out for Lisbon, where on his arrival he found preparing a fleet of three ships. Again, it is not certain on whom the chief command rested. Some, among them Varnhagen, say it was Don Nuño Manoel; others believe the fleet was in command of Gonçalo Coelho. We know at least that the three ships started from Lisbon on the 10th of May, 1501, and that Americus was in command of one.

Keeping along the coast of Africa until they reached 14½ degrees north latitude, they landed on the site of the present Gorée, not far from Cape Verd, where they remained eleven days, taking in water and fire-wood. Departing from this African port, they sailed in a southwesterly course, reaching land after sixty-seven days of storm and untoward weather. Here they met a people of very low civilization, and one of the crew was killed and roasted at a great fire, before their eyes. Unable to gain the consent of the chief captain to avenge this cruelty, the fleet departed on an east-southeast course, doubling Cape St. Augustine, which they reached on that saint's day, August 28; and on the 1st of November, which was All Saints' day, landed at a point which they called Bahia de Todos os Santos. Still coasting to the south, the fleet passed Rio de Janeiro, and later the Rio de la Plata, at which point the command of the fleet fell upon Vespucius. On the 2d or 3d of April they found themselves at a distance 500 leagues to the southeast of their starting-point, or about 52 degrees south latitude. On the 7th of April, when the nights were fifteen hours long, they reached an inhospitable land which is believed to have been the island of South Georgia, and which probably was not again seen by Europeans until Captain Cook rediscovered it in January, 1775. Here a terrible storm arose, great enough in its terror to draw from the sailors promises of pious pilgrimages if ever they reached home again. On the 10th of May they were at Sierra Leone, on their homeward journey, where they made a burnt-offering of one of their three ships, which had passed beyond a state of usefulness.

Of his four voyages, this—the third—was the most important and eventful. Starting from Lisbon, situated 38° 44' north latitude, and reaching the island of South Georgia, whose northernmost point is 54 degrees south latitude, the Florentine navigator had traversed an arc of longitude of more than 93 degrees, and, consequently, had accomplished the fourth part of the terrestrial circle. Vespucius, immediately upon his arrival at Lisbon, wrote to Lorenzo di Pier Francesco de' Medici, simply announcing his return and promising him a detailed account in a subsequent letter. This last is the famous "Epistola," the Italian text of which is lost, and of which so many Latin editions were printed during the years 1503 and 1504. In this letter Americus distinctly announces that he has discovered a new world,—not the prolongation of another continent, not the continuation of Asia, but a separate division which might well be called the fourth part of the world. He here speaks of "those new countries which we have sought and found, which it is lawful to call a new world, since among the ancients there was no knowledge of the same. If by any chance some have admitted it might be a continent, they have denied that it was peopled. This last journey of mine has proved the falsity of this notion, since I have found a continent in southern latitudes inhabited by a greater quantity of men and animals than Europe, Asia, or Africa." When, therefore, numerous editions of the "Epistola" made the account of the third voyage the common property of the scholars and geographers of Europe, it is the most natural thing conceivable that the editors and printers should entitle this the "Mundus Novus"; nor is it strange that a few years later the little coterie in the Vosgian Mountains, following the track of the Florentine sailor from 35 degrees of north latitude to 54 degrees of south latitude, should have thought it a seemly thing to have affixed to this new world the name not of its discoverer, but of its more complete explorer, Americus Vespucius. In the celebrated "Epistola" it must be remembered that Americus expressed his purpose to pass in a subsequent voyage—the fourth, and which he was then contemplating—to the eastern regions by way of the southern end of this new continent. This was a feat not destined for him, but vouchsafed in later years to a veritable Portuguese, Ferdinand Magellan. It is difficult to imagine, in view of what Vespucius himself has said, how Von Humboldt could have asserted that Vespucius, like Christopher Columbus, died in blissful ignorance of having visited any other land than a supplementary Asia. Whatever the extent of territory which Waldseemüller regarded as the New World, and to which he proposed to affix a name, it is evident that the early geographers intended to limit that name to the southern part, and it was not till 1538 that the name covered the entire continent. Withholding nothing from Columbus, but considering only the services of the Florentine, we may at least say that the naming of America was not absolutely without propriety.

Those were the days of long voyages and short tarryings at home. Early in the following spring, six ships sailed out from Lisbon under the command of Gonçalo Coelho. Juan Diaz de Solís, who had also left the Spanish service to enter that of Portugal, was one of the pilots. Vespucius himself was in charge of one of the ships. One might have thought that the discoveries made by Americus on the shores of the New World would have incited the Portuguese monarch to continue his explorations in that direction. But shortly after the return of Vespucius from his third voyage, some ships came in from the Indies laden with spices, and bringing word that this aromatic wealth was not the product of India, but had been gathered from some fragrant and mysterious isles to the eastward. It was to find these, and particularly to find Malacca, which was the purpose of this voyage. But fate was stronger than purpose, and, as the sequel will show, the New World drew him once more toward her. The fleet sailed southerly along the coast of Africa toward Sierra Leone, but the stormy weather prevented landing. Vespucius, in his account, lays the blame for even attempting Sierra Leone upon the incapacity of the captain of the fleet. Four days of fruitless effort led to the abandonment of the attempt and the adoption of a southwestern course, and, after sailing three hundred leagues, they reached the island of Fernando Noronha, where the customary wreck took place, the chief vessel, of three hundred tons, going ashore on a treacherous rock. Vespucius was ordered to seek a proper port, and in obeying his orders he lost sight of the other ships. Eight days afterward he fell in with one of the vessels of the fleet, and from that time on they sailed in company. It had been understood in the fleet that should the ships become separated, they were to make for the Bay of Todos os Santos, discovered on the preceding voyage. They reached this port after a voyage of seventeen days. For sixty-four days they waited patiently the arrival of the three other ships. Finally Vespucius and his fellow-captain started to explore to the south. Landing at Cape Frio, near Rio de Janeiro, they built a fort, stocking it with provisions for six months, and garrisoning it with twenty-four men who were part of the crew of the wrecked ship of the Admiral. It is said that this fort was still maintained in 1511. One Christovam Pires commanded the ship named *Bretoa*, which in that year visited Cape Frio and bore away a cargo of Brazil wood; and it is known by documents still existing in Portugal that other ships had visited the same place the preceding year. Departing on a direct course for Lisbon, after seventy-seven days of perilous voyaging they entered that port on the 18th day of June, 1504.

Vespucius did not remain much longer in the service of Portugal. It was now the turn of Ferdinand, King of Spain, to secure the successful Florentine and to bring him again into his service. Accordingly, at the beginning of the year 1505 he is found waiting upon the Castilian Cortes, which was holding its session in Toro. The odor from the land of spices had caught the fancy of the government, and an order was given to prepare an expedition of three ships. Varnhagen believes that it was about this time that Vespucius espoused a Spanish lady, Maria Cerezo. In a document dated April 11—a royal order appropriating 12,000 maravedis to defray the expense of his voyage—he is called *vecino* of Seville, and it is said that marriage with a native of that city entitled one to be so designated. On the 24th of April of that year, by letters patent he was made a naturalized Castilian, and was appointed captain in the navy, with an annual salary of 30,000 maravedis. The three ships mentioned above for this expedition were to have been constructed in Biscay. Philip the First, the successor of Ferdinand, on the 23d of August, 1506, made inquiry at the Casa de Contratacion in Seville as to the completion of these ships, and on the 15th of September received reply that the fleet would not be ready to start before February, 1507, Vespucius being charged with the personal delivery of this reply. Thereafter no mention or record of him is met with until the 24th of November of that year, when he was called by the court, in company with Juan de la Cosa, to Burgos. These voyagers bore with them a sum of gold from Darien, which has been estimated at 6000 ducats. Each received as an honorarium, by royal order, 6000 maravedis, and on the 22d of March, 1508, Americus was appointed *piloto mayor* of Spain.

By this time the fame of Vespucius had gone abroad over the world. The many editions of his letters and the "Cosmographia" issued by the St.-Dié press fixed attention on him as the most skilful living navigator. With fame came rest and, to him, the strange luxury of ease. It was easier to examine pilots and to issue to them certificates than to navigate a frail ship over the rough waves of the Ocean Sea. The respectful homage of the citizens of Seville was more to his taste than the wondering surprise of the Tabasco savages. Columbus, in his letter to his son Diego dated February 5, 1505, seems to echo a complaint from Vespucius of services unrewarded; but he was now dwelling in the midst of honor, fame, and emolument. Four enjoyable years were now his portion, until, on the 22d of February, in the year 1512, he entered upon the last voyage of all. His wife survived him, but he left no children. His nephew, Giovanni Vespucci, fell heir to his property, which consisted of maps rather than maravedis, and of diaries rather than ducats.

PART IV

The First Voyage of Vespucius

Its published Narration, with the Italian, Latin, and English Texts of the first Part of the famous Letter

Lettera di Amerigo vespucci delle isole nuouamente trouate in quattro suoi viaggi.

TITLE-PAGE OF THE FIRST (ITALIAN) EDITION OF THE LETTER OF VESPUCIUS DESCRIBING HIS VOYAGES.

CHAPTER I

The First Voyage of Americus Vespucius, with the Italian, Latin, and English Texts.

IN this part we give in parallel columns Vespucius's own account of his first voyage in the original Italian text from the very rare original entitled "Lettera di Amerigo Vespucci delle isole nuouamente trouate in quattro suoi viaggi," printed at Florence, 1505 or 1506, and also the Latin translation from the "Cosmographiæ Introductio," published in St.-Dié in April, 1507. Together with these two versions we give an English translation of the Italian original. This latter is taken from the admirable translation published by Bernard Quaritch in 1893.

[TEXT OF FIRST ITALIAN EDITION — CIRCA 1505.]

MAGNIFICE domine. Dipoi della humile reuerentia & debite recōmendationi &c. Potra essere che uostra Magnificentia simara uigliera della mia temerita, et usada uostra sauidoria, ch̄ tāto absurdamēte lo mimuoua a scriuere a uostra Mag. la p̄sente lettera tāto ꝓlissa: sappiendo che di cōtinuo uostra Mag. sta occupata nelli alti consigli & negotii sopra elbuon reggimēto di cotesta excelsa Repub. Et mi terra nō solo presumptuoso, sed etiam perotioso, in pormi a scriuere cose nō

[TEXT OF LATIN TRANSLATION PRINTED AT ST.-DIÉ, VII KALENDS MAY, 1507.]

Illustrissimo Renato. Iherusalem & Siciliæ Regi, duci Lothoringiæ ac Barn̄. Americus Vesputius humilē reuerentiā & debitā recōmēdationem. Fieri pōt, illustrissime Rex, vt tua maiestas mea ista temeritate ducatur in admirationē: propterea quod hasce litteras tam prolixas adte scribere non subuerear, cum tamen sciam te continuo in arduis consilijs & crebris reipublicæ negocijs occupatissimum. Atqʒ existimabor forte non modo præsumptuosus, sed etiam ociosus: id mihi muneris vendicans, ut res statui tuo minus con-

[ENGLISH TRANSLATION, FROM PRIMITIVE ITALIAN TEXT.]

Magnificent Lord. After humble reverence and due commendations, etc. It may be that your Magnificence will be surprised by my rashness and the affront to your wisdom, in that I should so absurdly bestir myself to write to your Magnificence the present so-prolix letter: knowing [*as I do*] that your Magnificence is continually employed in high councils and affairs concerning the good government of this sublime Republic. And will hold me not only presumptuous, but also idly-meddlesome in setting myself to write things, neither suitable to your station, nor entertaining, and written

conuenienti a uostro stato, ne dilecteuoli, & cō barbaro stilo scripte, & fuora dogni ordine di humanita: ma la cōfidentia mia che tengho nelle uostre uirtu & nella uerita del mio scriuere, che son cose nō sitruouano scripte ne p̄ li antichi ne p̄ moderni scriptori, come nel p̄cesso conoscera V. M. mifa essere usato. La causa principale c̄h mosse a scriuerui, fu p̄ ruogho del p̄sente aportatore, che sidice Benuenuto Benuenuti nostro fiorētino, molto seruitore secōdo che sidimostra, di uostra Mag. & molto amico mio: elquale trouandosi qui in questa citta di Lisbona, mi prego che io facessi parte a uostra Mag. delle cose per me viste in diuerse plaghe del mondo, per uirtu di quattro viaggi che ho facti in discoprire nuoue terre: edua per mando del Re di Castiglia don Ferrādo Re.vi. per el gran golfo del mare oceano uerso loccidente: et laltre due p̄ mandato del poderoso Re don Manouello Re di Portogallo, uerso laustro: Dicendomi che uostra Mag. nepiglierebbe piacere, & che in q̄sto speraua seruirui. Il perche midisposi a farlo: p̄che mirendo certo c̄h uostra Mag. mitiene nel numero de suoi seruidori, ricordādomi come nel tempo della nostra giouentu ui ero amico, & hora seruidore: & andando a udire eprincipii di grāmatica sotto la buona uita & doctrina del uenerabile religioso fratre di. S. Marco fra Giorgio Antonio Vespucci: econsigli & doctrina del quale piacesse a Dio che io hauessi seguitato: che come dice el petrarcha, lo sarei altro huomo da quel chio sono.

venientes non delectabili sed barbaro p̄rsus stylo (veluti amusus ab humanitatis cultu alienus) ad Ferdinandū Castiliæ Regem nominatim scriptas, ad te quoq̄ mittam. Sed ea quā in tuas v̄tutes habeo cōfidentia, & cōperta sequentiū rerū neq̄ ab antiquis neq̄ neotericis scriptarum veritas me corā t. M. fortassis excusabunt. Mouit me imprimis ad scribendum præsentiū lator Beneuenutus, M. t. humilis famulus, & amicus meus nō pœnitendus, qui dum me Lisbonæ reperiret precatus est vt t. M. rerū per me quatuor profectionibus in diuersis plagis mundi visarum, participē facere vellem. Peregi ēm bis binas nauigationes ad nouas terras inueniendas: quarū duas ex mandato Fernandi, inclyti regis Castiliæ, per magnū oceani sinum occidentē v̄sus fœci, alteras duas iussu Manuelis, Lusitaniæ Regis, ad Austrū. Itaq̄ me ad id negocii accinxi sperans q̄ t. M. me de clientum numero nō excludet: vbi recordabit́, p̄ oli mutuā habuerimus inter nos amicicia tēpore iuuentutis nr̄æ, cū grāmaticæ rudimētā imbibentes sub p̄bata vita & doctrina venerabiĺ & religiosi fratris de S. Marco Fra. Georgij Anthonij Vesputij, avunculi mei pariter militaremus. Cuius avunculi vestigia vtinam sequi potuissem, alius profecto (vt & ipse Petrarcha ait), essem q̄ sum. Vtcūq̄ tn̄ sit, nō me pudet esse qui sum. Semper ēm in ipsa v̄tute & rebus studiosis summā habui delectationē. Quod si tibi hæ narrationes omnino non placuerint: dicam sicut Plinius ad Mecenatē scribit olim facetijs meis delectari solebas. Et licet M. t. sine fine ī reipublicæ negocijs occupata sit, nihilominus tantū tēporis qn̄cq̄ suffuraberis, vt has res q̄vis ridiculas (quæ tamē sua nouitate iuuabūt) perlegere possis. Habebis ēm hisce meis lr̄is post curarū

in barbarous style, and outside of every canon of literature: but the confidence which I have in your virtues and in the truth of my writing, which are things [*that*] are not found written neither by the ancients nor by modern writers, as your Magnificence will in the sequel perceive, makes me bold. The chief cause which moved [*me*] to write to you, was by the request of the present bearer, who is named Benvenuto Benvenuti our Florentine [*fellow-citizen*], very much, as it is proven, your Magnificence's servant, and my very good friend: who happening to be here in this city of Lisbon, begged that I should make communication to your Magnificence of the things seen by me in divers regions of the world, by virtue of four voyages which I have made in discovery of new lands: two by order of the King of Castile, King Don Ferrando VI., across the great gulf of the Ocean-sea toward the west: and the other two by command of the puissant King Don Manuel King of Portugal, toward the south: Telling me that your Magnificence would take pleasure thereof, and that herein he hoped to do you service: wherefore I set me to do it: because I am assured that your Magnificence holds me in the number of your servants, remembering that in the time of our youth I was your friend, and now [*am your*] servant: and [*remembering our*] going to hear the rudiments of grammar under the fair example and instruction of the venerable monk friar of Saint Mark Fra Giorgio Antonio Vespucci: whose counsels and teaching would to God that I had followed: for as saith Petrarch, I should be

Quo modocunq; sit, non midolgho: perche sempre misono dilectato in cose uirtuose: et anchora che queste mia patragne nō siano conuenienti alle uirtu uostre, uidiro come dixe Plinio a Mecenate, Voi solauate in alcun tēpo pigliare piacere delle mie ciancie: anchora che uostra Mag.stia del continuo occupata nepublici negotii, alchuna hora piglierete di scanso di consumare un poco di tempo nelle cose ridicule, o dilecteuoli: et come ilfinocchio siconstuma dare in cima delle dilecteuoli uiuande p̄ disporle a miglior digestione, cosi potrete p̄ discanso di tante uostre occupationi mādare a leggere questa mia lettera: perche ui apartino alcun tanto della continua cura & assiduo pensamēto delle cose publiche: et se saro p̄lissoueniam peto Mag. signor mio. Vostra Mag. sapra, come el motiuo della uenuta mia in questo regno di Spagna fu p̄ tractate mercatantie: & come seguissi in q̄sto proposito circa di quattro anni: nequali uiddi & conobbi edisuariati mouimēti della fortuna: & come promutaua questi beni caduci & transitorii: & come un tēpo tiene lhuomo nella sommita della ruota: & altro tēpo lo ributta da se, & lo priua de beni che sipossono dire imprestati: di modo che conosciuto elcontinuo trauaglio che lhuomo pone in conquerirgli, con sottomettersi a tanti disagi & pericoli, deliberai lasciarmi della mercantia & porre elmio fine in cosa piu laudabile & ferma: che fu che midisposi dandare a uedere parte del mondo, & le sue marauiglie: & aquesto mi siofferse tempo fomēta & meditamēta negociorū nō modicā delectatiōe, sicut et ipse fœniculus prius sumptis esculentis odorē dare & meliorē digestionē facere asueuit. Enim vero si plus æq̄ p̄lixus fuero, veniā peto. Vale.

Inclitissime rex sciat t. M. quod ad has ipsas regiones mercādi causa primū venerim. Dumq; per q̄driennij reuolutionē ī eis rebus negociosus essem, et varias fortunæ mutatiōes animaduerterem, atq; vide rem quo pacto caduca & transitoria bona hominem ad tempus in rotæ sum̄o tenerēt, & deinde ipsum præcipitarent ad imū qui se possidere multa dicere poterat: constitui mecū, varijs taliū rerum casibus exanclatis istiusmo di negocia dimittere, et meorū laborum finem in res laudabiliores ac plus stabiles ponere. Ita disposui me ad varias mundi partes cōtemplandas, & diversas res mirabiles videndas. Ad quā rem se & tēpus & locus opportune obtulit. Ipse em̄ Castiliæ rex Fernandus tunc quatuor parabat naues ad terras nouas occidentem versus disco operiendas, cuius celsitudo me ad talia investiganda in ipsam societatē elegit. Et soluimus vigesima die Maij. MCCCC.xcvij. de portu Caliciæ, iter nostrū per magnū oceani sinū capientes: in qua profectione xviij. consumauimus menses, multas inuenientes terras firmas, & insulas pene innumerabiles vt plurimū habitatas, quarū maiores nostri mentionem nullam fœcerunt. Vnde & ipsos antiquos taliū non habuisse noticiā credimus. Et nisi memoria me fallat, memini me in aliquo legere, quod mare vacuum et sine hominibus esse tenuerint. Cuius opinionis ipse Dantes Poeta noster fuit, ubi duodeuigesimo capite de inferis loquens Vlyssis mortem cōfingit. Quæ autē mirabilia viderim, in sequentium processu T. M. intelliget.

another man than what I am. Howbeit soever, I grieve not: because I have ever taken delight in worthy matters: and although these trifles of mine may not be suitable to your virtues, I will say to you as said Pliny to Mæcenas, you were sometime wont to take pleasure in my prattlings: even though your Magnificence be continually busied in public affairs, you will take some hour of relaxation to consume a little time in laughable or amusing things: and as fennel is customarily given atop of delicious viands to fit them for better digestion, so may you, for a relief from your so heavy occupations, order this letter of mine to be read: so that they may withdraw you somewhat from the continual anxiety and assiduous reflection upon public affairs: and if I shall be prolix, I crave pardon, my Magnificent Lord. Your Magnificence shall know that the motive of my coming into this realm of Spain was to traffic in merchandise: and that I pursued this intent about four years: during which I saw and knew the inconstant shiftings of Fortune: and how she kept changing those frail and transitory benefits: and how at one time she holds man on the summit of the wheel, and at another time drives him back from her, and despoils him of what may be called his borrowed riches: so that, knowing the continuous toil which man undergoes to win them, submitting himself to so many discomforts and risks, I resolved to abandon trade, and to fix my aim upon something more praiseworthy and stable: whence it was that I made preparation for going to see part of the world and its wonders: and

& luogo molto oportuno: che fu, chel Re don Ferrando di Castiglia hauēdo a mandare quattro naui a discoprire nuoue terre uerso loccidente, fui electo per sua alteza che io fussi in essa flocta per adiutare a discoprire: et partimo del porto di Calis adi. io di maggio 1497. et pigliāmo nostro cāmino per el gran golfo del mare oceano: nel qual uiaggio stēmo 18. mesi: & discoprimo molta terra ferma & infinite isole, & gran parte di esse habitate: che dalli ātichi scriptori nō seneparla di esse: credo pche nō nheb bono notitia: che se ben miricordo, in alcuno ho lecto, che teneua che qsto mare oceano era mare senza gente: et di questa opinione fu Dante nostro poeta nel .xxvi. capitolo dello inferno, doue finge la morte di Vlyxe: nelqual uiaggio uidi cose di molta marauiglia, come intēdera uostra Mag. Come di sopra dixi, partimo del porto di Calis quattro naui di conserua: & cominciāmo nostra nauigatione diritti alle isole fortunate, che oggi sidicono la gran Canaria, che sono situate nel mare oceano nel fine dello occidente habitato, poste nel terzo clyma: sopra lequali alza elpolo del Septentrione fuora delloro orizonte, 27. gradi & mezo: & distāno da questa citta di Lisbona 280. leghe, per eluento infra mezo di, & libeccio: doue citenēmo octo di, prouedendoci dacqua & legne & di altre cose necessarie: et di qui, facte nostre orationi, cileuāmo & dēmo le uele aluēto, cominciādo nostre nauigationi pel ponente, pigliando una quarta di libeccio: & tāto

Terrarvm Insvlarvmqve Variarum Descriptio: quarum vestuti nō meminerūt autores Nuper ab anno incarnati domini. M.cccxcvij. bis geminis nauigationibus in mari discursis, inuentarū: duabus videlicet in mari occidentali per dominū Fernandum Castiliæ, reliquis vero duabus in Australi ponto per dominū Manuele Portugalliæ serenissimos reges, Americo Vespucio vno ex Naucleris nauiumqͥ præfectis præcipuo, subsequētem ad præfatum dominū Fernandum Castilliæ regem, de huiusmodi terris & insulis edente narrationem.

ANNO DOMINI. M.cccc.xcvij. xx, mensis Maij die, nos cum iiij. conseruantiæ nauibus Calicium exeuntes portum, ad insulas (olim fortunatas, nūc vero magnam Canariam dictas) in fine occidentis habitati positas in tertio climate: sup quo, extra horizontem earum, se. xxvij. gradibus cū duobus terijs, septentrionalis eleuat polus, distātesqͥ ab hac ciuitate Lisbona in qua cōscriptum extitit hoc præsens opusculum. cc.lxxx. leucis: vento inter meridiem & Lebeccium ventum spirante, cursu primo pertigimus. Vbi (nobis de lignis, aqua cæterisqͥ necessarijs prouidendo) cōnsumptis octo fere diebus nos (facta in primis ad deum oratione), eleuatis dehinc vento traditis velis, nauigationem nostrā per Ponentē incipiētes: sumpta vna Lebeccij quarta: tali nauigio transcurrimus, vt xxvij. vix elapsis diebus, terræ cuidā applicaremus, quā firmā fore existimauimus. Distatqͥ Canariæ magnæ ab insulis. M. (vel circiter) leucis: extra id quod in zona torrida habitatū est. Quod ex eo nobis constitit: qͥ Septētrionalē polū extra huiuscemodi telluris horizontē xvi. gradibus se eleuare, magisqͥ occidentalē. lxxv qͥ magnæ Canariæ īsulas gradibus existere cōspeximus: put instru-

herefor the time and place presented themselves most opportunely to me: which was that the King Don Ferrando of Castile being about to despatch four ships to discover new lands toward the west, I was chosen by his Highness to go in that fleet to aid in making discovery: and we set out from the port of Cadiz on the 10th day of May 1497, and took our route through the great gulf of the Ocean-sea: in which voyage we were 18 months [*engaged*]: and discovered much continental land and innumerable islands, and great part of them inhabited: of which there is no mention made by the ancient writers: I believe, because they had no knowledge thereof: for, if I remember well, I have read in some one [*of those writers*] that he considered that this Ocean-sea was an unpeopled sea: and of this opinion was Dante our poet in the xxvi. chapter of the Inferno, where he feigns the death of Ulysses: in which voyage I beheld things of great wondrousness, as your Magnificence shall understand. As I said above, we left the port of Cadiz four consort ships: and began our voyage in a direct course to the Fortunate Isles, which are called to-day *la gran Canaria*, which are situated in the Ocean-sea at the extremity of the inhabited west, [*and*] set in the third climate: over which the north pole has an elevation of 27 and a half degrees beyond their horizon: and they are 280 leagues distant from this city of Lisbon, by the wind between *mezzo di* and *libeccio:* where we remained eight days, taking in provision of water, and wood, and other necessary things: and from here, having said

nauicāmo, cħ alcapo di 37 giorni fumo a tenere una terra, cħ ia giudicāmo essere terra ferma: laquale dista dalle isole di Canaria piu allo occidente a circha di mille leghe fuora dello habitato drento della torrida zona: perche trouāmo elpolo del septentrione alzare fuora del suo orizonte 16. gradi, & piu occidētale che le isole di Canaria, secōdo che mostrauano enostri instrumenti 75. gradi: nel quale anchorāmo con nostre naui ad una legha & mezo di terra: & buttāmo fuora nostri battelli, & stipati di gente & darme: fumo alla uolta della terra, & prima che giugnessimo ad epsa, hauēmo uista di molte gēte che andauano alungho della spiaggia: di che cirallegrāmo molto: & la trouāmo essere gente disnuda: mostrorono hauer paura di noi: credo pche ciuiddono uestiti, & daltra statura: tucti siritrasseno ad un monte, & cō quāti segnali facēmo loro di pace & di amista, nō uollon uenire a ragionamēto con esso noi: di modo che gia uenēdo la nocte & pche le naue stauano surte ī luogo pericoloso, per stare in costa braua & senza abrigo, accordāmo laltro giorno leuarci di qui, & andare a cercare dalcun porto, o insenata, doue assicurassimo nostre naui: & nauigāmo per el maestrale, che cosi sicorreua la costa sempre a uista di terra, di continuo uiaggio ueggēdo gente perla spiaggia: tanto cħ dipoi nauigati dua giorni, trouāmo assai sicuro luogo p le naui, & surgēmo a meza legha di terra, doue uedēmo moltissima gente: & questo giorno medesimo fumo a terra co

mēnta oīa mōstrabāt. Quo ī loco (iactis de prora ācoris) classē nostrē, leuca a litore cū media distantē, restare coegimus: nonnullis solutis phaselis armis & gēte stipatis, cū quibus ipm vsqʒ ad littus attigimus. Quo qʒprimū puenimus: gentē nudam secundū littus euntem innumeram percæpimus. Vnde nō paruo affecti fuimus gaudio. Omnes eīm qui nudi incedere conspiciebant: videbant quoqʒ propter nos stupefacti vehementer esse. Ex eo (vt arbitror) q vestitos, alteriusqʒ effigiei qʒ forēt nos esse intuiti sunt. Hij, postqʒ nos advenisse cognouerunt, omnes in propinquū montē quemdam aufugerūt: a quo tunc nec nutibus, nec signis pacis et amicitiæ vllis, ut ad nos accederēt allici potuerīt. Irruente vero interea nocte, nos classem nostrā male tuto in loco (vbi nulla marinas aduersus procellas tuta residentia foret) cōsidere timentes: cōuenimus vna, vt hinc (mane facto) discederemus: exquireremusqʒ portū quempiam, vbi nostras statione in tuta collocaremus naues. Qua deliberatiōe arrepta, nos vento secundū collē spiranti traditis velis, postqʒ (visu terram ipsam sequendo, atqʒ ipso plagæ in littore, gentes cōtinue percipiendo) duos integros nauigauimus dies: locum nauibus satis aptum comperimus. In quo media tantū leuca distantes ab arida, constitimus: vidimusqʒ tunc inibi innumerabilem gentiū turbam, quam nos cominus inspicere & alloqui desiderantes: ipsamet die littori cū cymbis & nauiculis nostris appropiauimus, necnon & tunc in terram exiuimus, ordine pulchro .xl. circiter viri huiuscemodi gente se tamen a nobis & cōsortio nostro penitus alienam præbēte. Ita vt nullis eā modis ad colloquiū cōmunicationemue nostrā allicere valuerimus: præter ex illis paucos, qs multos post labores ob hoc sus-

our prayers, we weighed anchor, and gave the sails to the wind, beginning our course to westward, taking one quarter by southwest: and so we sailed on till at the end of 37 days we reached a land which we deemed to be a continent: which is distant westwardly from the isles of Canary about a thousand leagues beyond the inhabited region within the torrid zone: for we found the north pole at an elevation of 16 degrees above its horizon, and [*it was*] according to the shewing of our instruments, 75 degrees to the west of the isles of Canary: whereat we anchored with our ships a league and a half from land: and we put out our boats freighted with men and arms: we made toward the land, and before we reached it, had sight of a great number of people who were going along the shore: by which we were much rejoiced: and we observed that they were a naked race: they shewed themselves to stand in fear of us: I believe [*it was*] because they saw us clothed and of other appearance [*than their own*]: they all withdrew to a hill, and for whatsoever signals we made to them of peace and of friendliness, they would not come to parley with us: so that, as the night was now coming on, and as the ships were anchored in a dangerous place, being on a rough and shelterless coast, we decided to remove from there the next day, and go in search of some harbor or bay, where we might place our ships in safety: and we sailed with the maestrale wind, thus running along the coast with the land ever in sight, continually in our course observing people along the shore: till after having navi-

battelli, & saltāmo ī terra ben 40. huomini bene a ordine: & le genti di terra tuttauia simostrauano schifi di nostra conuersatione: et nō potauamo tanto assicurarli che uenissino a parlare cō noi: et questo giorno tanto trauagliāmo con dar loro delle cose nostre, come furono sonagli & specchi, cente, spalline & altre frasche, che alcuni di loro si assicurorono & uennono a tractare con noi: et facto cō loro buona amista, uenendo la nocte, ci dispedimo di loro, & tornāmoci alle naui: et altro giorno come sali lalba, uedēmo che alla spiaggia stauano infinite genti, & haueuano con loro le loro donne & figliuoli: fumo a terra, & trouāmo che tucte ueniuano carichate di loro mantenimenti, che son rali, quali in suo luogho sidira: et prima che giugnessimo in terra, molti di loro sigittorono a nuoto, & ciuennono a riceuere un tiro di balestro nel mare, che sono grandissimi notatori, con tanta sicurta, come se hauessino con esso noi tractato lungo tempo: et di questa loro sicurta pigliāmo piacere. Quanto di lor uita & costumi conoscēmo, fu che del tucto uanno disnudi, si li huomini come le dōne, senza coprire uergogna nessuna, nō altrimenti che come saliron del uentre di lor madri. Sono di mediana statura, molto ben proportionati: le lor carni sono di colore che pende in rosso come pelo di lione: et credo ch̄ se gliandassino uestiti, sarrebbon bianchi come noi: nō tenghono pel corpo pelo alcuno, saluo che sono di lunghi capelli & neri, & maxime le donne, che le rendon formose: nō sono di uolto

ceptos, tandem attraximus ad nos dando eis nolas, specula, certos cristallinos, aliaq̃ similia leuia, qui tum securi de nobis effecti, conciliatum nobiscum, necnon de pace & amicitia tractatum venerunt. Subeunte autem interim nocte, nos ab illis nosmet expedientes (relictis eis) nostras regressi sumus ad naues. Postea vero subsequentis summo diluculo diei, infinitam in littore virorum & mulierum, paruulos suos secum vectantium gentem rursum conspeximus, cognouimusq̃ multitudinē illam supellectilem suam secum deferre totam, qualem infra suo loco dicet̄. Quorum q̃plures q̃plurimum terræ appropiauimus, semet in æquor proijcientes cum maximi natatores existent) quantus est balistæ iactus nobis venerunt natantes obuiam, suscæperūtq̃ nos humaniter: atq̃ ea securitate et confidentia seipsos inter nos commiscuerunt ac si nobiscū diutius antea cōuenissent, & pariter frequentius practicauissent: pro qua re tunc haud parum oblectati fuimus. De quorum moribus (quales eos habere vidimus) hic, quando quidem se cōmoditas offert, interdum etiam interserimus.

DE MORIBUS AC EORUM VIUENDI MODIS.

qvantvm ad vitam, eorumq̃ mores omnes: tam mares q̃ fœminæ nudi penitus incedunt, tectis non aliter verendis quam cum ex vtero p̄dierunt. Hij mediocris existentes staturæ multum bene proportionati sunt, quorū caro ad rufedinē (veluti leonū pili) v̄git: qui si vestimētis operti mearēt albi (credo) tāq̃ nos extarēt. Nullos habēt in corpore pilos p̄ter q̃ crines, q̃s p̄cæros nigrescētesq̃ gerunt, & præsertim fœminæ, quæ propterea sūt tali longo nigroq̃ crine decoræ. Vultu non multū speciosi sunt, q̄m latas facies tartarijs adsimilatas habēt, nul-

gated for two days, we found a place sufficiently secure for the ships, and anchored half a league from land, on which we saw a very great number of people: and this same day we put to land with the boats, and sprang on shore full forty men in good trim: and still the land's people appeared shy of converse with us, and we were unable to encourage them so much as to make them come to speak with us: and this day we labored so greatly in giving them of our wares, such as rattles and mirrors, beads, balls, and other trifles, that some of them took confidence and came to discourse with us: and after having made good friends with them, the night coming on, we took our leave of them and returned to the ships: and the next day when the dawn appeared we saw that there were infinite numbers of people upon the beach, and they had their women and children with them: we went ashore, and found that they were all laden with their worldly goods which are suchlike as, in its [*proper*] place, shall be related: and before we reached the land, many of them jumped into the sea and came swimming to receive us at a bowshot's length [*from the shore*], for they are very great swimmers, with as much confidence as if they had for a long time been acquainted with us, and we were pleased with this their confidence. For so much as we learned of their manner of life and customs, it was that they go entirely naked, as well the men as the women, without covering any shameful part, not otherwise than as they issued from their mother's womb. They are of medium stature,

molto belli, pche tengono el uiso largo, che uoglion parere al tartaro: nō si lasciano crescere pelo nessuno nelle ciglia, ne necoperchi delli occhi, ne in altra parte, saluo che quelli del capo: che tengono epeli p brutta cosa: sono molto leggieri delle loro persone nello andare & nel correre, si li huomini come le donne: che nō tiene in conto na donna correre una legha, o due, che molte uolte le uedēmo: et in q̄sto leuon uantaggio grandissimo da noi christiani: nuotano fuora dogni credere & miglior le donne che gli huomini: pche li habbiamo trouati & uisti molte uolte due leghe drento in mare senza appoggio alcuno andare notando. Le loro armi sono archi & saette molto ben fabricati, saluo ch non tengon ferro, ne altro genere di metallo forte: et in luogo del ferro pongon denti di animali, o di pesci, ó un fuscello di legno forte arsicciato nella puncta: sono tiratori certi, che doue uogliono, danno: et in alcuna parte usano questi archi le donne: altre arme tenghono, come lance tostate, & altri bastoni con capocchie benissimo lauorati. Vsono di guerra infra loro con gente che non sono di lor lingua molto crudelmente, senza perdonare la uita a nessuno, se non per maggior pena. Quando uanno alla guerra, leuon con loro le donne loro: nō perche guerreggino, ma perche leuon lor drieto el mantenimento: che lieua una donna addosso una caricha, che non la leuera uno huomo, trenta, o quaranta leghe: che molte uolte le uedēmo. Nō costumano Capitano alchuno,

los sibi sinunt in supercilijs oculorumue palpebris ac corpore toto (crinibus demptis) excrescere villos, ob id quod habitos in corpore pilos quid bestiale brutaleq̃ reputant. Omnes tam viri q̃ mulieres siue meando siue currendo leues edmodum atq̃ veloces existūt: qm̃ (ut frequenter experti fuimus) ipsæ etiam mulieres vnā aut duas pcurrere leucas nihiliputāt, & in hoc nos christicolas multū præcellunt. Mirabiliter ac vltra q̃ sit credibile natant: multo quoq̃ melius fœminæ q̃ masculi quod frequenti experimento didicimus cum ipsas etiā fœminas omni prorsus sustentamine deficientes, duas in æquore leucas pernatare perspeximus. Arma eorum arcus sunt & sagittæ, quas multū subtiliter fabricare norunt. Ferro metallisq̃ alijs carent: sed pro ferro bestiarum pisciumue dentibus suas sagittas armant, quas etiam (vt fortiores existant) vna quoq̃ sepe præurunt. Sagittarij sunt certissimi. Ita vt quicquid voluerint, iaculis suis feriant: nonnullisq̃ in locis mulieres quoq̃ optimæ sagittatrices extant. Alia etiam arma habēt, veluti lanceas præacutasue sudes, necnō et clauas capita mirifice laborata habentes. Pugnare potissimū assueti sunt aduersus suos alienigenæ linguæ confines contra quos nullis parcendo (nisi vt eos ad acriora tormenta reseruent multum crudeliter dimicāt. Et cū in prælium properant suas secum vxores (non belligeraturas, sed eorum post eos necessaria perlaturas) ducūt, ob id q̃ sola ex eis mulier tergo sibi plus imponere possit, & deinde. xxx.xl. ve leucis subuehere (prout ipsi sæpe vidimus) q̃ vir (etiam validus) a terra leuare queat. Nulla belli capita nullosue præfectos habent: quinymmo, (cū eorum quilibet ex se dominus extet) nullo seruato ordine meant. Nulla

very well proportioned: their flesh is of a color that verges into red like a lion's mane: and I believe that if they went clothed they would be as white as we: they have not any hair upon the body, except the hair of the head, which is long and black, and especially in the women, whom it renders handsome: in aspect they are not very good-looking, because they have broad faces, so that they would seem Tartar-like: they let no hair grow on their eyebrows, nor on their eyelids nor elsewhere, except the hair of the head: for they hold hairiness to be a filthy thing: they are very light-footed in walking and in running, as well the men as the women: so that a woman recks nothing of running a league or two, as many times we saw them do: and herein they have a very great advantage over us Christians: they swim [*with an expertness*] beyond all belief, and the women better than the men: for we have many times found and seen them swimming two leagues out at sea without anything to rest upon. Their arms are bows and arrows very well made, save that they have no iron nor any other kind of hard metal [*wherewith to tip the arrows*]: and instead of iron they put animals' or fishes' teeth, or a spike of tough wood, with the point hardened by fire: they are sure marksmen, for they hit whatever they aim at: and in some places the women use these bows: they have other weapons, such as fire-hardened spears, and also clubs with knobs, beautifully carved. Warfare is used amongst them, which they carry on against people not of their own language, very cruelly, without granting life to

ne uanno con ordine, che ognuno e, signore di se: et la causa delle lor guerre nõ e, per cupidita di regnare, ne di allarghare etermini loro, ne per coditia disordinata, saluo che per una anticha inimista, che per tempi passati e, suta infra loro: et domandati perche guerreggiauano, non cisapeuono dare altra ragione, se nõ che lo faceuon p̄ uendicare la morte de loro antepassati, o de loro padri: questi non tenghono ne Re, ne Signore, ne ubidiscono ad alcuno, che uiuono in lor propria liberta: & come simuouino per ire alla guerra e, che quando enimici hāno morto loro, o preso alchuni di loro, sileua el suo parente piu uecchio, & ua predicando perle strade che uadin con lui a uendicare la morte di quel tal parente suo: et cosi simuouono per compassione: nõ usono iustitia, ne castigano elmal factore: ne cipadre ne la madre nõ castigano efigliuoli, & p̄ marauiglia o nõ mai uedēmo far questione infra loro: mostronsi semplici nel parlare, & sono molto malitiosi & acuti in quello che loro cuple: parlano poco, & cõ bassa uoce: usono emedesimi accenti come noi, p̄che formano le parole o nel palato, o ne denti, o nelle labbra: saluo che usano altri nomi alle cose. Molte sono le diuersita delle lingue, che di 100. in 100. leghe trouāmo mutamento di lingua, che nõ sintendano luna con laltra. El modo del lor uiuere e, molto barbaro, perche nõ mangiano a hore cerre, & tante uolte quante uogliono, et non si da loro molto che la uoglia uengha loro piu a meza nocte

regnandi dominiūue suum extendendi aut alterius inordinatæ cupiditatis gratia pugnant sed veterem solum ob inimiciciam in illis ab antiquo insitam: cujusquidem inimiciciæ causam interrogati nullā aliā indicant nisi vt suorum mortes vendicent antecessorum. Hæc gens sua in libertate viuens nulliq̃ obediens, nec regem nec dominū habet. Ad prælium autē se potissimum animant & accingunt, cum eorū hostes ex eis quempiam aut captiuum detinent aut interemerunt. Tūc em̃ eiusdem captiui interemptiue consanguineus senior quisq̃ exurgens, exit cito in plateas et vicos passim clamitans, inuitansq̃ om̃es & suadens vt cum eo in prælium consanguinei sui necem vindicaturi properent: qui omnes cōpassione moti mox ad pugnam se accingunt atq̃ repente in suos inimicos irruunt. Nulla iura, nullamue iusticiam seruant: malefactores suos nequaquam puniunt, quinymmo nec parentes ipsi paruulos suos edocent aut corripiunt. Mirabiliter eos inter sese conquaestionari nonnumq̃ vidimus. Simplices in loquela se ostentant, verum callidi multum atq̃ astuti sunt. Perraro, & submissa voce loquūtur, eisdē quibus vtimur accentibus vtentes. Suas vtplurimum voces inter dentes & labra formantes: alijs vtuntur vocabulis q̃ nos. Horū plurimæ sunt ydiomatū varietates quoniā a centenario leucarum in centenariū diuersitatem linguarum se mutuo nullatenus intelligentiū reperimus. Cōmessandi modū valde barbarum retinent: nec quidem notatis manducant horis, sed siue nocte siue die quotiens edendi libido saudet. Solo manducantes accumbunt, & nulla mantilia nullaue gausapa (cū lineamentis pannisq̃ alijs careant) habent. Epulas suas atq̃ cibaria in vascula terrea quæ ipsimet cōfingunt, aut in medias cucurbitarum testas ponunt.

any one, except [*to reserve him*] for greater suffering. When they go to war, they take their women with them, not that these may fight, but because they carry behind them their worldly goods: for a woman carries on her back for thirty or forty leagues a load which no man could bear: as we have many times seen them do. They are not accustomed to have any Captain, nor do they go in any ordered array, for every one is lord of himself: and the cause of their wars is not for lust of dominion, nor of extending their frontiers, nor for inordinate covetousness, but for some ancient enmity which in bygone times arose amongst them: and when asked why they made war, they knew not any other reason to give us than that they did so to avenge the death of their ancestors, or of their parents: these people have neither king nor lord, nor do they yield obedience to any one, for they live in their own liberty: and how they be stirred up to go to war is [*this*] that when the enemies have slain or captured any of them, his oldest kinsman rises up and goes about the highways haranguing them to go with him and avenge the death of such his kinsman: and so are they stirred up by fellow-feeling: they have no judicial system, nor do they punish the ill-doer: nor does the father nor the mother chastise the children: and marvelously [*seldom*] or never did we see any dispute among them: in their conversation they appear simple, and [*yet*] are very cunning and acute in that which concerns them: they speak little and in a low tone: they use the same articulations as we, since they form

cħ di giorno, che a tucte hore mangiano: ellor mangiare e, nel suolo senza touaglia, o altro panno alcuno, perche tengono le lor uiuande o in bacini di terra che lor fanno, o in meze zucche: dormono in certe rete facte di bambacia molto grande sospese nellaria: et ancora che q̄sto lor dormire paia male, dico cħ e, dolce dormire in epse: & miglior dormauamo in epse che ne coltroni. Son gente pulita & netta de lor corpi, per tāto continouar lauarsi come fanno: quando uaziano con riuerentia el uentre, fanno ogni cosa per non essere ueduti: & tanto quanto in questo sono netti & schifi, nel fare acqua sono altretanto sporci & sēza uergogna: pérche stando, parlando con noi senza uolgersi, o uergognarsi lasciano ire tal brutteza, che in questo non tenghono uergogna alchuna: non usano infra loro matrimonii: ciaschuno piglia quante donne uuole: et quando le uuole repudiare, le repudia, senza che gli sia tenuto ad ingiuria, o alla donna uerghogna, che in questo tanta liberta tiene la donna quanto lhuomo: non sono molto gelosi, & fuora di misura luxuriosi, & molto piu le donne che glhuomini, che silascia per honesta dirui lartificio che le fanno per contar lor disordinata luxuria: sono dōne molto generatiue, & nelle loro pregneze non scusono trauaglio alchuno: eloro parti son tanto leggieri che parturito dun di, uanno fuora per tucto, & maxime a lauarsi a fiumi, & stanno sane come pesci: sono tanto disamorate & crude, che se si adirono con lor

In retiaculis quibusdam magnis ex bombice factis et in aere suspēsis dormitant: quimodus q̄uis insolitus & asperior fortassis videri queat, ego nihilominus talē dormitandi modum suavem plurimum iudico. Etenim cum in eisdem eorū retiaculis mihi plurumq̨ dormitasse contigerit, in illis mihimetipsi melius q̄ in tapetibus quae habebamus, esse persensi. Corpore valde mūdi sūt et expoliti, ex eo q̨ seipōs freq̄ntissime lavant. Et cum egestum ire (quod salua dixerim reuerentia) coacti sunt, omni conamine nitunt̄ vt a nemine perspici possint: qui quidem in hoc quanto honesti sunt tanto in dimittenda vrina se in mundos inuerecundosq̨ tam mares q̄ fœminæ præbēt, cum siquidem illos nobiscum loquentes & coram positos suam impudicissime vrinam sæpius eminxisse perspexerimus. Nullā legē, nullū legitimū thori fœdus ī suis cōnubijs observāt, quinymmo quotquot mulieres quisq̨ cōcupiscit, tot habere & deinde illas, quandocūq̨ volet (absq̨ hoc q̨ id pro iniuria aut opprobrio habeant) repudiare potest. Et in hac re vtiq̨ tam viri q̄ mulieres eadē libertate fruuntur. Zœlosi parū, libidinosi vero plurimū extāt: magisq̨ fœminæ q̄ masculi: quarum artificia vt insatiabili suæ satisfaciant libidini, hic honestatis gratia subticenda censuimus. Eæ ipsæ in generandis paruulis fœcundæ admodū sunt: neq̨ dū gravidæ effectæ sunt, penas aut labores euitant. Leuissimo minīoq̨ dolore pariunt. Ita vt in crastinum alacres sanatæq̨ vbiq̨ ambulent: præsertimq̨ post partū in flumen quodpiam sese ablutū vadunt, tumq̨ sanæ mundatæq̨ inde (veluti piscis) apparent. Crudelitati aūt ac odio maligno adeo deditæ sūt, ut si illas sui forsitan exacerbauerint viri, subito certū quoddā efficiunt maleficiū:

their utterances either with the palate, or with the teeth, or on the lips: except that they give different names to things. Many are the varieties of tongues: for in every one hundred leagues we found a change of language, so that they are not understandable each to the other. The manner of their living is very barbarous, for they eat at no certain hours, and as oftentimes as they will: and it does not matter much to them that the will may come rather at midnight than by day, for they eat at all hours: and their repast is [*made*] upon the ground without a table-cloth or any other cover, for they have their meats either in earthen basins which they make therefor, or in the halves of pumpkins: they sleep in certain very large nettings made of cotton, suspended in the air: and although this their [*fashion of*] sleeping may seem uncomfortable, I say that it is sweet to sleep in those [*nettings*]: and we slept better in them than in quilts. They are a people of neat exterior and clean of body, because of so continually washing themselves as they do: when, saving your reverence, they evacuate the stomach they do their utmost not to be observed: and as much as in this they are cleanly and bashful, so much the more are they filthy and shameless in making water: since, while standing speaking to us, without turning round or showing any shame, they let go their nastiness, for in this they have no shame: there is no custom of marriages amongst them: each man takes as many women as he lists: and when he desires to repudiate them, he repudiates them without any imputation of wrong-doing

mariti, subito fanno uno artificio con che samazzano la creatura nel uentre, & si sconciano, & aquesta cagione amazano infinite creature: son donne di gentil corpo molto ben proportionate, che non siuede neloro corpi cosa, o membro mal facto: et anchora che del tutto uadino disunde, sono donne in carne, & della uergogna loro non siuede quella parte che puo imaginare chi non lha uedute, che tucto incuoprono cō le coscie, saluo quella parte, ad che natura non prouidde, che e, honestamente parlando, el pectignone. In cōclusione nō tenghon uergona delle loro uergogne, non altrimenti che noi tegniamo mostrare el naso & la boccha: p̄ marauiglia uedrete le poppe cadute ad una donna, o p̄ molto partorire eluentre caduto, o altre grinze, che tucte paion c̄h mai parturissino: mostrauansi molto desidero se di congiugnersi con noi christiani. In queste gente nō conoscēmo che tenessino legge alchuna, ne siposson dire Mori, no Giudei, & piggior c̄h Gentili: perche nō uedēmo c̄h facessino sacrificio alchuno: nec etiam non teneuono casa di oratione: la loro uita giudico essere Epicurea: le loro habitationi sono in comunita: & le loro case facte ad uso di capāne, ma fortemente facte, & fabricate con grandissimi arbori, & coperte di foglie di palme, sicure delle tempeste & de uenti: & in alcuni luoghi di tāta largheza & lungheza, che in una sola casa trouāmo che stauano 600. anime: & populatione uedēmo solo di tredici case, doue stauano quattro mila anime: di octo in dieci

cū q̊q̄ ingēti, ira p̄prios fœtus ī p̄prijs vteris necāṫ abortiūtq̃ deinde: cuius rei occasiōe īfiniti eorum paruuli pereunt. Venusto & eleganti p̄portione cōpacto corpore sunt Ita vt in illis quitquā deforme nullo inspici modo possit. Et quāuis disnude ambulent inter fœmina tamen earum, pudibunda sic honeste reposta sunt vt nullatenus videri quæant, præterquam regiuncula illa anterior, quā verecundiore vocabulo pectusculum ymū vocamus, quod & in illis vtiq̃ non aliter q̄ honeste natura ipsa videndum reliquit. Sed & hoc nec quidē curant, qm̄ vt paucis expediam nō magis in suorū visione pudendorū movenṫ q̄ nos in oris nostri, aut vultus ostentatiōe. Admirandā pervalde rem ducerent, mulierē in eis mammillas pulpas ve laxas aut ventrem rugatū ob nimiū partū habentē, cum omnes equæ integre ac solide post partū semper appareant ac si nūq̃ peperissent. Hee quidem se nostri cupientissimas esse monstrabant. Neminem in hac gente legem aliquam obseruare vidimus nec quidem iudæi aut mauri nuncupari solide queuut cum ipsis gentilibus aut paganis multo deteriores sint. Etenim nō persensimus q̃ sacrificia vlla faciant aut q̃ loca orationisue domos aliquas habeant. horum vitā (quæ omnino voluptuosa est) Epycuream existimo illorum habitationes singulis ipsis sunt communes, Ipsæq̃ illorum domus campanarum instar cōstructae sunt firmiter ex magnis arboribus solidate palmarū folijs desuper contectae & adversus ventos & tempestates tutissime, nōnullisq̃ in locis tam magnæ, ut in illarū vnica sexcentas esse personas inuenerimus. Inter quas octo populosissimas esse cōperimus, sic vt in eis essent habitarentq̃ pariter animarū decē milia. Octēnio quolibet aut septennio suas sedes

to him, or of disgrace to the woman: for in this the woman has as much liberty as the man: they are not very jealous, and are immoderately libidinous, and the women much more so than the men, so that for decency, I omit to tell you the artifice they practise to gratify their inordinate lust: they are very prolific women, and do not shirk any work during their pregnancies, and their travails in childbed are so light that, a single day after parturition, they go abroad everywhere, and especially to wash themselves in the rivers, and are [then] as sound as fishes: they are so void of affection and cruel, that if they be angry with their husbands they immediately adopt an artificial method by which the embryo is destroyed in the womb, and procure abortion, and they slay an infinite number of creatures by that means: they are women of elegant persons, very well proportioned, so that in their bodies there appears no ill-shapen part or limb: and although they go entirely naked, they are fleshy women, and, of their sexual organ, that portion which he who has never seen it may imagine, is not visible, for they conceal with their thighs everything except that part for which nature did not provide, which is, speaking modestly, the pectignone. In fine, they have no shame of their shameful parts, any more than we have in displaying the nose and the mouth: it is marvelously [rare] that you shall see a woman's paps hang low, or her belly fallen in by too much childbearing, or other wrinkles, for they all appear as though they had never brought forth children; they showed themselves

anni mutano le populationi: & domādato perche lo faceuano: per causa del suolo che di gia per sudiceza staua infecto & corropto & che causaua dolentia necorpi loro, che ciparue buona ragione: le loro riccheze sono penne di uccelli di piu colori, o paternostrini che fanno dossi di pesci, o in pietre biāche, o uerdi lequali simettono ple gote & ple labbra & orechi: & daltre molte cose cħ noi ī cosa alcuna nō le stimiamo: non usano cōmertio, ne comperano, ne uendono. In conclusione uiuono, & sicontentano con quello che da loro natura. Le riccheze che in questa nostra Europa & in altre parti usiamo, come oro, gioie perle & altre diuitie, non le tenghono in cosa nessuna: et anchora che nelle loro terre lhabbino, non trauagliano per hauerle, ne le stimano. Sono liberali nel dare, che per marauiglia ui nieghano chosa alchuna: et per contrario liberali nel domandare, quando si monstrano uostri amici: per el maggiore segno di amista, che ui dimonstrano, e, che ui danno, le donne loro, & le loro figliuole, & si tiene per grandemente honorato, quando un padre, o una madre traendoui una sua figliuola, anchora che sia moza uergine, dormiare con lei: et in questo usono ogni termine di amista. Quando muolono, usono uarii modi di exequie, & alchuni glinterrano con acqua & lor uiuande alchapo, pensando che habbino a mangiare: non tenghono, ne usono cerimonie di lumi, ne di piangere. In alcuni altri luoghi usono el piu barbaro & inhumano interramento: che e,

habitationesue transferunt, qui eius rei causam interrogati naturale responsum dederūt, dicentes q̇ phebi vehemētis estus occasionæ hoc facerēt, ob id q̇ ex illoꝶ longiore in eodem loco residentia aer infectus corruptusq̇ redderetur quæ res in eorū corporibus varias causaret ægritudines quæquidē eorū ratio nō male sumpta nobis visa est Eorum divitiæ sūt varioꝶ colorū auium plunæ, aut in modū lapillorum illoꝶ quos vulgariter pater noster vocitamus, lamine siue calculi quos ex piscium ossibus lapillis ve viridibus aut candidis faciunt & hos ornatus gratia sibi ad genas labia vel aures suspendunt. Alia quoq̇ similia futilia & levia pro divitijs habēt quæ nos omnino parvi pendebamus. Cōmutatiōibus aut mercimonijs in vendendo aut emendo nullis utunt̛ quibus satis est quod natura sponte sua propinat Aurum vniones iocalia cæteraq̇ similia quæ in hac Europa pro divitijs habemus nihil extimant imo pænitus spernunt nec habere curant. In dando sic naturaliter liberalissimi sunt vt nihil quod ab eis expetatur abnegent. Et quemadmodum in dando liberales sunt sic in petendo & accipiendo cupidissimi postq̇ se cuiquam amicos exhibuerint. Maximum potissimumq̇ amiciciæ sue signum in hoc perhibent q̇ tam vxoresq̇ filias proprias amicis suis pro libito habendas offerunt in qua re parens vterq̇ se longe honoratū iri existimat cum natā eius & si virginem ad concubitū suum quispiam dignatur & abducit & in hoc suam inter se amiciam potissimum cōciliant. Varijs in eoꝶ decessu multiq̇ modis exequijs vtuntur. Porro suos nōnulli defūctos in humo cum aqua sepeliūt & inhumant illis ad caput victualia ponentes quibus eos posse vesci & alimentari putant nullum deinde ꝓpter eos alium planc-

very desirous of having connection with us Christians. Amongst those people we did not learn that they had any law, nor can they be called Moors nor Jews, and [*they are*] worse than pagans: because we never saw them offer any sacrifice: nor even had they a house of prayer: their manner of living I judge to be Epicurean: their dwellings are in common: and their houses [*are*] made in the style of huts, but strongly made, and constructed with very large trees, and covered over with palm-leaves, secure against storms and winds: and in some places [*they are*] of so great breadth and length, that in one single house we found there were 600 souls: and we saw a village of only thirteen houses where there were four thousand souls: every eight or ten years they change their place of habitation: and when asked why they did so: [*they said it was*] because of the soil which, from its filthiness, was already unhealthy and corrupted, and that it bred aches in their bodies, which seemed to us a good reason: their riches consist of birds' plumes of many colors, or of rosaries which they make from fish-bones, or of white or green stones which they put in their cheeks and in their lips and ears, and of many other things which we in no wise value: they use no trade, they neither buy nor sell. In fine, they live and are contented with that which nature gives them. The wealth that we enjoy in this our Europe and elsewhere, such as gold, jewels, pearls, and other riches, they hold as nothing: and although they have them in their own lands, they do not labor to obtain them, nor do they value them. They are liberal in giving,

che quando uno dolente, o infermo sta quasi che nello ultimo passo della morte, esuoi parenti lo leuano in uno grande boscho, & corichano una di quelle loro reti, doue dormono, ad dua arbori, & di poi lo mettono in epsa, & li danzano intorno tucto un giorno: et uenendo la nocte, gliponghono alcapezzale acqua con altre uiuande, che sipossa mantenere quattro, o sei giorni: & dipoi lo lasciano solo, & tornonsi alla populatione: et se lo infermo si adiuta per se medesimo, & mangia, & bee, & uiua, si torna alla populatione, & lo riceuono esuoi con cerimonia: ma pochi sono quelli che schampano: senza che piu sieno uisitari, simuiono, & quello e, la loro sepultura: et altri molti costumi tenghono, che per prolixita non si dicono. Vsono nelle loro infermitadi uarii modi di medicine, tanto differenti dalle nostre, che cimarauigliauamo come nessuno scampaua: che molte uolte uiddi, cħ ad uno infermo di febre quãdo la teneua in augumẽto, lo bagnauano cõ molta acqua fredda dal capo alpie: dipoi glifaceuano un gran fuoco atorno, faccendolo uolgere & riuolgere altre due hore tãto che lo cansauano & lo lasciauano dormire, & molti sanauano: con questo usano molto la dieta, che stãno tre di senza mãgiare, & cosi elcauarsi sangue, ma nõ del braccio, saluo delle coscie & de lombi & delle polpe delle gambe: alsi prouocano el uomito con loro herbe che simettono nella boccha: & altri molti rimedii usano, che sarebbe lungho a contargli: pecchano molto nella flegma & nel sangue a causa

tum aut alias cerimonias efficientes. Alij quibusdam in locis barbarissimo atqȝ inhumanissimo sepeliendi vtuntur modo. Quippe cũ eorum quẽpiam mortis momento proximum autuman illũ eius propinquiores in siluam ingentem quamdam deferunt vbi eũ in bombiceis retiaculis illis in quibus dormitant impositum & recubantẽ ad duas arbores in aera suspendunt ac postmodum ductis circa eũ sic suspensum vna tota die choreis irruente ĩterim nocte ei aquã victũqȝ aliũ ex ɋ quatuor aut circiť dies viuere ɋat ad caput apponũt & deinde sic inibi solo pendẽte relicto ad suas habitatiões redeũt quibus ita pactis si isdẽ ægrotus postea mãducet & bibat ac inde ad cõvalescentiam sanitatemqȝ redeat & ad habitationẽ ppriam remeet illũ eius affines ac propinqui, cũ maximis suscipiũt cerimonijs. At perpanci suut qui tã grande prætereant periculũ cũ eos ibidem nemo postea visitet qui si tũc inibi forsan decedũt nullã aliam habent postea sepulturã. Alios quoqȝ complures barbaros habent ritus quos euitande plixitatis hic omittimus gratia. Diuersis varijsqȝ medicamibus in suis morbis & ægritudinibus vtuń quæ sic a nostris discrepant & discõueniunt vt miraremur haud parũ qualiter inde quis euadere posset Nempe vt frequenti didicimus experientia cũ eorũ quempiã febricitare cõtigerit hora qua febris eum asperius inquietat ip̃m in frigentissimã aquã immergũt & balneant postmodumqȝ per duas horas circa ignem validũ (donec plurimum calescat) currere & recurrere cogũt & postremo ad dormiendum deferunt quoquidem medicamento cõplures eorũ sanitati restitui vidimus. Dietis etiã (quibus tribus quatuor ve diebus absqȝ cibo & potu persistunt) frequentis-

for it is rarely they deny you anything: and on the other hand, free in asking, when they shew themselves your friends: the greatest sign of friendship which they show you is that they give you their wives and their daughters, and a father or a mother deems himself [*or herself*] highly honored, when they bring you a daughter, even though she be a young virgin, if you sleep with her: and hereunto they use every expression of friendship. When they die, they use divers manners of obsequies, and some they bury with water and victuals at their heads: thinking that they shall have [*whereof*] to eat: they have not nor do they use ceremonies of torches nor of lamentation. In some other places they use the most barbarous and inhuman burial, which is that when a suffering or infirm [*person*] is as it were at the last pass of death, his kinsmen carry him into a large forest, and attach one of those nets of theirs, in which they sleep, to two trees, and then put him in it, and dance around him for a whole day: and when the night comes on they place at his bolster, water with other victuals, so that he may be able to subsist for four or six days: and then they leave him alone and return to the village: and if the sick man helps himself, and eats, and drinks, and survives, he returns to the village, and his [*friends*] receive him with ceremony: but few are they who escape: without receiving any further visit they die, and that is their sepulture: and they have many other customs which for prolixity are not related. They use in their sicknesses various forms of medicines, so different from ours that we

delle loro uiuande, che elforte sono radici di herbe & fructe & pesci: nō tengono semente di grano, ne daltre biado: & alloro comune uso & māgiare usano una radice duno arbore, della quale fanno farina & assai buona, & la chiamano Iuca, & altre che la chiamano Cazabi, & altre ignami: mangion pocha carne, saluo che carne di huomo: che sapra uostra Magnificentia, che in questo sono tanto inhumani, che trapassano ogni bestial costume: perche simangiono tutti eloro nimici che amazzano, o pigliano, si femine come maschi, con tanta efferita, che a dirlo pare cosa brutta: quāto piu a uederlo come miaccadde infinitissime uolte, & ī molte parti uerderlo: & simarauigliorono udendo dire a noi che nō ci mangiamo enostri nimici: et questo credalo per certo uostra Mag. son tāto gli altri loro barbari costumi, che elfacto aldire uien meno: et pche in questi quattro uiaggi ho uiste tante cose uarie a nostri costumi, midisposi a scriuere un zibaldone, che lo chiamo le quattro giornate: nelquale ho relato la maggior parte delle cose che io uiddi, assai distinctamēte, secondo che miha porto el mio debile ingegno: elquale anchora nō ho publicato, perche sono di tanto mal ghusto delle mie cose medesime, che non tengho sapore in epse che ho scripto, ancora che molti miconfortino alpublicarlo: in epso siuedra ogni cosa p minuto: alsi che nonmi allarghero piu in questo capitolo: perche nel processo della lettera uerremo ad molte altre cose che sono particulari: questo basti

simis vtunť. Sanguinē quoqȝ sibi persepe comminuūt nō in brachijs (salua ala) sed in lumbis & tibiarū pulpis. Seipsos etiam ad vomitū cū certis herbis quas in ore deferunt medicaminis gratia plerūqȝ prouocant & multis alijs remedijs antidotisqȝ vtunť quæ longum dinumerare foret Multo sanguine multoqȝ flegmatico humore habundant cibariorū suorū occasiōe q ex radicibus, fructibus, herbis, variisqȝ piscibus faciunt. Omni farris granorūqȝ aliorum semine carent Cōmunis vero eorum pastus siue victus arborea radix quedam est quā in farrinā satis bonā cōminuunt & hanc radicem quidam eorum iucha alij chambi alij vero ygnami vocitant. Alijs carnibus, præterqȝ hominū per raro vescunť in quibusquidem hominū carnibus vorandis sic in humani sunt & inmansueti vt in hoc omnē feralem omnem ve bestialē modū superent. omnes em̄ hostes suos quos aut perimunt aut captos detinēt tam viros qȝ fœminas indistincte cum ea feritate deglutiunt vt nihil ferum, nihil ve brutū magis dici vel inspici queat quos quidē sic eferos īmanesqȝ fore, varijs in locis mihi frequentius contigit aspexisse mirantibus illis qȝ inimicos nostros sic quoqȝ nequaquam manducaremus. Et hoc pro certo maiestas vestra regia teneat Eoꝝ cōsuetudines (quas plurimas habent) sic barbare sunt vt hic nunc sufficienter satis enarrari nō valeāt. Et qm̄ in meis hisce bis geminis nauigatiōibus, tam varia diuersaqȝ ac tam a nostris rebus & modis differētia perspexi Idcirco libellū quēpiam (quē quattuor dietas siue quatuor nauigationes appello) cōscribere paraui conscripsiqȝ in quo maiorem rerū a me visarū partē distincte satis, iuxta ingenioli mei tenuitatē, collegi. Verūtamen non adhuc publicaui. In illo vero qm̄

marveled how any one escaped: for many times I saw that with a man sick of fever, when it heightened upon him, they bathed him from head to foot with a large quantity of cold water: then they lit a great fire around him, making him turn and turn again every two hours, until they tired him and left him to sleep, and many were [*thus*] cured: with this they make much use of dieting, for they remain three days without eating, and also of blood-letting, but not from the arm, only from the thighs and the loins and the calf of the leg: also they provoke vomiting with their herbs which are put into the mouth: and they use many other remedies which it would be long to relate: they are much vitiated in the phlegm and in the blood because of their food which consists chiefly of roots of herbs, and fruits and fish: they have no seed of wheat nor other grain: and for their ordinary use and feeding, they have a root of a tree, from which they make flour, tolerably good, and they call it Iuca, and [*there are*] others who call it Cazabi, and others Ignami: they eat little flesh except human flesh: for your Magnificence must know that herein they are so inhuman that they outdo every custom [*even*] of beasts: for they eat all their enemies whom they kill or capture, as well females as males, with so much savagery, that [*merely*] to relate it appears a horrible thing: how much more so to see it, as, infinite times and in many places, it was my hap to see it: and they wondered to hear us say that we did not eat our enemies: and this your Magnificence may take for certain, that their other barbarous customs are such

quanto allo uniuersale. In questo principio non uedēmo cosa di molto proficto nella terra, saluo alchuna dimostra doro: credo che lo causaua, perche nō sapauamo la lingua: che inquanto alsito & dispositione della terra, non sipuo migliorare: acchordāmo di partirci, & andare piu inanzi costeggiando di continuo la terra: nella quale facēmo molte scale, & hauēmo ragionamenti con molta gente: & alfine di certi giorni fummo a tenere uno porto, doue leuāmo grandissimo pericolo: Spiacque allo Spirito .s. saluarci: & fu in questo modo. Fumo aterra in un porto, doue trouamo una populatione fondata sopra lacqua come Venetia: erano circa 44. case grande ad uso di capāne fondate sopra pali grossissimi, & teneuano le loro porte, o entrate di case ad uso di ponti leuatoi: & duna casa sipoteua correre p tutte, a causa de ponti leuatoi che gittauano di casa in casa: & come le gente di esse ciuedessino, mostra rono hauere paura di noi, & disubito alzaron tutti eponti: & stando a uedere questa marauiglia, uedēmo uenire per elmare circa di 22. Canoe, che sono maniera di loro nauili, fabricati dun solo arbore: equali uēnono alla uolta de nostri battelli, come simarauigliassino di nostre effigie & habiti, & si tennon larghi da noi: & stando cosi, facēmo loro segnali cħ uenissino a noi, assicurandoli con ogni segno di amista: & uisto che non ueniuano, fumo a loro, & non ci aspectorono: ma si furono a terra, & con cenni cidixeno che aspectassimo, & che subito

omīa particulariter magis ac singillatim tangentur idcirco vniuersalia hic solūmodo ˏpsequens ad nauigationem nostrā priorem perficiendā a qua paulisper digressus fueram iam redeo.

IN HOC NAVIGII NOSTRI PRIMORdio notabiľ cōmoditatis res, nō vidimus idcirco (vt opinor) ꝙ eoꞃ linguā nō capiebamus præterꝗ nōnullā auri denotantiā, quod nōnulla indicia in tellure illa esse monstrabant. Heccine v̊o tellus quod ad sui situ positioneꝗ tam bona est vt vix melior queat. Cōcordauimus aūt vt illā derelinquētes lōgius nauigatione ˏpduceremus. Qua vnanimitate suscepta, nos dehinc aridā ipam collateraliter semp sectātes necnō gyros mľtos scalasꝗ plures circūeuntes & interim cū mľtis varijsꝗ locoꞃ illorū incolis cōferentiā habentes, tandē certos post aliquot dies portui cuidā applicuimus, in quo nos grandi a periculo altitono spiritui cōplacuit eripere. Huius ẽm modi portū ꝙprimū introgressi fuimus populatione unā eoꞃ hoc est pagū aut villā super aquas (vt Venetiæ) positā cōperimus, in qua ingētes. xx. edes aut circiter erāt in modū campanarū vt prætactum est effectæ atꝗ sup ligneis vallis solidis & fortibus firmiter fundatæ, præ quarū porticibus leuaticij pōtes porrecti erant per quos ab altera ad alterā tamꝗ per cōpactissimam strātā transitus erat. Igiť huiusmodi populatiōis incolæ ꝙprimū nos intuitu ita sunt magno propter nos timore affecti sunt, ꝙobrem suos confestim pontes omnes cōtra nos eleuauerunt & sese deinde in suis domibus abdiderunt. Quā rem ˏpspectantibus nobis & haud paꞃ admirantibus ecce duodecim eorū lintres vľ circiter, singulas ex solo arboris caudice cauatas (quo nauium genere vtunť) ad nos interim per æquor

that expression is too weak for the reality: and as in these four voyages I have seen so many things diverse from our customs, I prepared to write a common-place book which I name "Le Quattro Giornate": in which I have set down the greater part of the things which I saw, sufficiently in detail, so far as my feeble wit has allowed me: which I have not yet published, because I have so ill a taste for my own things that I do not relish those which I have written, notwithstanding that many encourage me to publish it: therein everything will be seen in detail: so that I shall not enlarge further in this chapter: as in the course of the letter we shall come to many other things which are particular: let this suffice for the general. At this beginning, we saw nothing in the land of much profit, except some show of gold: I believe the cause of it was that we did not know the language: but in so far as concerns the situation and condition of the land, it could not be better: we decided to leave that place, and to go further on, continuously coasting the shore: upon which we made frequent descents, and held converse with a great number of people: and after some days we went into a harbor where we underwent very great danger: and it pleased the Holy Ghost to save us: and it was in this wise. We landed in a harbor, where we found a village built like Venice upon the water: there were about 44 large dwellings in the form of huts erected upon very thick piles, and they had their doors or entrances in the style of drawbridges: and from each house one could pass through all, by means of the draw-

tornerebbono: & furono drieto a un monte, & nō tardoron molto: quādo tornorono, menauan seco 16. fanciulle delle loro, & intraron con esse nelle loro Canoe, & si uēnono a battelli: & ī ciaschedun battello nemisson 4. che tanto cimarauigliamo di questo acto, quanto puo pensare V. M. & loro simissono cō le loro Canoe infra nostri battelli, uenendo cō noi parlando: di modo che lo giudicāmo segno di amista: & andando in questo uedēmo uenire molta gente p elmare notando, che ueniuano dalle case: & come si uenissino appressando a noi senza sospecto alcuno, in q̄sto simostrorono alle porte delle case certe donne uecchie, dando grandissimi gridi & tirandosi ecapelli, mostrando tristitia: p ilche cifeciono sospectare, & ricorrēmo ciascheduno alle arme: & ī un subito le fanciulle cħ tenauamo ne battelli, sigittorono almare, & quelli delle Canoe sallargoron da noi, & cominciaron cō loro archi a saettarci: & quelli cħ veniano a nuoto, ciascuno traeua una lancia di basso nellacqua piu coperta che poteuano: di modo che conosciuto eltradimēto cominciāmo nō solo cō loro a difenderci, ma aspramēte a offendergli, & sozobramo cō li battelli molte delle loro Almadie o Canoe, che cosi le chiamano, facēmo ist agho, & tucti sigittorono anuoto, lassando dis.nanparate le loro canoe, cō assai lor damno si furono notando a terra: moriron di loro circa 15. o 20. & molti restoron feriti: & de nostri furon feriti 5. & tucti scamporono gratia di Dio: pigliāmo

aduentare conspeximus, quoꝶ naucleri effigiem nostrā habitūq̄ mirantes ac sese circū nos vndiq̄ recumferentes nos eminus aspiciebāt. Quos nos quoq̄ ex aduerso prospicientes, plurima eis amiciciæ signa dedimus, quibus eos, vt ad nos intrepidi accederent, exhortabamur, quod tn̄ efficere cōtēpserunt. Quā rem nobis p̄cipientibus mox ad eos remigare incæpimus, qui nequāq̄ nos præstolati sūt quinymmo ōīs cōfestim in terram fugerīt datis nobis interim signis vt illos paulisper expectaremus. Ipī em̄ extēplo reuersuri forent. Tumq̄ in montē quendā p̄perauerīt, a q̄ eductis bis octo iuuencuł & ī lintribus suis p̄fatis vna secū assūptis mox v̄sus nos regressi sūt. Et post hæc ex iuuēcuł ipīs q̄tuor ī singuł nauiū nr̄aꝶ posuerīt, quē faciē di modū noshaud paꝶ admirati tūc fuimus, put vr̄a satis p̄pēdere p̄t maiestas. Cæterūq̄ cū lintribus suis p̄æmissis int̄ nos nauesq̄ nr̄as cōmixti sūt & nobiscū sic pacifice locuti sūt vt illos amicos nr̄os fidelissimos esse reputaremus. Int̄ea v̄o ecce q̄q̄ ex domibus eoꝶ p̄mēoratis gens non modica per mare natitans aduentare cepit quibus Ita aduenientibus & nauibus nr̄is iam appropinquare incipientibus nec tn̄ proinde mali quitq̄ adhuc suspicaremur rursū ad earūdē domorū eoꝶ fores, vetulas nōnullas cōspeximus quæ immaniter vociferantes & cœlū magnis clamoribus implentes sibimet, in magnæ anxietatis indiciū proprios evellebāt capillos quæ res magnā mali suspectionem nobis tunc attulit Tumq̄ subitofactū est vt iuuencule ille quas in nr̄is imposuerant nauibus mox ī mare p̄silerent ac illi qui in lintribus erant sese a nobis elongantes mox contra nos arcus suos intenderent nosq̄ durissime sagittarent. Qui v̄o a domibus per mare natantes aduenieb̄ant singuli latentes in vndis lanceas

bridges which stretched from house to house: and when the people thereof had seen us, they appeared to be afraid of us, and immediately drew up all the bridges: and while we were looking at this strange action, we saw coming across the sea about 22 canoes, which are a kind of boats of theirs, constructed from a single tree: which came toward our boats, as if they had been surprised by our appearance and clothes, and kept wide of us: and thus remaining, we made signals to them that they should approach us, encouraging them with every token of friendliness: and seeing that they did not come, we went to them, and they did not stay for us, but made to the land, and, by signs, told us to wait, and that they would soon return: and they went to a hill in the background, and did not delay long: when they returned, they led with them 16 of their girls, and entered with these into their canoes, and came to the boats: and in each boat they put 4 of the girls. How greatly we marvelled at this behaviour your Magnificence can imagine, and they placed themselves with their canoes among our boats, coming to speak with us: insomuch that we deemed it a mark of friendliness: and while thus engaged, we beheld a great number of people advance swimming towards us across the sea, who came from the houses: and as if they were approaching us without any apprehension: just then there appeared at the doors of the houses certain old women, uttering very loud cries and tearing their hair to exhibit grief: whereby they made us suspicious, and we each betook ourselves to arms: and instantly the

due delle fanciulle & dua huomini : & fumo alle lor case, & entrāmo in epse, & in tutte non trouāmo altro ch̄ due uecchie & uno infermo : togliēmo loro molte cose, ma di pocha ualuta : & non uolēmo ardere loro le case, perche ci pareua caricho di conscientia : & tornāmo alli nostri battelli con cinque prigioni : & fumoci alle naui, & mettēmo a ciaschuno de presi un paio di ferri in pie, saluo che alle moze : & la nocte uegnente sifuggirono le due fanciulle & uno delli huomini piu sottilmēte del mōdo : & laltro giorno accordāmo di salire di q̄sto porto & andare piu inanzi : andāmo di cōtinuo allungho della costa, hauēmo uista dunaltra gente che poreua star discosto da questa .80. leghe : & la trouāmo molto differēte di lingua & di costumi : accordāmo di surgere, & andāmo cō li battelli aterra, & uedēmo stare alla spiaggia grandissima gente, che poteuano essere alpie di 4000. anime : & come fumo giunti cō terra, nō ciaspectorono, & simissono a fuggire p eboschi, dismamparando lor cose : saltāmo ī terra, & fumo per un cāmino che andaua alboscho : & ī spatio dun tiro di balestro trouāmo le lor trabacche, doue haueuon facto grandissimi fuochi, & due stauano cocendo lor uiuāde & arrostendo di molti animali & pesci di molte sorte : doue uedēmo che arrostiuano un certo animale ch̄ pareua un serpēte, saluo ch̄ nō teneua alia, & nella apparenza tāto brutto, che molto cimara uiglāmo della sua fiereza : Andāmo cosi p le lor case, o uero trabacche, & trouāmo

ferebant ex quibus eorū proditionē cognouimus Et tum nō solum nosmet magnanimiter defendere verū etiam illos grauiter offendere incepimus Ita vt plures eorum fasellos cum strage eorū nō parua perfregerimus & pænitus in ponto submerserimus ꝓpter quod reliquis faselis suis cū damno eorū maximo relictis per mare natantes omnes in terram fugerunt inter emptis ex eis .xx. vel circiter vulneratis ѷo pluribus & ex nostris quiq̇ dumtaxat lesis qui omnes ex dei gratia incolumitati restituti sūt Comprehēdimus autē & tunc ex pretactis iuuenculis duas & viros tres ac dehinc domos eoꝶ visitauimus & in illas introiuimus veꝶ ī eis quitquā (nisi vetulas duas et egrotantem virū unicū) non inuenimus. quasquidē eorum domos igni succendere nō voluimus ob id q̇ cōscientiæ scrupulū hoc ipsum esse formidabamus. Post hæc antem ad naues nostras cū prætactis captiuis quinq̇ remeauimus & eosdē captiuos, præterq̇ iuuenculas ipsas, in compedibus ferreis alligauimus. Eedē ѷo iuuencule captiuꝶq̇ viroꝶ vnus peruenienti nocte a nobis subtilissime evasreūt his itaq̇ peractis. Sequenti die concordauimus vt relicto portu illo longius secundū collem procederemus percursisq̇ .lxxx. fere leucis gentem aliā quamdam cōperimus lingua & conuersationæ pænitus a priore diuersam Cōuenimusq̇ vt classem inibi nostram anchoraremus & deinde in terram īpam, cū nauiculis nostris accederemus. Vidimus autē tunc ad littus in plaga gentiū turbam .iiij. M. personarū vel circiter existere qui cū nos appropiare persenserunt nequaq̇ nos præstolati sunt quinymmo cunctis quæ habebant relictis omnes in siluas & nemora diffugerūt. Tum vero in terrā prosiliētes, & viā vnam in siluas tendentē, q̄tus est baliste iactus, ꝑambulantes mox

girls whom we had in the boats, threw themselves into the sea, and the men of the canoes drew away from us, and began with their bows to shoot arrows at us : and those who were swimming each carried a lance held, as covertly as they could, beneath the water : so that, recognizing the treachery, we engaged with them, not merely to defend ourselves, but to attack them vigorously, and we overturned with our boats many of their skiffs or canoes, for so they call them, we made a slaughter [*of them*], and they all flung themselves into the water to swim, leaving their canoes abandoned, with considerable loss on their side, they went swimming away to the shore : there were killed of them about 15 or 20, and many were left wounded : of ours 5 were wounded, and all, by the grace of God, escaped [*death*] : we captured two of the girls and two men : and we proceeded to their houses, and entered therein, and in them all we found nothing but two old women and a sick man : we took away from them many things, but of small value : and we would not burn their houses, because it seemed to us [*as though that would be*] a burden upon our conscience : and we returned to our boats with five prisoners : and betook ourselves to the ships, and put a pair of irons on the feet of each of the captives, except the girls : and when the night came on, the two girls and one of the men escaped in the most subtle manner possible : and next day we decided to quit that harbour and go further onwards : we proceeded continuously skirting the coast, [*until*] we had sight of another tribe distant perhaps some 80 leagues from the former tribe : and

molti di questi serpēti uiui, & eron legati pe piedi, & teneuano una corda allo intorno del muso, cħ nō poteuono aprire la bocca, come sifa a cani alani, ꝑche nō mordino: eron di tanto fiero aspecto, che nessuno di noi nō ardiua di torne uno, pensando cħ eron uenenosi: sono di grandeza di uno cauretto & di lūgheza braccio uno & mezo: tēgono epiedi lunghi & grossi & armati cō grosse unghie: tengono la pelle dura &, & sono di uarii colori: elmuso & faccia tengon di serpēte: & dal naso simuoue loro una cresta come una segha, che passa loro ꝑ elmezo delle schiene infino alla sommita delle coda: in cōclusione gligiudicāmo serpi & uenenosi, & segli māgiauano: trouāmo che faceuono pane di pesci piccholi che pigliauon del mare, con dar loro prima un bollore, amassarli & farne pasta di essi, o pane, & li arrostiuano insulla bracie: cosi li mangiauano: prouamolo, & trouāmo che era buono: teneuono tante altre sorte di mangiari, & maxime di fructe & radice, che sarebbe cosa largha raccontarle ꝑ minuto: & uisto che la gente non riuentua, accordāmo nō tocchare ne torre loro cosa alcuna per miglior assicurarli: & lassamo loro nelle trabacche molte delle cose nostre in luogo che le potessino uedere, & tornamoci ꝑ la nocte alle naui: & laltro giorno come uenisse eldi, uedēmo alla spiaggia ifinita gente: & fumo a terra: & anchora che di noi simostrassino paurosi, tutta uolta si assicurorono a tractare cō noi, dandoci quāto loro domādauamo: & mostrandosi molto

tentoria plura inuenimus quæ ibidem ad piscandū gens illa tetenderat & in illis copiosos ad de coquendas epulas suas ignes accenderat, ac ꝑfecto bestias ac pꝉes variaꝶ specierū pisces jam assabat Vidimus autē inibi certū assari animal quod erat (demptis alis quibus carebat) serpenti simillimū tamq̃ brutū ac siluestre apparebat vt eius nō modicū miraremur feritatē. Nobis vero per eadem tentoria longius ꝑgredientibus plurimos huiuscemodi serpētes viuos inuenimus qui ligatis pedibus ora quoq̃ finibus ligata ne eadē aperire possent habebāt, ꝑut de canibus aut feris alijs ne mordere queant effici solet. Aspectū tam ferū eadē præ seferūt animalia vt nos illa venenosa putantes nullatenus auderemus cōtingere. Capreolis in magnitudine brachio vero cū medio in longitudine æqualia sunt. Pedes longos materialesq̃ multū ac fortibus vngulis armatos necnon & discolorē pellē diuersissimā habēt, rostrūq̃ ac faciē veri serpētis gestant, a quoꝶ naribus vsq̃ ad extremā caudam seta quedā per tergū sic protenditꝉ vt animalia illa veros serpentes esse iudicaremus, & nihilominus eis gens p̄fata vescitꝉ. Panē suū gēs eadem ex piscibus quos in mari piscāt efficiūt. Primū eɱ pisciculos ipsos inferuenti aqua aliquantisper excoquūt. Deinde vero contundunt & cōpistant & in panes cōglutinant q̊s super prunas insuper torrēt & tandē inde postea manducāt, hosquidē panes ꝑbātes q̃bonos esse repimus. Alia quoq̃ q̃mꝉta esculēta cibariaq̃ tam in fructibus q̃ in varijs radicibus retinent q̄ longū enumerare foret. Cum aūt a siluis ad q̄s aufugerāt nō redirēt nihil de rebus eoꝶ (vt amplius de nobis securi fierēt) auferre voluimus quinymmo in eisdē eoꝶ tentorijs ꝑm ꝉta de reculis nostris in locis q̄ perpēdere possent de-

we found them very different in speech and customs: we resolved to cast anchor, and went ashore with the boats, and we saw on the beach a great number of people amounting probably to 4000 souls: and when we had reached the shore, they did not stay for us, and betook themselves to flight through the forests, abandoning their things: we jumped on land, and took a pathway that led to the forest: and at the distance of a bow-shot we found their tents, where they had made very large fires, and two [*of them*] were cooking their victuals, and roasting several animals, and fish of many kinds: where we saw that they were roasting a certain animal which seemed to be a serpent, save that it had no wings, and was in its appearance so foul that we marvelled much at its loathsomeness: Thus went we on through their houses, or rather tents, and found many of those serpents alive, and they were tied by the feet and had a cord around their snouts, so that they could not open their mouths, as is done [*in Europe*] with mastiff-dogs so that they may not bite: they were of such savage aspect that none of us dared to take one away, thinking that they were poisonous: they are of the bigness of a kid, and in length an ell and a half: their feet are long and thick, and armed with big claws: they have a hard skin, and are of various colours: they have the muzzle and aspect of a serpent: and from their snouts there rises a crest like a saw which extends along the middle of the back as far as the tip of the tail: in fine we deemed them to be serpents and venomous, and [*yet*] they were used as food: we found

amici nostri, cidixeno cħ q̃ste erono le loro habitationi, & che eron uenuti quiui p̱ fare pescheria: & cipregorono che fussimo alle loro habitationi & populationi, pche ciuoleuano riceuere come amici: & simisseno a tanta amista a causa di dua huomini che tenauamo con esso noi presi, perche erano loro nimici: di modo che uista tanta loro importunatione, facto nostro consiglio, accordãmo 28. di noi christiani andare cõ loro bene a ordine, & cõ fermo proposito, se necessario fusse, morire: et dipoi che fumo stati qui quasi tre giorni, fumo cõ loro per terra drento: & a tre leghe della spiaggia fumo cõ una populatione dassai gente & di poche case, pche nõ eron piu che noue: doue fumo riceuuti cõ tante & tante barbare cerimonie, che nõ basta la penna a scriuerle: che furono con li balli & canti & pianti mescolati dallegreza, & con molte uiuande: & qui stẽmo lanocte: doue ci offerseno le loro dõne, cħ nõ cipotauamo difendere da loro: & dipoi dessere stari qui la nocte & mezo laltro giorno, furon tanti epopuli che per marauiglia ciueniuano a uedere, che erano senza conto: & li piu uecchi cipregauano cħ fussimo con loro ad altre populationi, che stauano piu drento in terra, mostrando di farci grãdissimo honore: per onde accordamo di andare: & nõ ui sipuo dire quanto honore cifeciono: & fumo a molte populationi, tanto che stẽmo noue giorni nel uiaggio, tãto cħ di gia inostri christiani cħ eron restati alle naui stauano cõ sospecto di noi: & stando

relinquẽtes ad naues nr̃as sub noctẽ repedauimus. Sequenti v̊o die cũ ex oriri titan inciperet infinitã in littore gentẽ existere p̱cæpimus ad q̃s in terrã t̃ũc accessimus. Et q̃uis se nr̃i timidos ostẽderẽt seip̱os tñ īter nos permiscuerũt & nobiscũ practicare ac cõuersari cũ securitate cœperũt amicos nr̃os se plurimũ fore persimulantes, insinuantesq̨ illic habitatiões eoᴙ non esse, veᴙ q̨ piscandi gr̃a aduenerãt. Et idcirco rogitãtes vt ad eoᴙ pagos cũ eis accederemus ip̃i etẽm nos tamq̨ amicos recipere vellent et hãc quidẽ de nobis cõcæperãt amiciciã captiuoᴙ quoᴙ illoᴙ (q̃s tenebamus) occasiõe, qui eoᴙ inimici erãt. Visa ãt eoᴙ magna rogãdi importunitate cõcordauimus .xxiij. ex nobis cũ ilℓ ĩ bono ap̱patu cũ stabili mente (si cogeret necessitas) oẽs strænue mori Cũ itaq̨ nobiscũ per tres extitissent dies & tres cũ eis ṗ plagã terrãq̨ illã excessissemus leucas, ad pagũvnũ novẽ dumtaxat domoᴙ venimus vbi cũ tot tamq̨ barbaris cerimonijs ab eis suscepti fuimus vt scribere penna nõvaleat, vtputa cũ choreis & cãticis ac plãctibus hilaritate & lœticia mixtis, necnõ cũ fercuℓ cibarijsq̨ mℓ'tis. Et ibidẽ nocte illa requieuimus vbi ṗprias vxores suas nobis cũ oĩ ṗdigalitate obtulerũt, q̃ quidẽ nos sic īportũe sollicitabãt vt vix eisdẽ resistere sufficeremus postq̃ aũt illic nocte vna cũ media die perstitimus, ingẽs admirabiℓq̨ pp̱ℓs absq̨ cũctatiõe stuporeq̨ ad nos inspiciẽdos aduenit q̃ᴙ seniores nos q̃q̨ rogabãt vt secũ ad alios eoᴙ pagos (qui lõgius in terra erãt) cõmearemus quod et quidẽ ãnuimus. Hic dictu facile nõ ẽ q̃tos ip̃i nobis īpẽdert̃ honores. Fuimus aũt apud q̃mℓ'tas eoᴙ populatões, per ītegros nouẽ dies cũ ip̃is euntes ob quod nobis nr̃i q̃ in nauibus remãserãt retulert̃ socij se idcirco pleruq̨ ĩ anxie-

---

that [*those people*] made bread out of little fishes which they took from the sea, first boiling them, [*then*] pounding them, and making thereof a paste, or bread, and they baked them on the glowing embers: thus did they eat them: we tried it, and found that it was good: they had so many other kinds of eatables, and especially of fruits and roots, that it would be a large matter to describe them in detail: and seeing that the people did not return, we decided not to touch nor take away anything of theirs, so as better to reassure them: and we left in the tents for them many of our things, placed where they should see them, and returned by night to our ships: and the next day, when it was light, we saw on the beach an infinite number of people: and we landed: and although they appeared timorous towards us, they took courage nevertheless to hold converse with us, giving us whatever we asked of them: and shewing themselves very friendly towards us, they told us that those were their dwellings, and that they had come hither for the purpose of fishing: and they begged that we would visit their dwellings and villages, because they desired to receive us as friends: and they engaged in such friendship because of the two captured men whom we had with us, as these were their enemies: insomuch that, in view of such importunity on their part, holding a council, we determined that 28 of us Christians in good array should go with them, and in the firm resolve to die if it should be necessary: and after we had been here some three days, we went with them inland: and at three

circa 18. leghe drēto infra terra, deliberāmo tornarcene alle naui: & alritorno era tāta la gente si huomini come dōne che uennon cō noi infino al mare, che fu cosa mirabile: & se alcuno de nostri sicansaua del camino, cileuauano in loro reti molto discansatamēte: & alpassare delli fiumi, che sono molti & molto grandi, con loro artificii cipassauano tanto sicuri, che nō leuauamo pericolo alcuno, & molti di loro ueniuano caricchi delle cose che cihauenon date, che eron nelle loro reti per dormire, & piumaggi molto ricchi, molti archi & freccie, infiniti pappagalli di uarii colori: & altri tracuano con loro carichi di loro mantenimenti, & di animali: che maggior marauiglia uidiro, che per bene auenturato siteneua quello, che hauendo a passare una acqua, cipoteua portare adosso: et giuncti che fumo a mare, uenuto nostri battelli, entrāmo ī epsi: et era tāta la calcha che loro faceuano p entrare nelli battelli, & uenire a uedere le nostre naui, cñ cimarauigliauamo: & con li battelli leuāmo di epsi quanti potēmo, & fumo alle naui, & tanti uēnono a nuoto, che citenēmo per impacciati per uederci tanta gente nelle naui, che erano piu di mille anime tucti nudi & senza arme: marauigliauonsi delli nostri apparecchi & artifici, & grandeza delle naui: et con costoro ciaccadde cosa ben da ridere, che fu, che accordāmo di sparare alcune delle nostre artiglierie, & quando sali eltuono, la maggior parte di loro p paura sigittorono a nuoto nō altrimenti che sifanno li ranocchi

tate timoreqȝ nō minīo extitisse. Nobis aūt bis novē leucis aut circiter ī eorū terra existētibus ad naues nr̄as repedare proposuimus Et quidē nostro in regressu tam copiosa ex eis virorū ac mulierū multitudo accurrit qui nos vsqȝ ad mare prosecuti sunt, vt hoc ipsum mirabile foret. Cumqȝ nostri quempiā ex itinere fatigatū iri cōtingeret ipsi nos subleuabāt & in suis retiaculis ī quibus dormitāt studiosissime subuehebant. In transitu quoqȝ fluminū quæ apud eos plurima sunt & maxima, sic nos cum suis artificijs securæ transmittebāt vt nulla usqȝ pericula pertimescerimus. Plurimi etiā eorū nos comitabant rerū suarū onusti, quas nobis, dederāt illas in retiaculis illis quibus dormiūt vectantes plumaria videlicet præditia necnō arcus multos, sagittasqȝ multas, ac infinitos diuersorū colorum psitacos Alij quoqȝ complures supellectilem suā totā ferentes animalia etiā fortunatū se fœlicemqȝ putabat qui in transmeandis aquis nos in collo dorso ve suo trāsuectare pœterat Quāprimū autē ad mare pertigimus & fasclos nostros conscendere voluimus in ipso faselorū nostrorū ascensu tanta ipsorum nos cōmitantiū et nobiscū ascendere cōcertantiū ac naues nostras videre cōcupiscentiū pressura fuit vt nostri Idem faseli pæne pre pondere submergerent, in ipsis autē nostris eisdem faselis recepimns ex eis nobiscū quotquot potuimus ac eos ad naues nostras vsqȝ perduximus Tanti etiam illorū per mare natantes & vna nos cōcomitantes aduenerūt vt tot adventare molestiuscule ferremus cū siquidē pluresqȝ mille in nostras naues licet nudi & inermes introiuissent, apparatum artificiūqȝ nostrū necnō & nauiū ipsarū magnitudinem mirantes Ast tunc quiddam risu dignū accidit Nam cū machinaꝶ, tormentorūqȝ bellicorū nostrorū

leagues from the coast we came to a village of many people and few houses, for there were no more than nine [*of these*]: where we were received with such and so many barbarous ceremonies that the pen suffices not to write them down: for there were dances, and songs, and lamentations mingled with rejoicing, and great quantities of food: and here we remained the night: where they offered us their women, so that we were unable to withstand them: and after having been here that night and half the next day, so great was the number of people who came wondering to behold us that they were beyond counting: and the most aged begged us to go with them to other villages which were further inland, making display of doing us the greatest honour: wherefore we decided to go: and it would be impossible to tell you how much honour they did us: and we went to several villages, so that we were nine days journeying, so that our Christians who had remained with the ships were already apprehensive concerning us: and when we were about 18 leagues in the interior of the land, we resolved to return to the ships: and on our way back, such was the number of people, as well men as women, that came with us as far as the sea, that it was a wondrous thing: and if any of us became weary of the march, they carried us in their nets very refreshingly: and in crossing the rivers, which are many and very large, they passed us over by skilful means so securely that we ran no danger whatever, and many of them came laden with the things which they had given us, which consisted of their sleeping nets, and

ch̃ stanno alle prode, che uedendo cosa paurosa, sigittonnel pantano, tal fece quella gente: & quelli che restoron nelle naui, stauano tanto temorosi, che cenepentimo di tal facto: pure li assicurãmo con dire loro che cõ quelle armi amazauamo enostri nimici: et hauẽdo folgato tucto elgiorno nelle naui, dicẽmo loro che sene andassino, perche uolauamo partire la nocte, & cosi sipartiron da noi cõ molta amista, & amore sene furono a terra. In questa gente, & in loro terra conobbi & uiddi tanti de loro costumi & lor modi di uiuere, che nõ curo dĩ allargharmi in epsi: perche sapra V. M. come in ciascuno delli miei uiaggi ho notate le cose piu marauigliose: & tutto ho ridocto in un uolume in stilo di geografia: & le intitulo le quattro giornate: nella quale opera sicontiene le cose p̃ minuto, & per anchora nõ sene data fuora copia, perche me necessario conferirla. Questa terra e, populatissima, & di gente plena, & dinfiniti fiumi, animali pochi: sono simili a nostri, saluo Lioni, Lonze, cerui, Porci, capriuoli & danii: & questi ancora tenghono alcuna difformita: nõ tẽghono caualli ne muli, ne cõ reuerentia asini, ne cani, ne di sorte alcuna bestiame peculioso, ne uaccino: ma sono tãti li altri animali che tẽghono, & tucti sono saluarchi, & di nessuno siseruono per loro seruitio, che nõsiposson contare. Che diremo daltri uccelli: che son tanti & di tanti sorte & colori di penne, che e, marauiglia uederli. La terra e, molto amena & fructuosa, pie na di grandissime

quedã exonerare cõcuperemus et p̃pter hoc (imposito igne) machinæ ipsæ horridissime tenuissent pars illorũ maxima (audito huiuscemodi tonitruo) sese in mare natitans percipitanit veluti solite sunt rane in ripa sidẽtes quæ si fortassis tumultuosum quitquã audiunt sese in p̃fundum luti latitaturæ immergũt, quemadmodum & gens illa tunc fecerunt illicq̃ eorũ qui ad naues aufugerantĩ sic tunc perterriti fuerũt vt nos facti nostri nosmet rep̃henderemus. Verũ illos mox securos esse fecimus nec amplius stupidos esse permisimus insinuantes eis q̃ cũ talibus armis hostes nostros perimeremus. Postq̃ aũt illos illa tota die in nauibus n̄ris festiuæ tractauimus ipsos a nobis abituros esse monuimus qm̃ seq̃nti nocte nos ab hinc abscedere cupiebamus. Quo audito, ip̃i cũ summa amicicia beneuolentiacq̃ mox a nobis egressi sunt. In hac gente eorũcq̃ terra q̃multos eoR ritus vidi cognouicq̃ in quibus hic diutius ĩmorari nõ cupio Cum postea nosse væstra queat maiestas qualiter in quauis navigationũ haR mærũ magis admiranda annotatucq̃ digniora cõscripserim ac in libellum vnũ stilo geographico collegerem quẽ libellũ quatuor dietas intitulavi & in quo singula particularit̃ & minutim notaui sed hactenus a me non emisi ob id q̃ illũ adhuc reuisere collationarecq̃ mihi necesse est Terra illa gente multa populosa est ac multis diuersiscq̃ animalibus & nostris paucissime similibus vndicq̃ densissima. Dẽptis leonibus vrsis ceruis suibus capreoliscq̃ & dãmis quæ & quidẽ deformitatem quãdã a nostris retinent equis ac mulis asiniscq̃ & canibus ac omni minuto pecore (vt sunt oues & similia) necnõ & vaccinis armẽtis pænitus carẽt, verũtamem alijs q̃ plurimis variorũ generũ animalibus (quæ nõ facile dixerim) habundantes

very rich feathers, many bows and arrows, innumerable popinjays of divers colours: and others brought with them loads of their household goods, and of animals: but a greater marvel will I tell you, that, when we had to cross a river, he deemed himself lucky who was able to carry us on his back: and when we reached the sea, our boats having arrived, we entered into them: and so great was the struggle which they made to get into our boats, and to come to see our ships, that we marvelled [*thereat*]: and in our boats we took as many of them as we could, and made our way to the ships, and so many [*others*] came swimming that we found ourselves embarrassed in seeing so many people in the ships, for there were over a thousand persons all naked and unarmed: they were amazed by our [*nautical*] gear and contrivances, and the size of the ships: and with them there occurred to us a very laughable affair, which was that we decided to fire off some of our great guns, and when the explosion took place, most of them through fear cast themselves [*into the sea*] to swim, not otherwise than frogs on the margins of a pond, when they see something that frightens them, will jump into the water, just so did those people: and those who remained in the ships were so terrified that we regretted our action: however we reassured them by telling them that with those arms we slew our enemies: and when they had amused themselves in the ships the whole day, we told them to go away because we desired to depart that night, and so separating from us with much friendship and love, they went away to land. Amongst that people and in their land, I knew and beheld so many of

selue & boschi: & sempre sta uerde, che mai non perde foglia. Le fructe son tante, che sono fuora di numero, & difforme altucto dalle nostre. Questa terra sta dentro della torrida zona giuntamente, o di basso del pararello, che descriue el tropico di Cancer: doue alza elpolo dello orizonte 23 gradi nel fine del secondo clyma. Vennonci a uedere molti popoli, & si marauigliauano delle nostre effigie & di nostra biancheza: & ci domandoron donde uenauamo: & dauamo loro ad intēdere, che uenauamo dal cielo, & che andauamo a uedere el mōdo, & lo credeuano. In questa terra ponēmo fonte di baptesimo: & infinita gente sibaptezo, & cichiamauano in lor lingua Carabi, che uuol dire huomini di gran sauidoria. Partimo di questo porto: & la prouincia sidice Lariab; & nauigāmo allungo della costa sempre a uista della terra, tanto che corrēmo dessa 870. leghe tutta uia uerso el maestrale, faccendo per epsa molte scale, & tractando con molta gente: & in molti luoghi rischartāmo oro, ma non molta quantita, che assai facēmo in discoprire la terra, & di sapere che te neuano oro. Erauamo gia stati 13. mesi nel uiaggio: & di gia enauili & li apparecchi erono molto cōsumati, & li huomini cansati: acchordāmo di comune consiglio porre le nostre naui amonte, & ricorrerle per stancharle, che faceuano molta acqua, & calefatarle & brearle dinuouo, & tornarcene per la uolta di Spagna: et quādo questo deliberāmo, stauamo giunti con un porto elmiglior del mondo:

sunt sed tamen omnia siluestria sunt quibus in suis agendis minīe vtunt. Quid pluraī Hij tot tantisq̉ diuersorum modorū ac colorū pænnarūq̉ alitibus fecūdi sunt vt id sit visu enarratuq̉ mirabile regio siquidem illa multum amena fructiferaq̉ est, siluis ac nemoribus maximis plæna quæ omni tempore virēt nec eorum umq̉ folia fluunt. Fructus etiam innumerabiles & nostris omnino dissimiles habent heccine tellus in torrida zona sita est directe sub paralello qui cancri tropicū describit uñ polus orizontis eiusdē se. xxiij. gradibus eleuat in fine climatis secundi. Nobis aūt inibi existentibus nos cōtēplatū populus multus aduenit effigiem albedinemq̉ nostram mirantes quibus vnde veniremus sciscitantibus e cœlo inuisende terre gratia nos descendisse respondimus quod & utiq̉ ipsi credebāt in hac tellure baptisteria fontesuæ sacros plures instituimus in quibus eorum infiniti seipsos baptisari fecerunt se eorū lingua charaibi hoc est magnæ sapientiæ viros vocantes. Et provincia ipsa Parias ab ipsis nuncupata est. Postea aūt portū illum terramq̉ derelinquētes ac secundū collē transnauigantes & terram ipsam visu semper sequentes. Dccc.lxx. leucas a portu illo percurrimus facientes gyros circuitusq̉ interim multos & cum gentibus multis conuersantes practicantesq̉. Vbi in plerisq̉ locis au℞ (sed nō in grandi copia) emimus cū nobis terras illas reperire & si ī eis au℞ foret tūc sufficeret cognoscere. Et quia tunc .xiij. iam mensibus in nauigatione nr̄a perstiteramus et naualia nr̄a apparatusque nostri toti penæ consumpti erant hominesq̉ labore perfracti. Cōmunem inter nos de restaurandis nauiculis nostris quæ aquā vndiq̉ recipiebant & repetunda hyspania iniuimus cōcordiam in qua dum persisteremus vnanimitatæ

their customs and ways of living, that I do not care to enlarge upon them: for Your Magnificence must know that in each of my voyages I have noted the most wonderful things, and I have indited it all in a volume after the manner of a geography: and I intitle it LE QUATTRO GIORNATE: in which work the things are comprised in detail, and as yet there is no copy of it given out, as it is necessary for me to revise it. This land is very populous, and full of inhabitants, and of numberless rivers, [and] animals: few [of which] resemble ours, excepting lions, panthers, stags, pigs, goats, and deers: and even these have some dissimilarities of form: they have no horses nor mules, nor, saving your reverence, asses nor dogs, nor any kind of sheep or oxen: but so numerous are the other animals which they have — and all are savage, and of none do they make use for their service — that they could not be counted. What shall we say of their different birds? which are so numerous, and of so many kinds, and of such variouscoloured plumages, that it is a marvel to behold them. The land is very pleasant and fruitful, full of immense woods and forests: and it is always green, for the foliage never drops off. The fruits are so many that they are numberless and entirely different from ours. This land is within the torrid zone, close to or just under the parallel which marks the Tropic of Cancer: where the pole of the horizon has an elevation of 23 degrees, at the extremity of the second climate. Many tribes came to see us, and wondered at our faces and our whiteness: and they asked us whence we came: and we gave them to understand that we had come from heaven, and that we were going to see the world, and they

nel quale entrāmo con le nostre naui: doue trouāmo infinita gente: laquale con molta amista ciriceue: & in terra facēmo un bastione con li nostri battelli & con tonelli & botte & nostre artiglierie, che giocauano per tucto: et discarichate & alloggiate nostre naui, le tiramo in terra, & le correggēmo di tucto quello che era necessario: & la gente di terra cidette grādissimo aiuto: & di continuo ciprouedeuono delle loro uiuande: che in q̄sto porto po che ghustāmo delle nostre, che cifeciono buon giuoco: perche tenauamo el mantenimento per la uolta pocho & tristo: doue stēmo 37. giorni: et andāmo molte uolte alle loro populationi: doue cifaceuono grandissimo honore: et uolendoci partire per nostro uiaggio, cifeciono tichiamo di come certi tempi dellanno ueniuano per la via di mare ī questa lor terra una gente molto crudele, & loro nimici: & contradimenti, o con forza amazauano molti di loro, & selimangiauano: & alcuni capriuauano, & glileuauan presi alle lor case, o terra: & cħ apena sipoteuono defendere da loro, faccendoci segnali che erano gente di isole: & poteuono stare drento in mare 100. leghe: et con tanta affectione cidiceuano questo, che lo credēmo loro: & promettēmo loro di uendicarli di tanta ingiuria: & loro restoron molto allegri di q̄sto: et molti di loro li offersono di uenire con esso noi, ma nō gliuolēmo leuare per molte cagioni, saluo che neleuāmo septe, cō conditione che si uenissino poi in Canoe: perche nō ciuolauamo obligare a tornarli

prope portū vnū eramus totius orbis optimū in quem cū nauibus nostris introeuntes gētem ibidē infinitā inuenimus quæ nos cū magna suscepit amicicia in terra autē illa nauiculā unā cum reliquis nauiculis nostris ac dolijs nouam fabricauimus ipsasq̃ machinas nostras ac tormenta bellica quæ in aquis undiq̃ pæne peribant in terram suscepimus nostrasq̃ naues ab eis exonerauimus & post hæc in terrā traximus et refecimus correximusq̃ & pænitus reparauimus. In qua re eiusdem telluris incole nō parvū nobis adiuuamen exhibuere quinymmo nobis de suis victualibus ex affectu largiti spontæ sua fuere propter quod inibi per pauca de nostris cōsumpsimus quāquidē rem ingenti pro beneplacito duximus cum satis tenuia tunc teneremus cum quibus hyspaniam nostram nō (nisi indigentes) repetere potuissemus. In portu aūt illo .xxxvij. diebus perstitimus frequentius ad populationes eorū cum eis euntes vbi singuli nobis non paruum exhibebant honorem. Nobis aūt portum eundem exire & nauigationē nostrā reflectere concupiscentibus conquesti sunt illi gentem quamdā valde feroce & eis infestam existere, qui certo anni tempore per viam maris in ipsam eorū terrā per insidias ingressi nunc ₚditorie, nunc ₚ vim q̄multos eorū interimerent manducarentq̃ deinde. Alios v̇o in suā terrā suasq̃ domos captiuatos ducerent, contra quos iр̄i se vix defendere possent nobis insinuantes gentē illam quamdā inhabitare insulā quæ ī mari leucis centū aut circiter erat. Quā rem ipsi nobis cū tanto affectu ac querimonia commemorauerūt vt eis ex condolentia magna crederemus, ₚmitteremusq̃ vt de tantis eos vindicaremus iniurijs, ₚpter quod illi lœtantes nō parū effecti, sese nobiscum venturos sponte sua propria

believed it. In this land we placed baptismal fonts, and an infinite [*number of*] people were baptized, and they called us in their language Carabi, which means men of great wisdom. We took our departure from that port: and the province was called Lariab: and we navigated along the coast, always in sight of land, until we had run 870 leagues of it, still going in the direction of the maestrale [*north-west*] making in our course many halts, and holding intercourse with many peoples: and in several places we obtained gold by barter but not much in quantity, for we had done enough in discovering the land and learning that they had gold. We had now been thirteen months on the voyage: and the vessels and the tackling were already much damaged, and the men worn out by fatigue: we decided by general council to haul our ships on land and examine them for the purpose of stanching leaks, as they made much water, and of caulking and tarring them afresh, and [*then*] returning towards Spain: and when we came to this determination, we were close to a harbour the best in the world: into which we entered with our vessels: where we found an immense number of people: who received us with much friendliness: and on the shore we made a bastion with our boats and with barrels and casks, and our artillery, which commanded every point: and our ships having been unloaded and lightened, we drew them upon land, and repaired them in everything that was needful: and the land's people gave us very great assistance: and continually furnished us with their victuals: so that in this port we tasted little of our own, which suited our game well: for the stock of pro-

a loro terra: & furon contenti: et cosi cipartimo da queste genti, lassandoli molto amici nostri: et rimediate nostre naui, & nauigando septe giorni alla uolta del mare p̄ ciuento infra greco & leuante: et alcapo delli septe giorni riscontrāmo nelle isole, che eron molte, & alcune populate, & altre deserte: & surgēmo con una di epse: doue uedēmo molta gente che la chiamauano Iti: et stipati enostri battelli di buona gente, & in ciaschuno tre tiri di bombarde, fumo alla uolta di terra: doue trouāmo stare alpie di 400. huomini & molte dōne, & tucti disnudi come epassati. Eron di buon corpo: & ben pareuano huomini bellicosi: perche erono armati di loro armi, che sono archi, saette & lance: et la maggior parte di loro teneuano tauolaccine quadrate: & di modo selepone uano, che non glimpediuono el trarre dello archo: et come fumo a circha di terra con li battelli ad un tiro darcho, tutti saltoron nellacqua a tirarci saette, & difenderci che non saltassimo ī terra: & tutti eron dipincti ecorpi loro di diuersi colori, & impiumati cō penne: & cidiceuano le lingue cħ con noi erano, che quādo cosi simostrauano dipincti & īpiumati, che dauon segnale diuoler cōbattere: & tāto perseueroron ī defenderci la terra, che fumo fforzati a giocare cō nostre artiglierie: et come sentirono el tuono, & uidono de loro cader morti alchuni, tucti sittasseno alla terra: per onde facto nostro cōsiglio, accordāmo saltare ī terra 42. di noi: & se ciaspectassino, combatter con loro: cosi saltati ī terra cō nostre armi, loro si uennono a

obtulerūt, quod plures ob causas acceptare recusauimus demptis septem quos data conditione recæpimus vt soli in suis lintribus ī propria remearēt, qm̄ reducendorū eorū curā suscipere nequaquā intendebamus cui conditioni ipsi q̄gratanter acquieuerūt. Et ita illos amicos nostros plurimū effectos derelinquētes, ab eis abcessimus. Restauratis aūt reparatisq̄ naualibus nostris, septē per gyrū maris (vento int' græcū & leuantē nos ducente) nauiguimus dies. Post quos plurimis obuiauimus insulis quarū quidē aliæ habitatæ aliæ v̄o desertæ erāt. Harū igitur vni tandē appropinquātes & naues nostras inibi sistere facientes, vidimus ibidem q̄maximū gentis aceruū qui insulam illā Ity nuncuparent quibus prospectis & nauiculis phaselisq̄ nostris viris validis & machinis tribus stipatis terræ eidem vicinius appropīquātes .iiijC. viros cū mulieribus q̄mƚtis iuxta littus esse conspeximus qui vt, de prioribus habitū est, om̄s nudi meantes, corp̄e strænuo erāt, necnō bellicosi plurimū validiq̄ apparebant, cum siquidē om̄s armis suis arcubus videlicet & sagittis lanceisq̄ armati essēt, quorum quoq̄ cōplures parmas etiā quadrataue scuta gerebāt, q̄bus sic oportune sese p̄muniebāt vt eos ī iaculādis sagittis suis in aliquo nō impedirēt. Cumq̄ cū phaselis nostris terræ ipsi q̄tus est sagittæ volatus appropiassemus om̄s citius in mare p̄silierunt & infinitis emissis sagittis sese contra nos strænue (ne in terrā descendere possemus) defendere occep̄t. Om̄s vero p̄ corpus diuersis coloribus depicti & varijs volucrū pēnis ornati erant, quos hij qui nobiscū venerāt aspicientes illos ad præliandū paratos esse quotiescunq̄ sic picti aut auium plumis ornati sunt nobis insinuerūt. Intantū aūt introitū terræ nobis impediēr̄t vt saxiuomas machinas nos-

visions which we had for our return-passage was little and of sorry kind: where [*i.e., there*] we remained 37 days: and went many times to their villages, where they paid us the greatest honour: and [*now*] desiring to depart upon our voyage, they made complaint to us how at certain times of the year there came from over the sea to this their land, a race of people very cruel, and enemies of theirs: and by means of treachery or of violence slew many of them, and ate them: and some they made captives, and carried them away to their houses, or country: and how they could scarcely contrive to defend themselves from them, making signs to us that [*those*] were an island-people and lived out in the sea about a hundred leagues away: and so piteously did they tell us this that we believed them: and we promised to avenge them of so much wrong: and they remained overjoyed herewith: and many of them offered to come along with us, but we did not wish to take them for many reasons, save that we took seven of them, on condition that they should come [*i.e., return home*] afterwards in canoes because we did not desire to be obliged to take them back to their country: and they were contented: and so we departed from those people, leaving them very friendly towards us: and having repaired our ships, and sailing for seven days out to sea between north-east and east: and at the end of the seven days we came upon the islands, which were many, some [*of them*] inhabited, and others deserted: and we anchored at one of them: where we saw a numerous people who called it Iti: and having manned our boats with strong crews, and [*taken*] three guns in each, we made for land: where we found

noi, & combattemo a circha duna hora, cħ poco uantaggio leuāmo loro, saluo cħ enostri balestrieri & spingardieri ne amazauano alcuno, & loro feriron certi nostri: & questo era, pche nõ ci aspectauano nõ altiro di lancia ne di spada: et tanta forza ponēmo al fine, che uenimo al tiro delle spade, & come ghustassino le nostre armi, simissono in fuga per emonti & boschi, & ci lascioron uincitori del campo con molti di loro morti & assai feriti: & per questo giorno non trauagliāmo altrimēti di dare loro drieto, perche stauamo molto affatichati, & cene tornāmo alle naui con tanta allegreza de septe huomini che con noi eron uentui, che nõ capriuano in loro: & uenendo laltro giorno, uedēmo uenire per la terra gran numero di gente, tutta uia con segnali di battaglia sonando corni, & altri uarii strumenti che loro usan nelle guerre: & tucti dipincti & impiumati, che era cosa bene strana a uederli: ilperche tucte le naui fecion consiglio, & fu deliberato poi che questa gente uoleua con noi nimicitia, che fussimo a uederci con loro, & di fare ogni cosa per farceli amici: in caso che nõ uolessino nostra amista, che li tractassimo come nimici, & che quāti nepotessimo pigliare di loro, tucti fussino nostri schiaui: et armatici come miglior potauamo, fumo alla uolta di terra, & non cidifesono elsaltare in terra, credo per paura delle bombarde: & saltāmo ī terra 57. huomini in quattro squadre, ciaschun Capitano con la sua gente: & fumo alle mani con loro: & dipoi duna lungha battaglia morti molti

tras in eos coacti fuerimus emittere, quaꝶ audito tumultu impetuꝗ viso necnõ ex eis plerisꝗ in terrā mortuis decidisse prospectis, oɱs interrā sese recæperunt. Tumꝗ facto inter nos consilio .xlij. de nobis in terrā post eos cõcordauimus exilire & aduersus eos magno animo pugnare quod & quidē fæcimus. Nā tū aduersum illos in terram cū armis nostris prosiluimus, cõtraꝗ illi sic sese nobis opposueꝶt vt duabus ferme horis cõtinuū inuicē gesserimus bellū, ꝑter id ꝗ de eis magnā faceremus victoriam demptis eorū perpaucis quos balistarij colubrinarijꝗ nostri suis interemerunt telis quod idcirco ita effectū ē quia seipsos a nobis ac lāceis ensibusꝗ nostris subtiliter subtrahebāt. Verūtamen tanta demū in eos incurrimus violentia vt illos cū gladijs mucronibusꝗ nostris cominus attingeremus. Quosquidē cū ꝑsensissent oɱs in fugā per siluas & nemora conuersi sunt, ac nos campi victores (interfectis ex eis vulneratisꝗ plurimis) deseruerunt. Hos aūt pro die illa longio, re fuga nequaquā insequi voluimus, ob id ꝗ fatigati nimiū tūc essemus quinpotius ad naues nr̄as cum tanta septem illorum quæ nobiscum venerant remeauimus læticia vt tantum in se gaudium vix ipsi suscipe possent. Sequēti aūt aduētāte die vidimus per insulam ipsam copiosam gentium appropinquare cateruam cornibus instrumentisꝗ alijs quibus in bellis vtuntur buccinantem, qui & quoque depicti omnes ac varijs volucrū plumis ornati erant. Ita vt intueri mirabile foret quibus percæptis ex inito rursū inꞇ nos deliberauimus cõsilio vt si gens hæc nobis inimicicias pararet, nosmet oɱs in unū cõgregaremus videremusꝗ mutuo semper ac interim satageremus vt amicos nobis illos efficeremus, quibus amiciciā nostrā nõ recipientibus illos quasi hostes

[*assembled*] about 400 men, and many women, and all naked like the former [*peoples*]. They were of good bodily presence, and seemed right warlike men: for they were armed with their weapons, which are bows, arrows, and lances; and most of them had square wooden targets: and bore them in such wise that they did not impede the drawing of the bow: and when we had come with our boats to about a bowshot of the land, they all sprang into the water to shoot their arrows at us and to prevent us from leaping upon shore: and they all had their bodies painted of various colours, and [*were*] plumed with feathers: and the interpreters who were with us told us that when [*those*] displayed themselves so painted and plumed, it was to betoken that they wanted to fight: and so much did they persist in preventing us from landing, that we were compelled to play with our artillery: and when they heard the explosion, and saw some of their number fall dead, they all drew back to the land: wherefore, forming our Council, we resolved that 42 of our men should spring on shore, and, if they waited for us, fight them: thus having leaped to land with our weapons, they advanced towards us, and we fought for about an hour, but we had little advantage of them, except that our arbalasters and gunners killed some of them, and they wounded certain of our men: and this was because they did not stand to receive us within reach of lance-thrust or sword-blow: and so much vigour did we put forth at last, that we came to sword-play, and when they tasted our weapons, they betook themselves to flight through the mountains and the forests, and left us conquerors of the field with many of them dead and

di loro, glimettēmo ī fuga, & seguimo lor drieto fino a una populatione, hauēdo preso circa di 250. di loro, & ardēmo la populatione, & cenetornamo con uictoria & con 250. prigioni alle naui, lasciando di loro molti morti & feriti, & de nostri nō mori piu che uno, & 22. feriti, ch̄ tucti scamporono, dio sia ringratiato. Ordināmo nostra partita, & li septe huomini che cinque ne eron feriti, presono una Canoe della isola, & cō septe prigioni che dēmo loro, quattro dōne & tre huomini, senetornorono allor terra molto allegri, marauigliādosi delle nostre forze: & noi alsi facēmo uela p̄ Spagna con 222. prigioni schiaui: & giugnemo nel porto di Calis adi 15. doctobre 1498. doue fumo ben riceuuti, & uendēmo nostri schiaui. Questo e, quello che miacchadde in questo mio primo uiaggio di piu notabile.

tractaremus, ac quotquot ex eis cōprehendere valeremus seruos nostros ac mancipia perpetua faceremus, & tunc armatiores ut potuimus circa plagā ipsam ī gyrū nos collegimus. Illi vero (vt puto præ machinarū nostrarū stupore) nos in terram tunc minime ₚhibuerunt exilire. Exiuimus igitur in eos in terram quadrifariam diuisi. lvij. viri simguli decurionē suū sequentes, & cū eis longū manuale gessimus bellum. Verūtamen post diuturnam pugnā plurimūcɜ certamen necnō interemptos ex eis multos, omnes in fugā coegimus & ad vscɜ populationē eorum vnam prosecuti fuimus vbi comprehensis ex eis .xxv. captiuis eandē eorum populationē igni cōbussimus & insuper ad naues nostras cū ipsis .xxv. captiuis repedauimus interfectis ex eadem gente vulneratiscɜ plurimis, ex n̄rs aūt interēpto dūtaxat vno sed vulneratis .xxij. qui oēs ex dei adiutorio sanitatē recuperauerūt. Cæterū aūt recursu ī patriā p̄ nos deliberato ordinatocɜ viri septem illi qui nobiscū illuc venerant quorū quincɜ in præmisso bello vulnerati extiterāt phaselo vno in insula illa arrepto cū captiuis septem (quos illis tribuimus) tres videlicet viros & quatuor mulieres in terram suā cū gaudio magno et magna viriū nostrarū admiratione regressi sūt. Noscɜ hyspaniæ viam sequentes Caliciū tandem repetiuimus portū cum. CC.xxij. captiuatis personis .xv Octobris die Anno dn̄i Mccclxxxxix. Vbi lætissime suscæpti fuimus, ac vbi eosdē captiuos nostros vendidimus. Et hæc sunt quæ in hac nauigatiōe nostra priore annotatu digniora cōspeximus.

a good number wounded: and for that day we took no other pains to pursue them, because we were very weary, and we returned to our ships, with so much gladness on the part of the seven men who had come with us that they could not contain themselves [*for joy*]: and when the next day arrived, we beheld coming across the land a great number of people, with signals of battle, continually sounding horns, and various other instruments which they use in their wars: and all [*of them*] painted and feathered, so that it was a very strange sight to behold them: wherefore all the ships held council, and it was resolved that since this people desired hostility with us, we should proceed to encounter them and try by every means to make them friends: in case they would not have our friendship, that we should treat them as foes, and so many of them as we might be able to capture should all be our slaves: and having armed ourselves as best we could, we advanced towards the shore, and they sought not to hinder us from landing, I believe from fear of the cannons: and we jumped on land, 57 men in four squadrons, each one [*consisting of*] a captain and his company: and we came to blows with them: and after a long battle [*in which*] many of them [*were*] slain, we put them to flight, and pursued them to a village, having made about 250 of them captives, and we burnt the village, and returned to our ships with victory and 250 prisoners leaving many of them dead and wounded, and of ours there were no more than one killed, and 22 wounded, who all escaped [*i.e., recovered*], God be thanked. We arranged our departure, and the seven men, of whom five were wounded, took an island-canoe, and, with seven prisoners that we gave them, four women and three men, returned to their [*own*] country full of gladness, wondering at our strength: and we thereupon made sail for Spain with 222 captive slaves: and reached the port of Cadiz on the 15 day of October 1498, where we were well received and sold our slaves. Such is what befel me, most noteworthy, in this my first voyage.

PART V

The Baptismal Font of America

St.-Dié, the little town in the Vosges Mountains where
the New World was christened

PART 4

The Bohemian Poet of America

St. Dié, the little town in the Vosges Mountains where the New World was Christened

VIEWS OF THE BAPTISMAL FONT OF AMERICA.

CHAPTER I

St.-Dié in Lorraine

THE Vosges are a range of mountains in the northeastern part of France, running northward along the west or left bank of the river Rhine. They look on Switzerland as they begin their ascent not far from Basle, and as they run northward they look on France to the west and on Germany to the east. In their strong hands they clutch the rock-salt and the ores of silver and copper which for centuries they have yielded grudgingly to the patient miner. On their eastern slope they nourish the vine half-way to their summit, and on their western side they send forth strong rivers to turn the miller's stone and the spindles of busy mills. Mountains with nourishment in their bosoms and wealth in their arms have missions to perform, and down their sides great movements make their successful way. These Vosges have been happily called the "baptismal font of America," for it was here that the New World first received its name, and it was because of their close relationship to neighboring countries that the appellation was quickly received and adopted for all time.

A little after the middle of the seventh century, not far from where the Meurthe, reinforced by the Fave and the Robache, becomes strong enough to be called a river, a pious ecclesiastic founded a chapel for prayer and meditation. In time this chapel became a cathedral, and the cluster of houses about it grew into a city, which took its name from Saint Deodatus, the founder of the chapel. It is the St.-Dié of to-day, an active little town of over ten thousand inhabitants. The chapel of Saint Deodatus, the pious bishop of Nevers, became a monastery and was dedicated to Saint Benoît and to Saint Colomban. Toward the beginning of the eleventh century it lost its purely religious character, and, becoming secularized, a collegiate institution was organized under the charge of an ecclesiastical official, a grand provost. It was enfeoffed by the conjoint authority of Rome and the German kingdom. Those were troublous times; the territory was border-land, and a priest without a sword could not hold his altar. So the collegiate chapter fortified itself, and as feudal lord of the neighborhood it strengthened itself by the arms of the people it assumed to guard. While there has come down to us no record of the work accomplished in education, we know the chapter did its full part in bringing on the revival of learning. In 1446 it is recorded that a *new* library was built over the cloister of the cathedral, and we can well believe that the old library had treasured for ages the manuscript writings of the Augustinian age and the religious works of the fathers.

We have no great interest in the history of St.-Dié until the end of the fifteenth century, when, under charge of the grand provost, Louis de Dommartin, it had gathered a few learned and ambitious men in its halls. Chief among them was Pierre de Blarru, the distinguished writer of "La Nancéide," the great national poem of Lorraine, celebrating in eternal verse the Battle of Nancy, which occurred on the 5th of January in the year 1477. This famous battle was fought by Charles the Bold and Duke René the Second, grandson of the Good King René. It resulted in the defeat and death of Charles, and the life of René was spared that he might become the most brilliant Mæcenas of his times. Two other men stand out as already specially distinguished at the time our interest in St.-Dié begins. The one was Jean Basin de Sendacour, the friend and companion of Pierre de Blarru, and whom the latter made his literary executor: he was himself the author of a treatise concerning the art of writing letters. The third distinguished member of this trio was Gualtier (Gualterus or Walter) Lud, the secretary of Duke René and the canon of the cathedral.

After the war with the Burgundians, Duke René gave his energies to cultivating again the devastated fields of his kingdom; and while assiduously employing the machines of peace, he found time to cultivate the arts which follow in their train. In this latter labor Gualtier Lud took the foremost part. In 1486 he obtained from Pope Innocent VIII. the dismissal of some ecclesiastical officials, and devoted their salaries to the maintenance of a music-teacher and to the teaching of the Latin language. Soon after, the field of education and learning opening before him as he went, he founded a learned society whose members came together for mutual improvement and for preparing and circulating scientific works. This society was known as the *Gymnase Vosgien*, and to the members above named were added Hugues des Hazards, the bishop of Toul; Louis de Dommartin, the provost of St.-Dié; Symphorien Champier, the physician and author; Johann Aluys, another of the numerous secretaries of René II.; Nicolas Lud, Mathias Ringmann, and Martin Waldseemüller. These last three merit more than a passing notice, and with one of them, Waldseemüller, we have much to do.

Alleged First Edition (Eyriès).	*Genuine First Edition (Thacher).*

[Ai] COSMOGRAPHIAE INTRODV-
CTIO/ CVM QVIBVS
DAM GEOME
TRIAE
AC
ASTRONO
MIAE PRINCIPIIS AD
EAM REM NECESSARIIS.
verso begins: MAXIMILIANO
Aij begins: DIVO MAXIMILIANO
  (but last l. begins: *ciēte/*)
verso 1st l. begins: *pręuiam*
Aiij 1st l. ends: *Ad*
  (but last l. begins: *Diamater*)
verso 1st l. begins: *trū circuli*
Aiiij 1st l. ends: *Igiť*
verso 1st l. begins: *Antarcticū*
  (but last l. ends: *anctoribus*)
[*Av*] 1st l. begins: *dicunť in ſpera*
verso 2d l. ends: *dig*
  (only fig. 4 in margin, op. 4th l. from bottom.)
[*Avi*] 1st l. ends: *trā*
verso last l. ends: *Vergilius in Geor*
B 1st l. begins: *gicis ait*
Bij last l. ends: *cancri. f.*
Biij last l. ends: *et. d. e.*
Biiij 1st l. begins: *Quarta quę*
a, b, c, d, in eights, *e* in fours, *f* in six, making 52 leaves in all.
12 lines on back of the diagram.
	[Ai] COSMOGRAPHIAE INTRODVCTIO/
	CVM QVIBVSDAM
	GEOMETRIAE
	AC
	ASTRONO
	MIAE PRINCIPIIS
	AD EAM REM NECESSARIIS
	verso 2d l. ends: GYNNASIVM VOS
	Aij 1st l. ends: *ex libris*
	verso 1st l. 5th w: *intelleximus.*
	Aiij 1st l. ends: *AD*
	  and last l. begins: *Diameter*
	verso 1st l. begins: *trū circuli.*
	Aiiij 1st l. ends: *Igiť.*
	verso 1st l. begins: *Antarcticū*
	  (but last l. ends: *auctoribus.*)
	[*Av*] 1st l. begins: *dicunter in ſphera*
	  and ends: *exi ʺ*
	verso 1st l. ends: *inferi*
	  and 2d l. ends: *di ʺ*
	  (fig. 3 in margin opposite 4th l. from bottom, and fig. 4 in margin opposite last line.)
	[*Avi*] 1st l. ends: *polos*
	verso last l. ends: *Virgilius in Geor ʺ*
	B 1st l. begins: *gicis aït*
	Bij last l. ends: *cancri. f.*
	Biij last l. ends: *et. d. e.*
	Biiij 1st l. begins: *Quarta quę*
	a, b, c, d in eights, *e* in fours, *f* in six, making 52 leaves in all.
	12 lines on back of the diagram.

Second Edition.	*Third Edition.*

[Ai] COSMOGRAPHIAE
INTRODVCTIO
CVM QVIBVS
DAM GEOME
TRIAE
AC
ASTRONO
MIAE PRINCIPIIS AD
EAM REM NECESSARIIS
verso 2d l. ends: GYMNASIVM
Aij 1st l. ends: *ex li ʺ*
verso 1st l. 5th w: *ītellexerimus.*
Aiij 1st l. ends: GEOMETRIAE
verso 1st l. begins: *trum circuli*
Aiiij 1st l. ends: *Igiť ſphera*
verso 1st l. begins: *Antarticum*
[*Av*] 1st l. begins: *dicuntur in ſphera*
  and ends: *exiſtē ʺ*
verso 1st l. ends: *inferio ʺ*
  and last l. begins: *maior eſt*
[*Avi*] 1st l. ends: *trāſiēs*
  verso last l. ends: *Georgi. ait.*
B 1st l. begins: *Quinq̃.*
Bij last l. ends: *ſcilicet*
Biij last l. ends: *&. d. e.*
Biiij 1st l. begins: *Quarta quae*
[*Bv*] and [*Bvi*], C and D in fours, another *A* in eights, *b* and *c* in fours, *d* in eights, *e* and *f* in fours, making 52 leaves in all.
15 lines on back of the diagram.
	[Ai] COSMOGRAPHIAE INTRODV-
	CTIO/ CVM QVIBVS
	DAM GEOME
	TRIAE
	AC
	ASTRONO
	MIAE PRINCIPIIS AD
	EAM REM NECESSARIIS
	verso begins: MAXIMILIANO
	Aij begins: DIVO MAXIMILIANO
	  (but last l. begins: *ciēte:*)
	verso 1st l. begins: *pręuiam*
	Aiij 1st l. ends: GEOMETRIAE
	verso 1st l. begins: *trum circuli*
	Aiiij 1st l. ends: *Igiť ſphera*
	verso 1st l. begins: *Antarticum*
	[*Av*] 1st l. begins: *dicunť in ſpera*
	verso 2d l. ends: *dig*
	  (fig. 3 in margin, op. 4th l. from bottom, and fig. 4 in margin, op. last l.)
	[*Avi*] 1st l. ends: *trā*
	verso last l. ends: *Vergilius in Geor*
	B 1st l. begins: *Quinq̃.*
	Bij last l. ends: *ſcilicet*
	Biij last l. ends: *&. d. e.*
	Biiij 1st l. begins: *Quarta quae*
	[*Bv*] and [*Bvi*], C and D in fours, another *A* in eights, *b* and *c* in fours, *d* in eights, *e* and *f* in fours, making 52 leaves in all.
	15 lines on back of the diagram.

COLLATIONS OF THE VARIOUS ST.-DIÉ EDITIONS OF THE "COSMOGRAPHIAE INTRODUCTIO."

CHAPTER II

The Coterie of Three

ICOLAS LUD was a name possessed at about the same period by three members of the important family of Lud of which Jean Lud de Pfaffenhoffen or Paffenhoven was the head, and who many years before had come from Alsace to establish himself in Lorraine. He was appointed superintendent or master-general of the valuable mines by the duke, and was possessed of wealth and influence. He had a brother, Nicolas Lud, Châtelain de Morsperg, who in April, 1493, was made secretary to the duke. Jean Lud's son Nicolas was admitted in 1490 among the apparently countless secretaries of René II., and still retained the position under Duke Anthony in 1508. A third Nicolas Lud, by letters patent under date of November 15, 1477, was nominated secretary to the Duke, and the assumption from the date is that he was an elder relative of the generation of Luds with which we have to do. It is likely that it is Nicolas Lud the second above mentioned who was so intimately associated with Ringmann, Waldseemüller, and Gualtier Lud in issuing the "Cosmographiæ Introductio." Ortelius, in his "Theatrum Orbis Terrarum," printed at Antwerp in 1570, makes a curious error in the name of Gualtier Lud, and enters Gualterus Ludovicus among the authors referred to in the "Speculo Orbis."

Mathias Ringmann, an Alsatian from the valley of the Orbey, was perhaps the most cultivated member of the coterie. He had been a pupil in Heidelberg under the famous philologian Jacques Wimpfeling de Schlettstadt, and afterward had studied in Paris under Jacques Lefebvre d'Etaples. He took for his nom de plume the Greek word *Philesius*, to which he added the adjective *Vogesigena* to indicate the place of his nativity. He was scarcely one-and-twenty when he wrote some verses "to the reader" for a new edition of the "Margarita Poetica" of Albertus Eyb, printed at the press of Johannes Pryss in Strasburg in 1503. His prose was likewise good, and probably the letters of Americus Vespucius on his four voyages were translated by him out of the common French, which in turn had been made from an unknown Italian version, and thus for the first time were these letters published in Latin in the little volume we are considering, and which goes under the title of its first tract, "Cosmographiæ Introductio."

Martin Waldseemüller was born in Freiburg in Breisgau about the year 1480, as we may judge from the record of his entrance into the primary department of the university, which record is dated December 7, 1490. He was doubtless the son of Conrad Waldseemüller of Freiburg, a man of position in his town in the middle of the fifteenth century, since he had been bailiff and treasurer. He early acquired the *trivium* of the course of education, or grammar, rhetoric, and logic, and then applied himself to the mastery of the *quadrivium*, or arithmetic, music, geometry, and astronomy, thus completing the gamut which made the scale of university knowledge and which students memorized in the following hexameter line:

Lingua, tropus, ratio; numerus, tonus, angulus, astra.

Following the custom of the scholars of the time, Waldseemüller turned his not unpleasant German name, meaning "miller of the forest lake," into its Greek equivalent "Hylacomylus," or, as it appears in the type of the St.-Dié and of the Strasburg presses, "Ilacomilus." The *Wald* becomes ὅλη, "woods" or "forest," and the *Müller* or *Miller* is easily turned into the soft μύλος. How the hard *c* found its way between these two mellifluous Greek words is a mystery. Abraham Ortelius, who, in his "Theatrum Orbis Terrarum," printed in 1570, drove the final nail which forever fastened the name of *America* to the new continent, fails fully to identify Martinus Ilacomilus with Martin Waldseemüller, and attributes a map of Europe, made somewhere in Germany, to the former, and a universal marine map, also published in Germany, to the latter. However, in a note he adds, after the latter's name, "puto hunc eundem esse cum Ilacomilo prædicto." Our Waldseemüller was not only a Latin and Greek scholar, but had made a special study of cosmography, and so impressed himself upon the other members of the Gymnase that they decided upon editing a new edition of the geography of Ptolemy. We shall see later that this idea was altered in the production of their first important work. In a printed note it is explained that Waldseemüller had been for some time engaged in translating and making a critical examination of a Greek manuscript of Ptolemy. Waldseemüller must have died shortly before the publication of the Ptolemy of 1522, for we read in that edition, on the verso of folio 100, in a brief address to the reader by the editor Laurentius Phrisius, these words: "Has tabulas e novo a Martino Ilacomylo pie defuncto constructas—"

CHAPTER III

The Press of St.-Dié

N the early part of the year 1507, a printing-press was set up for the first time in the Vosgian Mountains. This was the enlightened and progressive action of Gualtier Lud, who was wise enough to believe that the experiment would result in the composition and the circulation of books from the Gymnase, and who was rich enough easily to afford himself the luxury of the experiment. Much confusion has surrounded the time of establishment of this press. Gravier, the historian of St.-Dié, through want of bibliographical knowledge has been the cause of this confusion. A bull of Pope Paul II., made at Rome on the 16th of September, 1464, instituted a fête to commemorate the presentation of the Virgin in the temple. The prince-archbishop of Mayence, on the 3d of August, 1468, had published the bull, as well as a second bull carrying with it special indulgences, and dated from Rome, January 21, 1465. Gualtier Lud, in his ecclesiastical capacity as canon of the cathedral, interested himself in the proper performance of these imposing ceremonies, and from his own purse provided vestments and dresses for the actors, and all the necessary expenses of the fête, as well as its crowning function, an elaborate banquet. This fête took place for the first time on the 21st of November, 1494. Gravier, in his "Histoire de St.-Dié," tells of a copy of these bulls, printed upon three leaves in quarto with two columns to the page, in Gothic type, without signatures or catchwords; and in the absence of more definite information we are justified in presuming that the date and place of printing were also lacking. This copy contained in the autograph of Gualtier Lud a description of the institution and the successful observance of the fête. In the absence of this copy, which is lost, and failing more definite information which the historian Gravier might have given us concerning it, we have to conclude that the book was printed subsequently to 1507, and that the manuscript notes were placed there by Gualtier Lud, years after the institution of the fête, or else that the book was printed elsewhere than at St.-Dié,—perhaps at Strasburg or at

Freiburg. In the book we are soon to examine, the "Cosmographiæ Introductio," issued on the seventh of the Calends of May in the year 1507, we read in the preface: "Nobis qui librariam officinam apud Lotharingiæ Vosagum in oppido cui vocabulum est Sancto Deodato, *nuper ereximus*."

This language manifestly would not have been used if the printing establishment had been working since 1494, years before the famous coterie were brought together. Nor is there known any example of the St.-Dié press prior to 1507. The "Cosmographiæ Introductio" fortunately carries in its own arms, in the colophon which runs around the woodcut vignette, the settlement of this question:

> Urbs Deodate tuo clarescens nomine præsul
> Qua Vogesi montis sunt juga pressit opus
> Pressit, et ipsa eadem Christo monimenta favente
> Tempore venturo cætera multa premet.

> [The city, Deodatus, which is made illustrious by thy name, where the summits of the Vosgian mountains lift themselves, has printed this work, and by Divine favor, in the time to come, it will print many other monuments.]

This is appropriate language for the first issue of a promising and hopeful press, but it would have no meaning when spoken by a long-established and productive printing establishment.

There was said to be a distich on the back of the alleged imprint of 1494, containing in a rebus the name of Gualtier or Walterus Lud, and from that Gravier believed the entire manuscript to be in his hand.

> Post bis quinque sedens alter quem quinque sequuntur,
> Et tuba, cum Ludo (si caret orbe) vocor.

The riddle may thus be rendered:

> "Bis quinque" = V V or W
> plus "alter" = Walter
> "quinque" = V = Walteru
> "tuba" = s = Walterus
> "Ludo" (si caret orbe) = Walterus Lud.

The translation of "tuba" is an old-fashioned musical instrument in the form of the letter *S*.

Besides the "Cosmographiæ Introductio" there are but four or five other works known to have been issued by the St.-Dié press in the early part of the sixteenth century. They were published probably in the following order:

"Novus elegansque Conficiendarum epistolarum tractatus," composed by Jean

THE TOWN OF ST. DIÉ, IN LORRAINE. FROM A

AL DRAWING OF THE XVITH CENTURY.

Basin de Sendacour. No copy of this book is now known, but the historian Schöpflin once possessed one.

"Grammatica figurata octo partes orationis. Secundum Donati editionem et regulam Remigij ita imaginibus expressæ ut pueri iucundo chartarum ludo faciliora grammaticæ præludia discere et exercere queant."

"Chartiludium logice seu logica poetica vel memorativa," written by Thomas Murner, and reprinted from a copy published at Cracow in 1507. A copy of this was in the celebrated Schöpflin library at Strasburg, and was lost when that library was destroyed by fire. Lud dedicated this book to Bishop Hugues des Hazards, and the colophon is as follows:

> Est locus in Vogesò iam notus ubique per orbem. A Deodate, tuo nomine nomen habens. Hic Gualtherus Lud nec non Philesius ipse Presserunt miris hæc elementa typis. Anno Domini M. D. IX. Kalen. Junii.
> Renati secundi Siciliæ regis Lotharingiæ ducis vita per Johannem Aluysium Crassum Calabrum edita.

The above is on six quarto leaves, and the preface is dated, "ex oppido Divi Deodati MDX."

The paper, form, and type may easily be identified with the other publications from this press. A copy is in the library at Schlettstadt.

"Defensio Christianorum de Cruce, id est: Lutheranorum. Cum pia admonitione F. Thomæ Murnar, lutheromastigis, ordinis Minorum, quo sibi temperet a conuicijs et stultis impugnationibus Martini Lutheri. Matthæi Gnidii Augustensis Epistolæ item aliquot."

It is dated 1520, quarto, twelve leaves. Lud died in 1527, at the age of seventy-nine, and it is believed that some time before his death his printing establishment had been transferred to Johannes Schott, the printer at Strasburg. Another century passed before the art of printing was again practised in St.-Dié. It was not until 1625 that Jacques Marlier set up a press, and there published a little quarto in French, entitled, "Recherches de Saintes Antiquitéz de la Vosges."

Thus was brought together, in a spot removed from the distracting noise of the world, that famous coterie of literary men and scholars to which was permitted the unknown sensation of giving to a new world its appellation and of christening it with its never-to-be-forgotten name. And from among the members of this coterie it was preëminently Martinus Hylacomylus who set going in the cool refreshment of the Vosgian woods that mighty wheel of influence and power past which the stream has run, down the German river, out into the great ocean where America is known of, and hoped in, and prayed for by all good men in all the world.

PART VI

The "Cosmographiæ Introductio"

The Book which Conferred the Name America; with a Review of the Four Alleged Editions Printed at St.-Dié in 1507

CHAPTER I

The Inception of the Work

HE preparation and the publication of its first book gives solicitude to every printing establishment. When this establishment has been set up and the book has been composed by the owners themselves, who are true lovers of books, albeit amateurs in the great reproductive art, and when they await not silver or gold as the recompense for the days of their labor, the production of the book must be accompanied, like the coming of a new man into the world, by pain and travail and joy.

In the latter part of the month of April in the year 1507, an anxious group in the ancient town of St.-Dié stood about the first printing press ever erected in Lorraine and examined the sheets of the first book it issued to the world. It was an event of importance even beyond their purpose, for it was nothing less than the christening of a new land, the naming of a new continent, the baptism of a new world. Lud, the patron, Ringmann, the student, and Waldseemüller, the cosmographer, beheld the consummation of their labors with wonder and satisfaction. Lud saw the fecund machine he had contributed delivering copy after copy into their waiting hands. Ringmann read with delight the plainly lettered pages which faithfully repeated his poetic thoughts. Waldseemüller alone, while rejoicing that he had sent forth a timely treatise on geography, was fully conscious of its incompleteness, since it lacked the picture of the earth's surface and the outlines of the newly-discovered fourth part. If he had known that six long years must pass before the maps would be reproduced from his drawings, his ambitious soul would have been sad and fretful. The "Geography" of Claudius Ptolemy, made in the second century of our era, was the accepted text-book in that science, practically remaining unchanged and for the most part unedited until the maritime discoveries on the coast of Africa and in the western ocean suggested the addition of a few maps, in the latter part of the fifteenth century. The voyages of Prince Henry the Navigator, the discoveries of Columbus, disclosing, as they did, a new world, and the circumnavigation of the third division of the earth, or Africa, by Vasco da Gama, had impressed the little scientific coterie at St.-Dié with the necessity for a new edition of the works of the Alexandrian cosmographer, which in its completeness, in its recording for the first time in printed form the latest geographical knowledge, and in its elaborate and careful press work, should be worthy of the Vosgian Gymnase and its illustrious wise men. We do not know the exact date which found the Vosgian Gymnase beginning its task of translating and correcting Ptolemy. Harrisse quotes from d' Avezac's "Martin Hylacomylus Waltzemüller, ses Ouvrages et ses Collaborateurs," Paris, 1867, to prove that the coterie were engaged in this employment as early as 1505, and he seems to see Ringmann poring over Greek manuscripts, and Waldseemüller making globes and planispheres for several years before they announced their purpose and its abandonment in almost the same breath. As early as July, 1505, Ringmann, then in the University at Strasburg, was in possession of the Italian version of the "Voyages of Americus Vespucius," and at the same time he was studying the Ptolemaic maps and some new charts which were to go with a new edition of Ptolemy. In the "De Ora Antarctica," printed at Strasburg by Mathias Hupfuff in 1505, is a letter of Ringmann to Jacob Braun, whom he calls his bosom friend, his Achates.

M. Ringmannus Philesius A.
Jacobo Bruno suo Achati: S. P. D.

Cecinit in Eneide Virgilius noster, extra sydera jacere tellurem, extra anni solisque vias, ubi coelifer Atlas axem humero torquet stellis ardentibus aptum. Quam rem si quis forte miratus fuit hactenus, desinet certe identidem facere, ubi leget attentius quae Albericus Vesputius magni vir ingenii nec minoris experientiae de populo austrum versus sub antarctico quasi polo degente primus non falso prodidit. Gentem esse ait (ut ex ipso intelliges) nudam prorsus, et quae suorum hostium trucidatorum non solum (ut Carmanni Indiae populus) capita regi offert, sed ipsis quidem interfectis inimicis cupidissime solet vesci. Libellum ipsum Alberici casu nobis peroblatum perlegimus in transcursu, et singula ferme ad Ptolomeum (cujus tabulas ut nosti non versamus nunc indiligenter) comparavimus: subindeque de inventa nuper illa orbis ora breve quidem sed non minus cosmographicum lusimus poematulum quam poeticum. Id tibi mi Jacobe tanquam alteri Egoni mittimus legendum una cum libello, ut me tui non esse immemorem cognoscas. Vale. Cursim Argentinæ ex scholis nostris, Kal. Augusti anno M. D. V.

Master Ringmann Philesius to
Jacob Braun, his faithful friend.

Virgil, our poet, has sung in his Æneid, that in the region beyond where the stars have their home, beyond the pathways of time and the sun, there is a land where the heaven-lifting Atlas bears upon his shoulder the celestial regions bound together by the burning stars. If one should wonder at a thing like this, he will not restrain his surprise when he reads attentively that which a great man, of brave courage, yet small experience, Americus Vespucius, has first related without exaggeration of a people living toward the south, almost under the antarctic pole. There are people in that place, he says (as you shall presently read yourself), who go about entirely naked, and who not only (as do certain people in India) offer to their king the heads of their enemies whom they have killed, but who themselves feed eagerly on the flesh of their conquered foes. The book itself of Americus Vespucius has by chance fallen in our way, and we have read it hastily and have compared almost the whole of it with the Ptolemy, the maps of which you know we are at this time engaged in examining with great care, and we have thus been induced to compose, upon the subject of this region of a newly discovered world, a little work not only poetic but geographical in its character. We send to you, my friend Jacob, this work together with another book, so that you may know that you are not forgotten. Farewell. In haste, from our University, Strasburg, July 31, 1505.

This letter of Americus Vespucius, which so inspired Ringmann that he composed a poem upon that far-off region, which we feel to-day is quite mundane in its locality, was written to Laurentius Petrus Franciscus de Medicis, and was translated into Latin from Italian by Fra Giovanni del Giocondo, the famous architect who built the bridges over the Seine at Paris, the bridge of Notre-Dame and le Petit Pont, and of whom the poet Sannazar wrote:

> Jucundus geminos fecit tibi Sequana pontes:
> Jure tuum potes hunc dicere Pontificem.

> O Seine, for whom Jocundus
> Twin bridges fair hath walled,
> Let "Pontifex Anointed"
> Their builder long be called.

We shall presently meet with this poetical piece of Ringmann, since it was inserted in the "Quatuor Navigationes" of Americus Vespucius, which were printed to accompany the "Cosmographiæ Introductio." For the present our desire is to show that at least one of the future members of the Vosgian Gymnase was in the summer of 1505 not only interested in the cosmography of Ptolemy and in the geography of the new world, but was also profoundly impressed with the voyages and discoveries of Americus Vespucius.

It is easy to prove that the Luds, Ringmann, and Waldseemüller were intending to issue a Ptolemy before 1507, when they did issue the "Cosmographiæ Introductio," and it is easy to prove that after 1508 Ringmann and Waldseemüller, under new patrons, Jacob Aeszler and George Uebelin, the editors of the 1513 Strasburg Ptolemy, were actively employed in preparing it for publication. We take from Harrisse's valuable contribution, "The Discovery of North America," London and Paris, 1892, the following letter, discovered by Mr. Louis Sieber, the librarian of the Basle University Library, and first published by Dr. Charles Schmidt in 1875, in "Mémoires de la Société d'Archéologie Lorraine," Vol. III. It is written by Waldseemüller to Johannes Amerbach, a celebrated printer and publisher at Basle, where he set up his press in 1486.

Insigni viro M. Joanni Amerbachio literarum bonarum instauratori diligentissimo. Basileæ.
S. p. d. Non credo te latere nos Ptholomei cosmographiam, recognitis et adiectis quibusdam novis tabulis impressuros in oppido Divi Deodati.

Et cum exemplaria non concordent, obsecro te ut non tam mihi quam etiam dominis meis Gualthero et Nicolao Ludd morem gerere velis.

Id autem facies credo eo libentius quod ea res communi rei litterariæ proderit, pro qua tu et manibus et pedibus sine fine laboras.

Est apud prædicatores vobiscum in bibliotheca Ptholomei liber græcis caracteribus scriptus quem ego ut originale arbitror emendatissimum. Itaque rogo te ut quibus mediis id fieri possit procurare velis ut eum ipsum librum sive tuo sive nostro nomine per unius mensis spacium habere valeamus. Quod si opus fuerit vel vade vel recognitione, curabimus ut quodvis istorum actutum fiat. Sollicitassem et alios, nisi crederem te id oneris et libenter subiturum et etiam (namque potes) impetraturum. Solidum quod ad generale Ptholomei paravimus nondum impressum est, erit autem impressum infra mensis spacium.

Et si Ptholomei illud exemplar ad nos venerit, curabo ut solidum tale et alia quædam quæ filiis tuis prodesse poterunt ad te cum ipso Ptholomeo redeant.

Vale et cura ut non frustra te sollicitasse tuamque operam invocasse videamur.

Ex Divi Deodati oppido, ipso lunae post Paschae. Anno 1507.

Martinus Wualdsemuller alias Ilacomylus tibi ad vota subiectissimus.

To the distinguished man, Master Johannes Amerbach, the very diligent renovator of polite literature, at Basle, greeting:

I think you know already that I am on the point to print in the town of St.-Diey the Cosmography of Ptolemy, after having added to the same some new maps. But as the texts do not agree, I beg of you to comply with my wishes as well as those of the Messrs. Gaultier and Nicholas Ludd. I believe that you will do so with so much the more readiness as it will prove useful to our common literary studies, for which you labor with both hands and feet.

There is in the library of the Dominicans of your place a Greek text [of Ptolemy] which I deem to be as faithful as the original itself. That is the reason why I ask you to endeavor by all means to obtain, either in your name or in my own, that the said book [MS.] be allowed to remain with me during one month. If it be necessary to give a guarantee or a receipt, I shall try that one of the two be given at once. I would have appealed to some one else, had I not been sure that you would readily accept the task, and succeed, for you can do so.

The globe [*solidum?*] [comprising] Ptolemy in general, which we have prepared, is not yet printed, but will be so in a month. And if the manuscript I have just spoken of is sent to me, I shall see that it be returned to you, together with that globe and some other articles which may be useful to your sons. Farewell, and let it not appear that we have appealed to you in vain. From the city of St.-Diey, on Easter Monday [April 5], 1507.

Martin Wualdsemuller, alias Ilacomylus, your humble servant.

CHAPTER II

The Alleged Four Editions

E have said enough to show that at the beginning of the month of April, in the year 1507, the members of the Vosgian Gymnase were engaged in hurrying from their newly erected press an edition of Ptolemy. On the twenty-fifth day of April in the same year they issued the "Cosmographiæ Introductio" and the "Quatuor Navigationes." The Ptolemy had been suddenly abandoned, but it had been resolved to issue an elaborate map of the newly discovered lands. To aid in a proper understanding of the chart, a little treatise on cosmography was composed to accompany the map of the world. The map was not published, but the treatise was, and to it we owe the naming of the new continent. It is idle to speculate upon the reason for abandoning the project so long entertained by the Gymnase of printing a new Ptolemy. It may have been that the resources of the printing establishment were not equal to producing a folio book with engraved plates. It may have been that exaggerated rumors came to them of the early production of the Roman 1507–8 edition of Ptolemy with the Ruysch map, and that a consciousness of the unfinished state of their own work induced them to turn aside from their more pretentious purpose, and to content themselves with the speedy publication of the little tract on the science of geography and the four voyages of the Florentine discoverer.

The "Cosmographiæ Introductio"—including the "Quatuor Navigationes,"—is a small quarto of fifty-two leaves, spaced for twenty-seven lines to the full page, roman type, with signatures, but with no catchwords. These marks are common to the different editions of this book which issued from the St.-Dié press in the year 1507. The watermarks are two—a bull's head with a clover leaf at the top of a staff which rises from between the horns, and a large five-pointed star. Bibliographers think they recognize four distinct types of this book, two with the colophon dated VII Calends May (April 25)—and two dated IIII Calends September (August 29). The pagination of the so-called first two editions is as follows: Signature *A* is composed of six leaves;

B has four leaves; *a, b, c, d* have each eight leaves; *e* has four leaves, and *f* concludes the book with six leaves. There is in the Lenox Library to-day a copy of the "Cosmographia" which is unique. Some writers, for reasons to be mentioned further on, give it precedence over the other editions, and it has thus come to represent the first of the four alleged editions. It rests in a luxurious binding given it by Trautz-Bauzonnet. There was a time when, in torn sheep-skin, it slept, a vagrant and an outcast, in vulgar company, in the wooden stall of a dealer in second-hand books, on a quay by the side of the river Seine in Paris, and none passed by to do it reverence. One day a great geographer, who despised not small things, was rewarded of the Gods, and for twenty cents became the owner of a bibliographical treasure measureless in price. The geographer was Jean-Baptiste Eyriès, associated with Philippe de Larenaudière in publishing the "Annales des Voyages," afterwards conducted by Conrad Malte Brun. It was shown in 1836 to Alexander von Humboldt and played its part in the fourth volume of his "Examen Critique." After the death of Eyriès the book was catalogued in the sale of his library as "No. 649," and sold on the 30th of November in the year 1846 for only thirty-two dollars to the bookseller Tilliard, who was commissioned to buy it for a celebrated collector in Lyons, Nicolas Yéméniz. In 1867 the latter's library heard the dismal sound of the auctioneer's hammer, and it was bought from the catalogue, No. 2676, for the late Almon W. Griswold of New York for four hundred dollars. It afterwards went into the collection of Mr. Henry C. Murphy of Brooklyn, but before it could again be humiliated by appearing on the block, it was procured for the Lenox Library, where it is held the chiefest among rarities. It may not be the legitimate issue of the St.-Dié press; indeed we do not think it is. It stands alone, since there has never been found another to claim relationship with it, and soon we will examine its title to priority. Whatever its origin, it is curious, interesting, and important. We owe to Mr. Wilberforce Eames, the ideal librarian of the Lenox Library, the use of the accompanying table showing the differences between the so-called four editions. M. d'Avezac was content to distinguish these editions in the following manner, taking the first line of the title with the colophon:

	Title.	*Colophon.*
Edition I	Cosmographiæ Introdu	vij kl' Maij
Edition II	Cosmographiæ Introductio	vij kl' Maij
Edition III	Cosmographiæ	iiij kl' Septembris
Edition IV	Cosmographiæ Introdu	iiij kl' Septembris

No bibliographer could content himself with so meager a collation, and we shall give the reader not only Mr. Eames's admirable collation which is inserted at the beginning of this Part, but full-sized plates of such of the printed sheets as show the most important differences. By comparing these editions, it will be seen that the corresponding lines of the same color appear to have been printed from the same type, without resetting. The few other variations which are noted, like the preposition "Ad" at the end of the first line on the recto of *Aiij* of the first type in place of "AD" occupying the same space in the second type, may be taken for those accidents which were likely to happen in making corrections while the type was standing. If a capital *D* had been wanted somewhere else, it would have been released and a smaller one put in its place. It must be remembered that each sheet was printed by hand, independent of every other sheet, by a slow, laborious process, giving plenty of opportunity for those erratic differences between copies of the same book constantly occurring in early imprints.

By glancing at Mr. Eames's table it will be seen that the title of his Edition I, which is on *Ai*, differs from that of his Editions II and III, but is identical with that of Edition IV. It will also be seen that on the verso of *Ai*, in his Edition I, is printed the decastich addressed to the Emperor by the poet Ringmann reproduced in facsimile, on page 135 and of which the following is a translation.

Philesius of the Vosges to the Emperor Maximilian.

Since your majesty, O Emperor Maximilian, is venerated throughout all the world even to its furthermost confines — where the sun raises his glittering head from out the waves of the East — where he reaches the strait renowned by the name of Hercules — where the South is stifled by the burning constellation — where in the northern regions the surface of the seas is frozen; and since thou, O prince, more puissant than the greatest kings, when thou speakest dost behold thy words bearing fullest sway, therefore now, he who by his wonderful art hath prepared this work dedicates it to thee as a mark of his devotion.

The above poetical effusion is found in the same position on the verso of Ai in Edition IV. It was a happily constructed poem. It lauded the Emperor Maximilian the First to the furthermost constellations. There was no reason why it should not have been repeated in the so-called Editions II and III, if indeed it had been composed when these editions were printed. It was faithfully reproduced in the Strasburg edition of 1509. Ringmann was too brilliant a member of the coterie to have his excellent poem thrown out after its first appearance.

CHAPTER III

The Romance of the Unique Edition

ND just here we must tell the story which is told by those who claim priority for the so-called Edition I. Briefly told, it is that Waldseemüller wrote his dedication to the Emperor Maximilian and saw it leave the press with his name alone appearing as the author of the little treatise. He then left France, or the Vosgian village of St.-Dié, to go into Germany, and while he was away the Luds and Ringmann — or else some one must account for the latter's absence and thus acquit him of collusion — removed from the form the leaves *Ai* and *Aij* as well as leaves *Av* and *Avi*, and inserted the leaves which appear under corresponding signatures in Edition II, and in which the society itself, the Vosgian Gymnase, dedicated the work in hand to the Emperor Maximilian. A third edition appeared at the end of August, but at that juncture Waldseemüller, trembling with indignation, appeared and compelled his enemies to do him justice, and under the same date, the IIII Calends of September, August 29, a change was again made in the form, and an edition printed with his original dedication and Ringmann's ardent poem. The bitter complaint of Waldseemüller is found in the letter he wrote from Strasburg to Ringmann at Basle under date of February, 1508. It appears in a new edition of Ringmann's "Margarita Philosophica," printed by Johannes Grüninger at Strasburg, March 31, 1508.

The "Margarita Philosophica" was a sort of encyclopædia or circle of instruction which rapidly multiplied its editions at the beginning of the sixteenth century. It was edited by Gregorius Reisch, a graduate of the university of Heidelberg. The book was divided into twelve sections, three being devoted to the *Trivium*, four to the *Quadrivium* or the mathematical sciences, four to natural philosophy, and one, the last, to moral philosophy. It was first printed at Freiburg, in 1503, by Joannes Schottus. It was twice printed in 1504, and again in 1508. For this last edition Waldseemüller had been engaged to write an article which he entitled "Architecturæ et Perspectivæ Rudimenta."

In this article the above-mentioned letter appears as the prologue, preface, or dedicatory epistle, and is as follows:

Martinus Ilacomilus Friburgensis Philesio suo Salutem.

Cum his diebus Bacchanalibus solatij causa qui mihi mos est in Germaniam venissem ē Gallia: seu potius ex Vogesi oppido cui nomen Sancto Deodato ubi ut nosti meo potissimum ductu labore licet plerique alij falso sibi passim ascribant, Cosmographiam universalem tam solidam quam planam non sine gloria et laude per orbem disseminatam nuper composuimus: depinximus: et impressimus. collegi in angulo paulisper semotus: dum alij tumultuarentur: quædam ex diversis auctoribus de Scenographia quæ species est Architecturæ et de ipsa perspectiva positiva: quarum certe rerum non ignarum oportet esse eum qui se Geometriæ scium. Et id quidem rei tibi imprimis Phylesi dicare statui: cum et in Mathematicis sis pulchre eruditus: quippe qui fabrum Stapulensem omnis Matheseos peritissimum habuisti in Parhisiorum Lutecia præceptorem: et nunc in Academia Basiliensi Cosmographiam publice profitearis. Præterea etiam uti audio doctissimum principem Cristoforum de Utenheim sacrum Basiliensem Antistitem: studiosorum fautorem maximum eis in rebus privata lectione instruxeris. Vale mi Philesi: haec qualiacumque boni consulens et ea studia diligere non cessa quæ curant ne a platonico auditorio excludaris. Iterum Vale. Argentinæ.

Martin Waldseemüller of Freiburg to his friend Ringmann, greeting:

In those days of the Carnival, in order to refresh myself, as is my habit, I went into Germany from France, or more properly speaking, from that town in the Vosges known as St.-Dié, where, as thou knowest, *principally by my labor, although many others, here and there, falsely claim it for themselves*, we have lately composed, drawn, and printed a map of the entire earth, in the form of a globe as well as of a planisphere, and which is making its way over the world not without glory and praise. Retired for a little time in my seclusion, while others engaged in the activities of life, I have gathered knowledge from different authors concerning scenography, which is a branch of architecture, and also concerning perspective, of which surely no one should be ignorant who pretends to understand geometry. And it is to thee, Ringmann, that at the outset I am resolved to dedicate this, for thou thyself art most learned in the science of mathematics, thou who hadst at Paris as thy instructor Lefèbvre d'Étaples, so well skilled in all branches of mathematics, and who now dost occupy the chair of geography in the University of Basle, and who, moreover, as I hear, dost also give private instruction in these subjects to the most learned prince Christopher d' Utenheim, bishop of Basle, great patron of students. Farewell, my Philesius; do not cease, in caring for these other things, to diligently follow those studies which will keep thee in the school of philosophy. Again farewell. From Strasburg.

It is in the few words we have italicized above that some find the complaint of Waldseemüller against his treatment by the Vosgian Gymnase. This is not the language of one who has suffered a deadly wrong. It is simply a querulous utterance boxed up in a parenthesis. The adverbial expression *passim*, "here and there," is enough of itself to show that his accidentally dropped complaint was not directed against any one person or any one set of persons in any particular place. Ringmann himself was a member, or had until very lately been a member, of the Gymnase, and he could not have been the target for the shaft carelessly winged in the above paragraph. It leaves only Lud, or at best the two Luds, Gaulterus and Nicolas, as the guilty parties. But even they were not ubiquitous enough to be a "here and there"

COSMOGRAPHIAE INTRODV-
CTIO/CVM QVIBVS
DAM GEOME
TRIAE
AC
ASTRONO
MIAE PRINCIPIIS AD
EAM REM NECESSARIIS:

Insuper quatuor Americi Ves
spucij nauigationes.

Vniuersalis Cosmographię descriptio
tam in solido ꝗ̃ plano/eis etiam
insertis quę Ptholomęo
ignota a nuperis
reperta sunt.

DISTICHON.

Cum deus astra regat/& terræ climata Cæsar
Nec tellus nec eis sydera maius habent.

RECTO OF *Ai*, EYRIÈS'S COPY.

COSMOGRAPHIAE INTRODVCTIO,
CVM QVIBVSDAM
GEOMETRIAE
AC
ASTRONO
MIAE PRINCIPIIS
AD EAM REM NECESSARIIS

Insuper quatuor Americi Ves
spucij nauigationes.

Vniuersalis Cosmographiae descriptio
tam in solido ꝗ̃ plano/eis etiam
insertis quę Ptholomęo
ignota a nuperis
reperta
sunt.

DISTICHON.

Cum deus astra regat/& terræ climata Cæsar
Nec tellus nec eis sydera maius habent.

RECTO OF *Ai*, MR. THACHER'S COPY.

FACSIMILE PAGES OF THE "COSMOGRAPHIÆ INTRODUCTIO."

DIVO MAXIMILIANO CAESARI SEM,
PER AVGVSTO/GYNNASIVM VOS
AGENSE NON RVDIBVS INDO
CTISVE ARTIVM HVMANI
TATIS COMMENTATORI
BVS NVNC EXVL,
TANS: GLORIAM
CVN FOELICI
DESIDERAT
PRINCIPA
TV.

SI MVLTAS ADIISSE REGIONES/ET
populorū vltimos vidiſſe/nō ſolum voluptarium/
ſed etiam in vita conducibile eſt(quod in Platone/
Apollonio, Thyanæo atq̃ alijs multis philoſophis
q̃ indagandarū rerū cauſa remontiſſimas oras peti
Boetius uerunt/ darum euadit) Quis o Cæſar inuictiſſime
regionum atq̃ vrbium ſitus/ & externorum homi
num.
Quos videt condens radios ſub vndas
Phœbus: extremo veniens ab ortu:
Quos premunt ſeptem gelidi Triones:
Quos Nothus ſicco violentus æſtu
Torret ardentes recoquens harenas.

VERSO OF Ai, MR. THACHER'S COPY.

MAXIMILIANO CAESARI AVGVSTO
PHILESIVS VOGESIGENA.

Cum tua ſit vaſtum Maieſtas ſacra per orbem
Cæſar in extremis Maxmiliane plagis
Qua ſol Eois rutilum caput extulit vndis/
Atq̃ freta Herculeo nomine nota petit:
Quaq̃ dies medius flagranti ſydere feruet/
Congelat & Septem terga marina Trio:
Aciubeas regū magnorum maxime princeps
Mitia ad arbitrium iura ſubire tuum
Hinc tibi deuota generale hoc mente dicauit
Qui mira præſens arte parauit opus.

o Tλod,

VERSO OF Ai, EYRIÈS'S COPY.

FACSIMILE PAGES OF THE "COSMOGRAPHIÆ INTRODUCTIO."

DIVO MAXIMILIANO CAESARI AV GVSTO MARTINVS ILACO MILVS FOELICITA TE M OPTAT.

Si multas adijsse regiones/& populorū vltimos vidisse/nō solū voluptariū sed etiam in vita cōduci bile est(quod in Platone / Apollonio Thyanæo atq̃ alijs multis philosophis/qui indagandarū rerᵃ causa remotissimas oras petiuerūt /clarum euadit) quis oro inuictissime Cæsar Maximiliane / regio nū atq̃ vrbium situs /& externorum hominum   Boetius
Quos videt condens radios sub vndas
Phœbus extremo veniens ab ortu:
Quos premunt Septem gelidi Triones:
Quos Nothus sicco violentus æstu
Torret ardentes recoquens harenas.   Quis inquā illorū omniū ritus ac mores ex libris cognoscere iu cundū ac vtile esse inficias ibit: Sane(vt dicā quod mea fert opinio)sicut longissime peregrinari lauda bile est/ita de quis cui ipse terrarū orbis vel ex sola chartarū traditione cognitus est/nō absurde repeti identidē potest illud Odisseæ caput quod doctissi Home‑ mus poetarū Homerus de Vlisse scripsit.   rus
Dic mihi musa virū captæ post tempora Troiæ
Qui mores hominū multorum vidit & vrbes.
Hinc factū est vt me libros Ptholomęi ad exēplar Gręcū quorundā ope p̃ virili recognoscēte/& qua tuor Americi Vespucij nauigationū lustratões adij cięte/ totius orbis typū tā in solido q̃ plano(velut   A ij

Quis inquā illorū omniū ritus ac mores/ex libris cognoscere:iucundum ac vtile esse inficias ibit:Sa ne(vt sapientum fert opinio)sicut longissime per‑ egrinari laudabile est/ita de quouis mortalium cui præmensus ipsę terrarum orbis vel ex sola charta‑ rum traditione longę latęq̃ spectabilis atq̃ cogni‑ tus est non absurde repeti potest quod ab ipso poe tarum principe Homero musa Clyo de Naricio du Home‑ ce verbis istis rogabatur.   rus

Dic mihi musa virum captæ post tempora Troie
Qui mores hoīm multorum vidit et vrbes.

Hinc effectum est/vt nobis(qui librariam officia nam apud Lotharingię Vosagum in oppido cui vo cabulū est Sancto Deodato/nuper ereximus)Ptho lomęi libros post exēplar Gręcū recognoscēribus: necnon quatuor Americi Vespucij nauigationū lu strationes adijcientibus:totius orbis typū tam in so lido q̃ plano(velut pręuiam quandam ysagogen) pro communi studiosorum vtilitate parauerimus: Quę tuę sacratissimę maiestati/cū terrarum dn̄s ex istas dicare statuimus. Rati nosipsos voti compo‑ tes/& ab æmulorum machinamentis tuo (tamq̃ Achillis) clipeo tutissimos fore/ si tuę Maiestatis acutissimo in eis rebus iudicio/ aliquantula saltem   A ij

ANTELOQVIVM

ex parte nos fatiffeciffe intellexerimus. Vale cæfar in clytiffime. Ex fuperius memorato fancti Deodati oppido. Anno poft natum Saluatorē fupra fefqui- millefimum feptimo.

TRACTANDORVM ORDO

Cum Cofmographię noticia fine pręuia quadā aftronomiæ cognitione, & ipfa etiam aftronomia fine Geometrię principijs plęne habere nequeat: di cemus primo in hac fuccincta introductiōe paucu, la de Geometriæ inchoamentis ad fpheræ materia lis intelligentiam feruientibus:

2 Deinde quid fphera/axis/poli.&c.
3 De cœli circulis.
4 Quaudam ipfius fpheræ fecundum graduū ratio, nes Theoricam ponemus:
5 De quincq Zonis cęleftibus earundēcq & graduū cœli ad terram applicatione.
6 De Paralellis.
7 Declimatibus orbis.
8 De ventis, cum eorū & aliarū rerū figura vniuerfali
9 Nono capite quędam de diuifione terrę/de finibus maris/de infulis/& locorū abinuicē diftātia dicent Addecur etiam quadrans Cofmographo vtilis.

Vltimo loco qtuor America Vefpucij fubiūge: p̄, fectiōes. Et Cofmo.tā folidā cq̄ planā defcribemus.

VERSO OF *Aij*, MR. THACHER'S COPY.

ANTELOQVIVM

pręuiam quandā yfagogen) p̄ cōmuni ftudioforū vtilitate parauerim. Quē tuę facratiffimę maieftatī cū terrarū dn̄s exiftas dicare ftatui. Ratus me voti cōpotē/& ab æmulorū machinamentis tuo (tāncq̄ Achillis) clipeo tutiffimū fore/fi tuę Maieftatis acu tiffimo in eis rebus iudicio aliqua faltem, ex parte me fatis fœciffe intellexero.. Vale Cæfar inclytiffi. Ex oppido diui Deodati. Anno poft natū Saluato rem fupra fefquimillefimū feptimo.

TRACTANDORVM ORDO.

Cū Cofmographiæ noticia fine pręuia quadam aftronomię cognitione/et ipfa etiā aftronomia fine Geometriæ pricipijs plęne haberi neqat: dicemus primo in hac fuccicta itroductiōe paucula de Geo metrię inchoamentis ad fpheræ materialis intelligē (tiā feruientibus.
2 Deīde qd fphera/axis/poli &c.
3 De cœli circulis.
4 Quandā ipfius fpheræ fecundū graduū rōnes The (oricā ponemus
5 De quīncq̄ Zonis cęleftibus earundēcq̄ & graduū cœli ad terram applicatione
6 De Paralellis.
7 De climatibus orbis.
8 De ventis cū eorū et aliarum rerū figura vniuerfali
9 Nono capite quędā de diuifione terrę / de finibus maris / de infulis / et locor: abinuicē diftātia dicent Addet̄ etiā quadrans Cofmographo vtilis.

Vltio loco qtuor Americi Vefpucij fubiūge. p̄, fectiōes. Et Cofm. tā folidā cq̄ planā defcribemus.

VERSO OF *Aij*, EYRIÈS'S COPY.

FACSIMILE PAGES OF THE "COSMOGRAPHIÆ INTRODUCTIO."

sort of culprits, and so we have the right to infer that the cause of the not very serious difficulty was not confined to the Gymnase or to any trouble which had occurred there.

Returning to the unique edition: on the recto of *Ai* is the title-page. The first few lines of the four editions differ, and by referring to the accompanying facsimiles on page 134, the reader has an opportunity to note the variations between the title-pages of the two rival first editions.

The following is the translation of the title-page of the so-called first edition:

Introduction to Geography, together with some principles of Geometry and Astronomy necessary to the comprehension of the subject, to which are added the four voyages of Americus Vespucius. A description of the Geography of the entire world illustrated, as well by a globe as on a plane surface, to which are added those countries lately discovered and which were unknown in the time of Ptolemy. DISTICH. Neither the earth nor the stars possess anything greater than God and Cæsar, as God rules the stars and Cæsar the climes of the earth.

On the verso of *Ai* is the decastich of Ringmann, the translation of which we have already had on page 131.

On the recto and part of the verso of *Aij* of the so-called first edition is the dedication to the Emperor Maximilian by Martin Waldseemüller, which we have reproduced in facsimile on pages 136 and 137, and of which the following is a translation:

To the Emperor Maximilian Martinus Ilacomilus wishes all happiness.

Since it is not only pleasant but also profitable to have visited many countries and to have seen distant peoples (as was the case with Plato, Apollonius of Tyana, and various other philosophers who went to remotest parts of the world in quest of knowledge and so added to their fame): who then, I humbly ask, O invincible Emperor Maximilian, will deny the utility and pleasure of acquiring some knowledge of the countries and cities of those peoples whom, as Boetius says, "the sun sees when he hides his rays from us beneath the waves of the ocean, and when he rises again in the far East; over whom the seven stars of the Great Bear shed their cold beams, and whom the violent south wind scorches with his fervid breath, baking the burning sands?" Who, I ask, would deny the pleasure and profit of learning from books the customs and manners of all these peoples? Surely (if I may express my own opinion), as it is praiseworthy to travel to remote regions, so any one who knows the whole world or even has knowledge derived from maps may, without presumption, repeat those lines of the Odyssey which Homer, the most learned of the poets, wrote about Ulysses:

> "Tell me, O Muse, of that sagacious man
> Who, having overthrown the sacred town
> Of Ilium, wandered far and visited
> The capitals of many nations, learned
> The customs of their dwellers."

It thus happened that in collecting for my own work, aided by some others, the books of Ptolemy and collating them with the Greek text, and in proposing to add thereto an inquiry into the four voyages of Americus Vespucius, I have prepared for the common use of students, and as a sort of preparatory introduction, a figure of the entire earth, as well in the form of a globe as a representation on a flat surface; and I have resolved to dedicate it to Your Most Sacred Majesty, who holdeth in his hand the empire of the world. Hoping that my wish may be realized, *and that under the shelter of thy shield (as of that of Achilles) I would be safe from the designs of the envious*, should I be able to satisfy, at least in part, the judgment of Your Majesty, so discriminating in these matters. Hail, illustrious Emperor. From the city of St.-Dié, in the year after the birth of our Lord, 1507.

When one sets about building a card house, one is sometimes called upon to make a mole hill into a goodly mountain to shelter it from the winds of criticism. Having built up a theory that Waldseemüller had been robbed of his rights in the production of this book from the St.-Dié press, M. d'Avezac discovers in the phrase "ab æmulorum machinamentis," by the poetic license of inserting a personal pronoun where there is none, a violent crying out on the part of Waldseemüller to be protected against the intrigues of *his* rivals. The language is the common language of old-time dedications. Given the majesty of a protector, and one must have the humility of the protected. The outstretched wing must cover an abased head. If the story of Waldseemüller's wrongs as here narrated be true, if the first edition be the one before us, and if the dedication of the second edition in the name of the Vosgian Gymnase robbed him of his rights, then why have we any reference to his rivals in the first edition, before any injury had been perpetrated? Why the complaint before the cause?

CHAPTER IV

The real Priority of the alleged Second Edition

THIS is the proper place to examine the dedication found in the so-called second edition, made by the Vosgian Gymnase to the Emperor Maximilian, and which, it is claimed, replaced the dedication made by Hylacomylus and thus worked him a grievous wrong. The abbreviations found in the original are here, for the sake of ready understanding, written out in full, and furthermore the material variations between the dedications of the two editions are here indicated by italicized words in the second dedication. The text begins on the verso of *Ai*, and the reader will compare the words with the accompanying facsimile of the original on page 135.

DIVO MAXIMILIANO CAESARI SEM-
PER AVGVSTO, GYMNASIVM VOS
AGENSE NON RVDIBVS INDO
CTISVE ARTIVM HVMANI
TATIS COMMENTATORI
BVS NVNC EXVL-
TANS: GLORIAM
CVN FOELICI
DESIDERAT
PRINCIPA
TV.

SI MVLTAS ADIISSE REGIONES, ET populorum vltimos vidisse, non solum voluptuarium, sed etiam *in* vita conducibile est (quod in Platone, Apollonio Thyanæo atque aliis multis philosophis qui indagandarum rerum causa remontissimas oras petiuerunt, clarum evadit) Quis *o Cæsar inuictissime*, regionum atque vrbium situs, & externorum hominum,

        Quos videt condens radios sub vndas   (Boetius)
        Phœbus: extremo veniens ab ortu:
        Quos premunt septem gelidi Triones:
        Quos Nothus sicco violentus æstu
        Torret ardentes recoquens harenas.

Quis inquam illorum omnium ritus ac mores, ex libris cognoscere: jucundum ac utile esse inficias ibit? Sane (*ut sapientum fert opinio*) sicut longissime peregrinari laudabile est, ita de quovis *mortalium*

Ch. IV REAL PRIORITY OF THE ALLEGED SECOND EDITION

cui *præimensus* ipse terrarum orbis vel ex sola chartarum traditione longe lateque spectabilis atque cognitus est non absurde repeti potest quod *ab ipso* poetarum *principe* Homero *musa Clyo de Naricio duce verbis istis rogabatur.*

Dic mihi musa virum captæ post tempora Troie   (Homerus)
Qui mores hominum multorum vidit et urbes.

Hinc *effectum* est, ut *nobis* (*qui librariam officinam apud Lotharingie Vosagum in oppido cui vocabulum est sancto Deodato, nuper ereximus*) Ptholomæi libros *post* exemplar Græcum recognoscen*tibus*: *necnon* quatuor Americi Vespucij navigationum lustrationes adjicien*tibus*: totius orbis typum tam in solido quam plano (velut præviam quandam ysagogen) pro communi studiosorum utilitate paraveri*mus*. Quem tuæ sacratissimæ maiestati, cum terrarum dominus existas dicare statui*mus*. Rati *nos ipsos* voti compo*tes* et ab emulorum machinamentis tuo (tamquam Achillis) clipeo tutissi*mos* fore, si tuæ Maiestatis acutissimo in eis rebus judicio, aliqua*ntula* saltem ex parte *nos* satisfecisse intellexi*mus*. Vale cæsar inclytissime. Ex *superius memorato sancti* Deodati oppido. Anno post natum Salvatorem supra sesqui millesimum septimo.

The words *remontissimas oras* in the fifth line of the dedication in the so-called second edition are intended, manifestly, for *remotissimas oras*, and we find them so corrected, in the alleged first edition, by Waldseemüller. Moreover, in the other editions and in the Strasburg edition of 1509 the correction stands. This little error and its timely correction is a strong witness against the priority of the so-called first edition.

On the verso of *Av* of the so-called second edition the fourth word in the fifth line from the top is printed *ignorum*, a manifest error for *signorum*, and the error was naturally corrected in the so-called first edition when some one changed the sheets *Ai* and *Aij*. On the same folio, the verso of *Av*, the reader will observe that the fourth word in the tenth line from the bottom is wrongly printed *viris*. It should have been *uris*, and again the correction was made and remained corrected in the later editions. On the recto of *Avi* the fifth word in the eleventh line from the top is misprinted *ducentinm* for *ducentium*. On the verso of *Avi*, the last word in the third line from the bottom is wrongly printed *Nos*. It should have been *Hos*. On the same side of the folio, and in the fifth line from the bottom, the fifth word is misprinted *quaruor* for *quatuor*, and the second word in the line above is printed *celectis* for *celestis*. On the same side of the folio the sixth line from the top is written *Hnnc* for *Hunc*. Any practical printer would say that the edition which showed these typographical errors must have preceded one in which they were corrected. When the leaves were substituted with the dedication of Waldseemüller some one corrected the errors, and thus unconsciously put the stamp of priority on the carelessly printed so-called second edition.

But the strongest proof is still another bit of internal evidence. The reader will notice, by comparing the four editions in the collation at the beginning of this part, that the first and second leaves (*Ai* and *Aij*) of the first and fourth edition were printed from the same type without resetting, as were also the fifth and sixth leaves (*Av* and *Avi*) of the first and fourth edition. The red lettering indicates the similarity. The same can be said of leaves three and four (*Aiij* and *Aiiij*) of the first and second editions. The said practical printer would realize at once that, when the last or fourth edition was going through the press, some one, by design or accident, removed from the loosely piled sheets of a copy of the first edition, yet unbound, the full leaves *Ai*, *Aij*, *Av*, and *Avi*, putting in their place the corresponding leaves of the edition then in process of printing, and leaving the leaves *Aiij* and *Aiiij* as they were. This was done in the case of one copy, and of one only; by whom done or for what purpose we do not know.

On the verso of *Avi* of so-called edition I the last words are *Hinc & Vergilius in Geor-*. The words necessary to complete the sentence are the first words found on the recto of the new sheet *Bi*, namely, *gicis ait*. In the fourth or last edition—the second of the colophon, dated the fourth of the Calends of September—leaf *Bi* begins a new sentence, *Quinque*, etc. If therefore *Avi* in this made-up copy had been taken from the fourth edition, one might expect to find the ending of the last line of the verso to be "*Vergilius in Georgicis ait.*" But in fact it corresponds exactly with the last line of the verso of *Avi* as found in both of the first two editions, and consequently in the fourth there is a regular gap or lacuna between the ending of *Avi* and the beginning of *Bi*, and the word and a half, "*gicis ait*," are completely lost.

The chief distinction between the two forms of dedication is in the use of the personal pronouns. In the alleged first and fourth editions, the singular number of the pronouns and verbs is used. In the so-called second and third editions, the dedication is recited by the coterie, and the plural number is employed. But the essential sentiments and phrases are alike in all four, if we except the omission in the alleged first edition of any allusion to the printing press at St.-Dié, either *nuper erexi* or *nuper ereximus*. Even the remarkable expression *ab emulorum machinamentis* is in both dedications. The Strasburg edition of 1509 has the Waldseemüller dedication as taken from the last form of "Cosmographiæ Introductio," printed at St.-Dié. There are not wanting indications that Johannes Grüninger, the printer of the Strasburg edition, was acquainted with the peculiarities and differences of the various St.-Dié copies. For instance, in the passage which suggests calling the New World after Americus, the printer adopts for a marginal word the nominative case of the feminine form—*America*,—while in the September edition of the St.-Dié book the ablative case of the masculine form—*Americo*—is used.

The unique character of the so-called first edition is a witness against its legitimacy. In every essential feature, to the slightest nicety, the "made-up" copy agrees with the corresponding pages from the two editions used to create it. The unique copy was found, and a story was imagined to fit its strange appearance. If Waldseemüller desired protection *ab æmulorum machinamentis*, do we not find the members of the Vosgian Gymnase seeking protection also *ab emulorum machinamentis*. If Waldseemüller had secret enemies and dangerous rivals, do we not see the Vosgian coterie fearing the same hostile foes? If there were those who were envious of Waldseemüller, the envy could also make its way up the hill to St.-Dié, where the students were at work. It would seem as if Waldseemüller would have had his name appear in the colophon of the book with the same exclusive prominence as had been given it in the dedication, and yet in both these editions it is the Vosgian Gymnase which published the book, and which published it in "librariam officinam apud Lotharingie Vosagum in oppido cui vocabulum est sancto Deodato." The dedication and the colophon are in the one case in perfect harmony. In the other case they do not agree, and suspicion is aroused. If the reader will turn to our facsimile of the colophon, on page 166, he will notice that the intertwined letters M. I., the initial letters standing for Martinus Ilacomilus, are of larger dimensions than those letters which stand for the names of Nicolas Lud and his brother Gaultier Lud. The Gymnase itself recognized from first to last the labors and accomplishments of Waldseemüller. If the Gymnase had intended robbing Waldseemüller of his rights, it would have omitted his name from the colophon. The robber who steals a watch does not leave his victim in peaceable possession of his purse. No, this unique copy is a mongrel, yet swift and true as the light of the kennels; base, yet a gem; unacknowledged, yet full of honor.

The May (1507) edition of the "Cosmographiæ Introductio" may well form a fitting corner-stone on which to build an American library. There are some nine or ten examples of this edition known, of which all but three are in public libraries. Five of these copies are owned in the United States, while another is in the National Library of Rio de Janeiro. The example of this book which Cancellieri once saw in the Vatican, and which is referred to by Foscarini, Napione, d'Avezac, as well as by later writers, is believed to be now in this country. If this is so, the interment of a rare book in a public library does not remove it forever from the hope of the collector.

We close this bibliographical dissertation on the four editions by reprinting a note from the late Henry C. Murphy of Brooklyn, written to Henry Harrisse in 1872:

> I have had the opportunity of examining carefully all the copies of the "Cosmographiæ Introductio" printed at St.-Dié in the possession of Mr. J. Carter Brown, Mr. Griswold, and myself, and have arrived at a perfect conviction, which the minute actual comparison by inspection would

create in any mind used to the collation of books, that the Eyriès-Yéméniz copy [the unique example and so-called first edition] is not an original edition but is made up by the interpolation of four leaves (the 1st, 2d, 5th, and 6th), or rather substitution of them, in place of the corresponding leaves in the edition designated by M. d'Avezac as the second, and that the second and third editions according to his arrangement are the only original editions; his first [our so-called first edition] and fourth being variations alike made up from the second and third in the manner before stated.

Mr. Murphy at one and the same time had in his possession examples of the alleged four editions, a privilege not enjoyed by D' Avezac or by Harrisse, but which the kindness of the Trustees of the Lenox Library extended to the author, and which has permitted him, he ventures to hope, to definitely establish the priority of the alleged second edition.

CHAPTER V

The Baptismal Words

AFTER the dedication to Maximilian, the last lines of which occupy the upper part of the verso of *Aij*, comes the table of contents (Tractandorum ordo), or subjects of the nine chapters which compose the "Introductio Cosmographiæ." The Arabic numerals in the margin, beginning with 2, mark these nine heads. The following are the proper headings of the nine chapters:

1. De principiis Geometriæ ad spheræ noticiam necessariis.
2. Quid sphera, axis, poli &c. strictissime perdocet.
3. De circvlis cœli.
4. De quadam spheræ Theorica secundū graduum rationes.
5. De quinq̢ Zonis cœlestibus, earundemq̢ & graduū cœli ad terrā applicatione.
6. De parallelis.
7. De climatibus.
8. De ventis.
9. De quibusdam Cosmographiæ rudimentis.

Then comes the announcement that the four voyages of Americus Vespucius will follow the Introduction to Cosmography.

It is on the recto of *Aiij* that this little work really begins and forms the first chapter. On the verso of *Aiij*, at the bottom of the page, is the beginning of the second chapter.

CAPVT SECVNDVM QVID SPHERA, axis, poli &c. strictissime perdocet.

Anteaq̢ aliquis Cosmographiæ noticiā habere possit, necessum est vt spheræ materialis cognitionem habeat. Post quod vniuersi orbis descriptionē primo a Ptholomæo atq̢ alijs traditam, & deinde per alios amplificatā, nuper vero ab Americo Vesputio latius illustratā facilius intelliget.

Second Chapter, which treats of the sphere, the axis, the poles, etc., accurately explained.

Before any one can have knowledge of Geography, it is necessary he should become acquainted with the material sphere. After which one may more easily understand a description of the entire world as handed down to us first from Ptolemy and afterward more fully described by others, and in these latter days more widely disclosed by Americus Vespucius.

On the verso of *Bij* is a large woodcut figure of the axis of the earth and the axis of the zodiac, with the arctic and antarctic poles. On the verso of *Biij* occurs the following passage:

Sunt eṁ qui exustam torridamqȝ zonam nūc habitant multi. Vt qui Chersonesum auream incolūt, ut Taprobanenses, Aethiopes, et maxima pars terræ semper incognitæ nuper ab Americo Vesputio repertæ. Qua de re ipsius quatuor subiungentur nauigationes ex Italico sermone in Gallicum & ex Gallico in latinum versæ.

Indeed there are many now who dwell in the dry and torrid belt, as those who inhabit the golden Chersonese, as the inhabitants of Ceylon, of Ethiopia, and of the greatest part of the earth always hitherto unknown but lately discovered by Americus Vespucius. Concerning which latter there is hereto joined the narration of his four voyages rendered from Italian into French, and again from French into Latin.

On the recto of *Biiij* is another woodcut figure, 4⅝ inches in diameter, of the material sphere, showing the equatorial line, the two poles, the temperate, torrid, and frigid zones, and the six "climata." Between *Biiij* and *a*, in our copy, occurs the great folded woodcut figure of the sphere, 7⅜ inches in diameter. In the Eyriès copy this map is properly placed on the folded leaf immediately following *aiiij*. This is another illustration of the correction of an incorrect copy, and confirms the priority in time as to its issuing from the press of the incorrect or so-called second edition. For the sake of order we pass this remarkable double leaf to return to it in a moment.

On the recto of *aiij* is the following passage, reproduced in facsimile on page 158:

In the sixth climatic region, towards the Antarctic, are situated the extreme part of Africa lately discovered, and the islands of Zanzibar, Java Minor, and Seula, and the fourth part of the world (which, because Americus discovered it, it is proper to call Amerigen, that is, the land of Americus or America).

This, then, is that simple sentence composed by an unknown geographer and printed in an obscure town in a remote corner of the earth, which christened a new world and fixed upon it forever its pleasant sounding name. From the foundation of the world great things have come from mean places. No council of kings and wise men was called to name the newly discovered fourth part of the world. The holder of St. Peter's chair promulgated no bull to formally baptize the new continent. It was not the accidental association of a name and a thing. It was not a suggestion to make permanent some appellation which by chance had fallen on a land. A young German student, enthusiastic and imaginative, reading a narrative of distant voyages and magnifying the deeds of a skilful pilot and learned astrolabist, deemed it a mere act of justice to forever identify so marvelous a land with the traveler and discoverer. That he confounded Americus with the first discoverer of the new world is absurd, for the former in his narration distinctly credits Christopher Columbus with that distinguished honor.

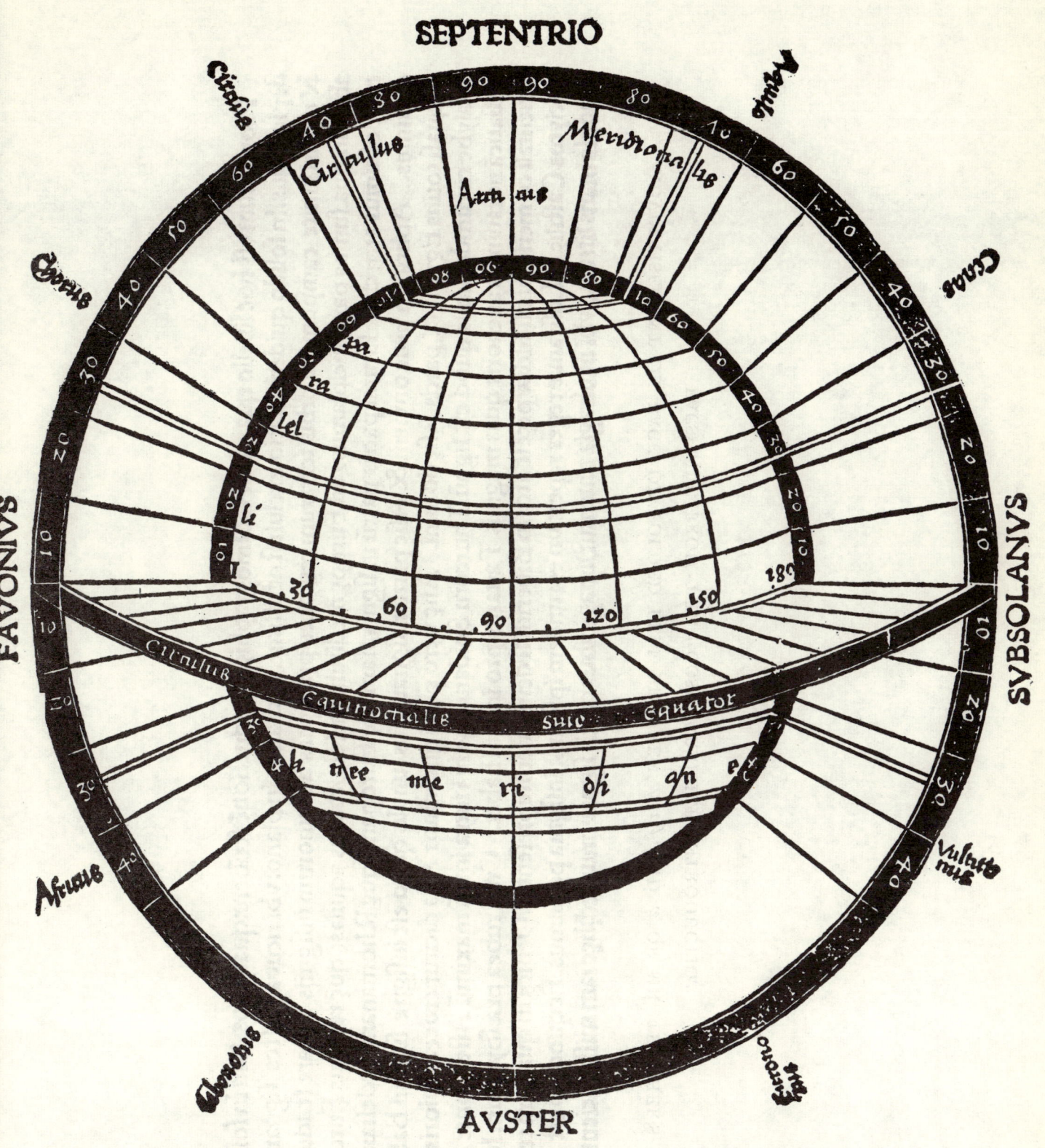

WOODCUT FIGURE ON FOLDED LEAF BETWEEN *Biij* AND *a* OF MR. THACHER'S COPY. FACSIMILE FROM THE "COSMOGRAPHIÆ INTRODUCTIO."

Propositum est hoc libello quandam Cosmographiæ introductionẽ scribere:quam nos tam in solido ɋ plano depinximus.In solido quidem spacio exclusi strictissime.Sed latius in plano:vbi sicut agrestes signare asueuerunt & partiri limite campum/ita orbis terrarum regiones præcipuas dominorum insignijs notare studuimus. Et(vt abea in qua sumus parte incipiamus)ad Europæ mediullium Rhomanas aquilas(quę regibus Europę dominan tur)posuimus atɋ claue summi patris patriũ ipsam fere Europam(quę Rhomanam ecclesiam profitetur) cinximus. Aphricam pene omnem & Asię domini. Asię vero parẽ quę minor Asia dicitur crocee coloris cruce iuncto ni quasi rotius Egypti & partis Asię domini. Asię vero parẽ quę minor Asia dicitur crocee coloris cruce iuncto chalybe circumdedimus quod est signũ Thurcorũ Soldani Scythia intra imaũ maximũ Asie monte & Sarmaticã Asiaticã notauimus anchoris quas magnus Tatarus pro insigni habet. Crux rubea præsbyterum Ioanne(qui et orientali & meridionali Indiæ præst atɋ in Biberith sedem tenet)repræsentat.Denique in quartam terre parte per inclyos Castilię et Lusitaniæ reges repertam eorundem ipsorum insignia posuimus. Et quod nõ est ignorandum vadosa maris littora(vbi naufragia timentur)imaginibus crucis signauimus sed hęc iam missa facientes.

ADVERTISEMENT ON BACK OF FOLDED LEAF BETWEEN *Biiij* AND *a* OF MR. THACHER'S COPY.

FACSIMILE FROM THE "COSMOGRAPHIÆ INTRODUCTIO."

CHAPTER VI

The Lost Map

ON the verso of *aiiij* occurs the following passage:

> Hucuscǫ de ventis dictū sufficiat. Ponamus nūc
> haʀ omniū figurā vniuersalē: in qua sint poli, axes,
> circuli cū maiores tum etiam minores, oriens, occi-
> dens, quincǫ zonæ, gradus lōgitudinis, latitudinis
> ★ tam ipsius terræ c̄p̄ cœli, paralleli, climata, venti, &c.

Enough has now been said about winds. We present now a universal figure of all these things: in which figure are poles, axes, circles, great and small, east, west, five zones, degrees of longitude and latitude of the earth itself and the heavens, parallels, regions, winds, etc.

On the left hand margin of this passage is a large black asterisk, and it is here, adjoining this page, that should be found the woodcut figure on the folded leaf which, we have said, appears in our copy between *Biiij* and *a*. A facsimile of this woodcut will be seen on page 147. On the back of this leaf, occupying twelve lines extending across the entire leaf, is an advertisement, reproduced in facsimile on opposite page, and the translation of which is as follows:

It is proposed in this book to write an introduction to the Cosmography which we have drawn upon a globe as well as upon a plane surface. In constructing the globe we have been very restricted as to space. But we have had more room in making our map; on which, in the same manner as the country people are accustomed to mark their fields and to define the boundaries thereof, we have been careful to distinguish the principal countries of the earth by means of the standards of their rulers. And (in order to begin with that country which we ourselves inhabit) we have placed in the central part of Europe the Roman eagles (which are symbols of authority among the kings of Europe) and we have marked part of Europe (which recognizes the church of Rome) by the keys, the characteristic symbol of the sovereign lord of the faithful. We have marked almost the entire continent of Africa and a part of Asia with the crescents which are the arms of the Sultan of Babylon, the sovereign of the whole of Egypt and of part of Asia. As to that part of Asia which is called Asia Minor, we have distinguished it by a cross, yellow in color, together with a sword, which are symbolic of the Sultan of Turkey. Scythia, the realm of the Imaus, the great mountains of Asia, as well as the Asiatic Sarmatia, we have designated by anchors, which are the arms of Great Tartary. A red cross represents Prester John, who rules over the Eastern and Southern Indies, and whose capital is in Biberith. Finally, in the fourth part of the world discovered by the illustrious kings of Castile and Portugal, we have placed the standards belonging to their kingdoms. And what is particularly to be noticed, we have marked those coasts which are fringed with shoals, and where consequently shipwreck is to be feared, with figures of the cross, which will serve to point them out.

It is at this point that we may consider a historical and bibliographical mystery. What has become of the map or planisphere here advertised? No copy of this map has ever been found, and if we have a trace, it is uncertain and unsatisfactory. We have seen Ringmann and his companions at Strasburg in the summer of 1505, deeply interested in the study of cosmography, and particularly and critically examining the maps of Ptolemy. We have read the letter of Waldseemüller to Johannes Amerbach, of Basle, written from St.-Dié, April 5, 1507, in which he says that they are engaged in printing a cosmography of Ptolemy and are adding thereto some new maps. We have the above formal advertisement announcing the forthcoming publication of the map with detailed information as to its contents.

In the famous "Speculum Orbis" of Gaultier Lud, printed at Strasburg in 1507, there is an interesting allusion to this map:

Accedamus nunc ad Speculi usum et commoditatem. Licet omnium primum in versatili et cosmographica rota (quæ maris, montium et fluviorum plena conspicitur) quæcumque famigeratissima terræ loca, insulas, pelagi tractus, quantum præsentis instrumenti captus potuit pati, clarissime videre. Fuit autem impossibile omnem pagum aut civitatem, quin etiam quamvis ignobilem regionem in re tam arcta comprehendere. Cernis vero partes terræ Europam, Asiam, Africam, et quamlibet illarum in nominatissimas urbes, montes, flumina et insulas divisam. Quia tamen propter spacii parvitatem non omnia loca introduci potuerunt extendimus eam saltem partem quam nos inhabitamus id est Europam, quæ versus polum arcticum et ipsum æquatorem xxx gradibus in latitudinem prætenditur ita quod quinque ejus gradus jaceant ultra circulum cancri; et in longitudinem lxxxiij grad. ab occidente orientem versus. Cujus principales partes sunt Germania, Italia, et Gallia usque ad Hispaniam, quas singillatim in civitates, montes, flumina, etc., partiti sumus.

Non tamen imus inficias in extensæ illius Europæ locum congruenter poni posse quem de ignota terra per Lusitaniæ regem pridem et post paratum Orbis Speculum inventa propere paravimus typum. De qua ora plura et veriora in Ptolomæo per nos et Martinum Ilacomylum talium rerum scientissimum cum multis additamentis recognito (quem nostris impensis mox Christo favente imprimemus) videre licebit. Quorum etiam regionum descriptionem ex Portugallia ad te Illustrissime rex Renate, gallico sermone missam Joannes Basinus Sendacurius insignis poeta, a me exoratus qua pollet elegantia latine interpretavit. Et circumferunt bibliopolæ passim ea de re nostri Philesii Vogesigenæ quoddam epigramma in libello Vespucii per Jocundum Veronensem qui apud Venetos architecti munere fungitur ex Italico in latinum sermonem verso impressum quod his subjicere libuit.

We come now to the use and advantage of this Mirror [of the World]. One may at first see very clearly upon the movable cosmographical disk (which is occupied by the sea, the mountains, and the rivers) all the most renowned places of the earth, the islands, the sea coasts, as well as the dimensions of the present diagram may permit. It was impossible, however, to include within such narrow limits every village, city, or even smaller provinces. You see here, nevertheless, the divisions of the world, Europe, Asia, and Africa, and in each of these are indicated the principal cities, mountains, rivers, and islands. As however, on account of the limitations of space, all these places could not be introduced here, we have enlarged that part which we inhabit, that is to say Europe, which extends over a latitude of thirty degrees between the arctic pole and the equator, in such a way that five of these degrees stretch beyond the tropic of Cancer; and over a longitude of eighty-three degrees from west to east; its principal countries are Germany, Italy, and France down to Spain, which countries we have respectively subdivided into their cities, mountains, rivers, etc.

We do not wish to deny that, in place of so greatly enlarging Europe, it might have been desirable to put the figure of the unknown world which we have hastily prepared, discovered by the King of Portugal recently, subsequently, however, to the preparation of this "Speculum Orbis." One will be able to see a more detailed and exact representation of this coast in the Ptolemy (which by the aid of God we shall soon publish at our expense), revised and greatly augmented by us and by Martin Waldseemüller, a most skilful man in such matters. A description of these regions, which has been sent you in the French language from Portugal, illustrious King René, has been, at my earnest request, translated into the Latin tongue by the eminent poet Jean Basin de Sendacour with that elegance of diction which distinguishes him. There circulate about the country, among the libraries, some verses of our Vosgian Ringmann upon this same subject, printed in the book of Vespucius, translated from the Italian into the Latin tongue by Giocondo of Verona, who practises his profession of architect at Venice. It has pleased us to repeat these verses here.

It is apparent from this book, published subsequently to the "Cosmographiæ Introductio," that the great map is not yet published, and also that there has been no rupture between the coterie belonging to the Vosgian Gymnase. Waldseemüller receives the highest praise from Gaultier Lud, and they are all working in union and harmony. This book was issued from the press of Johannes Grüninger in Strasburg, the printer of the 1509 edition of the "Cosmographiæ Introductio."

But where is this Waldseemüller map? We well remember a few days of exquisite anxiety when, after reading in the catalogue of a German antiquarian bookseller that there was for sale a copy of the "Cosmographia" containing the map of the world, we cabled wildly for the book, and knew no sleep until the cruel cable brought reply that the map of the world was only the folded woodcut of the poles and circles.

There is on record an interesting letter from the Benedictine priest John Heidenberg of Trittenheim, abbé of Saint Jacques in Würzburg, written on the 12th of August, 1507, to his friend, the theologian and mathematician William de Velde, himself the author of a geographical globe.

> Joannes Trithemius abbas divi Jacobi Herbipolensis, Wilhelmo Veldico Monapio plebano in Dyrmstein, theologo et mathematico nobis amicissimo salutem.
> . . . Orbem terræ marisque et insularum quem pulchre depictum in Wormatia scribis esse venalem, me quidem consequi posse optarem, sed quadraginta pro illo expendere florenos nemo mihi facile persuadet. Comparavi autem mihi ante paucos dies pro ære modico sphæram orbis pulchram in quantitate parva nuper Argentinæ impressam, simul et in magna dispositione globum terræ in plano expansum, cum insulis et regionibus noviter ab Americo Vesputio hispano inventis in mare occidentali ac versus meridiem ad parallelum ferme decimum, cum quibusdam aliis ad eam speculationem pertinentibus. . . . Ex Herbipoli duodecima die mensis augusti anno christianorum millesimo quingentesimo septimo.

. . . You write me that there is on sale at Worms a globe of the earth, seas, and islands, beautifully constructed, which I might desire to possess. But I could not easily be persuaded to expend forty florins for it. I obtained for myself a little time ago, for a moderate sum, a splendid map on a small scale lately printed at Strasburg, and at the same time a map of the earth in large size expanded as a planisphere, with islands and regions lately discovered by the Spaniard, Americus Vespucius, in the western ocean, toward the south almost to the tenth [50°] parallel, together with some other matters pertaining to this same exploration . . . Würzburg, the 12th day of August, in the year of our Lord 1507.

The tenth parallel is equal to the fiftieth degree of latitude, following the old custom of spacing the meridians and parallels by intervals of five degrees. The distinct declaration that the map was printed at Strasburg bears out the opinion we have always had, that the press facilities at St.-Dié would not admit of such a class of work as map printing on a large scale. It was but a step to Strasburg, an important center of the art of printing.

The planisphere to which reference is here made is also distinctly stated to be of large size. The term is relative, but those who were interested in the study of cosmography in those days had maps of various sizes from which to form comparisons. Manuscript maps at the beginning of the sixteenth century were generally very large. The Ptolemaic maps of 1478, 1482, and 1486 were of good size. A map the size of these could not have been intended for insertion in a book of the dimensions of the "Cosmographia." It may have been intended to accompany it in a folded form. If the various nations had their standards and arms printed in different colors, and if it embraced, as was advertised, the entire world, the map must have been larger than any printed map of that period which has been preserved to our day.

Trithemius was himself an amateur geographer, and evidently regarded his purchase as something unusual in its form as well as in the reasonable limit of its price. No other map is known to have been printed in Strasburg, and Ortelius speaks of Hylacomylus as having issued his map in Germany. St.-Dié was a French possession, while Strasburg was a well-known and important German city. Some writers have estimated the size of his map as equal to four of the Waldseemüller maps in the Ptolemy of 1513. There was published in 1511 at Strasburg a little work which will throw some light on this matter, and at least establish the approximate time at which the famous lost map was published.

This book is entitled:

INSTRUCTIO MANUDUCTIONEM PRESTANS IN CARTAM ITINERARIAM MARTINI HILACOMILI: CUM LUCULENTIORI IPSIUS EUROPAE ENARRATIONE A RINGMANNO PHILESIO CONSCRIPTA.

The book is a small quarto of twenty-two leaves. The following dedication to Duke Anthony, who succeeded his father on December 10, 1508, is on the recto of leaf II.

Illustrissimo Principi Anthonio Lothoringiæ ac Barri Duci: Martinus Hylacomylus sese humiliter commendat.

Mos fuit olim illustrissime princeps Parthorum reges salutare: sed id non sine munere. Ego quoque in præsentia cum te salutare instituissem: putavi id aliquo munusculo faciendum. Munusculo autem non aureo (neque enim tu auro eges: qui inter ceteros principes ut generis nobilitate ita etiam divitiis plurimum polles) sed cartaceo et eo quidem hujusmodi quo illustris genitor tuus Renatus ij Syciliæ rex: qui pridem e sæculo migrans hanc vitam cum celesti commutavit: mirum in modum delectatus fuisset. Erat enim optimarum artium studijs præstantium principum præstantissimus: et litterarum litteratorumque amantissimus: cui quicquid industrij ac sagacis acumen ingenij; præ se ferebat dici non potest quantum semper placuerit. Neque enim obliti sumus qua aurium clementia: quam hilari vultu et quam grato animo generalem orbis descriptionem: ac alia etiam litterarij laboris nostri monimenta sibi oblata a nobis susceperit. Et quia cuncti passim predicant per omnium virtutum gradus te ipsius vestigia insequi: nulli principum quam tibi nostram Europæ cartam offerendam existimaui: qua principaliores Christianitatis regiones: oppida: urbes: montes: flumina (ut quæque sita sunt) certis eorundem distantiis observatis: non sine regum ac principum insignibus: hominum oculis subjeci. Obsecro igitur supplex ut qualemcumque hunc laborem nostrum: una cum compendiosa ipsius enarratione a Philesio concinnata: faustissimo nomini tuo dicatum serena fronte excipere digneris. Quod ubi factum intellexero habunde mihi occasionem putabo datam ut et indefessa cura quædam id generis jam inchoata absolvam: et alacriori etiam animo cetera obire non dubitem. VALE princeps illustrissime.

Ex oppido Divi Deodati Anno Dni M. D. XI. kl, martii.

It was formerly the custom, illustrious prince, never to salute the Parthian kings except when bearing them gifts. I also, entertaining now the idea of saluting you, have thought that I ought to come bearing some present; not of gold (for you have no need of gold, you who are powerful among princes in possessions as well as in station), but with a gift in paper, and of a kind with which your illustrious father, René II, King of Sicily, who a few years ago departed this life to join the blessed saints, would have been extremely satisfied. He was indeed the most preëminent among those princes who are distinguished by reason of their excellent education; a great friend of letters and of the learned; and in whose sight any one of genius and ability was sure to find favor beyond our power to relate. For we have not forgotten with what indulgent attention, with what an agreeable countenance, and with what gracious disposition he accepted a general map of the world, and some other examples of our literary work, which we presented to him. And as all the world, without exception, declares that you are following in his footsteps in all ways meritorious, I have thought that to no other prince than you was due the offer of our map of Europe, in which I have put before the public the principal countries of Christendom, the villages and cities, the mountains and rivers, as to where all are situated, maintaining their relative distances, not omitting the arms of the kings and princes. I then humbly beg of you to accept with benevolence our work with the explanatory summary prepared by Ringmann, and let it have the valuable support of your name. When I shall have that assurance I will make it a fruitful occasion to finish carefully other works of the kind already in course of preparation, and undertake still others with more enthusiasm. Farewell, most illustrious prince. From the city of St.-Dié, March 1, 1511.

CHAPTER VII

The Lost Map, Concluded

E can thus fix the date when this map was issued as *after* April 25, 1507, the date when the "Cosmographiæ Introductio," advertising the forthcoming map, was first given to the world, and as *before* December 10, 1508, when, according to the above dedication, it had been already formally presented to, and graciously accepted by, King René II. If we can identify Waldseemüller's map with the one bought by Trithemius prior to August 12, 1507, it brings its date of publication only a little earlier than the so-called third and fourth editions of the "Cosmographiæ Introductio" dated August 29, 1507, in which the same proposition or advertisement is repeated. Moreover, it is worthy of note that, according to the subscription of the letter which closes the preceding chapter, Waldseemüller was still at St.-Dié on the first day of March, 1511, and apparently in a cheerful state of mind. The book itself, however, in which this letter appeared, was printed, as the colophon shows, the following month from the press of Johannes Grüninger, the printer of the 1509 edition of the "Cosmographiæ Introductio."

On leaf *V* of the same book is the following interesting letter from Ringmann to Waldseemüller:

Philesius Vogesigena Martino Hylacomylo S. P. D.

Cum Cosmographiæ noticia non parum conducibilis esse inveniatur: plurimum tibi devincis Martine studiosorum pectora. qui cum pridem generalem totius orbis typum dedalissime publicaveris: et non parvo jam tempore in describendis tabulis Ptolemei magnam locaveris operam: putans id satis non esse: nunc solam Europam latissime extensam hominum oculis conspiciendam miro ingenio parare voluisti. Ita ut partiales provinciæ: montes: flumina: civitates. Hispaniæ. Galliæ. Britanniæ. Germaniæ. Italiæ. Poloniæ. Hungariæ. Bohemiæ cæterarumque Europæ regionum paucis dumtaxat exceptis quæ hac in area tetragona comprehendi non poterant sub certa dimensione et miliarium ab invicem distantia clarissime intueri liceat adjectis omniquaque ad latera Cæsaris. regum. principum. ducum cæterorumque potentatuum armis (quæ propriis ac veris coloribus distincta conspiciuntur) non sine labore conquisitis. quæ omnia sunt allatura utilitatem pariter ac voluptatem non modicam spectatoribus talium rerum studiosis. Equidem nunc ipsum Europæ typum inspiciens et perpendens quam valida sit Hispania quam opulens et bellicosa Gallia: quam ampla pariter ac populosa robustissimorumque ferax virorum Germania: quam fortis Britannia quam audax Polonia: quam strenua Hungaria.

et (ut alia pleraque regna non pœnitenda prætereamus) quam dives et animosa rerumque bellicarum perita Italia: non potui non multum dolere acerbissima: pernitiosa: et funesta bella a nostris geri principibus: qui continuis dissidijs et privatis odijs inter se de agri possessione: de regno: de imperio: de gloria contendentes dum domi dissident: a Thurca et fidei nostræ hostibus Christianum sanguinem effundi: urbes deleri: vastari agros: sacras ædes incendi rapi virgines: violari matronas: et quæcumque immanissima scelera perpetrari patiuntur. Qui si hujusmodi graves periculosasque seditiones inimicicias et simultates tollerent: si unanimes essent et pacem inter se haberent: conjunctisque viribus adversus communem hostem arma sumerent: facile toti orbi frena imponerent: et Christum qui in Europa duntaxat: nec in ipsa quidem tota colitur (sicut ante adventum Christi notus solum in Judea Deus) omnibus gentibus præberent colendum. Sed quid laterem lavo? Cum mihi præsentata esset hæc Europæ pictura: eamque omniquaque lustrarem: et non mihi modo plus quam queat dici placeret: verumetiam a clarissimo atque doctissimo viro Andrea Reginio mirificis laudibus extolleretur: putavi me tibi et plerisque aliis harum rerum studiosis non ingratam facturum: si breviter atque in transcursu quodam: insigniores Europæ regiones: civitates: montes: flumina attingeremus: eaque ita in libellum collecta ad te mitteremus: ut si tibi ad rei intelligentiam nonnihil conducere visa fuerint pro libitu addas: demas corrigasque: et una cum ipso typo in lucem prodire patiaris. VALE. Cursim ex Nanceio.

Ringmann to Martin Waldseemüller, greeting:

Since it is acknowledged that the science of Cosmography is of great utility, you have won, Martin, the esteem of many studious people in having formerly published a general map of the entire world, very artistically made, and in having devoted yourself for so long a time to drawing the Ptolemaic maps; and finding that even that is not enough, you have wished to prepare with marvelous skill and to give to the public a very extensive map of Europe alone in such wise that one may see clearly, with their exact area and their relative distances in miles, the provincial subdivisions, the mountains, the rivers, the cities of Spain, France, Great Britain, Germany, Italy, Poland, Hungary, Bohemia, and of the other countries of Europe, with exception only of a few, which could not be put in, owing to the dimensions of the map, adding round about on the margin the arms of the Emperor, of the Kings, Princes, Dukes, and of the other potentates (represented with their true colors), verified with considerable difficulty; a thing which will be of much use and interest to people who are curious in such matters. For myself, in regarding this same map of Europe and considering how powerful is Spain, how rich and warlike is France, how great is Germany, and how robust are her men, how strong is Great Britain, how brave is Poland, how valiant is Hungary, and (in leaving unmentioned many States not to be despised) how rich, courageous, and experienced in the military art is Italy, I could not but regret most grievously the cruel, harmful, and dreadful wars which our princes wage, their perpetual dissensions and personal hates, disputing forever among themselves questions of territory, sovereignty, supremacy, and self-aggrandizement, while they leave the Turk and the enemies of our faith to spill Christian blood, destroy cities, devastate countries, burn churches, carry off our daughters, violate our wives, and commit the greatest crimes. On the other hand, if they would but give up these serious and perilous quarrels, these enmities and hates, if adopting peace and uniting their forces they would take up arms against the common enemy, they would easily subjugate the entire world and cause the blessed Saviour, now adored in Europe alone and not even in the whole of Europe (in like manner as before the coming of Christ the true God was known only in Judea), to be the object of worship by all nations. But why continue? When this map of Europe was shown me, when looking it over in all its aspects, not only did it please me more than I can tell, but was also the object of the most lavish praise by the celebrated and wise Andreas Reginius; I thought that I should be doing something which would not be disagreeable either to you nor to many other lovers of these things, if we should sketch briefly, as it were in passing, the principal countries, cities, mountains, and rivers of Europe, and if we should send you all this gathered together in one book in such a way that, should it seem to you to be of some use to the understanding of the matter, you might add to it, abridge it or correct it at your will, and might authorize its publication at the same time as that of your map. Farewell. In haste [dated] from Nancy.

We come now to where Waldseemüller is evidently preparing another and entirely different geographical work. It is a map of Europe alone, not only to be distinguished from the Ptolemaic maps, but to be distinguished from some former cosmographical work of Waldseemüller called a "map of the entire world." These are the maps found in the Ptolemy of 1513, printed in Strasburg at the press of Johannes Schottus. The following address to the reader is interesting as connecting this edition of Ptolemy with the work of the little coterie in the Vosgian Gymnase where, six years before, their geographical studies bore their first fruits. The name of Waldseemüller does not appear anywhere in this edition, and it was reserved for the 1522 edition of Ptolemy, printed by Johannes Grüninger, to do honor to the memory of Martinus Hylacomylus lately deceased. The following is the address to the reader:

AD LECTOREM.

Ne vero te Lector optime, nescio quis vel erroris, vel admirationis scrupulus seducat: placuit brevibus quæ scitu digna sint recensere. Ptolemæi Geographiam prima parte clausimus operis: ut incorruptior et selecta stet antiquitas sua. Verum quia temporis lapsus multa quidem labilitate quoque sua in dies mutat: plerisque visus est auctor notabilius a modernioribus deviasse. Id quod cernere licet in utraque Pannonia, quæ nunc Hungaria et Austria vocatur. Et quæ regio dum floruit unica appellatione Sarmatia, sive Sauromatia dicebatur: nunc divisim Poloniam, Russiam, Prussiam, Moscoviam et Lituaniam nominamus. Populorum denique usui placuit transmutatio vocabulorum. Quos enim vetustas Elvetios et Sequanos, nunc vulgo Burgundiones Suitensesque vocamus. Quædam et civitates primitivis nominibus orbatæ sunt. Quis enim juxta Rhenum fluvium, Canodurum, Augustam rauricum, Elcebum et Berthomagum urbes a Ptolemæo commemoratas digito monstrabit? Hæc vel his similia non est qui Auctoris imperitiæ subscribat. Quin potius hoc Supplemento modernioris lustrationis discat se ipsum certius informare. Qua tripartiti orbis explanationem planius ad tempora nostra videbit. Charta autem Marina, quam Hydrographiam vocant, per Admiralem quondam serenissimi Portugaliæ regis Ferdinandi, cæteros denique lustratores verissimis peragrationibus lustrata: ministerio Renati dum vixit, nunc pie mortui Ducis illustrissimi Lotharingiæ liberius prælographationi tradita est: cum certis tabulis a fronte hujus chartæ specificatis. Cujus item Ducis illustrissimi honori cedit extensa ad finem Dominii sui tabula studiosissime pressa. Nam ejus terræ latebris, Vosagi dico rupibus nobile hoc opus incœptum, licet quorumdam desidia ferme sopitum, a sexennali sopore per nos tandem excitatum est. In reliquis etiam tabulis non minus studium est adhibitum: quo limatius ex variis lustratorum prototypis transformarentur. Quod in Italia duplici planum est assentiri. Tabularum ergo harum neotericæ positiones Lector optime, sicubi a Ptolemæi traditionibus antiquis alienæ tibi videbuntur, non miraberis cum quæ Cæsareæ dedicationi supposita sunt in primæ partis protofolio studiosius ad hæc perlegeris. Cumque didiceris in his veram cœli latitudinem observatum. Regionum quippe longitudinem scrutari laboriosum est valde. Hinc variam causat situationem dimensio quoque varia. Tuum sit pro grata pietate quadrata longis aptare: ne vel illius antiquitatis, vel laboris nostri judiceris censor ingratus. Sufficiant inquam hæc post Majorum antiquitates fidelius lucubrasse, quæ sæculo suo certius respondeant. Vale.

In order, indulgent reader, that you may not be misled by a misconception or a mistaken anticipation, it seems best to state briefly that which it is essential to know. We have confined the Geography of Ptolemy to the first part of this work, in order that what is ancient should be kept distinct and separate from the rest. But as the course of time brings each day many changes, it has seemed to many people that the author would find himself drawn too far away from modern conditions; which is especially noticeable in the case of the two Pannonias, which are called to-day Hungary and

Austria; and the country which was formerly known by the single name of Sarmatia or Sauromatia, now bears the various names of Poland, Russia, Prussia, Moscovy, and Lithuania. The changes in the names of nations have also passed into common usage, and those who were once known as Helvetians and Sequanians, are now commonly called Burgundians and Swiss. Some cities have also lost their primitive names. Who, following the course of the Rhine, can put his finger now upon the cities Canodurum, Augusta Rauricum, Elcebus and Berthomagus mentioned by Ptolemy? These things and others like them should not be imputed to ignorance on the part of the author. It will consequently be better to inform oneself more accurately by means of this supplement devoted to modern explorations, where one will find a representation of the three parts of the world better adapted to our times. The marine map or hydrography, as it is called, corrected by means of exact navigations, first made by an admiral of the most serene King Ferdinand of Portugal [Castile(?)], and in later times by other explorers, was made possible for publication by the generosity of the illustrious René, then the reigning Duke of Lorraine, to-day, alas! dead; as were also certain other maps specified upon the frontispiece here opposed. To the honor of that illustrious Duke is due also the detailed map of his own states at the end of the volume, printed with particular care, for it was in a corner of that same country, I mean in the heart of the Vosgian Mountains, that the present work was commenced, which, in a measure forgotten through the negligence of some, is now finally awakened by us from a sleep of six years. No less care has been brought to the production of the other maps in order the better to revise them in accordance with the various accounts of travelers, as is easily authenticated in the case of the double map of Italy. If then, indulgent reader, the new positions on these maps appear to you different from the ancient traditions of Ptolemy, you will not be surprised, if you read attentively that which is said on this subject in the dedication to the Emperor, on the first page of the first part, and when you learn that the true astronomical latitudes have been observed in them. As regards longitudes, it is very difficult to determine them; thus it happens that differences of measure cause also differences of position. Kindly combine the surfaces with the distances, so that you may not appear as an unjust censor either of the works of the ancients or of our own labors. Let us be satisfied, say I, to have faithfully reproduced what, according to the traditions of the ancients, was in keeping with their age.

Henry Harrisse, in his "Discovery of North America," London and Paris, 1892, believes the lost 1507 Waldseemüller map would disclose a decided change of chartographical type so far as it relates to the New World, and a combination of Portuguese and German chartography. He believes that if one could find that map it would show a continuous coast line uniting North and South America, and that in every essential feature it would present the lines reproduced by the Stobnicza Ptolemy printed at Cracow in 1512, and the Waldseemüller Ptolemy printed in Strasburg in 1513. But the mystery of the map is a mystery still. Somewhere, in some dark corner of a monastic library, folded away in some oak-bound volume, a copy may be sleeping. The hand which awakens it will touch the most important of bibliographical prizes.

COSMOGRPHIAE

Capadociam/Pamphiliam/Lidiam/Ciliciã/Armenias maiorē & minorē. Colchiden/Hircaniam/Hiberiam/Albaniã: et pręterea mltas quas fingilatim enumerare longa mora esset. Ita dicta ab eius nominis regina.

Nūc v̄o & hę partes sunt latius lustratæ/& alia quarta pars per Americũ Vesputiũ (vt in sequentibus audietur) inuenta est/quã non video cur quis iure vetet ab Americo inuentore sagacis ingenij viro Amerigen quasi Americi terrã / siue Americam **Ameri-** dicendã: cũ & Europa & Asia a mulieribus sua for-**ca** tita sint nomina: Eius situ & gentis mores ex bis bi nis Americi nauigationibus quæ sequunt liquide intelligi datur.

Hunc in modũ terra iam quadripartita cognoscit̄ et sunt tres prinę partes cōtinentes/quarta est insula: cũ omni quaq mari circudata conspiciaī. Et licet mare vnũ sit queadmodũ et ipsa tellus/multis tamen finibus distinctum/& innumeris repletum insulis varia sibi noīa assumit: quę et in Cosmogra-**Prīscia-** phiæ tabulis cōspiciunt/& Prīscianus in tralatione **nus.** Dionisij talibus enumerat versibus.

Circuit Oceani gurges tamen vndiq vastus
Qui q̄uis vnus sit plurima nomina sumit.
Finibus Hesperijs Athlanticus ille vocatur
At Boreę qua gens furit Armiaspa sub armis.
Dicīt ille piger necnō Satur. idē Mortuus est alijs.

RVDIMENTA

Rhomes/ antidia Boristhenes: a gręca pticula anti q̄ oppositū vel cōtra denotat. Atq̄ in sexto climate Antarcticũ versus/& pars extrema Africæ nuper reperta &/Zamzibar/laua minor/& Seula insulę & quarta orbis pars (quam quia Americus inueuit **Ameri-** Amerigen /quasi Americi terrã / siue Americã nun **ca** cupare licet) sitæ sunt. De quibus Australibus dī ge matibus hęc Pomponij Mellę Geographi verba in telligēda sunt/vbi ait. Zonę habitabiles paria agūt **Pōpo-** anni tempora/verũ nō pariter. Antichthones alte- **Mellæ** ram/nos alteram incolimus. Illius situs ob ardorē in tercedentis plagę incognitus/huius dicendus est. Vbi animaduertendum est quod climatū quodq alios q aliud plerūq fœtus pducat/cū diuersę sint naturę/& alia atq alia syderũ virtute moderentur.

Vnde Virgilius.

Nec vero terrę ferre omnes omnia possunt **Vergi-**
Hic segetes/illic veniunt fœlicius vuę **lius**
Arboræi fœtus alibi/atq iniussa virescunt
Gramia. Nōne vides croceos vt Thmolus odores
India mittit ebur: mittūt sua thura Sabęi
At Calybes nudi ferrũ: virosaq pontus
Costerea. Eliadũ palmas: Epiros equarũ &c.

OCTAVVM CAPVT DE VENTIS.

Quoniã in superioribus ventorũ aliquando in cidenter memores fuimus (cū L. polū Boreũ/ polū Nothicũ/atq id genus alia diximus) & ipsorũ cor

a ij   in

CHAPTER VIII

The End of the Little Treatise on Geography

AFTER this digression let us return to our consideration of the "Cosmographiæ Introductio." On the verso of *av* is the celebrated passage which is regarded as the all-important baptizing phrase by those who are unacquainted with the preceding passage on the recto of *aiij*. Facsimiles of both these passages will be found on the opposite page. A translation of the passage on the recto of *aiij* we have already seen on page 146. The following is a translation of the passage on verso of *av*.

And now indeed these parts have been more widely explored, and another, a fourth part, of which we will presently speak more particularly, has been discovered by Americus Vespucius; I do not see why it may not be permitted to call this fourth part after Americus, the discoverer, a man of sagacious mind, by the name of Amerigen, that is to say, the land of Americus or America, since both Europe and Asia have obtained their names from women. Its situation and the customs of its people will be readily understood from the four voyages performed by Americus, and which here follow.

On the wide margin to the left the author adopts the feminine form of the name, and prints it in the nominative case, *America*. This is the first time this beautiful word was ever written by pen or engraved by tool or stamped by type. Therefore, perhaps, it is well to call this the christening sentence, the most important in the ritual of nomenclature. It is worthy of note that in setting up the edition or editions dated iiij of the Calends of September, the word used in the margin was *Americo*, the ablative case of the masculine form and occurring in the fourth line of the passage, the printer not noticing that the word in the margin of the May edition was not actually in the text, but was an addition suggested by the use of the accusative case of the feminine form. The nominative name is used again in the margin of the Strasburg 1509 edition. Harrisse, in his "Bibliotheca Americana Vetustissima," very truly says that but for this paragraph the western hemisphere might have been called "The Land of the Holy Cross"—as indeed it once was—or "Atlantis," or "Hesperides," or "Iberica," or "Columbia," or "New India," or "The Indies," as it is officially designated in

Spain to this day. The colophon of our book on the recto of *fvi* is dated *vij* Calends of May, 1507. The seventh of the Calends of May is the twenty-fifth day of April. This date is of the Julian calendar. In 1582 the calendar was reformed by Pope Gregory XIII., and adopting this corrected mode of reckoning, which for the rectifying of a date in the sixteenth century justifies the dropping of ten days, we have the fifth day of May as the baptismal or christening day of America. Thus we say the New World was born on the twenty-first day of October in the year 1492, and was baptized on the fifth day of May in the year 1507.

On the recto of *bi*, beginning with the eleventh line, is the following notice:

Hæc p inductione ad Cosmographiā dicta sufficiāt si te modo āmonuerimus prius, nos in depingendis tabulis typi generalis nō omnimodo sequutos esse Ptholomæū, præsertim circa nouas terras vbi in cartis marinis aliter animaduertimus æquatorem cōstitui q͞p Ptholomæus fæcerit. Et pinde nō debēt nos statim culpare qui illud ipm notauerint. Consulto eḿ fœcimus quod hic Ptholomeū, alibi cartas marinas sequuti sumus. Cū & ipse Ptholomæus quinto capite primi libri. Non omnes continentis partes ob suæ magnitudinis excessum ad ipsius peruenisse noticiam dicat, et aliquas quemadmodum se habeant ob peregrinantium negligentiam sibi minus diligenter traditas, alias esse quas aliter atq͗ alites se habere cōtingat ob corruptiones & mutationes in quibus p parte corruisse cognitæ sunt. Fuit igiť necesse (quod ipse sibi etiā faciundū ait) ad nouas temporis nostri, traditiones magis intendere. Et ita quidem temporauimus rem, vt in plano circa nouas terras & alia quæpiam Ptholomæū: in solido vero quod plano additur descriptionē Americi subsequentem sectati fuerimus.

These explanations of the introduction to cosmography will be sufficient if we but add here that we have not exclusively followed Ptolemy in the delineation of our general map of the world, especially as to the new lands in regard to which we have found the equator to occupy on marine maps a position different from that laid down by Ptolemy.

And those who may notice this should not reprove us. It is with full intention that we have followed sometimes Ptolemy and sometimes the marine maps. Ptolemy himself in the fifth chapter of his first book says that on account of their excessive vastness, certain parts of the continent have not come to his knowledge; and the condition of some lands has been by the negligence of travelers represented with little faithfulness, and there are still others which have fallen into other conditions on account of the revolutions and vicissitudes through which they are known to have passed. It has then been necessary (as Ptolemy himself said he intended to do in his own day) to keep account of the new relations of our own time. So we have divided the matter, following Ptolemy in the making of the planisphere, except concerning the new lands and some few other regions; but on the globe which accompanies the planisphere we have conformed to the description of Vespucius, which here follows.

On the verso of this same leaf is an appendix of twenty-one lines describing the method of taking the height of the pole by means of a quadrant or fourth of a circle, and on the recto of the next leaf, occupying two thirds of the page, is a woodcut figure of a circle, with its opposite quadrants marked off in degrees. At the bottom of the page, in four lines, is this sentence:

Hactenus exequuti capita proposita, hic ipsas longinquas expaciationes sequētur introducamus Vesputij, singulorum factorum exitum circa institutū tradentes.

Having thus accomplished the work proposed, we now proceed to introduce the distant voyages of Vespucius, narrating the events of each voyage as they occurred.

Ch. VIII THE END OF THE LITTLE TREATISE ON GEOGRAPHY

The work is closed with these two words, "Finis introductionis."

This concluded the "Cosmographiæ Introductio" and the work of Martin Waldseemüller. It has been said that the two works, the "Cosmographiæ Introductio" and the "Quatuor Navigationes," were printed separately, and that a copy is in the Grenville Library, British Museum, devoted to the voyages of Vespucius. R. H. Major, in a letter to M. d'Avezac dated July 24, 1866, stated that "it is catalogued as an integral work and has the appearance of so being." As the edition under consideration has the end of the "Cosmographiæ Introductio" on the recto of folio *bij*, and the beginning of the voyages, with the epistle of Philesius, on the verso of the same leaf, it is difficult to see how they could have been designed for separate issues.

CHAPTER IX

The Second Tract on the Four Voyages of Americus Vespucius

N the verso of *bij* are the eleven verses, each of two lines, composed by Ringmann, and addressed to the reader. We have seen that these elegiac verses, with a few changes, had appeared already in the "De Ora Antarctica," printed at Strasburg in 1505. On the margin of the page in the "Cosmographiæ Introductio" is a running guide of thirteen catchwords or phrases for the verses, as, for instance, Nilus, which heads the list of catchwords, and Amerige, which closes it. The following are the two versions:

(Preceding the letter of Vespucius in the "De Ora Antarctica" of 1505.)

De terra sub cardine Antarctico per regem Portugallie pridem inuenta. M. Ringmanni Philesij Carmen.

Rura papyriferus qua irrorat pinguia Sirus
    Et faciunt Lunæ stagna profunda nives,
Ad dextram montes sunt Ius, Danchis quoque Masche.
    Illorum Ethiopes inferiora tenent.
Aphrica consurgit quibus e regionibus aura
    Aflans cum Lybico feruida regna notho
Ex alia populo Vulturnus parte calenti
    Indica veloci per freta calle venit
Subjacet hic æquo noctis Taprobana circo
    Bassaque Prasodo cernitur ipsa salo.
Ethiopes extra terra est Bassamque marinam
    Non nota e tabulis o Ptolomee tuis.
Cornigeri Zenith cui fertur tropicus hirci
    Huic multæ comes est eiaculator aquæ.
At procul antarcto tellus sub cardine quædam est
    Tellus quam recolit nuda caterva virūm
Hanc, quem clara tenet nunc Portugallia regem,
    Inuenit missa per vada classe maris.
Et quid plura? situm gentis moresque repertæ
    Ille hic perparva mole libellus habet.
Candide sincero capias hunc pectore lector
    Et lege non naso Rhinocerontis. Ave.

Ch. IX THE SECOND TRACT ON THE FOUR VOYAGES

(Preceding the letters of Vespucius in the 1507 editions of the
"Cosmographiæ Introductio.")

Philesius Vogesigena
Lectori.

Rura papirifero qua florent pinguia Syro
  Et faciunt Lunæ magna fluenta lacus
Adextris mōtes sūt Ius, Danchis, quoꝗ Mascha
  Illorum Aethiopes inferiora tenent
Aphrica consurgit quibus e regionibus aura
  Afflans cum Libico feruida regna Notho.
Ex alia populo Vulturnus parte calenti.
  Indica veloci per freta calle venit.
Subiacet hic æquo noctis Taprobana circo
  Bassaꝗ Prasodo cernitur ipsa salo
Aethiopes extra terra est Bassamꝗ marinā
  Non nota e tabulis o Ptholomæe tuis.
Cornigeri Zenith tropici cui cernitur hirci
  Atꝗ comes multæ funditor ipsus aquæ.
Dextrorsum immenso tellus iacet æquore cincta
  Tellus, quam recolit nuda caterua virum
Hanc quem clara suum iactat Lusitania regem
  Inuenit missa per vada classe maris.
Sed quid plura? sitū, gentis moresꝗ repertæ,
  Americi parua mole libellus habet.
Candide syncero voluas hunc pectore lector
  Et lege non nasum Rhinocerontis habens.

Ο Τελοσ,

Where the crested papyrus blooms in fertile field, where the lakes of the moon form mighty rivers, there to the right lie the mountains of Io, of Danchis, and of Mascha. The Ethiopians occupy the lower regions, where rises the African wind which, with the Lybian blast, blows its hot breath on burning fields; and from other regions comes the Vulturnian [southeast] wind on speedy wing through Indian defiles upon a scorchèd people. Taprobane [Ceylon] lies under the equinoctial circle, and Bassa is discerned in the Prasodian sea. Far beyond the Ethiopians and the seagirt Bassa there lies a region, unknown to thy chartography, O Ptolemy, over which is seen in the tropical zenith Capricornus accompanied by the rainbringing Aquarius. To the right stretches a land surrounded by an immense sea, a land in which dwell a race of naked men. A king, of whom noble Portugal may well be proud, discovered this land by sending a fleet across the stormy sea. But why speak of these things? This booklet of Americus, little as it is in form, contains a description of this newly-found land and of the manners of its people. Gentle reader, peruse it in a spirit of fairness, and do not make, in reading it, "a nose of the rhinoceros."

The satyrist Martial in the fourth epigram of the first book of his "Epigrammata" alludes to the raised nose of the horned rhinoceros as the embodiment of all that could be put into disdain and scorn. It was delicate humor perhaps for the time of Domitian, but it now seems no more graceful than the animal to which the nose belongs.

QVARTA

ce multũ & vltraq̃ sit credibile festiuę suscepti fuiꝰ
mus:ob id q̃ ipsa ciuitas nos in mari disperdi-
tos esse existimabat/queadmodũ reliqui omnes de
turba nostra p̃ p̃fectu nr̃i nauiũ stultã preſumptio-
nẽ exiterãt. Quo superbia modo iustus omniũ cẽ
for deus cõpensat. Et ita nũc apud Lisbonã ipsam
subsisto ignorans quid de me sereniſſimus ipse rex
deinceps efficere cogitet/q̃ a tantis laboribus meis
iam ex nunc requiescere plurimũ peroptarem/hũc
nunciũ maiestati vestrę plurimũ quoq̃ interdũ cõ
mendans.   Americus Vesputius in Lisbona.

Vrbs Deodate tuo clarescens nomine praesul
Qua Vogesi montis sunt iuga pressit opus

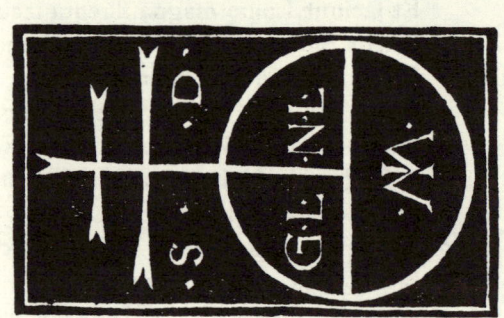

Pressit/& ipsa eadẽ Christo monimẽta fauẽte
Tempore venturo caetera multa premet.

Finitũ vij. kl̃. Maij
Anno supra sesqui
millesimum. vij.

QVATVOR AMERICI VE-
SPVTII NAVIGATIONES

Eius qui subsequentẽ ter-
rarum descriptio-
nẽ de vulgari
Gallico in
Latinũ
trãstu
lit.

Decastichon ad lectorem;

Aspicies tenuem quisquis fortasse logiam
Nauigium memorat pagina nostra placens;
Continet inuentas oras/gentesq̃ recenter
Lętificare sua quę nouitate queant.
Hęc erat altiloquo prouincia danda Maroni
Qui daret excelsę verba polita rei.
Ille quot ambiuit freta cantat Troius heros:
Sic tua Vesputi vela canenda forent.
Has igitur lectu terras visurus/in illis
Materiam librae;non facientis opus:
Item distichon ad eundem

Cum noua delectent fama testante loquaci
Quae recreare queunt hic noua lector habes

ὁ τέλος.

Ch. IX. THE SECOND TRACT ON THE FOUR VOYAGES

On the recto of leaf *biij* we have the title, which will be found reproduced in facsimile on the opposite page. The translation of the decastichon to the reader, which also appears on this page, is as follows:

Whoever thou mayest be, O reader, who perusest this little book, our pages tell of an interesting voyage; they describe coasts and people newly discovered, the novelty of all of which may charm thee. It were a task which might well be given some eloquent Virgil to embody so great a feat in harmonious song. The immortal Virgil sang of all the strange shores visited by the Trojan hero, and such as he, O Americus, should sing of thy voyages. Thou, O reader, who shalt in fancy visit those lands, think only of the tale, and not of him who has made it known to thee.

Distich. By common report new things give pleasure, and here, O reader, are things new which will indeed interest thee.

On the verso of the same leaf, *biij*, is the famous dedication which has done as much to rob Americus Vespucius of his due as the publication of the "Cosmographia" was instrumental in robbing the great Genoese of the honor which would perhaps otherwise have been paid him in giving his name to the New World. There must have been a spirit of mischief abroad in those Vosgian mountains, mixing the threads and colors of men and events. The dedication reads:

Illustrissimo Renato Iherusalem & Siciliæ regi, duci Lothoringiæ ac Barñ. Americus Vesputius humilē reuerentiā & debitā recōmēdationem.

The authorship of this letter and the historical matter of the four voyages have already been fully discussed. Nothing remains but to finish the bibliographical description of this work.

The dedication ends on the recto of leaf *bv* on the twelfth line from the top. Then begins, with a large woodcut initial letter *A*, the account of the first voyage. The signature *b* is in eights, *c* is in eights, signature *d* is likewise in eights. The account of the first voyage ends on the seventh line of the recto of *diij*. The relation of the second voyage ends on the last line of the recto of *ei*. The signature *e* is in fours. The narration of the third voyage ends on the fourteenth line from the top of the recto of *fiij*, and the signature is in sixes. The description of the fourth voyage ends on the eleventh line from the top of the recto of *fvi*, the fifty-second and last leaf. The oblong woodcut containing the initials of the Luds and of Martin Waldseemüller, or Hylacomylus, reproduced in facsimile on the opposite page, has already been explained.

PART VII

Scientific Geography

CHAPTER I

The Science Among the Ancients—The Computations of Eratosthenes

AN ancient writer has called chronology and geography the two eyes which adorn and serve the beautiful statue of History. Through them the impression of the times and places of great events is fixed. Dionysius Petavius entitled his history of the world "An Account of Time," but his editor acknowledged the incompleteness of the title, and added thereto "a geographical description of the world." To establish the exact locality where some eventful deed was exploited is the proper office of the historian. Geography has a still higher and more useful employment in so marking the pathways of the earth that man may find his way across lands and over seas. For when has man been content to know only his own and his father's home?

It is our purpose briefly to explain the mathematical process by which geography determines the position of places on the earth's surface and the relation of those places to each other, and also to follow the growth of the geographical knowledge of the New World, from the time of its discovery until with some definiteness its contours were established upon the map.

The rounded form of the earth was accepted as probable by the ancients several centuries before it came to be demonstrated. Pythagoras and his school taught that the earth, instead of being a plane, was a sphere, and that there were antipodes — a doctrine which may have been learned from Egyptian priests. Plato believed in the sphericity of both the universe and the earth, and one cannot read the "Phædo," "Timæus," or "Critias" without discovering this belief. It is probable that to his fancy the circumference of the earth was much greater than even the first mathematicians made it, and it is said of these latter, such as Eudoxus of Cnidos, and Calippus of Athens, that they estimated the circumference of the earth at 400,000 stadia. Aristotle not only adopted this theory as to the form of the earth, but accepted their calculation as to its size. This philosopher tells us something of the method by which this result was reached through the observation, when traveling from the north to the south, of new stars appearing in the south and the disappearance of other stars in the north. Pytheas, an inhabitant of Massalia, the modern Marseilles, living at the close of the fourth century before the Christian era, first made of geography a separate science. He first used the gnomon for observations, and by its use determined the latitude of Marseilles. In addition to possessing the most accurate scientific and geographical knowledge of his day, he was himself a traveler and discovered for the Greeks the island of Britain and the northernmost point of the habitable world, Thule, which probably was one of the Shetland Islands. Pytheas has left us no accurate measurements from which we can determine his calculations as to the circumference of the earth. Strabo, from whom we get the most of our knowledge concerning the Massalian geographer, is not at all clear as to the measurements of Britain which he imputes to him. By the time of Archimedes, the mathematicians had reduced the circumference of the earth to about 300,000 stadia, a calculation apparently accepted by Archimedes himself. Cleomedes, a Greek mathematician living in the second century of our era, gives the methods pursued in reaching this result. The distance between Lysimachia, a town of Thrace, and Syene in Egypt, the site of the present Aswân, under the first cataract, was measured and showed 20,000 stadia. Then it was observed that Syene lay under the sign of Cancer, and that Lysimachia was directly under the head of the constellation of the Dragon. It was estimated that the distance between these two points on the heavens was $\frac{1}{15}$ of a whole meridian. It followed, therefore, that the measurement of the earth would be fifteen times 20,000 stadia. It is unnecessary here to show the errors in their premises. The truth was drawing nearer all the time.

Eratosthenes, a native of Cyrene, living betwen 276 and 196 B. C., calculated with great care a measure of the earth. The distance measured was between the two points Alexandria and Syene, just below the first cataract on the Nile. The latter place was believed to be on the Tropic of Cancer, and it was known that at noon of the summer solstice a vertical stick set up at this point on the earth's surface would throw no shadow. The angular length of the sun's shadow at any other point at noon on this same day would give the angular distance of that point, or its geographical latitude.

The instrument used in this calculation was the gnomon, a semi-spherical bowl with a straight stick set in its lowest interior point, equal in length to the radius, and perpendicular to a plane tangent to the bowl's surface. It will be seen at once that in this method the shadow cast by the middle of the sun cannot be ascertained, and that the shadow cast by the northern limit was taken, thus introducing an error equal at least to the semi-diameter of the sun, or approximately fourteen or fifteen minutes.

Ch. I THE SCIENCE AMONG THE ANCIENTS

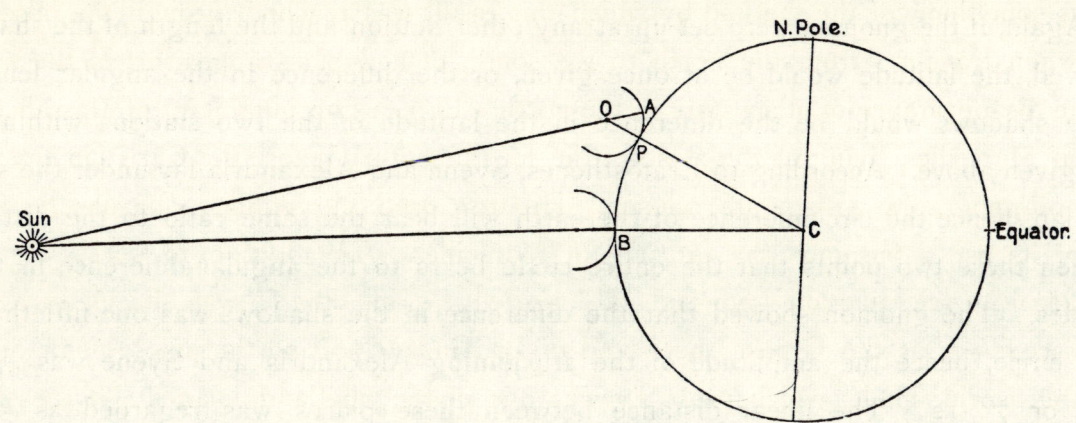

If in the figure B is a point on the equator and S the sun at noon on the equinoctial day, the peg in the gnomon will cast no shadow, but if on the same day a gnomon is set up at P the sun will cast a shadow whose angular length is $P\,O\,A$. Now, since the sun is infinitely distant from the earth in comparison to the distance $P\,B$, the lines of sun rays $S\,B$ and $S\,A$ are practically parallel (not true, of course, in a figure of the scale of the above); therefore the angle $B\,C\,P$ is equal to the angle $P\,O\,A$; but the angle $B\,C\,P$ is the latitude of P, hence the angle $P\,O\,A$ will be the latitude of the point P.

The latitude of a place is ordinarily found by taking the angle of elevation of the celestial pole above the horizon. This horizon is always a tangent to the earth's surface.

Suppose the figure below to represent a section of the earth—the relation of the lines somewhat exaggerated—P, P' the poles, and E, E' the equator.

Let the celestial pole for the point A be in the direction of $A\,S$, then the angle $S\,A\,D$ will be the latitude of A.

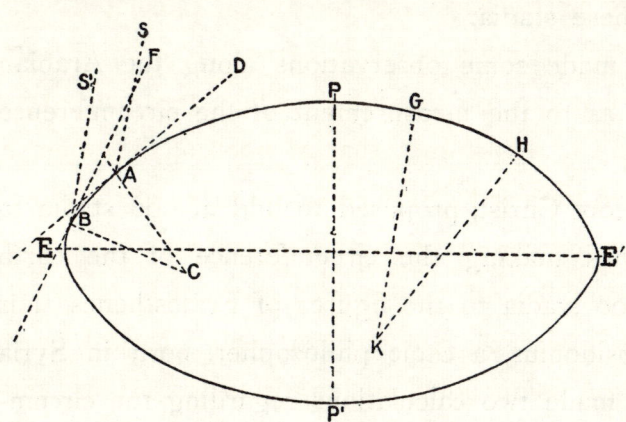

For the point B the latitude will be equal to the angle $S'\,B\,F$.

$A\,C$ is the normal for the point A, and $B\,C$ for the point B, and the angle $A\,C\,B$ is graphically the difference of latitude of the points A and B. Suppose this is 10°, then the arc $A\,B$ contains 10°. If these points were nearer the pole, say $G\,H$, the normals would intersect at K, they being longer; in order to have the angle $G\,K\,H$ equal to 10°, the arc $G\,H$ will be *longer* than the arc $A\,B$, or one degree near the pole will be longer than one degree near the equator.

Again, if the gnomon were set up at any other station and the length of the shadow observed, the latitude would be at once given, or the difference in the angular lengths of the shadows would be the difference in the latitude of the two stations within the error given above. According to Eratosthenes, Syene and Alexandria lay under the same meridian, hence the circumference of the earth will bear the same ratio to the distance between these two points that the entire circle bears to the angular difference in their latitudes. The gnomon showed that the difference in the shadows was one-fiftieth of a great circle, hence the amplitude of the arc joining Alexandria and Syene was $\frac{1}{50}$ of 360°, or 7° 12′. The linear distance between these places was regarded as 5,000 stadia, therefore the circumference of the earth must be 250,000 stadia.

Several Greek and Roman writers give as the result of this determination 252,000 stadia. It is quite likely that Eratosthenes added the 2,000 stadia so as to have one degree expressed in a round number, 700, instead of the awkward $694\frac{4}{9}$. Eratosthenes, unfortunately, did not employ reliable data, and the error in his conclusion was the result of the following specific errors found in his premises:

First.—The sun's semi-diameter was neglected, as indicated above.

Second.—The situation of Syene is not under the tropic, or in 23° 43′ north latitude, making allowances for the obliquity of the ecliptic in the time of Eratosthenes, but is in latitude 24° 5′ 53″.

Third.—The difference in latitude between Syene and Alexandria was not 7° 8′ 34″, but 7° 6′ 54″.

Fourth.—The meridian of Alexandria is about three degrees to the west of Syene, whereas Eratosthenes considered these two places as on the same meridian.

Fifth.—The distance in a straight line between Syene and Alexandria was not 5,000 Greek stadia, but about 4,583 of these stadia.

Pliny relates that Eratosthenes had made some observations along the Arabian Gulf which confirmed him in his opinion as to the measurement of the circumference of the earth.

Hipparchus, in the second century before Christ, proposed to add 26,000 stadia to the 252,000 as calculated by Eratosthenes, making the circumference of the earth 278,000 stadia. Pliny himself added 12,000 stadia to the figures of Eratosthenes, thus making the distance 264,000 stadia. Posidonius, a Stoic philosopher, born in Syria about 134 years before the Christian era, made two calculations regarding the circumference. The first result he reached through measuring the distance between the island of Rhodes and Alexandria, making it 5000 stadia. He found that the star Canopus, in the constellation of the ship Argo, was scarcely visible on the horizon at Rhodes, while at Alexandria it was $\frac{1}{48}$ of a circle above the horizon, whence he calculated the earth's circumference to be 240,000 stadia. Not only is Rhodes not on the same meridian as Alexandria, as Posidonius believed, but the distance between these two places is considerably less than 5000 stadia. Again, neither in its true nor in its apparent position was Posidonius correct in his observation of the star Canopus at Alexandria. By just what operation Posidonius reached his conclusion that the proper figure was 180,000 stadia we do not know. It is probable that he accepted his astronomical data as correct in both problems, and that the discrepancy must have been in the number of stadia between Rhodes and Alexandria, which would have been 3750 in order to have produced the result of 180,000 as the circumference of the earth. It is likely that he regarded 240,000 as the maximum and 180,000 as the minimum number of stadia.

Strabo, whose eyes saw the opening of the Christian era, adopted the measure of Eratosthenes as to the circumference of the entire globe, although he severely criticizes his measurement of the habitable part.

Marinus of Tyre lived in the second century of our era, and while there is little if anything of his original work which can be identified, the appropriation and use of his materials by Ptolemy make his name important in the list of geographers. Ptolemy, in the first book of his geography, frankly acknowledges his indebtedness to the Tyrian geographer, and is so full in his confession of obligation that for a long time many believed that he had plagiarized from Marinus. The principal labors of the latter were in carrying out the ideas of Hipparchus in laying down climata or parallels of latitude, and in measuring the length and breadth of the habitable world. Explorations, travels, and the tales of traders gave him added knowledge for this latter task.

CHAPTER II

Claudius Ptolemy, and his Contributions to the Science

HE most interesting figure among geographers is Ptolemy. For nearly 1300 years his writings on geography were standard. Claudius Ptolemæus was a native Egyptian, although not of the royal house, as his name might indicate. In the fields of pure mathematics, of astronomy, and of geography his name will be forever famous. Through the dates of his observations we are able to follow and determine twenty-six years of his eventful life, his last observation having been taken in the year 151 of our era. There is an Arabian tradition to the effect that Ptolemy lived eight and seventy years, and that there have been preserved some details of his personal appearance. It may be therefore that the woodcut portrait herewith presented contains some authentic features. It is taken from the "Margarita Philosophica" of Gregorius Reisch, printed by Johannes Grüninger at Strasburg in 1504.

There are no existing Ptolemaic maps known earlier than the thirteenth century. The manuscript map found in the Vatopedi monastery of Mount Athos is the oldest so far as we know, and probably was executed in the thirteenth century. It is a question if Ptolemy himself ever drew a map. Some think he designed the tables of latitudes and longitudes as simply so much material from which others could construct charts and maps. Some think that the lists of places given in the last books of his geography, with their latitudes and longitudes, were intended as an index to the maps. Agathodæmon, by some identified as a mathematician of the fifth century, is said to have made the earliest maps of which we have any record, and from which the ones still preserved and believed to date from the thirteenth century were copied. The first printed edition of Ptolemy was executed at Vicenza in 1475. All bibliographers are agreed that the alleged edition of 1462, edited by Philippus Beroaldus, and printed by Dominicus de Lapis at Bologna, is falsely dated. We know that Philippus Beroaldus was born in 1453, and he could scarcely be the corrector of a work of this kind at nine years of age.

Ch. II PTOLEMY, AND HIS CONTRIBUTIONS TO THE SCIENCE 175

We know that Balthazar Azzoguidi was the first Bolognese printer, and that the first issue of his press was dated 1471; and we also know that the first book printed by Dominicus de Lapis was issued in 1476. The book possesses signatures, and we know that signatures were not used until the Oxford press issued the "Expositio" of St. Jerome in 1468, or, as some bibliographers assert, until Johannes Koelhoff printed "Præceptorium divinæ

legis" at Cologne in 1472. Moreover, the preface to the Rome edition of Ptolemy, 1478, strongly suggests that Sweynheym, who prepared the copper-plate maps for that edition, was the first to apply himself to this art, and since the alleged Bologna edition has copper-plate maps it may be assumed that they were subsequent in their preparation to the work undertaken by Sweynheym and finished by Buckinck in 1478. The Bologna edition was probably printed in 1482.

The authentic first edition is that printed at Vicenza by Hermanus Levilapis in 1475. The Latin manuscript from which this edition was printed was translated from the Greek by Jacobus Angelus in Florence about the year 1409. It was dedicated to Pope Alexander V., who occupied the Apostolic chair only from June 26, 1409, to May 3, 1410, as we find Pierre d'Ailly in 1410 referring to it in his *Imago Mundi* and quoting therefrom Ptolemy's theory that India lay due west from Spain. This edition was issued without maps. It is said that the Grenville copy has an appendix of seven additional leaves. Dibdin describes the copy in the Bibliotheca Spenceriana as having an appendix of five leaves with a woodcut of the Arctic and Antarctic poles. Our copy ends with the colophon on the reverse of G. viii, and from the general appearance of the book itself we are inclined to think that the appendix was not a part of the book as originally printed.

The Rome impression of 1478 is the rarest of the editions. It is the first printed Ptolemy to contain maps. These are engraved on copper and are twenty-seven in number, as follows: one of the world, ten of Europe, four of Africa, and twelve of Asia. This map of the world we reproduce (see end of volume), as showing the extent of geographical knowledge at the time of the Columbian discovery. We learn from the dedication that Domitius Calderinus, the editor, carefully collated several Latin manuscripts with a very ancient copy which had been corrected by Gemistus.

The edition of Ptolemy issued at Ulm in 1482 from the press of Leonardus Hol is of interest to students of American geography because it gives for the first time on any engraved map any portion of the American continent. The map between the fourth and fifth maps of Europe, the eastern half of which we reproduce (see end of volume), gives as the northernmost land the peninsula of Greenland, called Engronelant, and makes it a prolongation of Europe toward the west. The maps are executed on wood and are thirty-two in number. They were the work of Nicolas Donis and are believed to have been undertaken as early as 1471. Ptolemy is no longer servilely followed, but Donis corrects his maps in the light of more modern knowledge. He adds five new maps of his own, Palestine, the Arctic regions, Spain, Italy, and France. It is said that these last four are found in a manuscript map dated 1481 and preserved in the public library of Brussels. The Ptolemy editions of 1486 printed at Ulm by Johannes Reger, and of 1490, printed at Rome by Petrus de Turre, are of no interest or special value; the first mentioned being a poor copy of the 1482 edition, and the second, although used by Nordenskiöld to illustrate an early Ptolemy, being only a reproduction of the 1478 edition. This completes the list of printed fifteenth century editions of Ptolemy, and those of the sixteenth century, with the beginnings of American geography, will hereafter be treated of at length. It may be here remarked that all these editions, and all those of the first part of the sixteenth century, were in

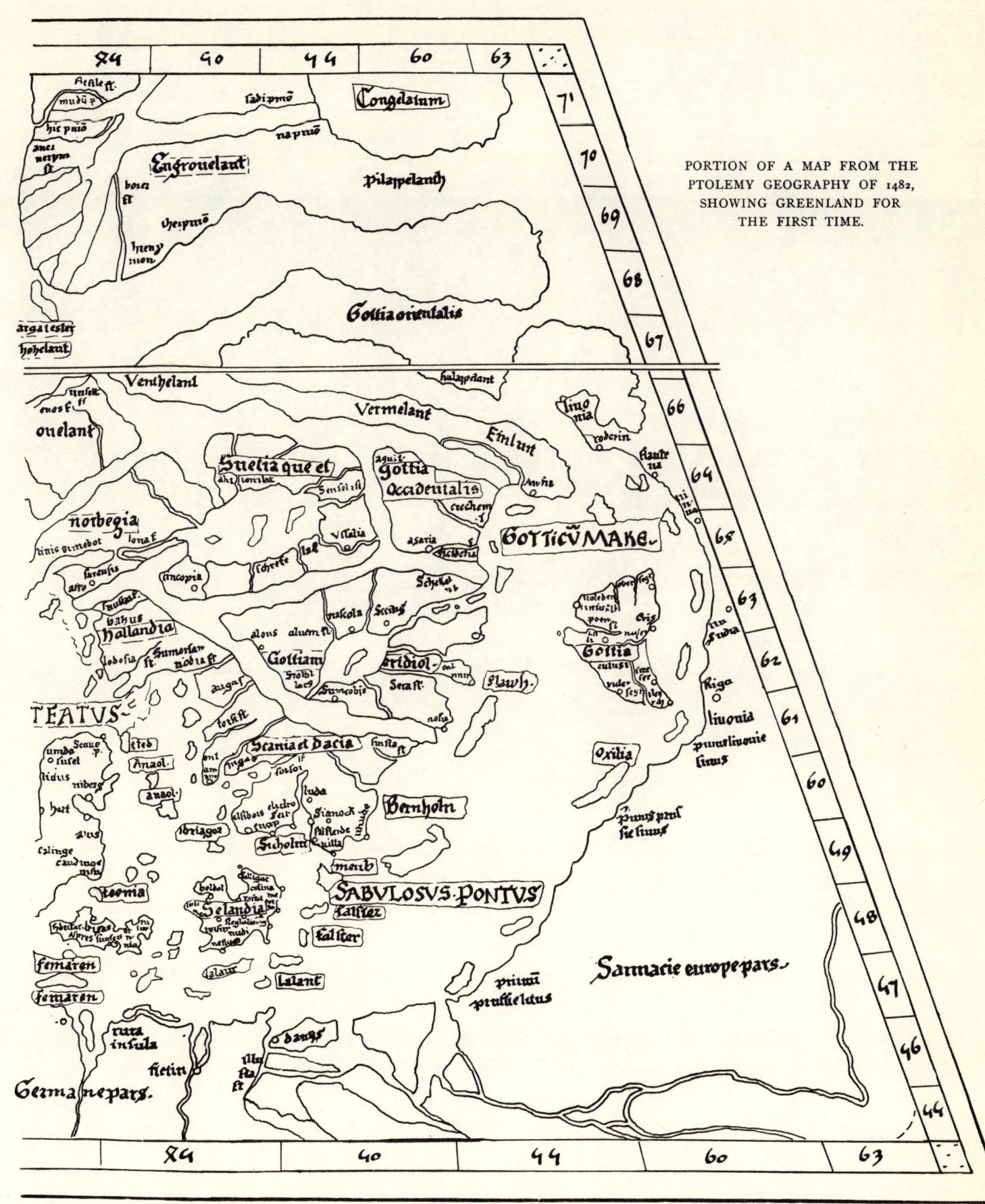

PORTION OF A MAP FROM THE PTOLEMY GEOGRAPHY OF 1482, SHOWING GREENLAND FOR THE FIRST TIME.

Ch. II PTOLEMY, AND HIS CONTRIBUTIONS TO THE SCIENCE

Latin. It was not until 1533 that a Greek edition of Ptolemy under the care of the learned Erasmus was published for the edification of scholars.

The Mediterranean Sea of Ptolemy is more than 20° too great in its length. It is 62° in his map, while its true length is but 41° 40′. The south-eastern projection of the European continent is made too small; the island of Ceylon, called Taprobane, is greatly magnified and forms a sort of Indian peninsula. In the maps, as produced in the fifteenth century, to the south of the Indian Ocean there is land called Terra Incognita. Ptolemy accepted the lesser calculation of Posidonius, viz., 180,000 stadia, as the correct measurement of the circumference of the earth, and divided the meridian into 360 degrees, counting his longitude east from the Fortunate Islands (Canaries). The maps of the world in the Rome edition of 1478, and in the Ulm edition of 1482, give us practically the boundaries of the habitable world up to the time of the new era of discovery opened up by the navigations along the south coast of Africa and the expeditions and travels into Further India and to the distant north. These newer discoveries waited for those across the Atlantic before making their appearance on the maps.

Ptolemy always gives the positions of places in degrees of longitude and latitude. To find in the unit of measure employed by him the distance between any two places on the same meridian marked in degrees, one must multiply each degree by 500 stadia. In determining longitude the labor even now is very great, and being wholly dependent upon differences of time, an error of one second in time will cause an error of *fifteen* seconds in longitude. Consequently no accurate fixing of longitude could take place until precise methods were elaborated for the determination, preservation and transmission of time. Prior to the existence of these conditions differences of longitude could only be known from the ratio of the distance between the two points to the length of one degree. Thus, if two places on the same parallel were 3500 stadia apart, and one degree was supposed to contain 700 stadia, their difference in longitude was regarded as 5°.

This method presumed that the earth was a sphere, and that a degree of latitude was equal to a degree of longitude. Even if these postulates were correct, accuracy would demand that the length of a degree of latitude be known with precision, that the exact air-line distance between the two places be accessible, and that the latitudes should be the same. These conditions could never be attained, and the errors in longitude were in proportion to the errors in the data, increased by the erroneous hypotheses underlying this method.

CHAPTER III

The Unit of Measure Employed by the Ancients

HE unit of measure employed by the ancient geographers was the stadium. It took its name from the arena or course in which the foot races were run. It represented the distance in a straight line from a square pillar set up at one end of the course to a like pillar at the other end. The ancient measure for this distance was six hundred times the length of the human foot. The earliest units of measure were taken from portions of the human body. It is a natural method of measuring. The smaller measures were the finger, the palm of the hand, the length of the arm, and, most commonly of all, the foot. The medium measures were the distance a stone or disk might be thrown, or for still greater measure, the distance traveled by a mule without resting. For very great distances, days and nights employed in navigation were used. The length of these courses differed, since the length of the human foot was not fixed. The stadium at Pisa near the Temple of Jupiter Olympus, the old writers declared, had been paced off by Hercules himself, and was six hundred times as long as one of his feet. We read in the "Noctes Atticæ" of Aulus Gellius that the philosopher Pythagoras determined from this course the dimensions of Hercules by reasoning that, as the foot of Hercules exceeded in length the foot of the ordinary man, so his height and proportions would exceed in the same ratio the ordinary human height and proportions. Herodotus is the earliest writer who used the stadium as a measure, but it is believed that the system of measures and weights was introduced into Greece and adopted about the ninth century before the Christian era. The foot contained four palms, and the palm contained four fingers. The simple step contained 2½ feet, and the double step, passus or pace, was equal to 5 feet; the perch contained 10 feet, the plethron was equal to 100 feet, and the stadium contained 600 feet. Phidon, king of Argos, is credited with having invented this system. The Attic foot was said to be found in the scale adopted in building the upper step of the basement of the Parthenon of Athens, upon which the pillars stood. The Parthenon itself was designated by some authors as *Heca-*

Ch. III THE UNIT OF MEASURE EMPLOYED BY THE ANCIENTS

tompedon. By others this term seems to have been applied to only the stylobate or basement, the upper step of which is believed to have contained 100 feet. It was here in the *cella* that the treasures were kept, and there may have been an exact relationship of the foot measures to the situation of the rich repository chambers. Attempts have been made to determine the Greek foot from the basement line. It has been thought by some writers to contain in its width of 100 Greek feet just 101 feet 1.7 inches, or 12.137 inches of our measure. The Greek foot is also, and probably much more accurately, calculated from the Roman foot, to which it bore a proportion of 25 to 24. Thus, if there were 600 Greek feet in the stadium, there were 576 Roman feet. If we assume the Roman foot to have contained 9708 of the English foot, a calculation which authorities sanction, the Greek foot would contain 1.01125, or 12.135 inches. We have now a unit of measure with which to follow the ancient geographers as they calculated the circumference of the earth. By turning back to the figures offered by Posidonius for the circumference of the earth, we find that for his maximum calculation he has given us 240,000 stadia, or 27,579 English miles, and for his minimum calculation he has given us 180,000 stadia, or 20,684 English miles. If now we take a mean between these two estimates we will be surprised how close to the measurement of the circumference as calculated to-day is that mean of 210,000 stadia, viz., 24,132 English miles.

From the time of Ptolemy until the ninth century of the Christian era, geography with the other sciences lay sleeping. The conqueror who wades through slaughter drags after him a triumphal car in which are seated the arts and sciences. The spread of knowledge follows the spilling of blood. The seat of learning is builded on the ruins of disaster. Thus we find the Caliphs of Bagdad, after conquering a large part of the habitable world, erecting a new edifice in which knowledge should be wooed and worshipped. Al-Mamun, the son and successor of Harun-al-Rashid, gave the study of geography into the special keeping of the wise men of his kingdom. In the year 819 two separate degrees of latitude were measured by Arabian astronomers between Tadmor and Raka, on the plain of the desert of Sinjar. Two parties started from a given point, and each traveled in an opposite direction, measuring the distances carefully with wooden rods. The one party traveled northward and stopped when the altitude of the pole was found to be exactly one degree higher than it was at the point where the measurements were begun. The length of this degree was just 56 miles. The second party traveled due southward and found that one degree measured 56⅔ miles. These Arab miles contained as nearly as possible nine stadia each, which would give for a degree of 56 miles, 504 stadia, and for the entire circumference of the earth nearly the measurements accepted by Ptolemy. The Arabian maps were not constructed with meridian lines, but were made on the circular disk system.

Then there came another long night to the science of geography, or at least to that mathematical part on which the true measurements of the surface of the earth depend. The adventuresome spirit in man has always existed, and after the fall of the Bagdad Caliphs travelers and merchants continued to explore the ends of the earth. The Northmen, whose traders had been in communication with the merchants of Arabia and India from the eighth to the eleventh century, pushed their way into unknown regions. The crusaders familiarized the common mind with adventure and travel. In Italy the various republics, particularly that of Venice, encouraged brave men to encounter danger in distant and unknown lands in the hope of commercial advantage. The travels of Marco Polo, a Venetian gentleman, in the middle of the thirteenth century, contributed more information to the store of knowledge concerning the distant parts of the earth than those of any other adventurer up to his time. Indeed, the historian Ramusio says of him and his companions, "And often in my own mind, comparing the land explorations of these our Venetian gentlemen with the sea explorations of the aforesaid Signor Don Christopher, I have asked myself which of the two were really the more marvelous." It was Marco Polo who put upon the map those siren names of Chipangu, Zayton, and Kinsay, which two and a half centuries later beckoned on the Genoese discoverer, and in the seeking of which he found a new world. The discovery of the polarity of the magnetic needle and the invention of the mariner's compass emboldened the navigator to leave the shores, along which he had been forced to coast for fear of losing himself, and secured for him a guided path across the seas even when he could see neither shore nor sky. Then came Prince Henry of Portugal, to whom history has justly awarded the title of "the Navigator," and after him came the greatest prince of all navigators, Christopher Columbus.

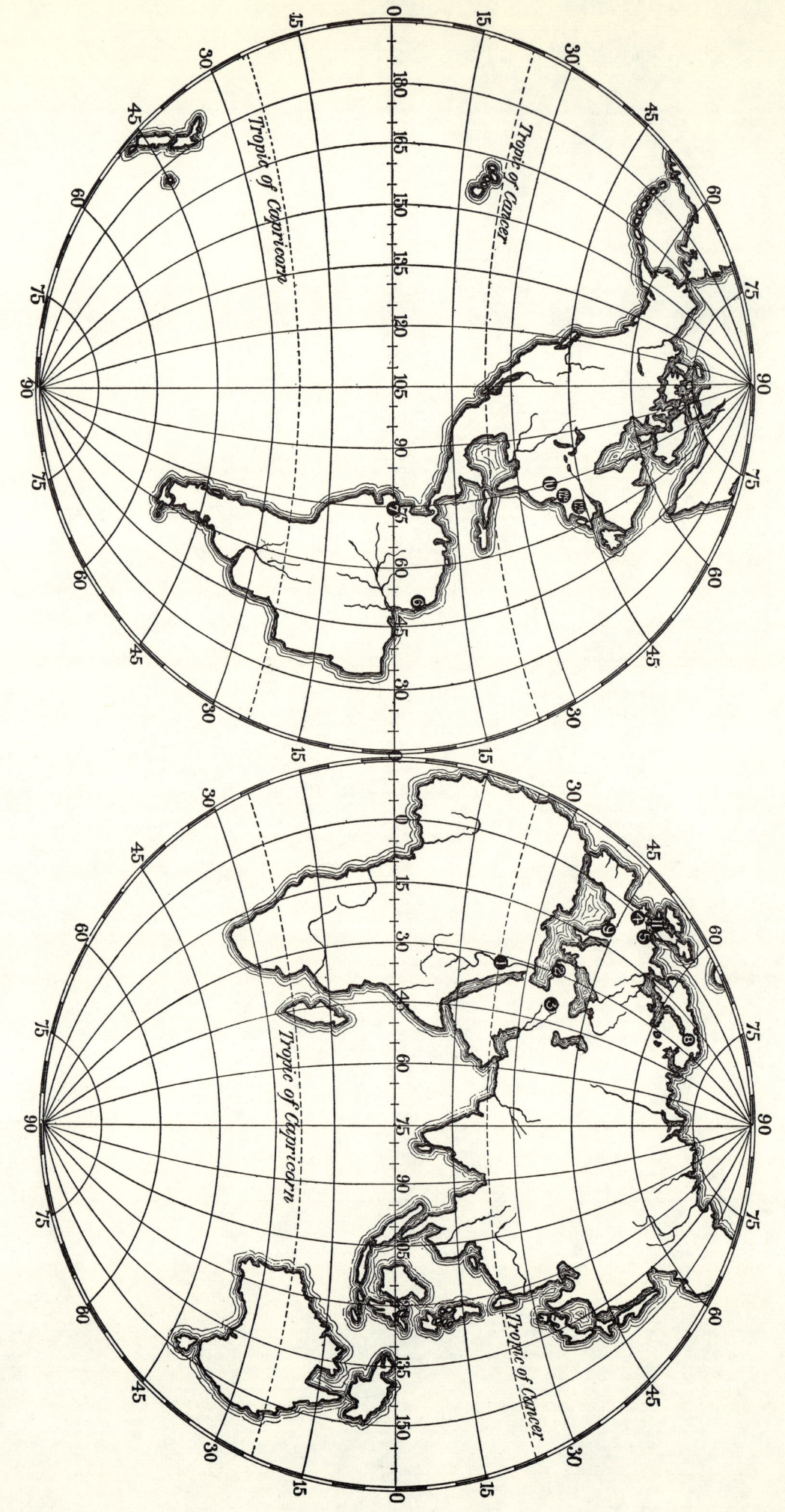

MAP OF THE WORLD, SHOWING LOCATIONS AT WHICH DEGREES OF LATITUDE HAVE BEEN MEASURED TO DETERMINE THE CIRCUMFERENCE OF THE EARTH.

KEY TO THE ACCOMPANYING DRAWING.

1. Egyptian measurement at Assouan by Eratosthenes in 216 B. C., Latitude 24° N., Longitude 32° E.
2. Measurement at Rhodes by Posidonius in 90 B. C., Latitude 36° N., Longitude 28° E.
3. Arabian measurement in Mesopotamia in 819 A. D., Latitude 36° N., Longitude 40° E.
4. Measurement near Paris by Fernell in 1525, Latitude 48° N., Longitude 2° E.
5. Measurement at Leyden by Snell in 1612, Latitude 52° N., Longitude 4° E.
6. Measurement at Cayenne, South America, in 1672, Latitude 5° N., Longitude 52° W.
7. Equatorial measurement at Quito in 1735, Longitude 78° W.
8. Lapland measurement in 1736, Latitude 66° N., Longitude 24° E.
9. Italian measurement near Rome in 1750, Latitude 43° N., Longitude 12° E.
10. Mason and Dixon measurement in Pennsylvania in 1764, Latitude 39° N., Longitude 75° W.
11. English Ordnance Survey measurement in 1801, Latitude 52° N.
12a, 12b. United States Coast Survey now in progress.

CHAPTER IV

Modern Geography, its Unit of Measure and the Length of a Degree

LL these discoveries added nothing to the exact science of measurements, and it was not until the early part of the sixteenth century that an attempt was again made to measure a degree. Jean Fernel, a native of Picardy and court physician to Henry II of France, had taught philosophy and mathematics at the College of Ste. Barbe. Probably soon after the globe had been circumnavigated by the Magellan expedition, Fernel set about determining the true measurement of its circumference. Having found the sun's meridian altitude at Paris or at some point near there, he traveled northward until the sun's altitude declared that he had advanced one degree. He is said to have verified the exact distance by counting on his homeward way the revolutions of a wagon wheel the circumference of which was 20 feet. These revolutions he counted as 17,024, whence he calculated the degree as 56,746 toises. A comparison of this measurement with the Arabian measurement will show a close agreement in the length of a degree of latitude and, by consequence, in the length of the circumference of the earth. A Dutch mathematician by the name of Willebroard van Royen Snell introduced the system of triangulation from a known base-line, and thus applied exact geodetic measurements for an arc of a meridian. This measurement extended over the distance between Alkmaar and Bergen-op-Zoom, and was completed in the year 1612. As a result of this measurement and others taken from Leyden to Alkmaar, a degree was found to have 28,500 Rhenish rods, or 55,072 toises, that is to say, 66.6 miles. The toise was the unit of measure employed by the scientists of that day and was equal to 6.3945 English feet, the Rhenish rod being equal to 1.9324 toises. The principle of triangulation adopted by Snell has since his time always been employed.

Jean Picard was selected by the Royal Academy of Sciences of Paris, at the request of Louis XIV, in the year 1660, as the proper person to calculate the measurement of the earth's circumference. About nine years were given to this work, and new and important instruments employed. The telescope used was provided with cross wires, and the base line was measured on the surface of the earth with two rods placed carefully end to end. The length of a degree was found to be 57,060 toises or 69.1 miles, giving for the circumference of the earth a length of 24,878 miles.

In 1672, under the auspices of the same scientific institution, Jean Richer, while making some observations with the pendulum of a clock in Cayenne, South America, defined the influence of the centrifugal force at the equator, thus demonstrating the spheroidal shape of the earth and the consequent difference in the length of a degree or the arc of a meridian according as the part of the meridian considered is near to or distant from the equator. The swing of the pendulum was retarded as the equator was approached. This could be accounted for only on the ground that the power of gravitation was lessened, and the lessening of this power could be accounted for only on supposing that the earth was pressed in or flattened at the extremities of its polar axis, and consequently extended or protuberant at the equator. The actual difference, as determined to-day in the length of the equatorial diameter as compared to the polar axis, is as 295 is to 294.

While the French Academy was studying this problem, Isaac Newton in England was laying down great eternal principles which were to be as essential in all calculations of the earth's form and size as were the telescope and the measuring rod. In the *Principia*, 1687, he proved theoretically that the earth must be an oblate spheroid, adopting in his calculations the measurements of Jean Picard as to the length of a degree, and the observations of Jean Richer on the retardation of the pendulum at the equator.

It was not until 1735 that the French Academy again made an elaborate attempt to measure a degree under circumstances which would disclose the influence of the centrifugal force and reveal the spheroidal shape of the earth. Two expeditions were sent out, the one in May, 1735, to Quito, in South America, to measure a degree at the equator, and the other in May, 1736, to Lapland, to obtain the length of a degree approaching the northern pole. Two iron toises were constructed of exact standard, and every precaution taken to have the instruments and methods employed as similar as possible. The first degree, counting from the equator, was found to measure 56,753 toises, while the degree of the meridian which is bisected by the Arctic Circle measured 57,438 toises. The measurements then made and discussed in 1738 by Pierre Louis Moreau de Maupertuis, the famous leader of the Lapland expedition, were received by the French Academy as closing the discussion as to the shape of the earth, and in 1742 these words were pronounced, "La Terre est aplatie; l'Académie a clos la discussion."

In the year 1750 Roger Joseph Boscovich measured a degree in Italy in latitude

43° and found the same to be 56,979 toises in length. In 1764 Charles Mason and Jeremiah Dixon were selected by the Royal Society of England to measure a degree in America. They had already been employed in making surveys in America, and were recommended for this more important work by Nevil Maskelyne, the Astronomer Royal. The location chosen for this measurement was near the boundary line between Maryland and Pennsylvania, in mean latitude 39° 11′ 56″, and the length of the degree was determined to be 56,888 toises, or 68 miles and 4723 feet. It may here be remarked that the popular idea of Mason and Dixon's line marking in after years, by the Missouri Compromise, the northern limit of slavery, is an erroneous idea. The Mason and Dixon line marking the boundary between Maryland and Pennsylvania is in 39° 43′ north latitude, while the line marking the northern boundary of slavery, as fixed by the Missouri Compromise of 1820, was in 36° 30′ north latitude.

In 1790 Barrow measured a degree near the Tropic of Cancer, and made it 56,725 toises, while in 1798 Nicolas Antoine Nouet, a French astronomer, measured a degree in latitude 27° 39′, and determined it to be 56,880 toises. During the latter part of the eighteenth century the French savants were particularly active in estimating the dimensions of the earth. The chief result of their labors was the happy adoption of the mètre as a unit of a new system of measurement. A quadrant of the meridian, or the distance from the equator to the pole, was divided into ten million equal parts, and each of these parts was to be a mètre. It was decided to measure the meridian between Barcelona and Dunkerque. The figures obtained from this measurement were then submitted to a committee of twenty, consisting of nine Frenchmen and eleven representatives from other nations. The committee found that a mètre contained 39.3707904 English inches. England declined to participate in the calculations or to accept the results. At the beginning of the present century two measurements were made under the auspices of the English astronomers. The length of a degree in latitude 52° 2′ was 57,068 toises, and in latitude 51° 25′ it was 57,109 toises. In the year 1820 Carl Friedrich Gauss, a German mathematician, found the length of a degree the latitude of whose midde point was 52° 2′ to be 57,126 toises. In the year 1842 Friederich Wilhelm Bessel, a German astronomer, calculated from all the known measurements the dimensions of the earth, and established the fact that the earth was a spheroid. He determined the equatorial semi-diameter to contain 3962.8 miles and the polar semi-diameter 3949.5 miles. The length of an equatorial degree he found to be 69.164 miles, the equatorial circumference 24,899 miles, and the meridian circumference 24,858 miles. Until a few years ago these values were in general use, and by many are still retained.

In 1880, General A. R. Clarke of the English Royal Engineers, having before him the figures of all the accurately measured arcs then known, calculated anew the dimensions of the earth with the following results: the equatorial semi-diameter he found to measure 3963.4 miles, the polar semi-diameter 3949.8 miles, the length of an equatorial degree 69.173 miles, the equatorial circumference 24,902 miles, and the polar circumference 24,859 miles. These measurements are now preferred by many specialists to those made by the German astronomer Bessel. For many years an International Commission, representing the most important European powers, has been engaged in measuring great distances on the earth's surface and in calculating therefrom the dimensions of the earth. In our own country most important measurements have been made under the direction and authority of the Congress of the United States. While the original title of the United States Coast and Geodetic Survey would seem to confine its labors to shore and boundary work, yet in order to correct the points on the Pacific and Atlantic coasts in their relationship to each other, it was determined to run a chain of measurements across the Continent, and this important work is now progressing. One can comprehend the interest with which the scientific world awaits the completion of the measurement of this immense arc. The following are the four principal measurements undertaken by the government:

(1) *The Nantucket Arc of the Meridian* (proposed for extension to the St. Lawrence river). Extends from Farmington, Maine, in latitude 44° 40′ 12″ and longitude 70° 9′ 50″, to Nantucket, Mass., in latitude 41° 17′ 33″ and longitude 70° 6′. Amplitude, 3° 22′ 39″. Has 6 sub-divisions. Length, 233 statute miles, or 24,835 for the circumference of the earth.

(2) *The Pamlico Chesapeake Arc of the Meridian* (proposed for extension to the St. Lawrence river). Extends from Principio, Md., in latitude 39° 35′ 33″ and longitude 76° 0′ 16″, to Portsmouth Island, N. C., in latitude 35° 4′ 3″ and longitude 76° 3′ 42″. Amplitude, 4° 31′ 30″. Has 13 sub-divisions. Length, 312 statute miles, or 24,822 for the circumference of the earth.

(3) *The U. S. Central Arc of the Parallel.* Extends from Point Arena, Cal., to Cape May, N. J., or from latitude 38° 57′ 2″ and longitude 123° 44′ 7″ to latitude 38° 55′ 9″ and longitude 74° 57′ 7″. Amplitude, 48° 47′ of longitude. There is a gap at 105° to 109° of west longitude. This gap will be completed during the current season. Length, about 4226 kilometres, or 2626 statute miles. There are 19 sub-divisions. This arc passes by or includes Cincinnati, St. Louis, Denver, Virginia City, etc. It is the completion of this great arc which is expected this year, and which will be of inestimable value to science.

(4) *The Oblique Arc of the Atlantic.* Extends from Eastport, or Calais, Maine, to Montgomery, Alabama, but is to be extended to the Gulf of Mexico. Calais is in

latitude 45° 11′ 6″ and longitude 67° 16′ 53″, and Montgomery about latitude 32° and longitude 87°. Present amplitude, 20° 15′, and when completed 22° 30′. Completed length, 2252 kilometres, or 1399 statute miles, giving 24,871 statute miles as the circumference of the earth.

Accompanying this is an outline of the two hemispheres on which we have indicated the various locations where the most important measurements of degrees and arcs have been made.

It is also to be noticed that it was in the New World, in latitude 5° to the north of the equinoctial line, that the first suggestion was vouchsafed to man that this round earth of ours is not a perfect sphere but a spheroid. While the shape of the earth is determined as spheroidal and not spherical, its exact form and its true dimensions can only be determined when the equatorial regions of Africa and South America shall for a time hold back danger, disease and death, and suffer the hand of man to measure their unknown sides, and when in the regions of the frozen north a degree of latitude shall be measured near the pole. Until that time the heart of every true geometer shall be drawn by invisible currents to the mysterious girdle and to the veritable end of that spheroid we call our earth.

CHAPTER V

Geographical Instruments in Use in the Time of Columbus

F all instruments used by them who go down to the sea in ships, the compass is the most useful and indispensable. It is the instrument most familiar to us in the list of aids to navigation. Without the compass, a ship might as well bid adieu to port and sail away rudderless. This instrument is of great antiquity. In its earlier form it consisted of a magnetized piece of iron attached to some light substance, like thin wood, straw, or cork, floating in a vase or basin of water. In this form it was manifestly unfit for use on the tossing ocean, and the ingenuity of Flavio Gioja in the latter part of the thirteenth century gave to the needle a more stable support by attaching to it a card and suspending it on a center. By some this Flavio Gioja is credited with the improvement of placing this card and needle in an inclosed box. The principle of the compass existed before; the attachment to a card was only an improvement and development. In the beginning this card had marked on it simply the four cardinal points. The next step was to add the four — palpably misnamed — collateral points. Later, the card had marked on it thirty-two points to designate the more minute variations from the true north to which the prow of the ship might be turning. This must have been an early improvement, inasmuch as the poet Chaucer speaks of the sailors reckoning thirty-two points of the horizon.

The quadrant was an instrument employed very early for measuring angles and in taking the height of the pole. It consisted of an arc the fourth part of an entire circle and marked with degrees or parts of degrees; probably in its earliest form it was of stone, polished on one side and marked with degrees and graduations. In time this instrument took a more convenient and portable form, and its principle was incorporated in the more elaborate instrument known as the astrolabe.

In classic use the baculus was a general term applied to a stick or rod, whether used as a staff to support the steps of the aged — as for instance where Œdipus asks his daughter for such an aid in his walking, or where in his *Metamorphoses* Ovid makes the Gods, when they disguised themselves as old women, lean upon the baculus — or whether used as a crook when it served as the third and long reaching arm of the shepherd; or whether carried on the Roman stage, where the baculus became a truncheon and spoke with the voice of authority; or whether it was employed like the virga, and was recognized as the symbol of magical powers. Later, this term was applied particularly to the rod used in measuring distances, but it is doubtful if it had a fixed value like the toise. In the *Margarita Philosophica* printed at Strasburg in 1504, the baculus is represented and described as an instrument employed for determining the height of inaccessible places. It is there represented as a rod several feet in length, with holes or clefts cut at certain points, into which an upright stick or peg could be inserted.

The baculus may have been unnecessary where the *cross-staff*, called by the Spaniards *ballestilla*, was used. The vertical bar together with the horizontal staff would seem to perform all the functions of the baculus. The staff of the ballestilla was much more elaborately constructed than its plainer relative. Scales of degrees were carefully marked along its upper side, and probably each staff was accompanied with crosses of various sizes to facilitate the taking of smaller or larger angles as the case required. The cross-staff was certainly one of the instruments carried by Columbus on his eventful voyage.

A word may be said of the manner of determining geographical positions at sea in the time of Columbus. Latitude was determined by observing the meridian altitude of the sun or pole star, but as no device was at that time known for simultaneous observations on the horizon and of a star, all measurements were made from the vertical giving the co-latitude. The astrolabe, improved by Martin Behaim, was undoubtedly the instrument used by Columbus. It was graduated from the zenith, and held freely suspended from a point directly over the 360° mark; it can thus be seen that the accuracy of any reading depended largely upon the precision with which the point of suspension was placed in the vertical of the starting point of the graduation, and the coincidence of the line of gravity with the opposite, or 180° mark on the ring. The division of the ring was in degrees, with perhaps an approximation to half-degrees.

In observing, one person held the astrolabe, which hung from his thumb by the ring attached to the point of suspension; another person made the pointing by moving the alidade, or pointer, until the two terminal sights were in line with the object observed, and a third person read the angle. As no means of clamping was then employed, it was necessary, because of the rolling of the ship, that the circle should be read at the instant the sights were brought into line, and likewise it was essential that the latter should be done only when the instrument was in a truly vertical position — two important conditions difficult of simultaneous fulfilment.

It would be impossible to determine theoretically the errors which would result from the use of the astrolabe, but by comparing the latitudes of places as given by the voyagers of this epoch with the correct latitudes, the average error appears to be about *sixty* geographical miles.

Longitude was derived solely by dead reckoning, using for this purpose the mean course for the day, as shown by the compass, and the speed of the vessel obtained by estimation. The log and line did not come into use until a century later. In getting the speed a sandglass was used for timing, but no account was taken of *currents;* thus it is that the longitudes are greatly in error, and the "overruns" so numerous in the early voyages.

Another source of error in longitudes results from the false hypothesis, held at that time, that degrees of longitude were equal at all latitudes; however, this class of errors is somewhat corrected by the employment of a value for the earth's circumference too small by about 33 per cent.

It is therefore impossible to arrive at or even estimate the average error in the determination of longitudes, but the minimum error appears to be $1°$, while in one case the position of a place is out $8°$ in longitude.

In addition to these feeble instruments Columbus had a table of the sun's declination, a correction for the altitudes of the sun and, lastly, an imaginary chart of an unknown sea. In all the universe there is nothing so independent as a great soul. In a little ship, with meager helps, Columbus made brave venture of his fate and found a new world.

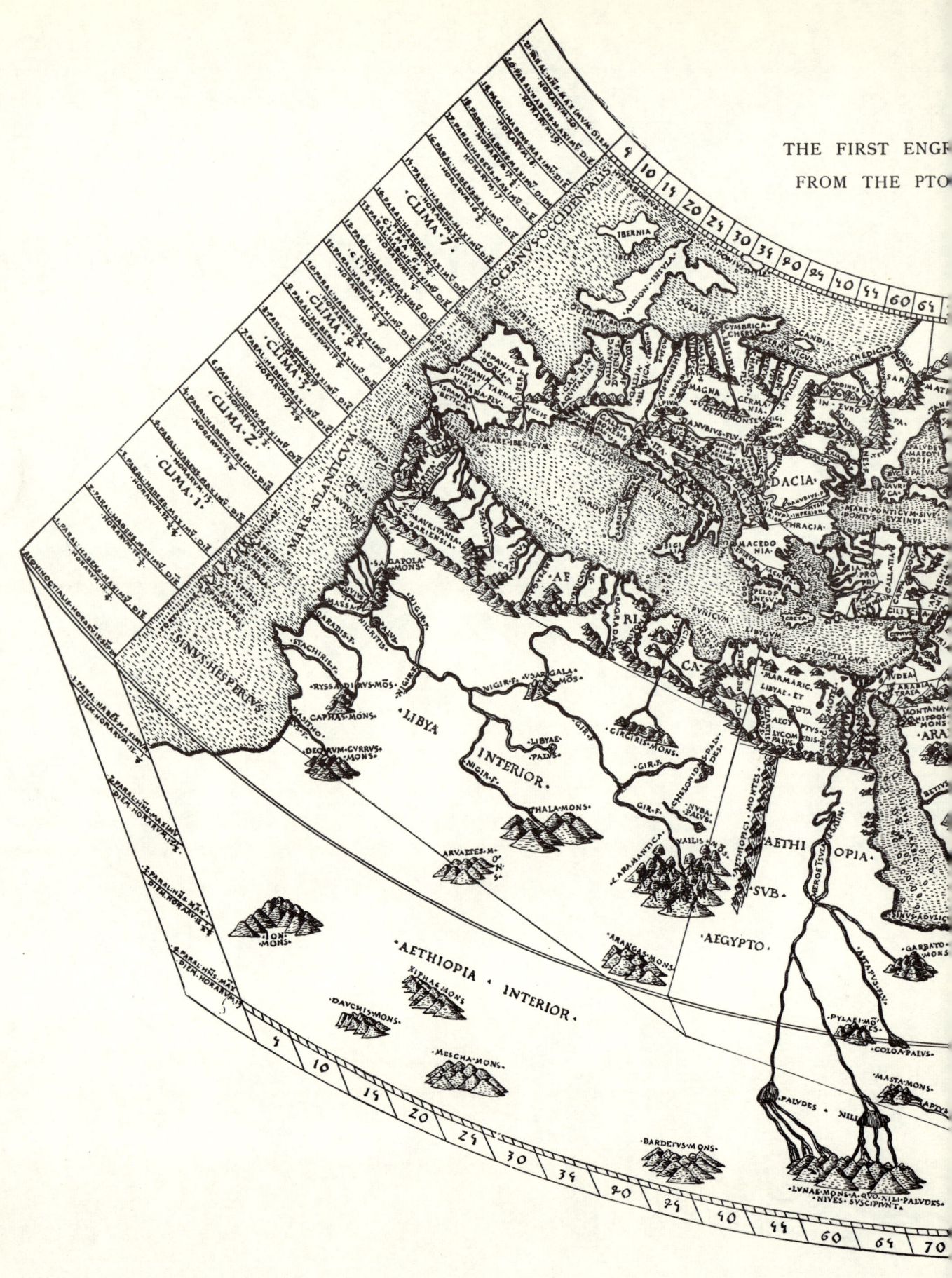

THE FIRST ENGR[AVED MAP]
FROM THE PTO[LEMY]

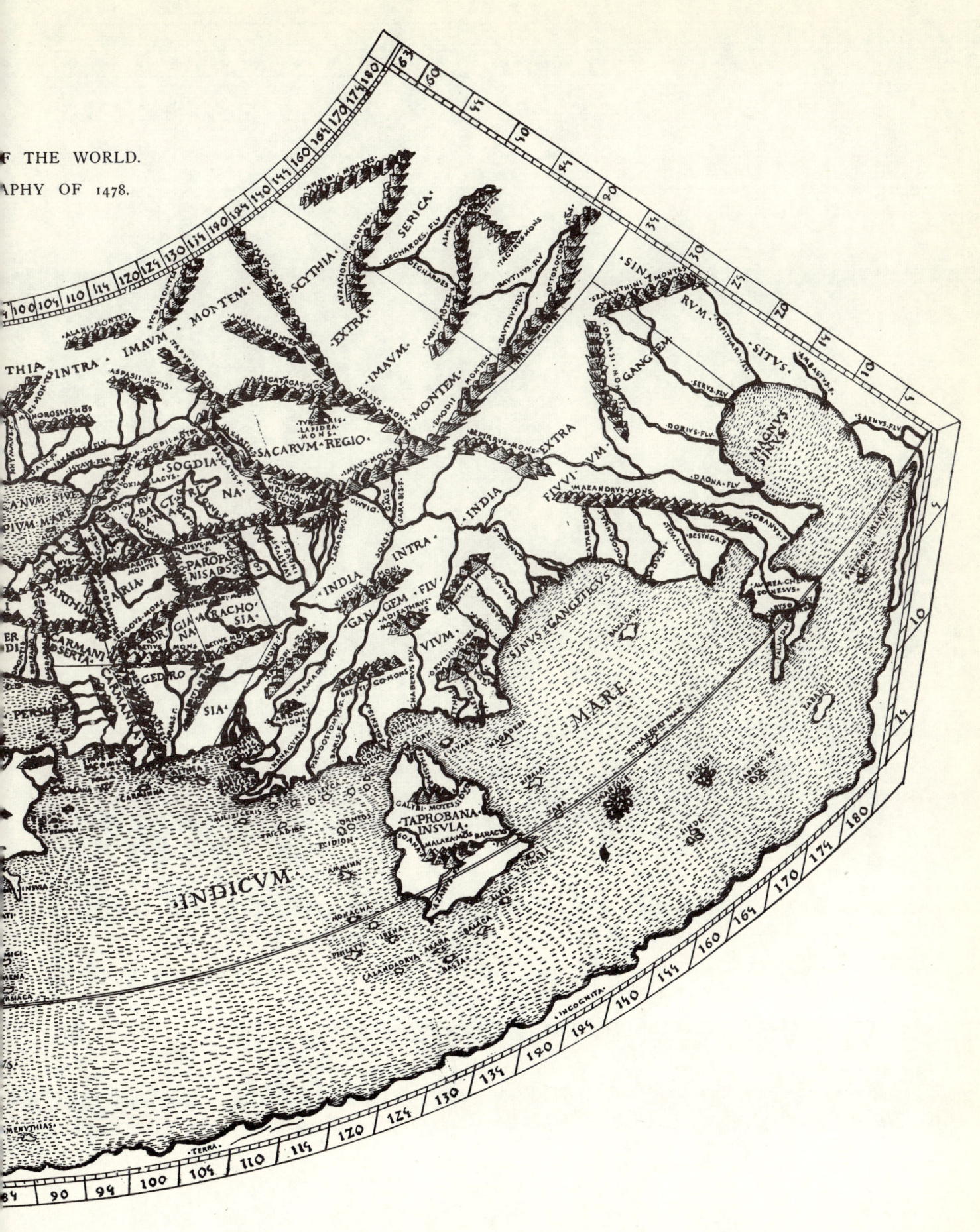

CHAPTER VI

Mercator's Projections

IF the earth were cylindrical in form, then a map of its surface could be represented with exactness upon a plane, with the one condition that the ratio of the length of the plane to its width should be equal to the relation of the length of the cylindrical earth to its circumference.

As the figure of the earth differs from the cylinder, the task of representing its surface upon a plane increases in difficulty—a difficulty which came to be experienced just as soon as men found it necessary to map or plot any considerable area. A small area can be represented on a map upon the hypothesis that the earth is flat without introducing any serious error, but a section containing one degree square cannot be accurately drawn upon a plane surface.

This impossibility becomes apparent when it is realized that because of the convergence of the earth's meridians—all meeting at both poles—the distance between any two meridians is diminishing as we recede from the equator; that is, a section of the earth which is a degree wide in latitude and a degree long in longitude, is not square.

Another illustration can be found in the figure which would be formed from the rind of an orange. If the rind is removed by making incisions extending entirely around the orange and passing through the point at which it was attached to the stem and a point directly opposite to this, and these pieces placed upon a table so that they may touch along a line half way between their tip ends, it will be seen that the rind covers a portion of the table in a shape somewhat like a double-edged saw.

In order to make these pieces cover a rectangular portion of the table, it would be necessary that they be elastic, and that their elasticity increase towards the tips, where the greatest extension would be needed. So it is with the problem of projecting the earth's surface or depicting it upon a plane; those sections which lie near the pole must be subjected to contortion if the equatorial regions retain their proper relative positions and contour.

Gerard Krämer, or Gerardus Mercator, in the Latinized form of his name, was born in the year 1512 at Rupelmonde, in Flanders. We have a double interest in him, first, in that he first applied the word *America* to the entire Western Hemisphere in his globe of 1538, and, second, because of the method first adopted by him of displaying upon a flat surface the figure of our globe. This method is known as Mercator's projection, and is still employed in the making of the marine charts of to-day. In the little town of Duisburg, near Düsseldorf, in Rhenish Prussia, Gerardus Mercator published his famous "Mappemonde" in the month of August of the year 1569. It is of exceeding rarity, and the only copy of which we have knowledge is that preserved in the Bibliothèque Nationale at Paris. Mercator, like others before him, employed a certain cordiform projection in his double-heart map of 1538, which the reader will find reproduced in this volume, and in the "Ptolemy" printed at Strasburg in 1525 the learned Pirkheimer speaks of a new cylindric projection; but the devising of cylindric projections with latitudinal curves, "Latudini crescenti," was the invention of the Flemish geographer Gerardus Mercator, and was first published in 1569.

In the Mercator projection meridians are represented by equi-distant parallel straight lines, and the parallels of latitude by straight lines perpendicular to them. From this it naturally follows that the course between two points, *or rhumb line*, will be a straight line, and will cut all meridians at the same angle. Because of these advantages the Mercator charts have retained their popularity with seamen.

The construction of this projection is made on the principle that, since the meridians are regarded as equi-distant parallel lines, the scale on which a degree of longitude is represented must continually increase as the pole is approached; and hence, to avoid unfortunate disagreements in the longitudinal and lateral distances, the scale of latitude must also be increased in the same proportion.

It is apparent from this that the degree is the unit, and that all points that are a degree apart in longitude will on a Mercator chart be at the same distance from one another, irrespective of their latitudes, whereas, if a mile should be taken as the unit, or the scale of the map should be thirty miles to the inch, a degree of the equator would be approximately two inches, while a degree on the fortieth parallel would be about one and one-half inches. The reader will thus understand that a chart drawn on this projection is not a safe map on which to measure distances. The scale by which one would reckon distances would have to be changed as one moved about on the surface of the earth.

The problem is somewhat complicated when we are required to determine the scale for an earth that is not spherical but spheroidal, nor can this problem be accurately solved until the earth's exact figure is known. Thus it is that our charts are inaccurate, and ships will sail to their destruction upon erroneously plotted courses, and states and nations war over disputed boundaries, until the geodesist determines the earth's true shape and size.

It may interest the reader to see a holograph letter of Gerardus Mercator, especially since its subject matter is the edition, issued the following year at Cologne, of his famous work *Tabulæ geographicæ ad mentem Ptolemæi restitutæ et emendatæ*.

TRANSLATION OF LETTER OF GERARDUS MERCATOR.

S. P. [Salutem Plurimam.] When, O most noble man, some two months ago, I was considering in the presence of James Wicham, the chamberlain of the most illustrious prince, my intention of securing the privilege in regard to my Ptolemy (i. e., to print it), he (J. W.) declared that by no one were you excelled in philanthropy both in benevolence and promptness in action, and that while you had both influence and zeal, actuated at the same time by the most honorable motives, you also entertained the most favorable opinions towards me and my geographical attempts. He (J. W.) informed me that when an opportunity in regard to this matter presented he would act with you and would see that on instruction of your lordship a letter should be written to his Majesty, and that with the addition of your intercession my supplication should be brought to his notice, and he thought that by your skill the matter would be disposed of and arranged. And so a little while after I sent my own draft of a supplication drawn up somewhat rudely to Sir James, praying him that he would, after kindly polishing it and making any additions, exhibit it (to his Majesty). This, I learned, was afterwards done, and letters have already been sent to His Majesty, and it is hoped that in a short time this privilege may be sent. Wherefore, when now the time of the Frankfort Fair draws nigh, in which, if it can be done, I would hawk about freely (i. e., get subscribers to) this work of Ptolemy, I await eagerly the granted privilege for which I have made supplication, especially if it is conceded to me in the same form as asked for at the Brabantine court. In both quarters that privilege must be obtained for me before I can publish. I pray, therefore, O most distinguished man, that, if you have not yet in hand the concession of the privilege, you will be present on the earliest opportunity at the royal council, where this may be settled as soon as possible. And that you may keep in mind myself and my cause, I send you a map of Europe mounted on cloth and made distinct with colors, so that I may be the more deserving of your benevolence, with whom I shall have brought this work to light. Farewell, thou most to be cherished among nobles.

Duisburg, 22d of June, 1577.

To the most distinguished H. T.

Most ready for every service,

GERARD MERCATOR.

To the Honorable Paulus, Secretary to the illustrious Duke of Juliers.

PART VIII

The Chartography of the New World

The Contour of the Continent as it was developed on the early Maps

PART VII

CHAPTER I

The First Map of the Old and New Worlds

WHOSE fingers traced the first map of the New World? We know that Christopher Columbus was a draughtsman — not an artist, but a proficient chartographer. The artistic pen-and-ink sketch preserved in the city hall of Genoa and attributed to him is apocryphal. According to M. Jal and M. Margry, the sketch presents Columbus and Providence in a shell-like galley, with allegorical figures of Tolerance, Constancy, Christianity, Victory, and Hope in and above the waves. These writers believe the names of the figures were inscribed by Columbus on the sketch in his own hand. We do not recognize the handwriting as that of Columbus.

The hand that drew this sketch was that of a master. That master had taken the three degrees of fancy, grace, and strength. Both Columbus and his brother Bartholomew supported themselves by their skill as map-makers. Yet to-day there probably exists no specimen of the admiral's chartographic handiwork. We cannot doubt that many maps were drawn by him not only to accompany his letters and to facilitate his explanations of the discovery, but to permanently record the results of his voyage. None of these has come down to us. In the spring of the year 1893 the author was offered an opportunity to buy a map of the island of Hispaniola alleged to be a holograph of Columbus. The map purported to have been discovered in Seville on the four-hundredth anniversary of its making, bearing the date of 1492. The mysterious fullness of time in which it appeared, together with the fact that it was dated at a time when Columbus could have known nothing of the topography of the island beyond its northern side, led to a few inquiries which never were answered, and which withdrew the interesting relic from our immediate market. Harrisse had already effectively disposed of the remarkable Columbian forgery known as the "Bank of St. George letter." The reader will remember that some years ago the literary world was excited over the discovery of a holograph letter of Columbus, which to-day

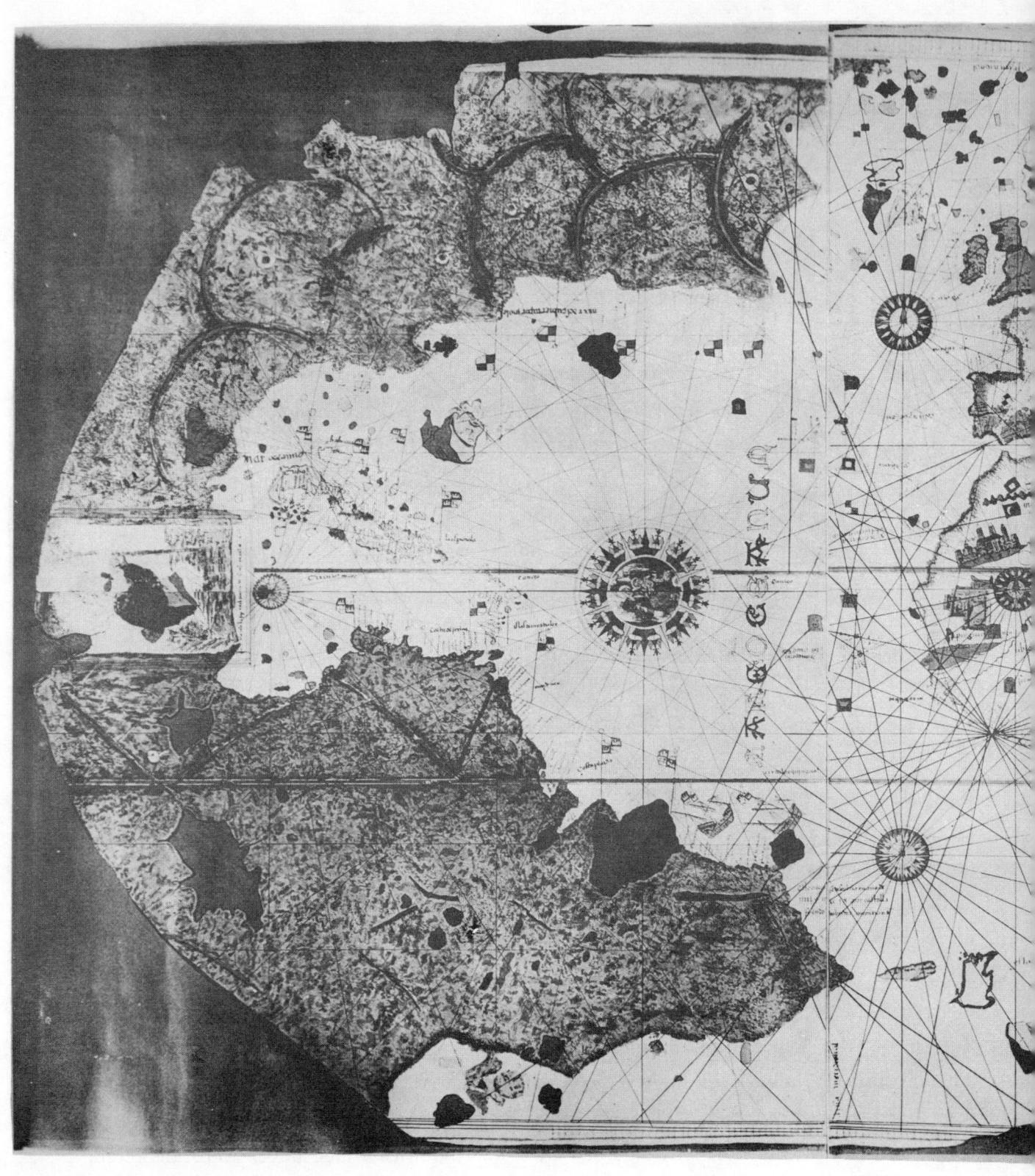

THE MAP OF JUAN DE LA COSA, DRAWN ABOUT 1500 C

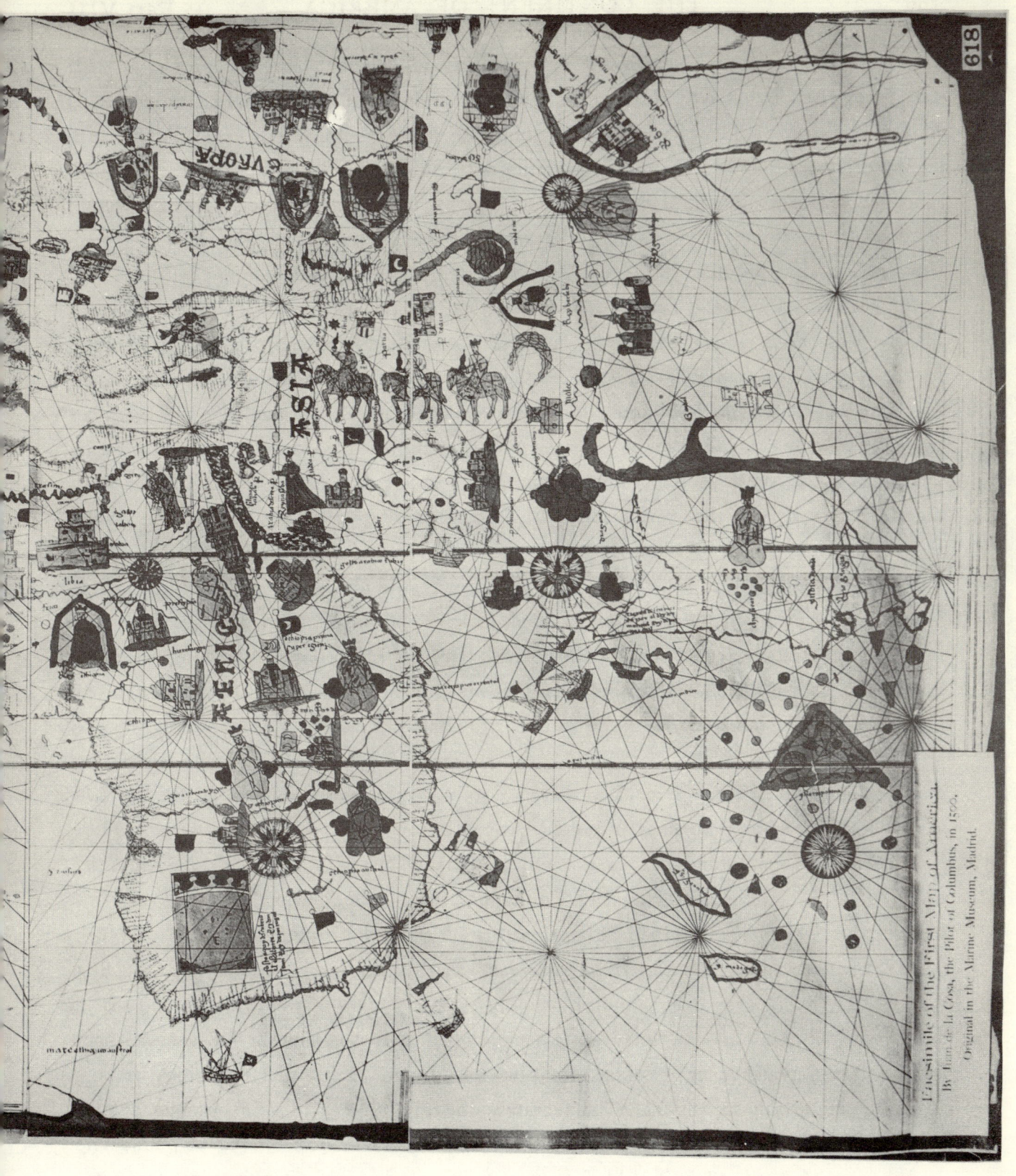

THE FIRST MAP SHOWING THE NEW DISCOVERIES.

is said to be hidden in New York city awaiting a rich but careless purchaser. It was recognized by Henry Harrisse as a clever facsimile of an original letter preserved in the Bank of St. George in Genoa. Harrisse kept his knowledge to himself until an American friend was about to be victimized into the purchase of the alleged letter, when he wrote a most interesting and instructive Columbian brochure, proving beyond shadow of question the fraudulent character of the document and at the same time surrounding that proof with a great crowd of delightful and entertaining witnesses.

There was a versatile character on the first expedition of Columbus with whom map-making was one of several trades. Juan de la Cosa was born in Santa Maria del Puerto, in the province of Santander, on the northern coast of Spain, a little town now known as Santoña. It was a land whose bold shores had been ever at war with the Biscayan waves, and many a ship caught between the two mighty combatants had gone to its death. To this day the historians of Santander honor the name of La Cosa not so much because he was the companion of the Genoese discoverer, nor because he owned the caravel named after his native town and which bore the standard of Spain and the admiral's flag at its masthead, and which was the first ship to reach the New World; nor yet again because he obtained more royal favor than any Biscayan follower of the sea ever got from Spanish king; not so much for these things do they honor him as for the fact that he was the first to make a chart of the dangerous Cantabrian coast, and, as says the author of "Breve Relación de los lauros, hechos gloriosos é hijos afamados de Santoña, ó Santonia" (1677), "rendered to sea-faring men the most important of services, helping to save thereby the lives of his brother sailors and preventing the loss of countless costly cargoes."

The Baron von Humboldt, in the fifth volume of his "Examen critique de l'histoire de la Géographie du Nouveau Continent," speaks of a "document entirely unknown, the *mappemonde* of Juan de la Cosa, dated 1500, the great importance of which M. Walckenaer and I discovered in the year 1832." This now famous map, the first map of the world ever made, after having been lost for three centuries, turned up in a Paris bric-à-brac shop in the year last mentioned, and was bought for a small sum by the Baron Walckenaer. Public attention was drawn to its chartographical importance by Humboldt in 1837, and immediately the great piece of skin became famous, and it is small wonder that, when after the baron's death it was offered at public sale on the 21st of April, 1853, it sold for 4020 francs, and went with singular propriety, and as the result of unusual official foresight, to the Spanish government, the minister of marine of that country bringing about its purchase. To-day it hangs in the Naval Museum at Madrid, a precious jewel in the Spanish crown. In the catalogue of the Museum it is marked "553," with the following description:

Ch. I   THE FIRST MAP OF THE OLD AND NEW WORLDS   197

Chart of the part appertaining to America, designed by Juan de la Cosa in the second voyage of the Genoese discoverer in 1493, and in the expedition of Alonso de Ojeda in the same year; stolen from Spain, it was in the possession of Baron de Walckenaer, whose executors sold it in public auction, where it was bought for the Hydrographic Department, whose Director, at the time Señor George Lesso de la Vega, kindly had it deposited in this Museum in order that the public might admire a document so curious and of such merit, considering the epoch in which it was made.

What is perhaps a reference to this identical map is found in Peter Martyr's account of his visit to Juan Rodriguez de Fonseca, the bishop of Burgos, in 1514, in whose house he saw a beautiful marine chart made by Juan de la Cosa. This same Fonseca had been at the head of that maritime department which afterward was organized as the celebrated *Casa de Contratacion* in Seville, the official trading bureau in which La Cosa had himself long served. It is easy to imagine Fonseca's coming into possession of this very map or one like it. Peter Martyr well described it as beautiful. To-day it is faded, torn, and frayed. When it was in possession of Fonseca it was rich in blue and gold, and illuminated after the departing fashion of the medieval manuscripts. The map is not on parchment, as is generally asserted, but on ox-hide. It is five feet and nine inches in length and cut square at the tail of the hide, where the width is three feet and two inches. At the neck the hide is rounded. Evidently it was intended to go upon a roller, as was the custom in constructing an ancient *portolano*. Three hundred and sixty degrees of longitude are supposed to be laid off on the map, each degree measuring fifteen Spanish leagues. The Tropic of Cancer runs vertically through the middle of the map, the top of which is the extreme west and includes the Caribbean Sea and the Gulf of Mexico. This space in the map, instead of being devoted to geographical description, is occupied by a rectangular piece of rather rude drawing, $7\frac{1}{4}$ by $4\frac{7}{8}$ inches, representing St. Christopher bearing the Christchild, in imitation of the famous woodcut engraving so long preserved in the *Bibliotheca Spenceriana* and dated 1423. There have been writers who fancied La Cosa intended to preserve in the face of St. Christopher the features of the great Admiral, and hence reference is sometimes made to this as the first portrait. It is needless to say that there is no foundation for the belief. Manifestly this picture was suggested by the name of the saint and by the folio woodcut made early in the century and for a long time regarded as the earliest specimen of wood engraving. There are thin lines bordering the picture to answer for a frame. It is much faded and in the upper left-hand corner is somewhat torn. Beneath the picture, but within the border, are the words:

Juan de la cosa la fizo en el puerto de S^a M^a en año de. : 500.
Juan de la Cosa made this in the Port of Santa Maria in the year 1500.

Directly under the picture, its upper edge touching the lower part of the frame, is a small mariner's compass one inch and three sixteenths in diameter. The green of the land has been allowed carelessly to run over the border of the picture. Following down the axis, here called the circle of Cancer, for ten and seven eighths inches from the lower border of the frame, we touch a little to the right of its own axis a larger ring in the form of a mariner's compass, four and three fourths inches in diameter, having sixteen points. Here is drawn by a more skillful hand than was employed in the rectangular picture an illuminated Madonna and child, two other figures appearing in the background. In all the reproductions we have seen there has been faulty copying. The right hand of the child is raised in the original, extending away from the body, the bended arm forming a square, while in the reproductions the right arm is across the body. The feet of the Virgin show in the original, and are covered in the reproductions. The right hand of the Virgin is impossible in the reproductions, while in the original it is natural. Aggravating liberties are also taken with the background of the vignette. Just beneath this mariner's compass, running in beautiful letters across the map, are the words MARE OCEANUM, the tropical line passing between the third and fourth letters of the second word. Four inches below the rosette, as it may be called, and still following down the tropic of Cancer, we come to the meridian line running at right angles to it. From this line to the top of the map, that is virtually to the top of the rectangular picture, is 27¼ inches, while the meridian line measures 37½ inches. It is this part of the map which particularly concerns America. The meridian line is that imaginary boundary wall which was to divide the fair lands of the New World into Portuguese and Spanish possessions. The famous document authorizing this partition was dated the fourth day of May, 1493. The line was one hundred leagues west of the Azores and Cape Verd Islands, and all westward thereof was to belong to Spain. By the treaty of Tordesillas, concluded on the seventh of June, 1494, between Spain and Portugal, this line was moved so much further westward in the interests of the Portuguese as to fall 370 leagues west of the Cape Verd Islands.

CHAPTER II

The First Map—Continued

IT must be remembered, however, that this map of La Cosa is intended to delineate upon a planisphere the entire world as known at the end of the fifteenth century. Accordingly we find the three continental areas laid down under their respective names, Europe, Asia, and Africa. The artist, when once his hand was drawn away from the green planes of the New World, the green denoting unknown lands, gave a freer course to his brush, and we find the surface of the map richly ornamented with cities, castles, and cathedrals, with ships and caravels, with banners, crowns, and sceptres. The Queen of Sheba is marveling at the glories of Palestine, and the three crowned kings are riding out of the East, following closely a shining golden star. Away to the extreme east are two mysterious and gigantic figures, the one a human figure with the head of a dog, called *Got*, and the other a hideous nondescript, with his eyes in his breast and his mouth in his stomach, entitled *Magot*. These are the Gog and Magog of the Scriptures, typifying the monsters with which the unknown regions were believed to be peopled. In the "Chronicon Nurembergense," printed in Nuremberg in the year 1493, are many figures of similar strange creatures whose existence was vouched for by Martin Behaim and, back of him, by Marco Polo. To understand this map one must remember that the vignette of St. Christopher is occupying and covering up the space intended for the Gulf of Mexico, and that the first projection of the main land to the right of the lower left corner of the vignette—really the lower right corner as it faces us—is intended for Florida. From that point on, the coast is northward. It was evidently the purpose of La Cosa to embody on this map the results of seven important voyages to the New World, as follows:

First, The Voyage of Discovery by Columbus, begun August 3, 1492.

On this voyage, the first recorded expedition made to the New World, Columbus discovered the Bahama Islands, landing first on Watling Island, and after naming and examining three others of the Bahama group, reached the north side of the large island of Cuba and coasted it to its eastern extremity, and also coasted the north side of the island of Haiti.

Second, The Second Voyage of Columbus, begun September 25, 1493.

On this voyage the Admiral opened to the world the lesser Antilles, landing at Guadalupe, Marigalante, Santa Cruz, Porto Rico, nearly reaching the western extremity of Cuba, and really completing the circumnavigation of Haiti.

Third, The First Voyage of Vespucius, begun May 10, 1497.

The door of the new continent was then opened by the Florentine adventurer for the first time. On this voyage Americus landed in the Bay of Honduras, having passed to the south of Cuba, thus proving to himself and La Cosa, the pilot of Columbus on the first two voyages, that it was an island; skirted the Gulf of Mexico, rounded Florida, and skirted the coast as far as Cape Hatteras, in thirty-six degrees of north latitude.

Fourth, The First Voyage of John Cabot, begun May, 1497.

On this voyage the elder Cabot sailed from Bristol, England, with a crew of eighteen men in a small vessel, passing the southern extremity of Ireland and turning to the northward for a time, finally taking a westward line, which brought him to a point on the coast of Labrador. Cape Clear, the southern extremity of Ireland, is on a more northerly parallel than the north coast of Newfoundland. The adventurers were back in Bristol before the beginning of August, 1497, and it is evident there was small time for explorations or coasting to the southward. It is safe to say that on this, the first voyage of the Cabots, no land to the south of Labrador was seen by them.

Fifth, The Second Voyage of Cabot, begun April, 1498.

This expedition sailed out of Bristol in April, 1498, and consisted of a fleet of five or six ships. We do not know if this expedition was in charge of John Cabot or his son Sebastian. The latter always claimed to have led it. Nor do we know the extent of the explorations made. The voyage was to the southward of the first expedition. The testimony of Sebastian Cabot is too contradictory to be reliable. Summoned before the Council of the Indies in December, 1535, he declared under oath that he did not know of his own knowledge whether or not there was an uninterrupted continental coast line from the Gulf of Mexico northward to the Baccalaos. Although occupying the position of pilot major to Spain and the censor of geographical and chartographical descriptions, he never questioned the claim made for Ponce de Leon that the latter first discovered the fair land of Florida. On the other hand, Sebastian Cabot did declare at one time that he himself had sailed as far south as the latitude of Gibraltar, which would have taken him not far from Cape Hatteras; and at another time he declared he had gone as far south as Florida.

Sixth, The Third Voyage of Columbus, begun May 30, 1498.

On this voyage Columbus discovered the Island of Trinidad, and in passing around it his eyes saw for the first time that which had been the desire of his heart, continental land; the Pearl coast was followed, and the islands of Margarita and Cubagua visited. It was on this voyage that the Gulf of Paria received its name, which, by identifying it with the Province of Lariab on the coast of Mexico, led to inextricable confusion and for a long time to the dishonoring of the name and fame of Vespucius.

Seventh, The Second Voyage of Vespucius, begun May 16, 1499.

On this voyage the equatorial line was crossed, and Cape San Roque, on the Brazilian coast and in south latitude about five degrees, was reached by the Spanish expedition. It must be remembered that La Cosa himself was pilot in this fleet.

To these voyages may be added that made by Pinzon, who set out in December, 1499, and visited Brazil, working about three degrees lower down than the point reached by Americus on his second voyage; also the voyage made at the beginning of the year 1500 by Diego de Lepe, a native, like Pinzon, of the holy port of Palos, who added two degrees of latitude to the map of the Brazilian coast; and finally the famous expedition of Pedro Alvarez Cabral, which, starting for Hindustan, was by the winds of chance driven to the shores of the New World, thus effecting an unintentional Portuguese discovery. A point sixteen and a half degrees south of the equator, or about the site of Porto Seguro, was reached on this occasion, the report of the voyage having been borne back to Portugal by Gaspar de Lemos in the early summer of 1500.

We have now before us the sources of geographical information concerning the New World from which La Cosa builded his map. Strangely enough the last bit of information, latest in point of time and covering the lowest point of southern land then discovered, enables us to approximately fix the northern limit of the discovery made by John Cabot. From the tropic of Cancer to the lowest southern point of the Cabral discovery is thirty nine and a half degrees. The northern limit of the English discoveries, the most northerly of the English flag stations on the map, is as far distant to the north from the tropic of Cancer as the Cabral discovery is to the south. This would fix the Cabot landfall at sixty-two and a half degrees of north latitude, or in the neighborhood of Frobisher Bay. Cape Farewell, the most southerly point of Greenland, is situated in sixty degrees of north latitude, and the most northerly point of Labrador is but a trifle further to the north. Whatever knowledge of the north coast of America the map of La Cosa indicates, we are assured he obtained that knowledge from an English source, and therefore from John Cabot. La Cosa must have kept himself thoroughly acquainted with the spread of geographical knowledge, to which he himself was contributing so liberally.

Henry Harrisse, more carefully and completely than any one else, has copied from this map its list of names and places, bays and streams, and systematically arranged them in three divisions, the Northeastern Continent, the North Coast of the Southern Continent, and the Brazilian Coast as then known. (See "Discovery of North America," London, 1892.) We have availed ourselves of his labors. The readings on the map to-day are faded and uncertain. Harrisse was at pains to compare the nomenclature here given with what was reported as on the map when it was unearthed by Von Humboldt in 1832, and as read by him, and by Rembiélinski and by Ramon de Sagra in subsequent years, while the map was still in fair condition.

NORTHEASTERN CONTINENT.

Y. verde	Isla de la trenidat	Iusquei
S. grigor	R.º longo	Requilia
Cauo de ynglaterra	Forte (or Fonte)	C.º de S. luzia
C. sastanatre	Argare (or Argair)	Ansro
Agron	Menistre	Lagofori
Cauo de S. iohan	S. luzia	C.º de S. Jorge
S. nicolas	C.º de lisarte	Cauo descubierto

NORTH COAST OF THE SOUTHERN CONTINENT.

M. de S. eufemia	Gigan	M. tasado
Sato de uerbos	Y. de ge	3. echo
C. de la bela	M. alto	Canpina
Almadabra	C. de la mota	Yllas de sana
C. de espera	P. flechado	G. de las perlas
Venuçuela	Aldea de turme	Margalada
Y. de brasil	Costa parej	Tres or
	Boca del drago	

BRAZILIAN ELBOW.

R. de la posesion	El macareo	Costa pareja
Mar de agua duce	G. de S. mjª	M. negro
Rio del obpā	Ysla de S. telmo	Rº negro
Tres hermanos	Mas alta la mar que la tierra	G. de arecifes
Plaia de cordoba	Costa plaida	Rº dº se fallo una cruz
Rº de holganca	. . . . anca	Punta del medano
C. de S. dº	. . . . plata	Cº de St mja
Las planosas	Costa de arena	Motas arenosas
Tierra de S. anbrosio	Rº de arboledos	Rº de bazia bariles
Costa anegada	P. fermoso	Plaia de arena

It is apparent at once that this nomenclature has not been preserved in subsequent maps of the American mainland and is to-day almost entirely unintelligible. The names given by Harrisse and copied from early readings of the La Cosa map are largely imaginative. Even when Von Humboldt first saw it, the chart was faded and in many places illegible. The great German savant promised to give his own rendering of this nomenclature, but he never completed his work. It is certain that the northeast coast marked by the English flags was never seen by La Cosa, and its description must have been obtained from English sources, and presumably from one of the Cabots himself. If Cabot communicated to him the general course of the mainland from the sixty-third degree of north latitude, reached in his first voyage of 1497, to about the thirty-sixth degree, reached in his second expedition of 1498, it would give the coast-line to the point where La Cosa might take it up and complete it from his own personal observation preserved in notes and on hastily drawn charts. But as we read this remarkable map the last English flag to the south is far north of Cape Hatteras. If the extremity of Florida is taken as the point nearest the words Mar Oceanus, ten degrees more of latitude should bring us to Cape Hatteras; but this distance would be almost as far from the most southerly English flag as it is from the Florida point. Computing by the scale of relative measures we find that the peculiar horn-like piece of land taken by Dr. Kohl for Cape Cod is far too much to the south to answer the situation of that marked projection. If the latter is really intended for Cape Cod it must have been seen by the Cabots, and in that case the line of English flags should have come further south. Of course this may have been an omission on the part of the artist who embellished the map. Dr. Kohl, in his "History of the Discovery of Maine," Portland, Me., 1869, accounts for this discrepancy in the appearance of relative distances by the old-fashioned method of projection, permitting the coasts in north latitude to be drawn out more from west to east. Dr. Kohl has decided that the point marked by the most northerly of the English flags, and called on the map *Cauo de Ynglaterra*, is Cape Race. But the latter is only in forty-six and one half degrees of north latitude, or sixteen degrees too far south for the projection of La Cosa's map. As this cape was the nearest point of land to England, its name, Dr. Kohl thinks, was naturally suggested. If this point is not Cape Race, as the low latitude of the latter leads us to doubt, it is the north extremity of Labrador, and the trend of the land westward may be meant for Hudson Bay.

When we look at the nomenclature of the northern part of South America we find the name of The Isle of Giants given to an island situated about where Curaçao is in the group of Leeward Islands in the Caribbean Sea. This island was discovered and named by Americus Vespucius on his second voyage, in which La Cosa himself took part. The reader will notice that to the extreme south is an island with the inscription "This island was discovered by the Portuguese." Harrisse in his "Discovery of North America" identifies this simply with the Brazilian coast then just discovered by Cabral and reported as stated above by Gaspar de Lemos, who sailed from Porto de Seguro in May, 1500. To us it seems like a later addition, and to refer to the third voyage of Vespucius (1501–1502), during which he discovered the Island of South Georgia. Harrisse is not the first to be puzzled by the strange nomenclature of this famous map, or to doubt, in view of the meaningless names, not only in the northern part but in the region visited by La Cosa himself, whether the latter really drew and inscribed the chart, or whether it might not have been the handiwork of some contemporaneous chartographer working a few years later from an original by La Cosa. A manuscript map always lacks the authentic stamp of date found in a printed or engraved map. The same hand or a later hand can easily elaborate a document in manuscript, and of which there can be but one original. We already have evidence that different hands probably embellished and ornamented portions of this particular map. However this may be, the La Cosa map must always have the liveliest interest for the student of American geography.

The interest in geography awakened by the Columbian discovery and the subsequent explorations was not confined to Spain and Portugal. Manuscript maps made in those countries were distributed over Italy and among the northern nations. It is stated that the chartographers of Portugal were not permitted to copy the official maps for duplication and communication to foreign nations, but it is equally a fact that such copying was extensively done. Where commerce and science unite in demanding knowledge the edict of no king can keep it hidden. We have seen the influence early Spanish and Portuguese manuscript maps had upon German geographers, such as Ruysch and Waldseemüller. Indeed, no correct knowledge of the lands of the New World could have come from any other source. The student of chartography and nomenclature can discover the origin of inspiration governing each geographer.

CHAPTER III

The Cantino and Canerio Manuscript Maps

ESIDES the map of La Cosa there are two other manuscript charts which have had important influence on early chartography. One is known as the Cantino map. It takes its name from Alberto Cantino, the envoy to the court of Portugal of Hercules d'Este, Duke of Ferrara. Cantino had communicated to his patron in the fall of 1501 the latest news of the discoveries, and had doubtless related the account — perhaps repeated by the voyager himself — of the first two expeditions of Americus Vespucius, together with the information that he had sailed in the spring of that very year to follow up the discovery of Cabral, the Portuguese pilot; and with this information Cantino had told of the voyage to the north of another bold Portuguese, Gaspar Corte-Real.

This Cantino chart is a planisphere on vellum, considerably larger than the La Cosa map, measuring 86½ inches by 39⅜ inches. It is rich in colors and gilt, and is evidently the work of an Italian artist. The map was executed in Lisbon between December, 1501, and October, 1502. In a letter written by Cantino to the Duke of Ferrara and dated from Rome, November 19, 1502, the map is stated to have been contracted for at twelve gold ducats, but the cost had been equal to "twenty narrow ducats." Harrisse relates the romantic history of this map. For nearly 100 years it retained its place in the Ducal library. In the year 1592, when, by direction of the Pope Clement VIII., Cæsar d'Este was deprived of his duchy, it was removed to Modena. It was at one time employed on a frame as a screen, to adapt itself to which it was forced to part with considerable of its upper portion. It was stolen during the municipal riot of 1859, and some years afterward was discovered by Signor Boni, the librarian, playing some greasy part in a pork shop in the Via Farini. It is needless to say the rare chart was rescued and now is a bright ornament in the *Biblioteca Estense* at Modena.

The portion of this map devoted to the New World is an advance on that of the La Cosa in some respects, and falls short of its fullness in others. No scale of latitude whatever is given; it may have existed on the lost portion. The Columbian Islands are accurately described, and the insularity of Cuba and its true position correctly shown. The northwest continental land is plainly marked from the southern point of Florida to a point near Hudson's river. A large peninsula, the land we now call Greenland, reaches beyond the arctic circle, extending to sixty-two degrees north latitude. On this stretch of territory are depicted the discoveries of Gaspar Corte-Real. There can be no doubt as to the source of information which led to the drawing of the extreme northern coast-line. The second voyage of Gaspar Corte-Real, made in 1501 and reported in the autumn of the same year, afforded all this knowledge. Indeed, an inscription is added, in another hand from that which traced the map, that "It is feared he [Gaspar Corte-Real] is lost." On the southern coast the discovery made by Cabral is recorded, and the chartographer has permitted his imagination to extend the coast-line south of Porto Seguro, the point at which Cabral's expedition sailed for the Cape of Good Hope.

Whatever doubt there may be in the La Cosa map of the long coast-line there depicted being intended for America or Asia, there can be no such doubt as to the Cantino chart, for its Asiatic line is clearly defined, and in addition we find traced in its proper position what can only be the eastern continental coast of America. The question may well be repeated here,—from what voyager's explorations did the map made in 1502 secure its northeast continental information? If Florida and the adjoining northern coast were not visited until 1513 by Ponce de Leon, how came they on a map in 1502? If the insularity of Cuba was not ascertained until 1508, when it was explored by Sebastian de Ocampo, how comes it that on the Cantino, as on the La Cosa map, it appears clearly as an island? Surely some ship sailed to the south of Cuba into the Gulf of Mexico, around the point of Florida, and well up the northeast coast before the beginning of the sixteenth century. No one ever claimed to have done these things except Americus Vespucius.

The other manuscript map which we will notice is the planisphere made or copied by Nicolay de Canerio, a Genoese. There is nothing to indicate the date when or the place where it was executed. The descriptive matter on the map is in Portuguese, and the inference is that either it was made in Portugal, or that it was an immediate copy from a Portuguese original. In the "Bulletin de la Société de Géographie," Lyons, 1890, is the announcement of the finding of this map by Mr. L. Gallois of Lyons, in the *Archives du Service hydrographique de la Marine* at Paris. It is a map of the entire world and measures 88½ inches by 45¼ inches.

While the date of the making of this map is uncertain, it may be referred to a period between 1502 and 1504. It follows the Cantino map in contour and in nomenclature, but with some changes. The Corte-Real discoveries in the extreme north and the description of the "Land of the True Cross" are the same as in the latter. The southern coast is extended ten degrees further south than in the Cantino map, or to thirty-five degrees south latitude. If Nicolay de Canerio, or whoever may have made the map, had obtained his knowledge of this coast from Americus Vespucius, he would have known that the third voyage of the Florentine explorer had carried him to the fifty-second degree of south latitude. The configuration of the northwest coast is carried seventeen degrees farther south than in the Cantino map. Again proof is given of the early knowledge of the insularity of Cuba. The northwest coast of that island is marked with small crosses to indicate after the manner of marine charts the presence of reefs and dangerous submerged rocks. This part of Cuba was not explored by Columbus, and yet, prior to its exploration by Ocampo, it was known to be an island. This map shows imperfectly the Gulf of Mexico and the Yucatan country. The Florida peninsula is well defined, and its relative position to the northwest coast of Cuba. Harrisse considers the prototype of this map as having had more influence on the German chartographers than any other chart, Spanish or Portuguese. The nomenclature adopted in the engraved maps is more directly traceable to the Canerio than to any known Spanish chart.

These two Portuguese manuscript charts, or the originals of which they may be copies, are regarded by Harrisse as the prototypes of the printed maps which soon after began to appear in Central Europe. There were doubtless scores of others as important and trustworthy as these. If the Duke of Ferrara could have one made for "twenty narrow ducats," there were other lords with gold pieces, and there were universities and seats of learning eager to acquire the recorded results of each new discovery. The learned throughout Europe were inquiring for knowledge of the New World, and correspondents in Seville and Lisbon were busy sending, by authority or surreptitiously, copies more or less accurate of the official charts. There had as yet been produced no engraved maps containing the discoveries in the New World. Indeed, since 1482 and until 1508 there had been but two editions of Ptolemy, the one simply a new edition in 1486 of the Ulm imprint of 1482, and the other an edition in 1490 of the famous Rome Ptolemy of 1478. Facts were so difficult to determine that all were waiting before engaging on the important work of introducing the Alexandrian geographer to a New World.

One impressive fact is established by these three manuscript maps — the La Cosa, the Cantino, and the Canerio — drawn between 1500 and 1504, and that is the knowledge of the existence of a continental land lying between Europe and Asia. We have been taught by careless historians that the early discoverers had no conception of what they had discovered, and went to their graves ignorant of the great geographical enlargements they had been instrumental in opening. Columbus is represented as mourning in his dying moments over an unsubstantial Cathay, and we are asked to believe that Americus Vespucius died in the assurance that his own Lariab and the Paria of Columbus were but two distant points on the same eastern coast of Asia. Yet the latest of these manuscript maps was made at least two years before Columbus died and eight years before Americus passed away. Truly, who knew so well as these great souls the import of what they had accomplished!

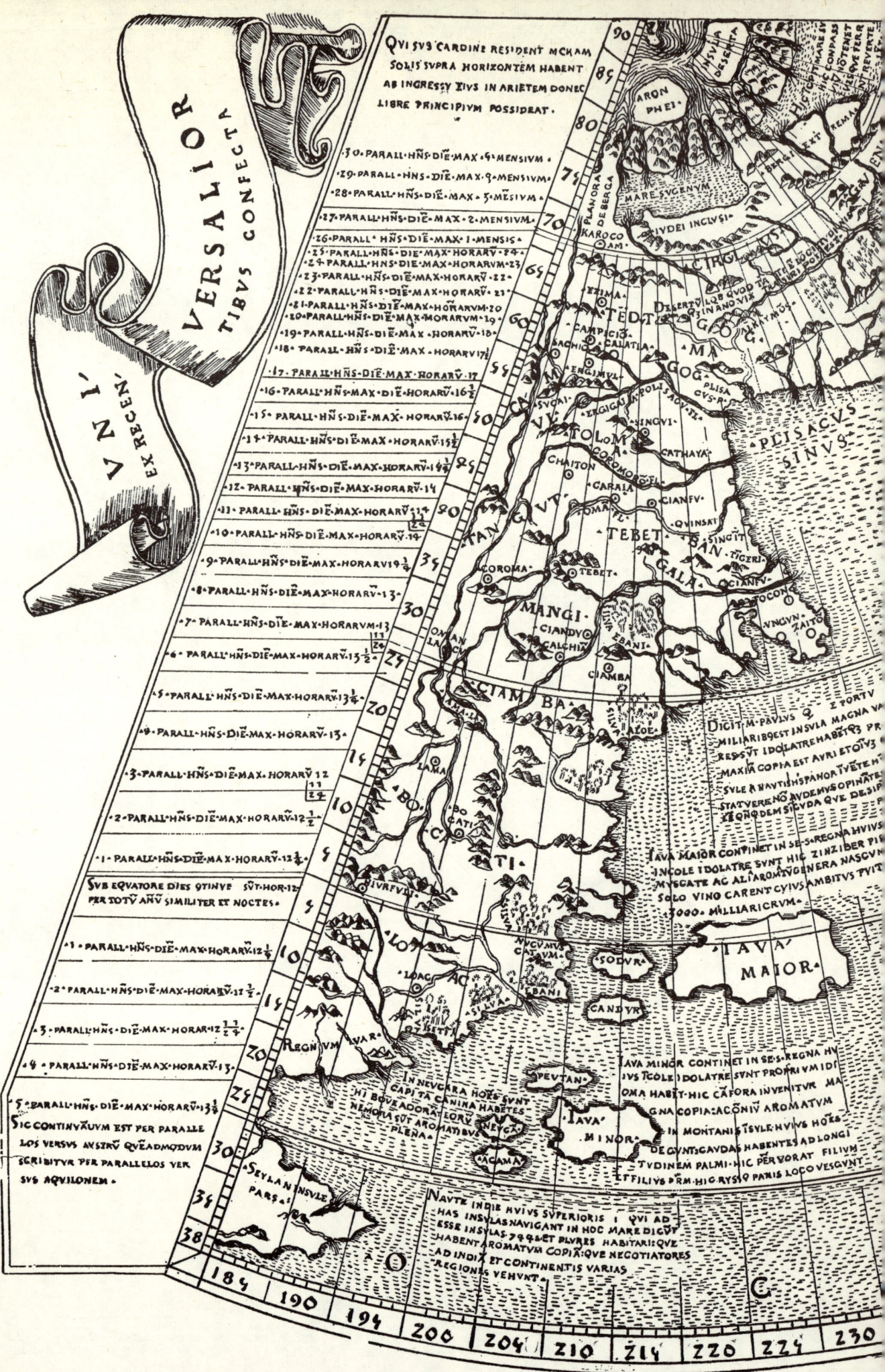

PORTION OF THE MAP OF THE WORLD BY JOHANNES
THE FIRST ENGRAVED MAP S

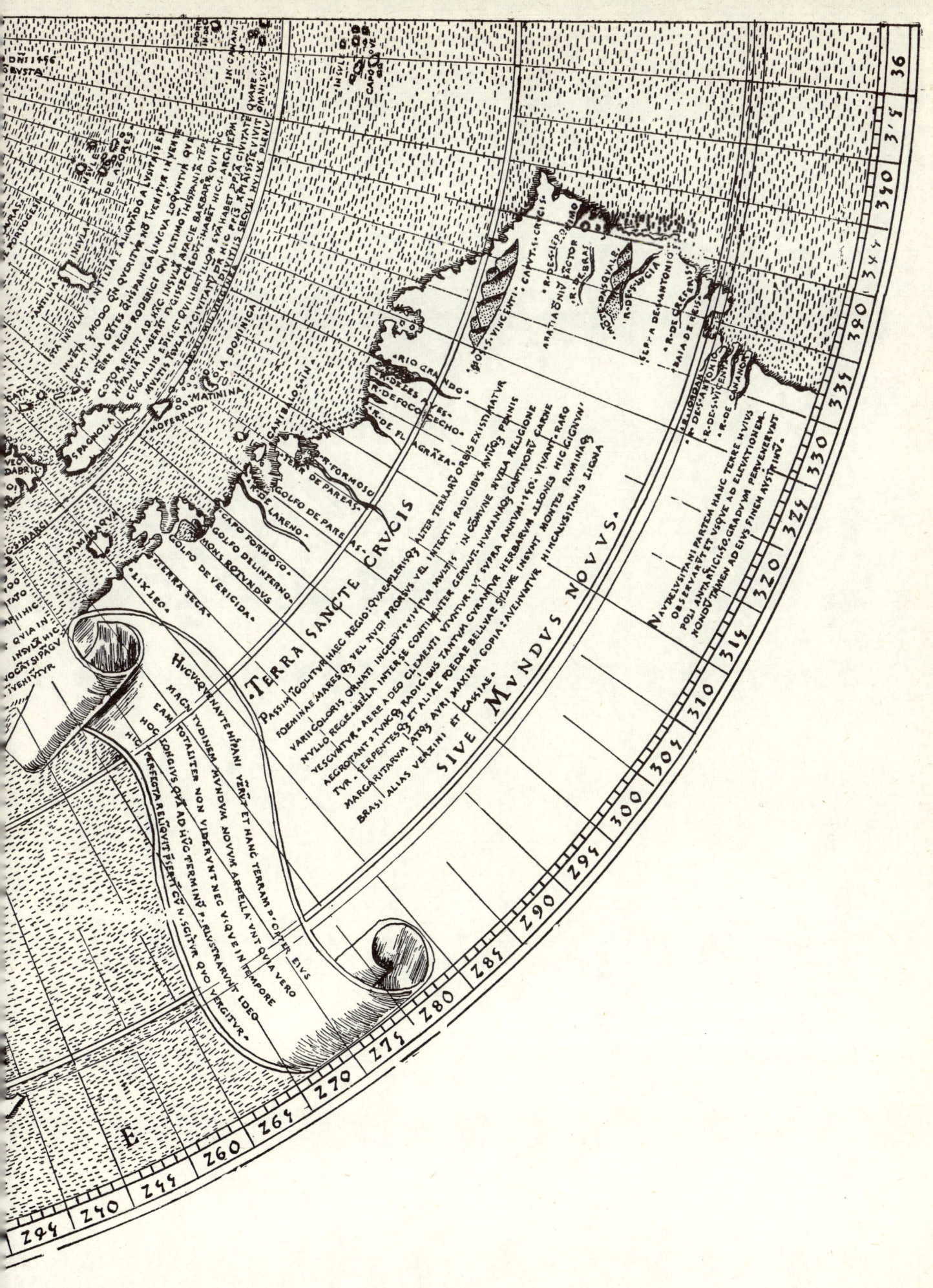

FROM PTOLEMY'S GEOGRAPHY OF 1507-1508.
THE NEW WORLD.

CHAPTER IV

The Ruysch Map

HEN we leave the field of manuscript maps to examine those which have been engraved and printed we are upon more certain and assured ground. The manuscript map, not being subject to the limitations of book form, affords opportunity for detail and particularity which is denied the largest printed folio. But in the manuscript map there is always uncertainty as to the date of its execution, and there is the possibility of subsequent additions and amendments. The La Cosa map, for instance, shows indications of two distinct hands. A false date may be put upon a hand-written map; the coast-line may be altered, a bay may be inserted, a river may be drawn down to the sea. And all these modifications of an original map may be made to imply earlier knowledge of important discoveries than really at the time existed. In the case of an engraved published map changes are practically impossible. Once sent out into the world in two or three hundred copies, the opportunity for alterations is gone forever. That different states of the same engraved plate frequently exist is well known, but the period of the change can almost always be accurately determined. An instance of this, curiously enough, occurs in the engraved map we now first consider, and on which map, off the eastern coast of Asia, the words *Plisacus Sinus* are inserted in some copies and omitted in others. On the eighth of September, 1507, there issued from the press of Bernardinus Venetus de Vitalibus in Rome an edition of Ptolemy's geography. Bernardinus Venetus set up his press in Venice in the year 1494, and in 1498 printed, in partnership with Matheus Venetus, under the name of Li Albani, the first volume of the "Enneades" of Marcus Antonius Sabellicus, followed in 1504 by the second volume, in which, eighth book of the tenth Enneade, occurs the first biographical sketch of Christopher Columbus ever printed. This edition of Ptolemy, as the title informs us, was prepared under the direction of Marcus Beneventanus, a monk of the Celestine order, and John Cotta of Verona. There are thirty-three maps, including the twenty-seven which are found in the Rome edition of

1478, and in addition six more maps, one each for Italy, France, Spain, Livonia, and the Holy Land, and one on which is most of the territory comprising the present empires of Germany, Russia, and Austria. There is no map of the New World found in the examples bearing the date of 1507 on the title. That it was intended there should be such a map is evident from the permission or exclusive permit to sell granted to the publisher Tosinus by Pope Julius II., and which permission is granted as a recompense for the expense Tosinus was under in securing a map of the new regions. This permission is dated July 28, 1506. It may be that this order or permission will account for the failure on the part of the coterie in the Vosgian Gymnase to issue the map of the New World they were preparing in 1507. The civil jurisdiction of the Pope did not reach into Lorraine, but the Lud brothers and the others were ecclesiastics or semi-ecclesiastics, and only too ready, doubtless, to obey the will of the head of the Church. Be this as it may, in the Rome printing office the map was not yet ready when the first copies were printed. Shortly after, with a title page bearing simply the date of 1508, but with the colophon still dated September 8, 1507, copies were issued announcing that Marcus of Benevent had prepared a description of the New World and of the ocean pathway from Lisbon to the Indian Ocean, and that accompanying the description was a map of the entire known world by Johannes Ruysch, a German. Therefore copies of this later edition have thirty-four maps, the same thirty-three that are in the first edition, and the additional map of the world entitled:

VNI | VERSALIOR | COGNITI ORBIS | TABVLA
EX RECEN | TIBUS CONFECTA | OBSERVATIONI | BUS

This title is on a many-folded scroll at the top of the map, and the words are placed on four of these folds as indicated by the perpendicular lines. The map is 21¼ inches by 16 inches, and is shaped like a fan. We have only given the western half of this map, but it is reproduced in exact size of the original.

The following is a brief bibliographical description of this rare volume:

The book is a large folio, 16⅞ by 11½ inches. The water mark used in the paper is a figure of an ostrich-like bird, a crown resting on its head and a large key lengthwise under its feet. The book consists of 142 leaves exclusive of the maps, and is printed in double columns. A, B, C, F, G, H, I, K, L, M, N, and O have each eight leaves, while D and E have six. *Aa* and *Bb* have eight leaves each, while *Cc* has four. Sheet *a* has six and *b* has eight. The initial letter of the preposition *In* of the title on the recto of *Ai* is an ornamented woodcut about 2⅜ inches in width and about 11¾ inches in length. There are 35 preliminary leaves, and the first book of the geography begins on the recto of the thirty-sixth leaf, or *Evi*. *Ni* has on the recto a "sphæra in plano" covering the entire page. On the verso of *Nviii* is an epistle from Marcus of Benevent to Johannes Baduarius explaining the connection of Johannes Cotta with the great work he had in hand. The colophon, which is the same in the editions of 1507 and 1508, is found in eight lines on the recto of folio *Ovii* and is as follows.

Explicit planisphærium Ptholemæi recognitum diligentissime a Marco Beneuentano Monacho Cælestinorum quod antea in multis etiā antiquis exemplaribus latinis corruptissimum reperiebantur. Nec nō Claudii Ptholemæi a plurinis uiris utriusq̃ linguæ doctiss. emendatū cum multis additionibus Romę Nouiter impressum per Bernardinū Venetū de Vitalibus. Expēsis Euāgelista Tosino Brixiano Bibliopola. Impante Iulio. II. Pont. Max. Anno. III. Pōtificatus sui. Die VIII. Septēbr. M.D.VII.

Folio *Oviii* is blank. The register "de tribus orbis partibus" begins on *Aa* and runs to the recto of *Cciv*. The recto of *ai* (unnumbered) contains an epistle from Tosinus, while on the verso is an epistle from Marcus of Benevent to Marianus. On the recto of *a2* begins the "nova descriptio orbis," by Marcus Beneventanus, which ends on the recto of *bviii*, the verso being blank. On the recto of *a3* is the following passage, interesting because of its reference to Columbus and also to Johannes Ruysch:

Quāuis aūt nostra habitabilis ad ortū ulterius tractū non habeat tamē nostra orbis assignatio pluribus in parallelis cognita est ad circuli quātitatē iuxta Columbi nostræ ætatis Nauarchi diligentissimi obseruata: qui dixit se Gadibus nauigasse per mesonyctiū ad ortus littera: Tum in subparallelo in quo sita est ea insula quā Spagnolam uocāt, qui distat ab subęqtore subgr̄. ferme. 29 ad boreā tū ultra tropicū cancri ad eleuationē poli aquilonii gr̄. 15. ubi sita est terra sanctæ Crucis. Ioānes' Ruschi Germanus Geographo℞ meo iudicio pitissimus: ac in pingendo orbe diligentissimus cuius adminiculo in hac lucubratiuncula usi sumus. dixit: se nauigasse ab albionis australi parte: & tā diu quo ad subparallelū ab subæquatore ad boreā subgr̄ 53. p̃uenit: & in eo parallelo nauigasse ad ortus littora per angulū noctis atq̃ plures insulas lustrasse. qua℞ inferius descriptionē assignabimus. Erit igī nostra descriptio uniuersalis nec ad perticularia nisi ad noua quędā descēdemus: quo℞ apud antiquos: aut nulla: aut admodū parua extabat cognitio. Atq̃ p̄mhanc descriptionē quidq̃d cōtinentis est: quidq̃d oceani notatu dignū recensebimus, nō quo ad historias: sed quo ad situm & positurā: quo nam pacto sese habet.

Although our earth is not known farther to the east, its limit is ascertained in many parallels, and its extent lately observed by Columbus, a most famous admiral of our time, who said that he himself had sailed from the Straits of Gades by the reckoning of the stars to the shores of the east from that parallel: in which is situated the island called Hispanola, and which is distant from the equator nearly 29 degrees of north latitude, even beyond the tropic of Cancer as far as 15 degrees north of the equator, where is situated the territory called the Land of the Holy Cross. Johannes Ruysch, a German, in my judgment most learned of geographers and well skilled in depicting the globe, of whose assistance we have availed ourselves in our arduous labor, said that he himself had travelled from the south of England, and when he had attained to the parallel which is about 53 degrees of north latitude, had navigated by the sole aid of the stars until he came to the shores of the east and discovered many islands, an account of which we will give further along. Therefore our description will not be given in detail except when we come to certain new parts, of which no knowledge or but little existed among the ancients.

In accordance with our proposition we intend to take note of whatever in this description may be of interest concerning the continent and the ocean, not with regard to their history but with respect to their geographical situations.

CHAPTER V

Legends on the Ruysch Map

THE entire map is covered with legends and descriptive text. Beginning with the one furthest to the north, beyond the Arctic circle, we have:

> Hic īcipit Mare Svgenv̄
> Hic compassus naviv̄ nō tenet
> nec naves qve ferrvm tenent
> revertere valēt.
>
> Here begins the Sugenum Sea.
> Here the compasses of the ships
> lose their power, and it is not
> possible for ships which have iron on board
> to return.

The reader, knowing that the Cabots had first visited this territory, might infer from this note that they had first noted and commented on the variation of the magnetic needle. But the credit for registering this observation does not belong to either of the Cabots. Nor yet does it belong to Columbus. It is recorded in his journal, as printed in the "Historie," written by his son, Fernando Columbus, and printed first in Venice in 1571, that on the evening of September 13, on his memorable first voyage, and when the fleet was in about 28° of north latitude, in the parallel of the Canary Isles, he noticed the needle declining toward the northwest, and that this declination was increased on the morning following. By the third day thereafter this variation had amounted to a "wind's quarter," or "meza quarta," as it is in the original edition of the "Historie," and the frightened pilots were with difficulty persuaded that natural and not diabolical causes were at work. But a knowledge of the susceptibility of the magnetic needle to change must have come to the mariners who sailed into strange seas long before the time of Columbus. Not only the captains and pilots, but even the common sailors must have been familiar with the turning of the needle from the north. What Columbus and his sailors discovered was not a mere declination of the needle, but its response to the presence of the magnetic meridian when their fleet was passing for the first time. It was as great a change as would be an observation of the thermometer which should suddenly disclose, to one accustomed in a temperate zone to see only slight variations of the mercury, a fall below the zero mark. It was a sight which might well have disquieted the souls of the brave navigators.

Mare Sugenum is not easily interpreted. We take it as from the Latin verb *sugo*, *sugere*, conveying the idea of a force drawing the sea toward some center, as in a whirlpool. There is a legend in the broad upper border of this map, but at the beginning of the right hand quadrant, and therefore not shown in this reproduction, which may throw some light upon this strange term. "One may read in the book entitled 'Inventio Fortunata' that under the arctic pole there is a lofty rock of magnetic stone thirty-three German miles in circuit. The fluid Sugenum Sea encircles this in the form of a vase emitting water from its mouth."

The book here mentioned was composed by Nicholas de Linna, or Nicholas of Lynn, in England. It records his voyages from 54° north latitude "to the inflowing regions about the pole." In the first book of Hakluyt's Voyages the reader will find an account of these expeditions of Master Nicholas to the north, begun in 1360 and continuing over several years. If this voyager had found his way into Baffin's Bay, or that region, especially Engroenlande, from the northern parts of America, and had beheld the gigantic tides rising 120 feet only to fall and suck back the disturbed waters, he could have described the phenomenon in no more remarkable words.

To the southward of this interesting body of enchanted water is a region marked *Judei inclusi*, the supposed abiding place of the lost ten tribes of Israel. In the early manuscript maps the location of these tribes is sometimes confounded with the joint empire of Gog and Magog. There was still preserved a few years ago in the Borgian Museum in Velletri a map of the earth engraved and enameled on copper, and believed to have been executed about 1452. The author was devoted to history as well as geography, and placed this legend on the northern part of Asia:

Provincia Gog, in qua fuerunt Judei inclusi tempore Artaxercis regis Persarum. Magog: in istis duabus, sunt gentes magni et gigantes, pleni omnium malorum morum: quos Judeos, Artaxas rex collegit de omnibus partibus persarum.

South of the arctic circle and east of Greenland, and referring to an island, we have the following legend:

Insvla hec in āno dñi 1456
Fvit totaliter cōbvsta.

This island in the year of our Lord 1456
Was totally destroyed by fire.

It is believed that reference is here made to that island discovered by Gunnbjörn, and which through volcanic action disappeared in the year 1456, leaving dangerous skerries as a menace to navigators.

South of Greenland, and in the great bay running west, is a description of some islands, the translation of which we give:

> Felarufeie also called Cibes. They say that when sailors have visited these islands they have been so enchanted by demons that they have escaped with difficulty.

South of Newfoundland and west of the Azores is seen the island of Antilia, with a legend, which we translate as follows:

> This island Antilia was discovered by the Portuguese, and now when it is sought it is not found. In this island are people who speak the Spanish tongue, and who in the time of King Roderic (who ruled in Spain in the last time of Gothic power) are believed to have fled to this island from the Barbarians who at that time invaded Spain. Here dwelt an archbishop with six other bishops, each one of whom had his own particular city. Wherefore this island is called by many "seven cities." This people lived most piously in the full enjoyment of all the riches of this time.

If the reader will compare this reading with the legend as latinized by Dr. K. Kretschmer in his "Festschrift der Gesellchaft für Erdkunde" (plate IX of his Atlas), a decided difference of opinion will be noticed as to the meaning of words and the values of abbreviations. As the student of this valuable German Atlas is given no opportunity to see the original of the legend, and as no other writer has been at pains to translate the same, it is no wonder it has escaped criticism.

Across the South American Continent is a legend to this effect:

> Land of the Holy Cross or the New World. This country, which is generally considered another continent, is inhabited in scattered settlements. The men and women go either entirely naked or adorned with interwoven fibers of wood (roots) and birds' feathers of various colors. Many live in common: they have no religion and no king: they wage war among themselves continually. They devour flesh — that of captives in war: they breathe so mild an air that they live to be over 150 years: they are rarely sick, and then they are cured by roots of herbs only: lions are found here: serpents and other foul beasts. There are forests, mountains and rivers: there is the greatest abundance of pearls and gold. Brazil wood, otherwise called Verzini, and cinnamon are exported hence by the Portuguese.

To the left of this last legend, and running at right angles to it, is a large scroll defining the geographer's ideas as to the western boundary of this New World. The following is a translation of the legend upon this scroll:

> Thus far Spanish sailors have come, and because of its magnitude they call it a new world, for indeed they have not seen the whole of it nor at this time have they explored beyond this limit. Therefore this map is left incomplete for the present, since we do not know in which direction it trends.

Above the northern end of this scroll, and covering the ocean space between Asia and the New World, is the following legend:

> Marco Polo says that 1500 miles east of the harbor of Zaiton is a vast island generally called Sipango, whose inhabitants are idolaters, who have a king of their own, and who are tributary to no one. The greatest abundance of gold and of all kinds of gems is there to be found. But because the islands discovered by the Spanish sailors occupy this locality, we do not dare to locate this island there, thinking that what the Spaniards call Spagnola they call Sipango, inasmuch as the particular things described as existing in Sipango are found existing in Spagnola except the idolatry.

To the south of this is the island of Java Major, over which appears a legend which we translate as follows:

> Java Major contains in itself eight kingdoms, whose inhabitants are idolaters. Here grow ginger, pepper, nuts, muscats, and all other kinds of spices. They lack wine alone. This island is 3000 miles in circumference.

Southwest of Java Major is Java Minor, attached to which is a legend which we translate as follows:

> Java Minor contains eight kingdoms whose inhabitants are idolaters: each kingdom has its own language: here camphor is found in great abundance: there are spices of all kinds. There are men living in the mountains of the island who have tails the breadth of one's hand in length: here father devours son and son devours father: they live upon rice in place of bread.

Once again to the southward is a legend to the following effect:

> Sailors to this higher India who sail to these islands relate that in this sea there are 7443 islands, many of which are inhabited, and in which there is an abundance of spices, which the traders carry to India and the various countries of the continent.

Reference has already been made to the brief legend on the scroll which forms the western boundary of the disconnected portion of the northeast continental land which reads:

> Thus far the ships of Ferdinand, King of Spain, have made their way.

There remains one important legend to describe. It is on the extreme southeastern part of the New World, and is of interest as recording the results of the third voyage of Americus Vespucius — the first of his two voyages under the King of Portugal. We translate as follows:

> Portuguese sailors have explored this country even to the 50th degree of south latitude, but nevertheless they have not reached its southern termination.

CHAPTER VI

Nomenclature of the Ruysch Map

THREE portions of the western hemisphere stand out prominently in this map. Here are recorded the discoveries of the three great navigators of the fifteenth century — all Italian born — Christopher Columbus, Americus Vespucius, and John Cabot. To the extreme north we see the results obtained from the voyages of Cabot and his successors, the Corte-Real brothers. Greenland, Labrador, and Newfoundland are clearly outlined. Greenland is carried from the north to its southern extremity, or to the sixtieth degree of north latitude. The extreme point, Cape Farewell, is not named. The great bay between this cape and Labrador is undoubtedly the entrance to Davis Strait. Newfoundland is called *Terra Nova*, and Cape Race is called *C. de Portogesi*, or Cape of the Portuguese, in order to identify the discoveries of the Corte-Reals, and not to indicate, as some writers have assumed, the most easterly point on the coast of the "new land," and therefore the nearest land to Portugal. From this point the land runs almost due east, forming the northern line of a gigantic bay called *Plisacus Sinus*, and possibly the Amur river of to-day, — the Polisanchin river in the map of Fra Mauro of 1457 — having its source in Mongolia and forming the northern border of Manchuria, the most northern province of the Chinese empire. To the south of this great river lay Cathay, that mysterious land, the home of Prester John and the islanded and forgotten eastern repository of the Christian religion according to the weird tales of Marco Polo; Cathay, dreamed of by the students and travelers of Europe for two hundred years; Cathay, the country of spices and gold, of jewels and rich cities, of arts and devices; Cathay, sought for by the bravest sailor of all the ages, who in the seeking found a new world and an eternal abiding place for peace and liberty.

South of the land described above, and extending from twenty-five degrees to thirty-five degrees north latitude, is a strip of continental land in the shape of a triangle, its base running north and south and its apex pointing to the east. Along its base, as if marking the limit of its explorations, is the scroll with its legend, "thus far the ships of Ferdinand, king of Spain, have made their way." Southeast of the apex are several islands, the largest of which is called Spagnola, the Santo Domingo of to-day. Both the Bahama group and the greater Antilles are shown. The mystery of this map — and every early map boasted its mystery — is the absence of the island of Cuba from its place in the Caribbean Sea. Many writers have sought to identify the triangular land with that island, and have claimed that Ruysch intended to represent Cuba. If in the year 1500 the insularity of Cuba was known to La Cosa and two years later was incorporated in the Cantino chart, it must have been known to Ruysch, and he would not have introduced it with any such configuration as we find on this map, and certainly not with the scroll on the west which was generally used to indicate unknown or unexplored territory. The nomenclature also forbids our mistaking the land for Cuba. Columbus on his first voyage gave the name of "Alpha and Omega" to the extreme easterly point of Cuba, now called Cape Maysi. This point was *Omega* to the citizen of Cathay, and it was *Alpha* to the adventurous Genoese. It seemed to Columbus that it was the last land to the traveler going eastward, and the first land to him journeying from the east toward the west. If the land on the Ruysch map is intended for Cuba, how is it that its eastern point is called *C. de Fundabril* or *Cabo do Fim do Abrill?* Both Las Casas and Ferdinand Columbus in his "Historie" fix the date of this christening of the easterly point of Cuba by the name of "Alpha and Omega" as December 5, 1492, so that no occurrence of April 30, either in the year 1492 or any other year, could have suggested to Columbus or his companions calling this point after "the last day of the month of April." This date, however, does correspond with the time in the spring of 1498 when Americus Vespucius and his companions Pinzon and Solis turned the point of Florida on their way up the northeast coast of the continent.

South of this middle continental land, and about eight degrees south of the tropic of Cancer, is a vast continent called *Terra Sancte Crucis* or *Mundus Novus*. This great mass is bordered on the west by a large scroll bearing the legend translated above, and which distinctly announces that the Spanish sailors called the country a "new world." We have followed in another chapter the voyage of the Florentine sailor, who, now under the Spanish flag and now under the Portuguese standard, opened up the two continental lands above and below the tropic of Cancer, and who from the most northerly point of his first voyage, Cape Hatteras, here called *C. Elicontii*, to the southern limit reached on his third voyage, 52 degrees of south latitude, had traversed a longer arc on the surface of the globe than any other explorer, a record of voyaging which was not surpassed until in the year 1520 Fernando de Magellan, unfortunate in the hour of his triumph, first put a girdle around the globe. We have also seen in another chapter that four years or more before this map was published there appeared a little quarto tract of six leaves, entitled *Mundus Novus*, containing the letter of Americus Vespucius to Laurentius Petrus Franciscus de Medicis with an account of his third voyage, which letter Fra Giocondo of Verona, but then living in Paris, translated from Italian into Latin. This little work was reprinted nine times within the next two years, showing that it must have excited interest. One of these editions was printed in 1504 by Jean Otmar in Augsburg, and another in 1505 by Matthias Hupfuff in Strasburg. These German editions must have been known to Johannes Ruysch, the German geographer. Thus Americus Vespucius is seen to have been the first to suggest a name, not his own, for the newly discovered lands, and that name was duly inscribed upon this map — *Mundus Novus*.

The following nomenclature is taken from Harrisse's "Discovery of North America."

NORTHWESTERN CONTINENTAL REGION

Cantino	*Ruysch*	*Canerio*
C. d. licotu	C. Elicontii	C. dellicontir
Cornejo	Corveo	Comello
C. do fim do abrill	C. de fvndabrill	Cauo do fim de abrill
C. lurcar	Cvlcar	Cauo lurcar
G. do lurcor (?)	Anterlinoi	Gorffo do lineor
	Lago de loro	Lago del lodro
	C. S. Marci	

SOUTHEASTERN COAST

Kunstmann No. 2 (A Portuguese map made about 1503.)	*Ruysch*	*Canerio*
delisleo	lix leo	
terra seccha	terra seca	
G. de Uenetia	golfo de vericida	
monte retondo	mons rotvndvs	
G. de inferno	golfo delinferno	Gorffo do linferno
aide venada	capo formoso	
cavo frenoso	rio de lareno	
rio de arena	golfo de pareas	
c. de pario	canibalos in[sula]	y de los canbales
	terr de pareas	
	r. formoso	Gorffo fremoso
de alegroza (?)	r. de flagrāza	
	r. de foco cecho	
rio de le aues	r. de les aves	
	rio grando	Rio grande
monte de S. uincenzo	mos s. vincenti	Monte de Sam Visenso
Capo de Sancta ✝	caput s. crvcis	Cabo do Sta. croxe

SOUTHEASTERN COAST — *Continued*

Kunstmann No. 2	*Ruysch*	*Canerio*
rio de saō hieronymo	r. de s. ieronimo	rio de Sam Jeronimo
a baia de tutti santi	abatia ōniv. sāctorv.	baie de tutti li santi
rio de brazil	r. de brasil	rio de brazil
monte de pasqual	mōte pasqvale	mont passqual
rio de Sta Lucia	r. de s. lvcia	Rio de Sta. Lucia
serra de santhome	serra de s. antonio	Sierra de Sam Tome
rio de arefeces	rio de oreferis	rio da resens
bova de reis	baia de reis	baie de reis
rio jordan	r. iordan	rio Jordam
rio de são antonio	r. de s. antonio	rio de Sto. Antonio
punta de san uincentio	r. de s. vicent	porto de Sam Visenso
rio de cananor	r. de cananor	rio de cananor

In the Latin edition of the Four "Voyages of Americus Vespucius," printed at St.-Dié in 1507, in relating the adventures of the fourth voyage, allusion is made to that "Bay of All Saints" discovered in the previous voyage and appropriately named after the day of discovery. In the Portuguese map of Canerio the bay is properly designated, but in the above Latin edition it became *Abbatia omnium sanctorum*. Ruysch evidently had read this edition, and so translated the Portuguese phrase *Bay of All Saints* into that impossible and most confusing expression *The Abbey of All Saints*. The alternative designation of the *Mundus Novus* as *Terra Sancte Crucis* is a strong evidence of the Portuguese origin of Ruysch's map. In the Spanish maps this latter name was never given. It was first used by Cabral to mark his discovery of the Brazil Coast, April 23, 1500.

From this map as executed by Ruysch we deduce three conclusions:

First, Ruysch believed that the northern part of America from Greenland to Nova Scotia was part of Asia, and that the remainder of the newly discovered lands was separate from the Asiatic coast and distinctly continental;

Second, that Ruysch had knowledge of the voyagings and writings of Americus Vespucius;

Third, that the chartography of the New World in Ruysch's map is essentially Portuguese in its origin and not Spanish, and that this fact is particularly determined by its nomenclature.

CHAPTER VII

The Ptolemy and Peter Martyr Maps of 1511

ERNARDUS SYLVANUS, a native of Eboli, a little town of southern Italy not far from Naples, had at the close of the fifteenth century acquired renown as a skilled geographer and map-maker. There is still preserved in the National Library in Paris a manuscript Ptolemy map on vellum and dated 1490, which presumably was made by his own hand, although a strict reading might interpret it to have simply been made under his supervision in his own studio. In the preface, or the epistle to Aquævivus, in the edition of Ptolemy we are about to examine, Sylvanus gives the motive which induced him to undertake that work:

> I, most illustrious Duke, when I observed that Ptolemy among other writers of geography wrote most carefully of the situation and distances of places, I wondered especially that his tables agreed in so few instances with the voyages undertaken in our own time; and I marveled more since I believed that whatever Ptolemy did write was the result of information obtained from the early voyages. As my mind dwelt often on the subject, I gathered from all over different Greek and Latin copies of his work, and I discovered in all the examples which came into my possession the greatest differences in the figures by which the intervals of places were designated. Turning this over in my mind, I began carefully to examine the exact language of Ptolemy where in many places the numbers or figures were at variance with the words themselves. I knew that the words of Ptolemy agreed almost always with the navigations and for the most part disagreed with the figures. When I saw this, moved by an audacity which perhaps was not justified, comparing the writings of Ptolemy with the voyages themselves, I corrected the figures which were able to be, and which were likely to be, easily distorted.

Sylvanus hit upon the true basis of geography in adopting, or endeavoring to adopt, the actual observations of travelers and navigators. Before the time of Ptolemy two expeditions under Roman generals had made their way into the interior of South Africa, and the furthest point visited received the name of one of these generals (Agisymba) and appears upon the maps of the Old World in the Sylvanus edition of Ptolemy, 1511, the one under consideration, as Agisinba, in about fifteen degrees of

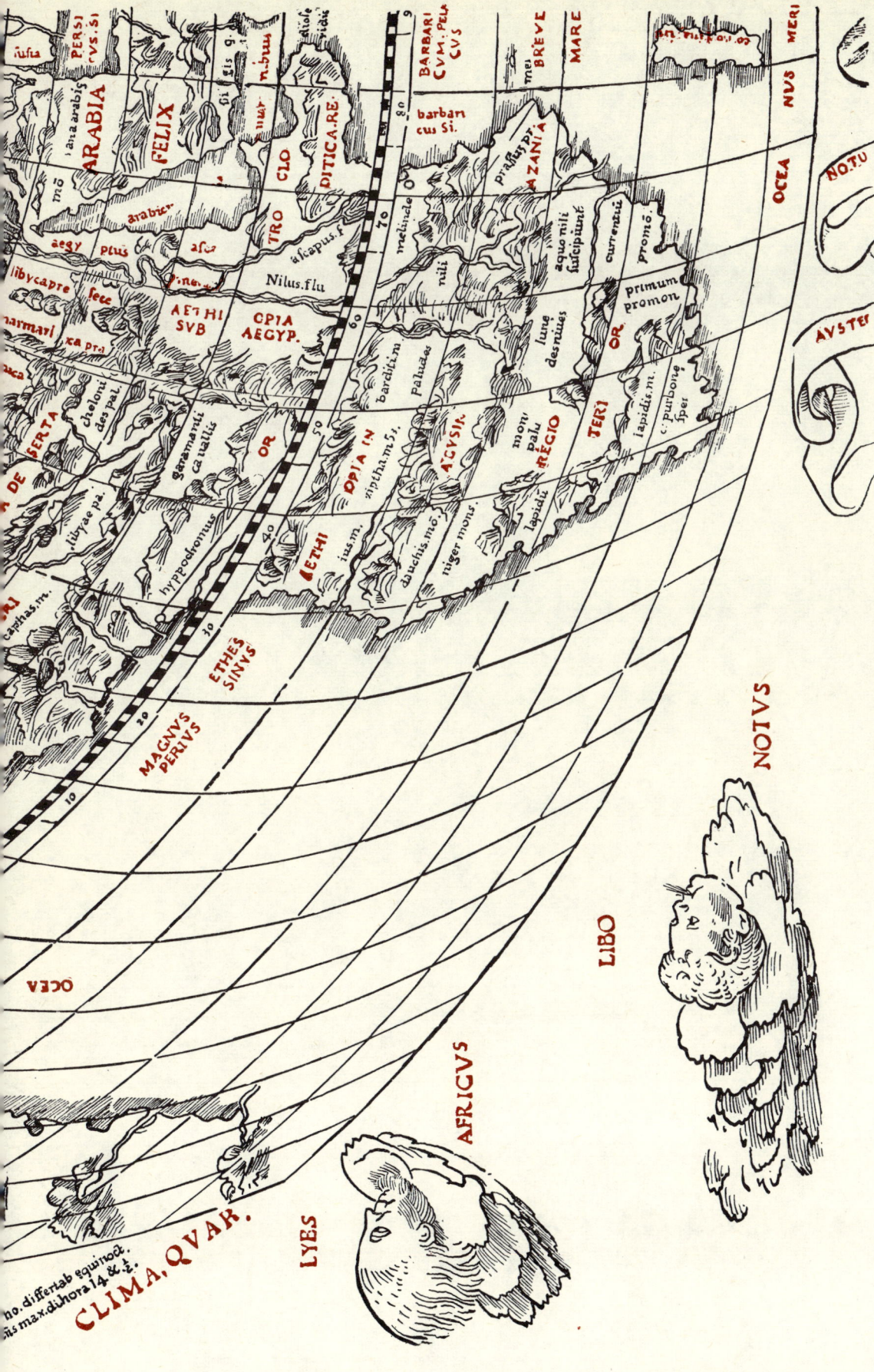

MAP OF THE NEW WORLD.
FROM THE SYLVANUS PTOLEMY OF 1511.

south latitude and about thirty-five degrees of east longitude. This designation is not found in the map of the world in the edition of Ptolemy printed in 1478 at the press of Arnold Buckinck in Rome, but it is found in the fourth map of Africa in that edition. Who can doubt, in the light of modern discovery, that Ptolemy had taken from the lips of some explorer an account of the two great lakes and the Mountains of the Moon which feed the river Nilus? Traders in the East had brought home stories of the regions of silks and gold and spices which the learned Alexandrian called Sera and Cattigara. The latter he placed about eight and a half degrees south of the equator, but the furthest east of any known part of Asia. It first appeared in a printed map in the Rome edition of 1478, and is found in the eleventh map of Asia. A little north of it is the designation for the country of Sinae or China. To the north, in mid-Atlantic, adventurous spirits had found Thule, and from their description of this, the last land of the north, he placed it in sixty-three degrees of north latitude. The sailors who told Ptolemy of the Fortunate Islands must have been strangely inexact, since he gives them a space extending beyond six degrees within which to have their home. They formed the western limit of the known world when Ptolemy wrote his eight books, or when Agathodæmon drew his maps. And it was from the Fortunate Islands or Canaries that Ptolemy began to count his lines of longitude. We find in the first printed edition of Ptolemy from the press of Hermanus Levilapidis, Vicenza, 1475, that the latitude and longitude of ninety-five separate provinces are distinctly given. The Mediterranean is allowed by Ptolemy a length of sixty-two degrees, and this error of nearly twenty degrees is due to the difficulty Ptolemy met with in calculating the distances in longitudes on the surface of the earth. More than fifteen degrees of this discrepancy is to the westward. As Sylvanus himself says, moved by these discrepancies and somewhat by audacity, he proceeded to correct the errors and to establish his own as authentic readings. Joachim Lelewel in his "Géographie du Moyen Age," Brussels, 1852, shows how the Italian commentator, by arbitrarily giving new latitudes and longitudes to localities wrongly marked by Ptolemy, contributed more than any other writer to the confusion and derangement of places and geographical situations. He gives a table of forty important localities from Ptolemy together with the changed figures which Sylvanus inserted and offered as substitutes. It is, however, in his observations and recording of the new discoveries in the south of Africa and in the New World that we are more interested.

It is well to give a brief bibliographical account of the edition of Ptolemy edited by Sylvanus and printed for him in Venice in the year 1511. The volume is folio in form, measuring 15⅞ inches in height by 10¾ inches in width. There are two watermarks in the paper used in this book. The one is a circle 1⅞ inches in diameter, a double fluked anchor occupying the entire circle. The other is a circle of the same size, but within, instead of the anchor, is a triple-arched crown, the middle arch extending an inch and a half beyond the circle and terminating in a cross. There are four preliminary leaves without signatures or catchwords. The title is on the recto of the first leaf and is printed in red.

CLAVDII PTHOLEMAEI ALEXANDRINI LI
BER GEOGRAPHIAE CVM TABVLIS ET
VNIVERSALI FIGVRA ET CVM AD
DITIONE LOCORVM QVAE A
RECENTIORIBVS REPER
TA SVNT DILIGENTI
CVRA EMENDA
TVS ET IM
PRESSVS

On the verso of this leaf are thirty-seven lines of verse by Joannes Aurelius Augurellus, an Italian Latin poet who died in 1524 at the age of eighty-three years. At the top of the second folio begins an epistle from the author Bernardus Sylvanus to the illustrious Andrea Matteo Acquaviva, Duke of Atria, who had made a literary name for himself as the commentator of Plutarch. This letter occupies a little more than two thirds of the page, the text filling the page in single column. Then follow a series of annotations occupying the whole of that and the following leaves. The text falls into double columns on the recto of the fourth leaf, and ends with a table of contents on the verso of the fourth folio. The title is partially repeated in red at the bottom of the folio. Then follow fifty-eight leaves of text, sheets *A* and *I* being in eights, while *B, C, D, E, F, G,* and *H* are in sixes. On the recto of *Ii* is the figure of the earth on a sphere 6⅛ inches in diameter. The eighth and last book ends on the recto of *Iviii*, the colophon being:

Venetiis per Jacobum Pentium de leucho
Anno domini M. D. XI. Die. XX.
Mensis Martii.

There is one peculiarity of printing in this book so far as the maps are concerned. After the wood-plates had been cut, names for the identification of places were stamped in, the ink used being red and the type of a heavier letter than the style elsewhere employed. The winds are represented by heads of cherubs and are skilfully drawn. The arrangement of some of the maps varies in the different copies. The first map is of the Eastern Hemisphere, extending from the Fortunate Islands on the west 180°

to the *Terra Incognita* on the east, and from about 18° south of the equator to 63° of north latitude. The mappamundi is of chief interest. This map is sometimes found directly after the map of the Old World, but in some copies, as in ours, it is at the end of the book. It extends from 290° of longitude counting from the Fortunate Islands eastward to 360° east of those islands. It extends from 40° south of the equator to 80° of north latitude. The map is cordiform, the first instance of this kind of projection. Only the western half, in which we are especially interested, is shown. On the extreme north Greenland is made a part of Europe. Iceland is situated to the westward. Southwest of Iceland Labrador is represented as an island, separated from a land the western portion of which is abruptly cut off, and which is called *Regalis Domus* or Royal House, latinizing the patronymic of Gaspar Corte-Real. This latter land is intended to embody the discoveries of the Portuguese in 1500-1501. South of this, but still quite north of the tropic of Cancer, are two large islands: the western one, almost cut off by the western border of the map, is called *Terra Cubæ*. The other is called *Ispania*. Harrisse, in his "Discovery of North America," classifies the early American charts into five distinct types, the distinguishing features of which are:

1. The New World represented in the form of an archipelago, with Cuba as an island and at its westernmost point.

2. Cuba in insular form, with a continental region close to it but extending south only to 20° 30′ north latitude.

3. A map like the second type, but with a northeastern coast prolonged five degrees further south through a gulf.

4. A map extending the said coast-line about eleven degrees still further south.

6. A map in which both sections of the American continent are connected by a continuous coast line.

In addition to the general resemblances of contour serving to establish identity and admitting readily of classification, the nomenclature employed is of the greatest assistance. When we look at this map of 1511 we find but few names to guide us, and none on the northeast coast. For the most part writers follow Harrisse and place this map in his first type. The little *Terra Cubæ* would seem to indicate continental land, and we know the northeast coast was sometimes denominated Cuba. But besides being represented as an island it resembles much that peculiar hook in the southwest corner of the island so often seen in pictures of Cuba, and notably in the Waldseemüller map of 1513, which the reader must remember was executed previous to 1508.

A few days after the Sylvanus edition of Ptolemy had issued from the Venetian press of Jacobus Pentius de Leucho, there was printed in Seville by Jacobus Cromberger (or Corumberger) the "First Decade" of Peter Martyr. It is a folio volume of 74 leaves, as follows: title (a), a*ii*, a*iii*, a*iiii* + 4 blank (*i. e.*, without signatures); b, b*ii*, b*iii*, b*iiii* + 4 blank; c, c*ii* + 2 blank; 2 blank leaves with the map and errata; d, d*ii*, d*iii*, d*iiii* + 4 blank; e, e*ii*, e*iii*, e*iiii* + 4 blank; f, f*ii*, f*iii*, f*iiii* + 4 blank; g, g*ii*, g*iii* + 3 blank; h, h*ii*, h*iii*, h*iiii* + 4 blank; i, i*ii*, a*iii* (sic pro i*iii*), i*iiii* + 4 blank; k, k*ii*, k*iii* + 3 blank.

The title is on the recto of the first leaf:

> P. MARTYRIS ANGLI
> MEDIOLANENSIS OPERA
> LEGATIO BABYLONICA
> OCCEANI DECAS
> POEMATA
> EPIGRAMMATA
> CUM PREVILEGIS.

That is to say: The works of Peter Martyr of Milan, the embassy to Babylon, the decade of the ocean, poems, epigrams. With privilege.

On the recto of the twenty-first leaf is the famous map of the Western World which we will soon describe. On the verso of this same leaf is the dedication to Cardinal Ximenes. The next leaf is devoted to a table correcting errors which had occurred as far as signature *f*. On the verso of the seventy-third leaf, or the next to the last, is the colophon:

> "Impressum Hispoli cũ summa dilgencia per Jacobũ corrum-
> berger alemanũ. Anno. Millessimo quingentessimo. xi. mẽse
> vero Aprili."

Jacobus Cromberger, or, as the writer calls himself in this instance, Corumberger, had a press in Seville as early as 1508. In 1526 he printed in partnership with Juan Cromberger, who has the honor of having established the first printing-press ever set up in the New World, the place being the City of Mexico and the time being about 1540. There are six copies known of this "First Decade" with the map. While our copy has the two leaves of the map and errata inserted between the last blank leaf of signature *c* and the first leaf of signature *d*, in another of the six copies these two leaves are found after the forty-fourth leaf. The map is a rather poor woodcut 11⅛ inches in length, or running east and west, and 7⅝ inches in width, or from north to south. There are no meridian lines and no scale of distances. On the back of the map is the dedication to Cardinal Ximenes. Peter Martyr describes the principal fea-

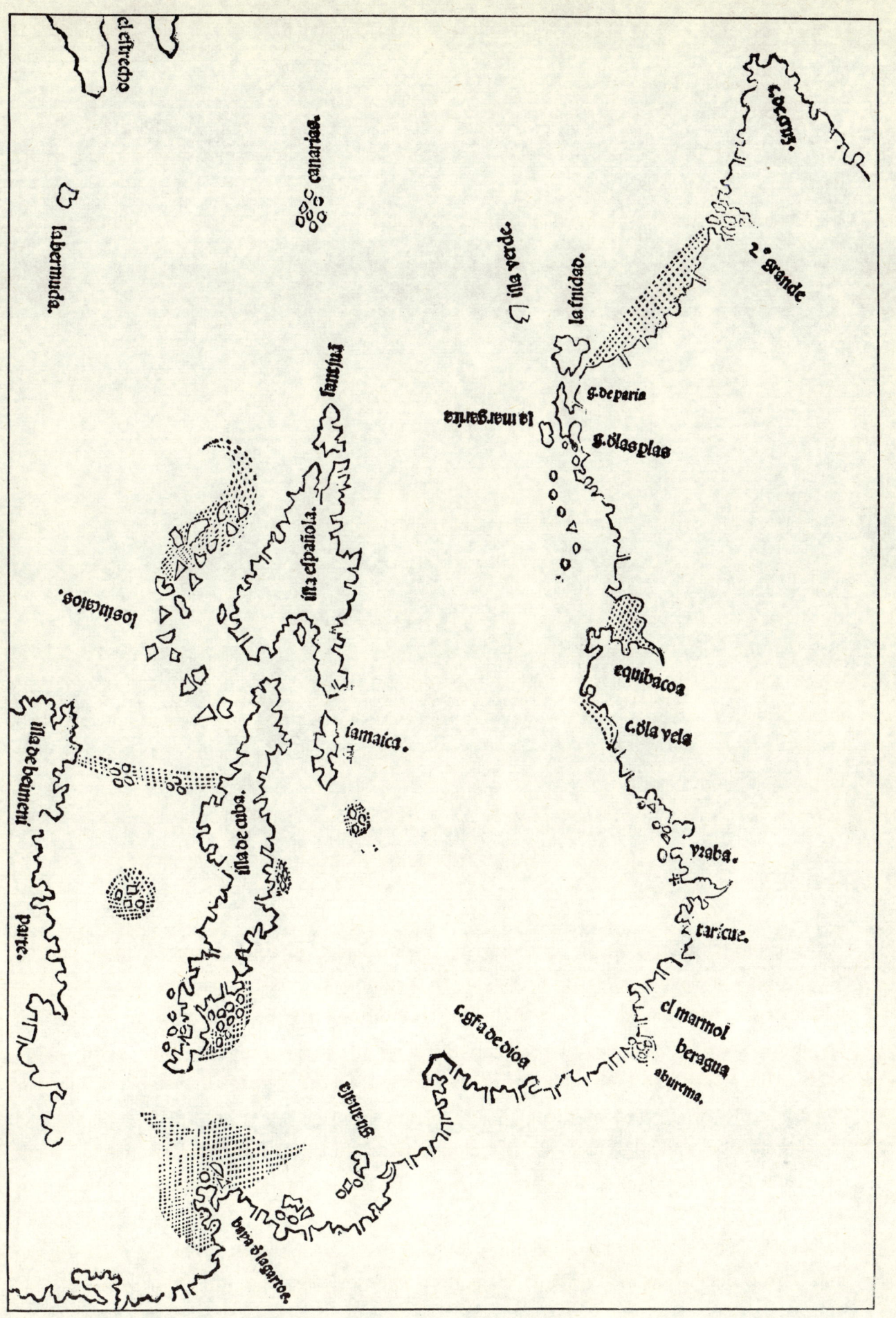

MAP OF THE NEW WORLD, FROM PETER MARTYR'S "FIRST DECADE," SEVILLE, 1511, SHOWING THE COAST OF FLORIDA BEFORE THE PONCE DE LEON DISCOVERY.

MAP FROM THE PTOLEMY GEOG

...NTED IN CRACOW ABOUT 1512.

tures of the map. After speaking of "the Dragon's mouth," Paria, Curiana, Cauchiet, Cuquibachoa, Urava, Beragua, and the other very large provinces which are said to be the Indian Continent, he proceeds as follows: "The land to the west of Hispaniola, surrounded on all sides with islands (like a hen with a brood of chickens), is Cuba, a great island. To the left and adjoining both these is Jamaica, sufficiently described by us. To the north wonderful lands and marvelous regions have been discovered, engraved tracings of which you can perceive on the right." This marvelous land to the north, bearing the legend "parte, isla beimeni," is none other than our own Florida. The reader will observe that this "land to the north" is no small or insignificant territory. Only a portion is shown, the northeastern side being suddenly cut off because of the limited space given to the map, but that portion is far greater in extent than Cuba. We wish that Peter Martyr had been a little more definite and had told us when and by whom these lands had been discovered. It could not have been by Juan Ponce de Leon, for the letters patent under which his expedition sailed were not granted until February 23, 1512, and this map had then been long published. From the moment that Ponce de Leon viewed the new land it was known as *Florida*, and if the account of this land had come from him it would not have been designated as *Beimeni*. In the first decade of Herrera we read that Ponce de Leon decided to go and make discoveries to the north because he had learned that lands had already been found in that region. There is no detailed account of any voyage to, or discovery of, land to the north except that given by Americus Vespucius concerning his first voyage in 1497. There was a rumor, as appears in Las Casas, that two ships with a company of fifty or sixty men had sailed from Puerto de Plata early in the year 1511, and had seen and landed in a certain country "which," says Las Casas, "was unquestionably the country and seaboard which we call Florida." Rude as is the Peter Martyr map, it could not have been made and inserted in this edition if it resulted from information given by this doubtful expedition of 1511. It is true that the map-folio and the second folio which accompanies it give indication of having been inserted subsequent to the printing of some copies, but not a long time after, not months after nor even weeks after. The printer would have had time to correct the text and would likely have changed the date of the month, if the insertion of the map had long succeeded the issuing of the earliest copy. We believe we have here a strong confirmation of the truth of the first voyage of Americus Vespucius.

CHAPTER VIII

The Stobnicza Ptolemy of 1512

HE rarest edition of Ptolemy, when found complete, is the one published at Cracow in the year 1512. Cracow, the capitol of the ancient kingdom of Poland, while sharing in the vicissitudes of that unfortunate country, possessed the delightful consolation of a famous university where the serenity of science was undisturbed by the sounds of war. It appears to have been founded by Casimir III., surnamed the Great, in the year 1364, thus antedating in its foundation the universities of Germany, except that of Prague, and preceding, although by only one year, the establishing of that celebrated university which ornaments the capitol of Austria. A printing-press had been set up at Cracow in the latter part of the fifteenth century, the exact date of its establishment being in dispute. We have no specimen with a veritable date earlier than the year 1500. With few exceptions the early issues of this press were philosophical and educational rather than religious, and the probability is that the university largely sustained and supported the printing establishment. Among the learned teachers of the university was Johannes de Stobnicza, who, as early as 1508, published at the Cracovian press a treatise on logic and another on natural philosophy in 1513, besides editing several other books between these years. The possession by Cracow of an important seat of learning, and the character of the works published by its flourishing printing-press, remove the surprise we feel at finding an edition of Ptolemy coming from this far-away Polish town. The scientific attainments of its editor, Stobnicza, and his probable intercourse with brother professors at other schools of learning, will perhaps account for the advanced knowledge or for the correct geographical surmises which distinguished this edition of Ptolemy over all others issued in the early part of the sixteenth century.

The volume is a quarto, with one leaf on which is the title, one leaf unnumbered, followed by leaves numbered i–xl. The title as recorded by Panzer in the "Annales Typographici," Vol. VI., page 454, is:

> *Introductio in Claudii Ptholomei*
> *Cosmographiam: cum longitudinibus*
> *& latitudinibus regionum. Cum*
> *Carmine Sapphico Rudolphi*
> *Agricolae ad Episcopum Posnani-*
> *ensem Joannem Lubranski.*
> *Impressum Cracoviae per Florianum*
> *Unglerium Anno Domini MCCCCC*
> *XII.*

Harrisse in his "Bibliotheca Americana Vetustissima" copies the title as given by Panzer, but in the "Additions" to the same work, published in 1872, the following correct title is given as taken from the copy in the Vienna Imperial Library:

> *Introductio in Ptholomei Cosmo*
> *graphiã cũ longitũnibus & latitũnibus regio*
> *num & civitatum celebriorum*
> *Epitoma Europe Enee Silvii.*
> *Situs & distinctio partium tocius Asie per brachia Tauri mõ*
> *tis et Asia Pii secundi.*
> *Particularior Minoris asie descriptio et eiusdem Pii Asia*
> *Sirie compendiosa descriptio : ex Isidoro*
> *Africe brevis descriptio : ex paulo orosio*
> *Terre sancte & urbis Hierusalem apertior descriptio : fratris*
> *Anselmi ordinis. Minorum de observancia.*

On the last leaf is the colophon:

> *Impressum Cracovie p. Florianũ*
> *Ungleriũ. Anno dñi M. D. XII.*

There is a second copy of this book in the Vienna Imperial Library which has the last four leaves unnumbered, and which is without any date. That Stobnicza had before him the "Cosmographiæ Introductio" of Waldseemüller is beyond question. On the verso of folio vii is a passage taken almost bodily from the "Cosmographia":

Non solũ aũt p̄dictę tres p̄tes nũc sunt latius lustrate, verũ & alia quarta pars ab Americo Vesputio sagacis ingenii viro, inserta est, quã ab ip̄o Americo eius inuentor amerigem quasi americi terram siue americã appellari volunt, cui latitudo est sub tota torrida roua, etc.

The chief interest in this edition is in one of its two maps, a copy of which is here introduced. The original map is engraved on wood and measures 15 inches by 10⅝ inches.

The earth in the original map represents the two hemispheres for the first time in a printed or engraved map, although in 1495 Jaume Ferrer de Blanes sent to Ferdinand and Isabella on January 27, 1495, a manuscript map on which "los dos Emisferios" were pictured. This latter map is now lost. The one before us we may call the prophetic map, for not only does it plainly connect the two continents of the Western Hemisphere, but it gives their general contour with an accuracy which is marvelous. It reaches from 70° north latitude to 40° south of the equator. The north continental land terminates at about the fiftieth degree of north latitude, but there is a land represented ten degrees further north and considerably to the east, which is no doubt intended for the land of Labrador as put down in the Ptolemy of 1511. The islands of Hispaniola and Cuba are both shown, and on the mainland the east coast of Florida is designated as Isabella. The coast-lines are unbroken from north to south, and the Gulf of Mexico is plainly traced. The few words engraved on the map are easily traced to the Waldseemüller map which we have already established as engraved many years before, although not attached to a printed book until 1513. On the north continent, at about the fortieth degree, is the designation *Cabo de bona Ventura*, which is found on the Waldseemüller map. On the south continent, *Arcay, Caput de stado, Gorffo spermosa, Caput S. Crucis* and *Monte fregoso* are names of places taken directly from the Waldseemüller map. The last name on the map, placed a little above the fortieth degree of south latitude, is Allepego, which Harrisse interprets for Pagus Sam Pauli. The name, the Village of St. Paul, is first found in the Canerio manuscript map executed somewhere between the years 1502 and 1504. In that map it is named *Alapego de Sam Paullo*. In the Waldseemüller map of 1513 it is printed *Pagus S. Pauli*, and in the Schöner globe constructed about 1515 the same spelling is used. The reader need not be told how difficult a task it is, after nearly three centuries, to read correctly the names on globes and manuscript maps. Time is far less cruel to engraved maps shut away from the light and air within well-bound printed books. Enough has been said, however, to indicate that the geographical knowledge possessed by Stobnicza came from St.-Dié in the Vosgian Mountains, from the little treatise on cosmography published there in 1507, and from the engraved map of Waldseemüller which was prepared there as early as that same year.

The author has no copy of this edition, nor is there, so far as we can learn, another copy with the map known outside of the Imperial Library in Vienna. Frederick Müller & Co. of Amsterdam published a few facsimiles of this map, and it is not impossible to meet with one of these in catalogues of early and rare books.

CHAPTER IX

The Waldseemüller Ptolemy of 1513

THE Ptolemy of 1513 and the Waldseemüller map have frequently been mentioned in the progress of this work. The volume is a large folio measuring 18 inches by 12⅛ inches. The watermark is what is known in the nomenclature of old water marks as petite fleur-de-lis, nearly 1⅜ inches high by 1 inch broad. The title is on the recto of the first leaf and consists of thirty-eight lines, the first two of which are in large gothic lettering, while the other thirty-six are in smaller and round type. This leaf and the one following are not numbered.

CLAUDII PTOLEMEI
VIRI ALEXANDRINI
Mathematicę disciplinę Philosophi
doctissimi
Geographię opus novissima traductione e Gręcorum archetypis castigatissime pressum: cęteris
ante lucubratorum multo pręstantius.
Pro Prima parte continens
1 CL. Ptolemęi Geographiam per octo libros partitam |
ad antiquitatē suam | integre & sine ulla corruptione.
2 Vna cum collatione dictionum gręcarum e regione
ad latinas certissima graduum calculatione.
3 Registrationem item nouam regionum | prœfecturarum
ciuitatum | fluminum | marium | lacuum | portuum | siluarum | oppidorum | villarum ac gentium | ad ordinem
chartarum & columnarum | singula certissime monstrans, indice.
℞ Quā breuis & doctissima Gregorii Lilii. subsequitur instructio de Gręcoʀ numerali supputatione | in traductione gręcâ res scitu aurea.
5 Tabularum dein Auctoris vigintiseptem ordo hic est
Generale orbis juxta descriptionē Ptolemęi.   Vna
Europę tabulę.   Decem.
Aphricę tabulę.   Quattuor.
Asię tabulę.   Duodecim.

Est & una corporis Spherici in plano juxta finẽ. 7. li
Pars secunda | modernorium lustrationum Viginti tabu-
lis | veluti supplementum quoddam antiquitatis obso-
letę | suo loco quę vel abstrusa | vel erronea videban-
tur | resolutissime pandit.

Adnexo ad finem tractatu sicuti lectu jucundissimo |
ita & utilissimo de variis moribus & ritibus gentium : eorundem ↄȝ ac localium nominū originibus.

Breuis continentia Libri.
Oppida | regna | lacus | montes | & ęquora | siluas
ac hominum mores hic Ptolemęus habet.

Cum gratia & priuilegio Imperiali
per ♃ annos.

On the verso of the first leaf is a letter dated 4th Calends September 1508, from Joannes Franciscus Picus, Count of Mirandula, to Jacobus Æszler and his associates (*et complicibus*). We know from the letter of the editors as well as from the reference to the very next line of this same letter, where the words *utriusque vestrum* are used, that the associates must be narrowed to a single partner, Georgius Uebelin, a famous ecclesiastical counselor at Strasburg. The letter explains the journey of Mathias Ringmann (Philesius) into Italy and his access to an original Greek manuscript of Ptolemy's geography, by means of which the Latin version of Jacobus Angelus de Scarparia, made early in the fifteenth century, was collated and corrected. On the recto of the second leaf is the dedication of the editors, Jacobus Æszler and Georgius Uebelin, to the Emperor Maximilian. This is dated from Strasburg, March 15, 1513, notwithstanding that the colophon itself, as we shall soon see, is dated March 12. Thus, as so often happens, new hands present to the world the labor of others, and two lawyers of Strasburg,—for Æszler as well as Uebelin was of this profession,—take the credit which really belongs to Waldseemüller and Ringmann and the coterie of the Vosgian Gymnase. On the verso of this second leaf is an index to the seven books of Ptolemy with a line at the bottom announcing that the eighth book has its own index. The geography begins with Chapter I. of Book I. on the recto of the third leaf, which is marked "B." The leaves are numbered as follows:

B, C, D, E, F, G, H, I, K, and *L* are in sixes. *M* is in fives, and is numbered in the Arabic style. *N* begins on *Nii* and ends on *Nvi*, the last two leaves not numbered but of course belonging to *N*. On the verso of *Ki* is a *Sphera in Plano* covering the entire page. The colophon is on the verso of folio *Nvi*, and is as follows:

Anno Christi opt. Max. MDX iii, March Xii
Pressus hic Ptolemęus Argentinę Vigilantissima casti-
gatione, industriaȝ Joannis Schotti ur-
bis indigenę.

Then in our copy follow four blank leaves which are entirely of a later period of manufacture, and probably are not to be found in other copies. After this is the general map of the Old World on two uncut leaves. Then follow ten maps of Europe, all folding or double folio in form. After these come four maps of Africa and twelve maps of Asia, all double folios except the last one of the twelve Asiatic maps, which is on a single folio.

Then follows the new matter, beginning with a second title on the recto of the folio:

IN CLAUDII PTOLEMEI
SUPPLEMENTUM

followed by thirty-nine lines, for the most part an index of the supplementary matter. Included in this page are the subjects of the twenty maps which follow. The first is entitled:

HYDROGRAPHIA, SIVE CHARTA MARINA: CONTINENS TYPUM ORBIS
UNIVERSALEM JUXTA HYDROGRAPHORUM TRADITIONEM.

This is said to be the first time the word *charta* is employed in printed form, although we find it designating maps in manuscripts before this period. On the verso of this leaf is a notice to the reader which we have already introduced in Part VI. of this book.

Then comes the great "Charta Marina," covering two folios. It gives besides the Old World an unnamed region southwest of "Gronland," and which probably is intended for the Corte-Real discoveries, although placed too far to the east. South of this, but far to the west, are the two islands "Spagnolla" and "Isabella," and then a very large part of South America, with a few names such as "Cambales" and "Caput de Crucis." Greenland is the belonging of Europe and has not cast in her lot with the New World.

Lelewel, in the book of maps accompanying his "Géographie du Moyen Age," published at Brussels in 1852, has attempted to reconstruct a *Hydrographia Charta Marina Portugalensium* which might have been a prototype of the map now under consideration. Lelewel's Geography, however, while invaluable to the student, must be studied with care and caution, since it does not pretend to reproduce the ancient maps in facsimile, but in an altered and corrected form. The *Charta* of the 1513 Ptolemy has evidently been cut off at its western side, and that border runs through the west end of the island of Cuba. Consequently, none of the Gulf of Mexico or the continental land to the west of Cuba is shown. The latitudes are marked, but there are no degrees of longitude given. The degrees number 90 north and 80 south of the equatorial line, but the southern continent extends only to about forty degrees. The tropics of Cancer at 25° north of the line, and of Capricorn at the same distance south of the line, are the only parallels given. There is a scale at the bottom of the map giving divisions in which there are ten long German miles to fifty Italian miles, but the points in the scale are not very clear.

It is in the next map in the Ptolemy of 1513 that we have most interest It is reproduced by us in exact fac-simile. Here the reader has the nearest connecting link to the lost map of Martin Waldseemüller. As we have already said in another part of this book, the editors of the Ptolemy of 1522 distinctly state that this map, there reproduced on a smaller scale and in a somewhat more elaborate style, was drawn by Waldseemüller. It is certain that neither the map in the Ptolemy of 1513 nor in that of the 1522 edition is an exact reproduction of the map which the St.-Dié coterie proposed issuing in 1507. The reader will recall that in the advertisement of the "Cosmographiæ Introductio" it was proposed that upon this map the principal countries of the earth should be distinguished by the standards of their rulers. The Roman eagles were to mark the German Empire. The keys were to be the symbol of the Church's power. The crescents, the arms of the Sultan of Babylon, were to cover Africa and part of Asia, while Asiatic Sarmatia was to be designated by anchors, which the Great Tartar had for his arms. Even the home of good Presbyter John was to be known by a red cross. Finally, in the fourth part of the world discovered by the illustrious Kings of Castile and Portugal were to be placed the standards belonging to their kingdoms. Then, too, we are told that on these maps coasts which might be dangerous for the mariners were to be marked "with figures of the cross which will serve to point them out." None of these symbols, banners, and standards anywhere appears in the Ptolemy of 1513, in either the "Charta Marina" or the "Tabula Terre Nove." In the Ptolemy of 1522, which follows this rather closely, the later map has the single standard of Castile placed over the Island of Cuba. It will be remembered that the early manuscript portolani were distinguished by standards, pictures of kings, castles, animals, and idols, while their parchment surfaces were crowded with inscriptions and explanations. If the advertisement to the reader in the "Cosmographiæ Introductio" was written before the map had progressed enough for Waldseemüller to discover the impossibility within reasonable limits of depicting all these things on a single map, it may account for the marked but essential departure made by Waldseemüller in the actual construction of his map. The dimensions of the largest book were not suited for reproducing the gigantic maps and charts drawn or painted on oxhide, and sometimes as high as the stature of a man.

The "Tabula Terre Nove" is a large map, being within its borders 14⅝ inches in length by 17½ inches broad. Both the east and west borders carry degrees of latitude, running from 55° north latitude to 35° south of the equator. The tropics are here very correctly placed. The continental land of North America begins just below the fifty-fifth degree north latitude and is marked *C. del mar usiano*, which has been interpreted to mean Cape of the Ocean Sea. The land runs in a straight line until it reaches a point which we take to be our Florida. The upper region marked *C. del mar usiano* we believe is intended to mark the most northerly point reached by Vespucius on his first voyage in 1498. The map was constructed to exhibit the discoveries made by Columbus and Vespucius and the possessions in the New World of the Kings of Castile and Portugal. The reader should study the several types of early maps as classified by Harrisse in his "Discovery of North America." This present map is his fifth type and illustrates the union of the northern and southern continents.

It has been shown that Waldseemüller was under the influence of the spell cast upon any one who reads the four voyages of Americus Vespucius, and it may well be that the purpose of the German geographer was accomplished when he depicted upon his map all that region which he believed, from his reading of the voyages of Columbus and Vespucius, really constituted the New World. The lands to the north may have been in the mind of Waldseemüller but part of Asia, and thus not to be included in a "Tabula Terre Nove." The point of land here called *C. doffim de abril*, or *C. de Fundabril* as it is in Ruysch (Cape of the End of April), is, we believe, Cape Sable, which Vespucius would have reached at that date on his way from the land of Lariab. We are aware that those who believe in the bodily transfer of the nomenclature belonging to the island of Cuba to the mainland, account for this name by attributing its christening to Columbus on his second voyage, when he went from Spagnolla to the east end of Cuba. But it will be recalled that Columbus had already named this point on his first voyage and christened it *Alpha et Omega* because, believing that Cuba was the coast of Asia, this extreme eastern end of the land would be the *last* of the earth to those traveling from the west to the east, and the *first* to those traveling from the east to the west. Whatever may be said in claiming a Cuban right to the other names of the mainland, certainly the name of the Cape of the End of April never did belong lawfully to Cuba. The coast of Louisiana and the Gulf of Mexico are given, and the continental land is drawn, an uninterrupted and unbroken line, to the thirty-fifth degree of south latitude. There is no nomenclature of the coast from the mouth of the Mississippi until we reach *Arcay*, the eastern boundary of the Gulf of Venezuela on the north coast of the southern continent. From here on we have some forty-four names, eighteen of which are on the north coast and twenty-six on the southeast coast. South of *Arcay*, below the equator and stretching nearly across the continent, is the phrase which gives to Columbus the honor of discovery:

HEC TERRA CUM ADJACENTIBUS INSULIS INVENTA EST PER COLUMBUM
JANUENSEM EX MANDATO REGIS CASTELLE.

(This land with the adjoining islands was discovered by Columbus the Genoese under the authority of the King of Castile.)

Below this inscription are the two words describing the interior of the New World, *Terra Incognita*. The nomenclature is a mixture of Spanish and Portuguese. The fourth place named on the southeast coast is S. Maria de Rabida. Beyond doubt this point is named after the convent of La Rábida near Palos, and as the Pinzons, and indeed many of the sailors on these early voyages, were from that one-time busy maritime village, it is quite natural it should be remembered by its venturesome citizens in christening some distant spot in the New World. When we try to connect the naming of this place with Americus Vespucius we meet with some difficulty, since he could never have seen it while sailing under Spanish colors and with Spanish sailors. His third voyage took him there, but it was made under the Portuguese flag. It is not known with certainty who were the ship captains and pilots on this expedition, and it may be there were some Palos people connected with it. The name first appears on a manuscript map known in Harrisse's list as *Kunstmann No. 3*, and which was probably executed before 1505. It is found for the first time in a printed or engraved map in this edition of Ptolemy. The eleventh name down the eastern coast is of peculiar interest to us, and reference has already been made to it in a preceding chapter. In the Latin edition of the "Four Voyages" of Americus Vespucius, and incorporated in the "Cosmographiæ Introductio" printed at St.-Dié in 1507, the phrase *Abbatia omnium sanctorum* is used to designate a point on the east coast of South America where Americus Vespucius and his companions made a rendezvous on his fourth voyage. In speaking of this circumstance he is made to say, each ship "should make for the land that we discovered in the previous voyage,"— his third voyage,— "at a harbor to which we gave the name of the Abbey of All Saints." It may be here remarked that the church in the city of Florence in which Vespucius worshiped, and in which his family lie buried, was called Church of All Saints. This Latin version, it is stated in the book itself, was translated from the French, which, in turn, had been taken from the original Italian of Vespucius made by him at Lisbon. This original has this same error, and instead of using the Italian *Baja*, bay, the word *Badia*, Abbey, is employed. The error is the work of a careless type-setter, a careless proof-reader, or, possibly, a careless Vespucius. At all events the word "bay" was turned into "abbey," and the error has proved of infinite service in tracing the connection between the hand of Vespucius and the early maps made in Germany and throughout northern Europe. The word is spelled *Abbatia* on this Waldseemüller map. Another name on this same coast of interest to us is the *Rio de St. Augustine*, but our interest in it comes from some having identified it with the name *Cabo de St. Augustine*. The latter, strangely enough, does not appear on this map, an omission which is not easily accounted for on the theory that the map is the work of Vespucius. Cabo de St. Augustine should appear on the point near the eighth degree of south latitude and here called Caput Sanctæ Crucis, as it is also named in the "Charta Marina." Americus himself—so says Garcia de Toreno, a celebrated geographer who made some important maps while in the house of Vespucius—declared that the said cape was situated in 8° of south latitude. In the disputes over the line of demarkation between the possessions of Spain and Portugal this cape bore an important part. It was also the point of arrival in the New World of Magellan, from which he took a southerly course for the straits. Americus Vespucius, and others who had sailed with him, claimed to have named this point while in the service of Portugal. Lopez de Gómara, the author of "Historia de las Indias," in speaking of this claim, took occasion to soundly berate Vespucius for his claims, and boldly asserted that *others*, naming the editor of the Ptolemy printed at Lyons in 1535, agreed with him in pronouncing the Florentine as something of a pretender. The editor of the Lyons Ptolemy of 1535 was Michael Servetus. He severely criticized the bestowal of the Florentine's name on the New World, declaring that he first visited it long after Columbus and, what was more, that he sold his services to Portugal. Vespucius had departed this life and could not defend himself nor show that he had never by word or sign, directly or indirectly, taken jot or tittle from the honor belonging to Columbus. But the gods were with the Florentine and sweetly avenged him. Servetus had copied from the Ptolemy of 1522 a statement concerning the Holy Land to the effect that, notwithstanding the authority of Moses, it was a sterile and unhappy region. Supposing it to be original with Servetus, this statement formed one of the charges of heresy brought against him and resulted in his prosecution by John Calvin and his wretched death at the stake.

At the bottom of the map, and to the right of the border, is another scale with the notice: "Quelibet har. divisionū continet Mil. Ital. 10." In the history of chartography the "Charta Marina" of this edition of Ptolemy has come to be known as the "Admiral's Map" from a passage in the address to the reader. See Part VI., where it is given in full.

"Charta autem Marina, quam Hydrographiam vocant, per Admiralem quondam serenissi Portugaliæ regis Ferdinandi cæteros denique lustratores verissimis peragratiōnibus lustrata."

Who was this admiral? The one early navigator who was always distinguished by that title was Christopher Columbus. From the day of the discovery he was in the Spanish language "El Almirante," whether spoken of by the King and Queen of Spain or by the sailors on his caravels. But of course Columbus was never admiral to Ferdinand, King of Portugal. The latter died October 22, 1383. The explanation is that Spain, or Castile, is here intended instead of Portugal. The adverb *quondam* might be used in the sense of "the late" or "deceased," a meaning post-classic, as "Valeriani quondam centurionis testamentum."

This notice to the reader must have been written subsequent to the death of Duke René, 1508, for the latter is referred to as "of pious memory." Some have imagined that Pedro Alvarez Cabral is the Admiral to whom allusion is made. Others, and not without argument, have insisted that this admiral was Vespucius. *Quondam* may be then interpreted *at one time*, and the phrase rendered — "by an admiral at one time in the service of Ferdinand, King of Portugal." This necessitates the substitution of the name of Manuel for that of Ferdinand, as the former was the king of Portugal at the time of the service of Vespucius under the Portuguese crown. While Vespucius was never admiral, he did occupy an important post in the marine service of Portugal. At one time he was put in command of a fleet, and the title might be attached to him by courtesy. The fact that he had been in the employ of Portugal, and had returned afterward to the service of Spain, might justify the expression "at one time an admiral." It must be remembered that the men who prepared these maps were believers in Vespucius, and that the map which follows the Admiral's, and which probably emanated from the same source, the "Tabula Terre Nove," is full of evidences of a Portuguese origin; its nomenclature is Portuguese, and the coast-line, both north and south, is an outline sketch of the four voyages of the Florentine navigator. If we read this passage literally and assume that the writer meant just what he said, we would have the statement that beginning with the discoveries or rather voyages under an admiral of Ferdinand, king of Portugal, who died in 1383, and continuing with credible accounts of other voyages, the results thereof had been placed upon this marine chart. Why not? It is said that just before King Ferdinand I. went upon the throne, the Portuguese had made their way to the Azores, and certainly there should have been at least a full generation of daring mariners before a nation could have produced such a grand sailor as Prince Henry the Navigator. Gil Eannes, one of the admirals of Prince Henry, for the first time in the authentic history of navigation doubled Cape Non, and yet at that time, suggestive of long years of attempt, there existed among the Portuguese this proverb: *Quem passa o cabo de Não ou Tornara ou não* (He who passes the cape of Not (Não) may return, or he may not). In a portolano at one time belonging to the Baron Walckenaer, and dated 1351, this cape is put down in its proper position.

The one important geographical fact for the reader to grasp is that when this so-called Admiral's map was drawn, the continental land west and north of Cuba was known to be connected with, and to form part of, the *Terra Nova*, or the land to the south, and which up to that time—1507—had been believed to be separate from the region to the north. It was a great step in the onward march of geographical knowledge. As to the idea prevailing at the time of the western boundary of the New World we have only the Stobnicza map to guide us. This last seems beyond doubt to have been copied from the map of Waldseemüller—the original map—which probably gave his notion of the western boundary, but which boundary was cut off in both the "Charta Marina" and the "Tabula Terre Nove," and since this Stobnicza map is found in only one of the several copies known, there is a cloud upon its title, at least as to the date.

It will not be strange if our interest in this volume shall now flag, but we must continue a brief bibliographical account of the remaining portion. A new map of Ireland, England, and Scotland comes next. Then follow:

A modern Map of Spain.

A modern Map of France, and parts of Germany and Italy, but to distinguish the territory belonging to the former, it is ingeniously delineated here in an inverted position. Next there is a modern map of Germany, with the Vosgian mountains filling an important boundary between that country and France. A modern map of Austria, Russia, and Poland follows, and after that we have a map of northern Europe with the Engronelandt and the Mare Congelatum in the extreme north. Two maps of Italy and one of Greece follow. Then there come two maps of Africa, followed by a new map of Asia Minor. Next there is a map of the Holy Land. There is an inscription a little to the east of the middle of the map, and covering the land reaching to the Mediterranean, as follows:

Tota ista terra cesarea usque lida vocat.

Sarona et est fertil.

This is repeated, as we shall see, in the Ptolemy of 1522, and also in the edition of 1535. Next there is a new map of India upon which are inscribed many legends. Following this is a series of three remarkable topographical maps, one of Switzerland, another of the upper Rhine from Basle to below Heidelberg, and a third of Crete. The last map in the book is a one-folio representation of Lorraine, comprising the territory between the rivers Meuse and Rhine, and extending from Plombières to Trèves. The south of this region is placed at the top of the map, where are found two large circles inclosing arms of princes, the one on the right bearing the legend *Ducatus Lotharingie*, and the one on the left *Dominii Vasti Regni*. At the top of the map — really the south — one finds Toul and Nancy, while at the bottom, or the north, is the region about Metz denominated in great red letters *Vastum Regnum*. Around the border are shields carrying the arms of the lesser lords and barons of the country. Humboldt interpreted this *Vastum Regnum* as if Waldseemüller had intended to magnify the importance of Lorraine by terming it a *Vast Realm*, and D'Avezac has taken grim satisfaction in pointing out that it was simply equivalent to calling the region around Metz the West Reich, covering the territory between Lorraine, Alsace, the electorate of Trèves, and the palatinate of the Rhine.

At the bottom of this folio is the inscription:

Secundæ partis Ptolemæi finis: opera Joannis Schotti Argentineñ.
ANNO CHRISTI OPT. MAX. 1513.

The verso of this folio is blank. There follow sixteen folios, the first beginning

LOCORUM AC MIRABILIUM

and the last leaf blank. The numbers are *a* in sixes, *b* in fours, and *c* in sixes. We have thus faithfully tried to give a detailed bibliographical collation of a very rare volume, and which will aid the reader — should he be so happy as to meet with this book on the Quai or in the auction room — to identify it and to determine its completeness.

Thus far we have deduced two important facts:

First, the discoveries made by the Spaniards and Portuguese in the great Ocean Sea disclosed a new world; and,

Second, this new world was an unbroken continental land reaching from about forty-five degrees north latitude to about forty degrees south latitude.

In addition to these two facts we hope we have presented with some force the theory that much of the geographical knowledge here contained came directly from, and embodied, the personal experiences of Americus Vespucius.

CHAPTER X

The First Map with the Name of America

A LATIN grammarian, Caius Julius Solinus, who flourished at the end of the first century, gathered the curious matters in the Natural History of Pliny and made a book therefrom. There were at least nine editions of this work printed during the fifteenth century, first under the title
"*De Situ Orbis et Memorabilibus Mundi,*"
and later under the comprehensive title of "Polyhistor." The first edition in the sixteenth century was issued in 1520 from the Vienna press of Joannes Singrenius and at the expense of Lucas Alantse, a famous bookseller of that city. Two years before they had given to the world an edition of Pomponius Mela's "*Libri de Situ Orbis Tres.*" This edition of Solinus was accompanied with valuable commentaries by Johannes Camers, who had come from Umbria and who was afterward a professor of theology in Vienna. The bookseller Lucas Alantse caused a map of the world to be prepared, and its execution was intrusted to Petrus Apianus, or Bienewitz, a native of Leisnig, near Meissen, in Saxony. The map is engraved on wood, and is 16 inches in length by 11 inches in height, measuring within the borders. It is not certain that the map was engraved in the Vienna printing establishment of Singrenius, but there can be no question as to the map having been prepared for this edition of the "Polyhistor." It is invariably found between the eighth and ninth folios, which would not be the case if the map had been made independently of the book and inserted at random by the different purchasers. The water-mark is the same in our copy both in the map and in the different folios of the book, but the style of woodcutting employed in the map does not seem to be the same as that in the initial letters found in the book itself. Moreover, if Joannes Singrenius had used his shop and tools for the work he would have managed to identify himself with the important map by placing his name or initials somewhere on its surface. This printer, Singrenius, was a man of standing in his profession. He had his own elaborate printer's mark and arms, and

was of enough importance to himself address eight lines of valedictory to the readers, in which he styles himself *Calcographus*. On the other hand two persons besides Petrus Apianus evidently had the making of this map in hand. At either extreme lower corner is a wreath with a scroll. In the sinister corner the scroll within the wreath bears the monogram of Lucas Alantse with the initials *Jo. K* underneath the wreath. The wreath in the dexter corner has an empty scroll and, underneath, the initials *L. F.* These latter initials are identified by Harrisse as belonging to Laurentius Friess, the maker of the maps in the Ptolemy of 1522. Petrus Apianus in 1527 had a printing establishment at Ingolstadt, in Upper Bavaria, in the university of which he was professor of mathematics; and the first printer in that town at the close of the fifteenth century was Johannes Kacheloffen. There may possibly have been a connection between these persons. But the theory we think much more probable is that the map was printed in Strasburg at the press of Johannes Knobloch, who began to print in that town as early as 1497, and who in this very year of 1520 printed eight out of the total of twenty-three Strasburg imprints for that year. The brothers Leonardus and Lucas Alantse were booksellers and not printers, and at their expense they had various printers make books for them.

Before proceeding to describe the map it will be well to speak briefly of the book itself. This edition of the "Polyhistor" is a folio, the title

JOANNIS
CAMERTIS MINORI
TANI, ARTIUM ET SA
CRAE THEOLOGIAE
DOCTORIS, IN. C. JULII
SOLINI PoλΥϊΣΤΩPA
ENARRATIO
NES.

is on the recto of the first leaf and inclosed within a woodcut border. In the center of the lower panel is a monogram of the initial letters of Lucas Alantse. The upper panel contains two large wreaths of conventionalized design, each inclosing a helmeted human head. The two side panels inclose each a pillar, the dexter column having a scroll wound around its base which is wanting in the pillar on the opposite panel. On the verso of this folio is the Imperial permit to the printer, running more than half-way down the recto of folio *ii*, and dated July 20, 1518. On the verso of folio *vii* is a *Life of Solinus* by the editor Johannes Camers. The text of Solinus begins on the recto of folio *ix*. The notes of Camers surround the text, the latter oftentimes consisting of but a few lines placed in the middle of the page. The volume has its pages — not folios — numbered, beginning on the recto of folio *ix* and running to page 336. The next folio is not numbered and contains *Errores Textus*. After this is a folio, also not numbered, containing on the recto the library woodcut plate of Lucas Alantse. The verso of this folio is blank. Then follow fifteen folios of index, *a a* in sixes, *b b* in sixes, and *c c* in threes; the last not marked and containing on the verso the wood-cut printer's mark of Joannes Singrenius.

We may now return to a description of the map of Apianus. The title to the map runs lengthwise across the top of the map, but within the border:

TIPUS ORBIS UNIVERSALIS JUXTA
PTOLOMEI COSMOGRAPHI TRADITIONEM
AME // RICI VESPUCII ALIORUMQUE
LUSTRATIONES A PETRO APIANO
LEYSNICO ELUCUBRAT //
AN. DO. M. D XX

The figure of the entire earth according to the teaching of the cosmographer Ptolemy, and according to the voyages of Americus Vespucius and others, prepared by Peter Apianus of Leisnig.

The map is of the cordiform projection type, with the latitudes marked in spaces of ten degrees, showing land in the New World from a little above fifty degrees south latitude to a little above fifty degrees north latitude, while the longitudes are marked in spaces of thirty degrees each, the first meridian running through the Fortunate Islands. The earth is entirely surrounded by water from the *Mare Congelatum* on the north to the *Mare Prassodum* on the south, and from the sea which holds Zipanga on the east to the ocean which is west of the continental lands in America. The word *OCEANUS*, cut up into letters at a distance from each other, is stretched around the globe.

The reader will at once observe that the chief interest in this map lies in its presenting for the first time on any engraved representation of the earth the name of *America*. It is in large letters just north of the tropic of Capricorn. So far as is known, this is the first chartographical adoption of the name suggested by Waldseemüller in 1507, and its first application to the New World. The undated globes are of doubtful authority. Every few years some wealthy collector has found unearthed from the forgotten archives of some remote village or ancient monastery a metal, wooden, or paper-covered globe, unique in every feature save that of forgery. If the collector entertains doubt because of its having no date, it will come back to him with the date 1511 (or thereabouts) in minute figures, and which he is told escaped his scrutiny on his first introduction to the globe. If he lays much store in a name he can have *America* cut on his globe without an increase in cost. Shall we, for instance, doubt the date of the Hauslab Globe? It is at present in the collection of Prince Liechtenstein at Vienna, and he had it from the collection of General von Hauslab. Strictly speaking, it is not a globe, but a set of strips or gores so cut that when placed upon a hard, rounded surface they meet and completely cover said surface. D'Avezac saw this set and pronounced the date of its execution as of the year 1509, and from this simple expression of opinion it is now confidently ascribed to that early date by writers on chartography. These gores bear the name *America*, and if identified as made in 1509 would record the name for the first time on a picture of the earth's surface. The reader may consult Dr. Nordenskiöld's Atlas for a facsimile of these. We have lately seen a clumsily constructed globe with the year 1509 inscribed upon it—a palpable forgery. The manuscript gores found some years ago at Windsor among papers which are believed to be autographs of Leonardo da Vinci, are also undated and are simply ascribed to the year 1515 by reason of a note in his hand referring to a map apparently owned by him in Italy and from the fact that he left Italy at the close of the year 1515. He did not die until 1519, and no one can tell what subsequent hand may have inserted the word *America*. And so with the globe of Johann Schöner, the Nuremberg mathematician, spoken of always as the globe of 1515; there is no evidence that the only one known was executed in that year. There is a certain probability that *a* globe was made to accompany the "Luculentissima Descriptio," written by Schöner and printed in Nuremberg in the year 1515, but it depends largely upon the interpretation of a passage in the "permit," so to speak, and which may refer to the mounted globe depicted on the fifteenth folio of the book. It was in this latter book that Schöner said Americus Vespucius had discovered the New World in the year 1497.

The Schöner globe of 1520 is dated, but the word *Asia* and the four figures composing the date are of different style from the other lettering on the globe. We do not say these particular globes are not genuine. We simply direct the attention of the reader to the uncertainty surrounding a unique specimen of a wooden or metal globe on the one hand, and on the other hand the probability of genuineness in a dated map engraved from a plate and issued in large numbers. An afterthought might easily alter or modify the one. The other must be corrected throughout all its copies or else be at once detected in the fraud. For instance, it would be easy, since the names on the Sylvanus map of 1511 were all printed in subsequent to the engraving of the plate, to print or stamp in the name of *America*, but what good would it do to so alter the map when all the other copies of Sylvanus stored in public or private libraries would declare the apparent cheat? The present map by Apianus, and plainly dated in the year 1520, is the first engraved chart and authentic map to bear the name of *America*.

That the maker of this map was acquainted with the Vespucian voyages is certain. On the northern continent the Spanish flags mark the southern and the northern limit of his first voyage. Just north of the former is *Parias*, so called from the error in the Latin editions of the "Cosmographiæ Introductio," instead of *Lariab* in the original. Cuba is here called *Isabella*. The island of Spagnolla bears an interesting legend to the effect that it is *Insula in qua reperitur Guaiacum Lignum*. The first published use of the bark of this wood as a specific for the *morbus gallicus* was in an anonymous pamphlet printed in Augsburg in 1518, and soon after in the "Lucubratiuncula" of Leonard Schmaus, printed in Augsburg in the same year.

At 10° north of the equator is an apparent strait. Then the land begins again and runs uninterrupted to below the fortieth degree of south latitude. Just below the equator is the legend that in the year 1497 the land there, with the adjacent islands, was discovered by Columbus the Genoese under the authority of the King of Castile, thus mixing up the original Columbian discovery with the date of the first Vespucian voyage. The oceans meet at the southern end of the continent, and the author of this map intended the public should know that in his opinion the New World was separated from the shores of Asia by a sea. To emphasize this idea he placed a gallant ship in full sail making its way up the western coast toward the equatorial line. But how did Apianus in 1520 know that there was water communication between the two oceans? It was not known in Europe until 1522 that Magellan had found and passed through a strait from ocean to ocean in November, 1520. The discovery of the Pacific Ocean by Balboa in 1513 made it reasonably certain that the New World was entirely cut off from Asia. Doubtless the instinct of the geographer supplied Apianus with the remaining elements of his faith, and he confidently islanded the great western world.

There have been added, then, to the store of geographical knowledge two important facts:

First, the waves of the Pacific Ocean are seen washing the western shores of the New World, and,

Second, the name suggested by the little coterie of scholars at St.-Dié, April 25, 1507, is, for the first time on any engraved map intended for general distribution, applied to the New World; and the *novus mundus* to which it is applied is the southern part of the Western Hemisphere.

CHAPTER XI

𝔉ata 𝔙iam 𝔍nvenient

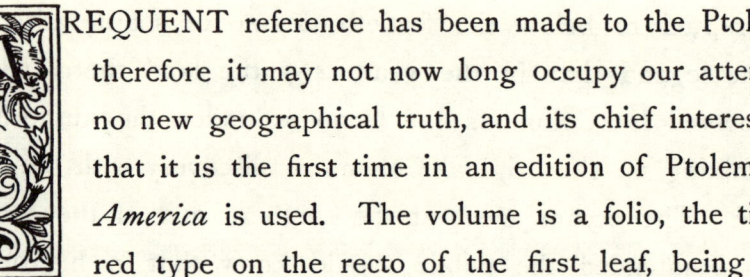REQUENT reference has been made to the Ptolemy of 1522, and therefore it may not now long occupy our attention. It teaches no new geographical truth, and its chief interest lies in the fact that it is the first time in an edition of Ptolemy that the name *America* is used. The volume is a folio, the title, in black and red type on the recto of the first leaf, being within a border executed with the elaborate designs so common to the press of Grüninger. The verso is blank, and on the recto of *A2* is the preface of Thomas Aucuparius in which he praises our Vespucius as the *nobilissimus inventor, visitator et Primus Hospes* of the New World. The register begins on the recto of *Aiii* and runs through to $\frac{E}{F}2$. *A* and *B* are in sixes, while the next leaves, which are in sixes, are numbered $\frac{C}{D}$, followed by $\frac{E}{F}$ in fours. This extraordinary pagination we have never observed before in any book. On the recto of $\frac{E}{F}3$ is a letter of the editor Laurentius Frisius to the pious reader. The text of Ptolemy begins on *Gi* and runs to *R3*, on the verso of which is a large *Sphera in Plano* covering the entire page. On the verso of the next folio (*Riv*) is the notice to the reader by Laurentius Frisius to the effect that the maps were constructed *a Martino Ylacomylo* (Waldseemüller) *pie defuncto*, and that they were reduced somewhat in form from those which he originally made. Book *VIII* and last ends on the verso of *Rv*. The recto of *Rvi* is blank, while on its verso is a list of some twenty maps which are to follow. Then come ten double folio maps of Europe, on the other sides of which one finds the explanatory text, for the most part bordered with most elaborate and artistic designs, among which are the earliest masonic symbols we have ever met with in printed books. Many of the designs are signed by the monogram of the artist *J. H.*, and he is identified as Johannes (or Hans) Holbein. After the European maps there come four maps of Africa and twelve maps of Asia. Next there is a general chart of the world according to Ptolemy. Then we have the "Tabula Terre Nova" reduced from the same map in the Ptolemy of 1513,

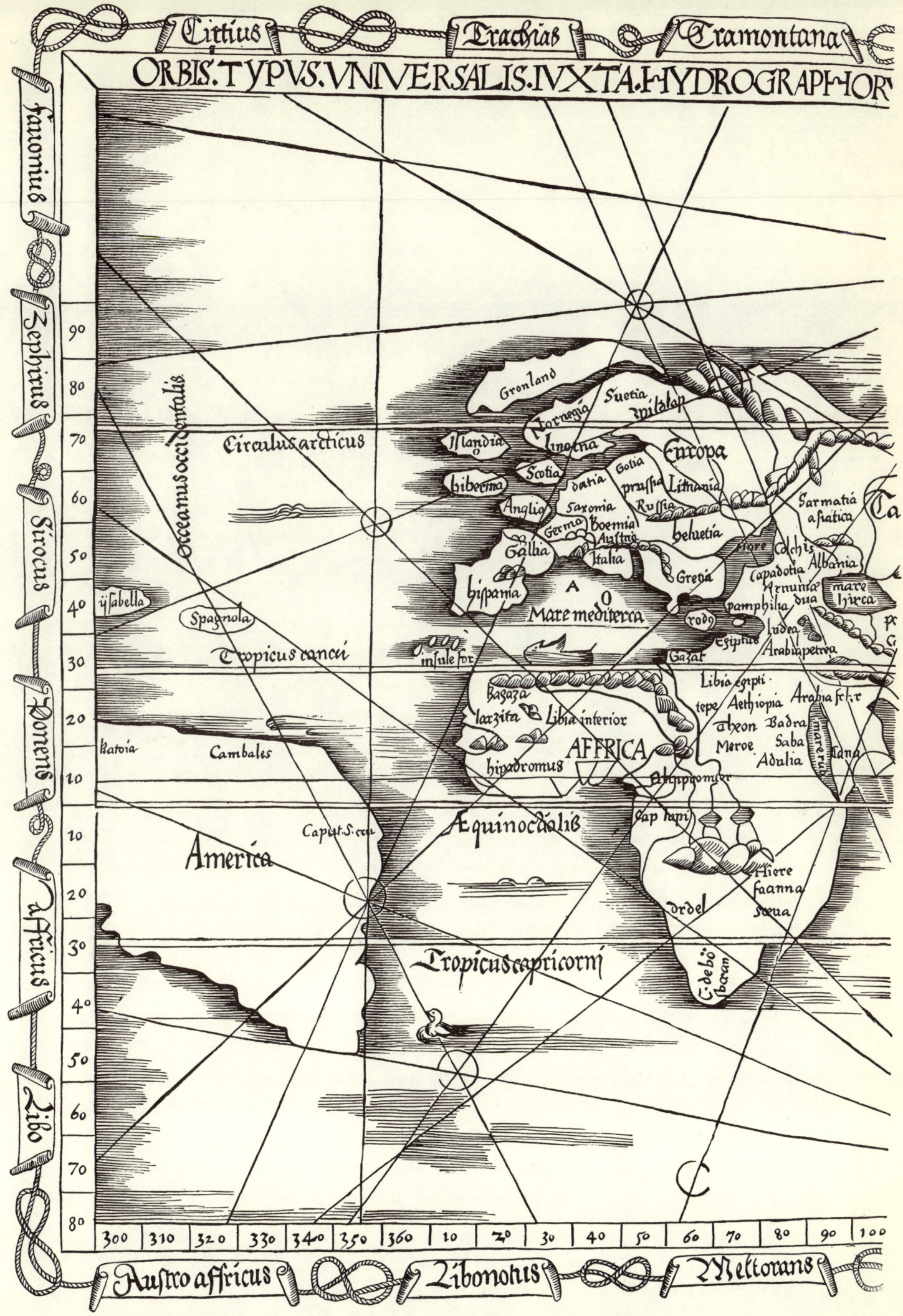

PORTION OF A MAP FROM THE PTOLEMY GEOGRAPHY OF 1522.

MAP OF

MADE IN 1531, AND PUBLIS

PARIS GRYNAEUS OF 1532.

but embellished with a picture of a huge female wolf and another of a group of feasting cannibals. The word *Parias*, wanting in the 1513 edition, is here inserted in the province of the true Lariab. The nomenclature is almost identical with the earlier edition, a few names only being omitted owing to the reduced space. The text on the back of the map — on both folios — is in German script, and this nowhere else appears in the book. Then follow ten more maps of Europe, two of Africa, five of Asia, and one each of Switzerland, of the Rhenish provinces, and of Crete. Next a map of the Old World and a reduced copy of the Waldseemüller "Orbis Typus Universalis" are found, with the word *America* south of the equator. Then the book is completed with eight more folios, on the recto of the last of which is the colophon, stating that the book is printed at Strasburg by Joannes Grieninger (Grüninger), March 12, 1522. In the text accompanying the "*Tabula Terrae Sanctae*" it is stated that, notwithstanding what Moses had said about the Holy Land, it was sterile and unprofitable. At this time Michael Servetus was only a lad of thirteen at school in Spain. Because, thirteen years later, in editing the Ptolemy of 1535, he copied verbatim this passage, he had it counted against him in the indictment for heresy. As we said before, the reader will learn nothing new of the growth of cosmography from this edition of Ptolemy.

The book now to be considered is the "Novus Orbis" of Simon Grynæus, printed at Basle in the month of March, 1532. The reader is referred to Harrisse's "Bibliotheca Americana Vetustissima" (171) for the copy seen and described by him. There were three editions of this book issued in the year 1532, the one described by Harrisse and printed at Basle in March, and another printed at Paris on the viii Kalends of November, and still a third printed by Jean Petit. In the first or Basle edition is found the large map generally ascribed to Sebastian Munster. In the Paris edition is found the celebrated double hearted map of Orontius Finæus. In the Basle edition of 1537 the former map is also found, differing only in the fact that the word *Asia* is printed in a kind of type somewhat different and smaller. For purposes of identification we will speak of the map found in the Basle edition as the Munster map, to distinguish it from the map made by Orontius Finæus. The former, then, the Munster map, is very interesting from the quaint wood-cut adornments about its borders. Two figures are represented at either pole turning a crank which revolves the earth upon its axis. Both the Munster and the Finæus maps bear the name of America covering the same stretch of land, but as to the importance of the two maps there is no comparison. The Munster map is scarcely more than a reproduction of the type from which the Stobnicza map was taken. While much more exact in reality than the Finæus or than most of the maps issuing for many years after its date, it represents the results not of knowledge but of happy speculation. It is important to trace the acceptance of the truths, step by step, as they became accepted, and to show the seasons of doubt and uncertainty and even the backward flights, recorded in the maps of the old geographers.

The title of the book before us is:

NOVUS ORBIS REGIO-

Num ac insularum Veteribus incognitarum
Unā cum tabula cosmographica, & aliquot aliis consimilis
Argumenti libellis quorum omnium catalogus.
Sequenti patebit pagina.

The printer's mark is a pillar or pedestal on which are mounted the busts of three helmeted men (modified in the 1537 edition) and underneath is the motto:

Fata viam invenient.
Basileae Apud Io. Hervagium.   Mense
Martio.   Anno M D XXXII.

On the verso of this first folio is a catalogue of the contents of the book. The second of the chapters is entitled:

IN TABULAM COSMOGRAPHIÆ INTRODUCTIO PER
SEBASTIANUM MUNSTERUM.

In reality it is the third chapter or division — not the second. On the next folio is a letter from Simon Grynæus. The compilation of voyages included under the title of this book has come to be known as the work of Grynæus, although scholars to-day recognize in it the labor of Johannes Huttich, a celebrated German archæologist. Then follow twenty-three folios distinguished by Greek letter signatures and 585 pages numbered. The map in our copy is found just before the *voyages* on page 1. It is folded on two folios. This collection includes the voyages of Columbus, the four voyages of Vespucius, and those of Pinzon and others.

In the *Declaratio Cosmographiæ*, or, as the table of contents calls the chapter, *In tabulam cosmographiæ introductio*, by Sebastian Munster, on the recto of δ2, occurs the following interesting passage:

Quin & in oceano occidentali ferè novus orbis nostris temporibus ab Alberico Vesputio & Christophoro Columbo, multis que aliis insignibus viris inventus est, qui non abs re quarta orbis pars nuncupari potest, ut jam terra non sit tripartita, sed quadripartita, cum hæ Indianæ insulæ sua magnitudine Europam excedant, præsertim ea quam ab Americo primo inventore Americam vocant.

We should expect to find the map prepared by Sebastian Munster to accompany this book designating the land discovered by Vespucius as Novus Orbis, and this is precisely what we find in the Munster maps accompanying the Ptolemy of 1540 and that of 1552. In the most of the copies of the Basle edition of Grynæus, 1532, the New World is called *Terra Nova* (the word *America* of course being over it), and the general appearance of the entire western half of the map indicates a servile copy of either the Stobnicza map or its prototype. When we reach the Ptolemy of 1540 the geographical ideas of Munster will be fully disclosed.

It is in the map of Orontius Finæus in the Paris Grynæus, 1532, that we find an advanced step in geography. This edition is a trifle larger folio than that printed at Basle. The title is the same, but instead of the printer's mark (the pedestal with the three helmeted heads) there is substituted the mark of the Paris printer Galeoti à Prato — a galley propelled by silhouetted oarsmen, and the legend *Vogue la Galee* on a streamer from the masthead. There are twenty-four preliminary leaves, 515 pages, with the colophon on the recto of the next and last folio, and which is as follows:

>   Impressum Parisiis apud Antonium Augerellum impensis Johannis
>   Parvi & Galeoti à Prato Anno M. D. XXXII. VIII
> Calen. Novembris.

There is an edition of this date made at Paris by Jean Petit with his name recorded as printer. Antonius Augerellus, the real printer of the Paris book, may have intended concealing some secret by means of a cipher, for a more grotesque pagination was never seen out of the Shakespeare folio than this book exhibits after page 474. If some other copy is found with these faults corrected it may be the means of reaching a conclusion as regards the priority of the Munster or Finæus map.

The map is 16¼ inches wide by 11¼ inches high. It is a double heart projection of the globe. The title runs across the top of the map in a scroll:

NOVA, ET INTEGRA UNIVERSI ORBIS DESCRIPTIO.

The following advertisement is in a square at the bottom of the map:

>   ORONTIUS F.: DELPH:
>   ad lectorem.
> Offerimus Tibi, Candide
> Lector, universam orbis terrarum descriptionem,
> Juxta recentium Geographorum ac Hydrographo
> rum mentem, servata tum Æquatoris, tum pa
> rallelorum ad eas quæ ex centris proportione,
> gemina cordis humani formula in plano coexten
> sam: quarum læua borealem, dextra vero au
> stralem Mundi partem complectitur. Tu igitur
> munusculum hoc liber aliter excipito: habetoque
> gratias Christiano Wechelo, cujus favore et
> impensis hæc tibi communicarimus.
>   Vale. 1531.
>   Mense Julio.

Orontius Finæus of Dauphiny (he was a native of Briançon, in Dauphiny) to the reader:

We offer to thee, gentle reader, a universal description of the entire earth, according to the ideas of the latest geographers and hydrographers, arranged with a due proportion between the lines of the equator and of the parallels relative to the lines which run from the center, and included in two human-heart-shaped forms. The one on the left encircling the north part of the world and that on the right encircling the south part. Receive, then, this little work and give thanks to Christianus Wechel, by whose generosity and at whose expense we are able to communicate it to thee.

Farewell. 1531.
In the month of July.

The left-hand heart has the north pole for its center, while the south pole is the center of the right-hand heart. Across the top of the south pole is this legend:

TERRA AUSTRALIS RE
center inventa, sed nondum plenè cognita.

There is no such a thing in the mind of Finæus as a *novus orbis* in the sense of a new continent. One could walk from the north pole to the south pole without wetting his feet except for the Straits of Magellan. Finæus sees a great stretch of land opened up and explored by adventurous sailors. The land narrows at about ten degrees of latitude north of the equator, and he learns from the conquistador Balboa that the land other geographers have called a *novus orbis*, or a new and gigantic island, is simply part of the land of the north, and that the land to the north has come out of the Asiatic fields. This gulf of Uraba washes the Isthmus of Darien, and this thin neck of terra firma unites the southern part of the land to the northern part. A little below the fiftieth parallel is the first representation on any printed map of the straits discovered by Magellan, and in honor of him who found a way about the globe the western sea was called *Mare Magellanicum*.

The reader now has discovered the backward step taken in the march of geographical knowledge. The light which was flashed on the Western Hemisphere disclosed for a moment the north and south continental lands freed from all connection with Europe and Asia. Many geographers saw it and caught its meaning. Then the light was withdrawn, doubt and uncertainty again controlled men, and until the contrary was absolutely affirmed through the experiences of bold and intelligent voyagers it seemed safer to anchor the newly discovered lands to the solid foundations of ancient Asia.

But we shall see that, if Orontius Finæus could not discover the truth to the northward, he had seen the full effect of its light to the southward. This Finæus was a remarkable man. He had been carefully trained in the sciences and moreover had a natural aptitude for mechanics. He invented many useful instruments, so many that a printed catalogue was made to inventory the number. His studies were carried on in

Paris, and as early as 1514 he edited a work on arithmetic. In 1523 he is said to have edited an edition of the "Margarita Philosophica." It is evident that he was in no indebtedness to Sebastian Munster for his geographical notions, yet we find J. Baptista Benedictis, in his book on dialing published at Turin in 1574, accusing him of plagiarizing from Munster, particularly in the use of a projection upon a globe. Two years before he died, in 1553, Finæus invented a certain marvelous clock, which brought him much fame but added nothing to his fortunes, for it is said he died in something approaching poverty.

We are now to receive from Finæus two new truths, and to add them to the sum of geographical knowledge:

First, the southern land which Americus Vespucius called *Novus Mundus*, and which Waldseemüller baptized America, is not separate from, but a part of, the lands directly to the north; and

Second, this land is not an impassable barrier between east and west, but a way has been found from sea to sea. This means more than the knowledge brought by Balboa, that the sea which washed the shores of Cathay also lapped serenely the western coast of the new lands. This knowledge and this fact were of no importance until a passage of communication was opened. And behold, Magellan found this way. In the words of the Basle printer of the first Grynæus:

FATA VIAM INVENIENT.

CHAPTER XII

The Backward Step Regained

FOR a long time the first map to apply the name of America to the north and south parts of the continent was believed to be that made by Gerard Mercator in 1541. Then there was found by the late James Brevoort a double cordiform map dated 1538 and made by Mercator when only twenty-six years of age. This was long pointed out as unique, and to-day occupies a resting-place in the treasures of the American Geographical Society. The late James Lenox was once looking through a consignment of book gems forwarded him by the hunters on the other side of the water, when in a copy of the Grynæus printed by Jean Petit at Paris in 1532, and loosely folded next to the usual Finæus map of 1531, was a beautiful specimen of the Mercator 1538. The border is not quite so full, some binder having cut it in his efforts to fit it to some particular book, but it is otherwise in a better state of preservation than its only sister — the one preserved in the Geographical Society rooms. As a geographical contribution it is of no great importance, since it so closely follows the double heart-shaped Finæus map. Its interest lies in the happy extending of the name *America* so as to include what is now recognized as the Western Hemisphere. The reader must not regard this or the map of 1541 as specimens of what is known as Mercator's projection. It is for the first time in the edition published in Duysburgh in 1569 that the form of projection which bears his name was introduced. It is not known where this map of 1538 was constructed. The water-mark, which is somewhat indistinct, appears on each of his connected folios, and is about as long as (and not entirely unlike in appearance) a woman's thimble. The map measures 20½ inches in width by 13 inches in height within the border.

The next book to come under our observation is the Ptolemy of 1540. Its editor was Sebastian Munster, a man who covered in his day a goodly bit cf ground. Born at Ingelheim in the Palatinate in 1489, he was educated in Heidelberg and Tübingen. He was a theologian first within the Church of Rome and afterward in the embrace of

MAP OF THE WORLD, BY AP
THE FIRST MAP C

M SOLINUS POLYHISTORIA, 1520.
THE NAME AMERICA.

Lutheranism. He preached before a court in Heidelberg, and he taught before a class in Basle; he edited the Hebrew Bible and composed geographies; he published a dictionary in three tongues, and he wrote a treatise on mathematics. The good people called him the German Ezra, and the wise people called him the German Strabo. He received his degrees from the universities, and his works obtained admission to the "Index Librorum Prohibitorum." In several books of his in our possession some sensitively pious soul has written in each, opposite his name, in very big and very black letters, the dreadful word *Damnatur*. The title begins on the recto of the first unnumbered leaf:

GEOGRAPHIA
Universalis, Vetus et Nova
Complectens.

CLAUDII PTO.
Lemæi Alexandrini enarratio
Nis Libros viii.

(Then follow seven subjects, the fourth of which is: *succedunt tabulæ Ptolemaicæ, opera Sebastiani Munsteri novo paratæ modo.*

Basileæ Apud Henricum Petrum
Mense Martio Anno
M. D. XL.

The verso of this folio is blank. Six leaves of index marked with an asterisk and eighteen leaves of the first book marked *a, b, c* in sixes, bring us to *Liber II*, at which the pages begin to be numbered and run to page 155, the next page being blank. Then follow forty-eight double folio maps — the first, entitled

TYPUS ORBIS UNIVERSALIS,

gives in general the features which appear in detail in the forty-fifth map, and in addition, over the land called Francisca, appears a strait and an open water-way into the oceanus orientalis. A legend says *Per hoc fretum iter patet ad Molucas*. Gómera tells of many expeditions sent out by Spain and Portugal to find a way to the Moluccas by the north, and the coast of Labrador was searched faithfully for this passage. Verrazzano in 1524 and Cartier in 1534 sought this short route to the land of spices. From what source did Munster get his belief in a strait in the northern latitudes? Was it simply the belief which the old geographers had that all seas were connected by water? Have not the cosmographers ever been in advance of the discoverers? It was the long fulfilment of a dream from the story of Verrazzano and the sketching of Maggiolo to the accomplished voyage of Vitus Bering. Something of discovery has been reserved for each age and each great nation, and this proof of the separation of terrestrial divisions was the reward to a great king of a rising northern nation, although his ears never heard the tale from the lips of the Danish sailor.

The forty-fifth map is entitled:

NOVAE INSULAE, XVII. NOVA TABULA.

This is the seventeenth of the new maps, but they are not numbered in strict order, No. 14, for instance, being inserted between 15 and 16. The *Novus Orbis*, as it is here called, is a continent, the northern and southern portions connected by an isthmus. The north part is cut off from both Europe and Asia, and is called Francisca, beyond doubt recording the voyage of Verrazzano under the standard of Francis I. Across the south part is the legend:

Insula Atlantica quam vocant Brasilii & Americam.

The legend is inconsistent with the contour of the land on the map, unless the author intended to apply this phrase to the continent; that is, to the country from the Straits of Magellan to the north coast of Francisca. Against this theory is the application of the term *Novus Orbis* to the whole region, and the association of America with the well-known situation of Brazil. To the west of the Straits of Magellan the words *Mare pacificum* christen the western ocean. There is a relic of the old Asiatic connection in the placing of the word *Catigara* on the western coast. The great galley which is represented as plowing the waves is wanting in some of the maps found in this edition, according to Harrisse. That there must have been many impressions of this map is apparent from the character of the wooden blocks when the later editions were struck, the blocks being worn and much broken.

The backward step taken by Orontius Finæus has been regained, and the rude but suggestive map teaches

First, the continuity of the land, north and south; and,

Second, the integral character of this continental division.

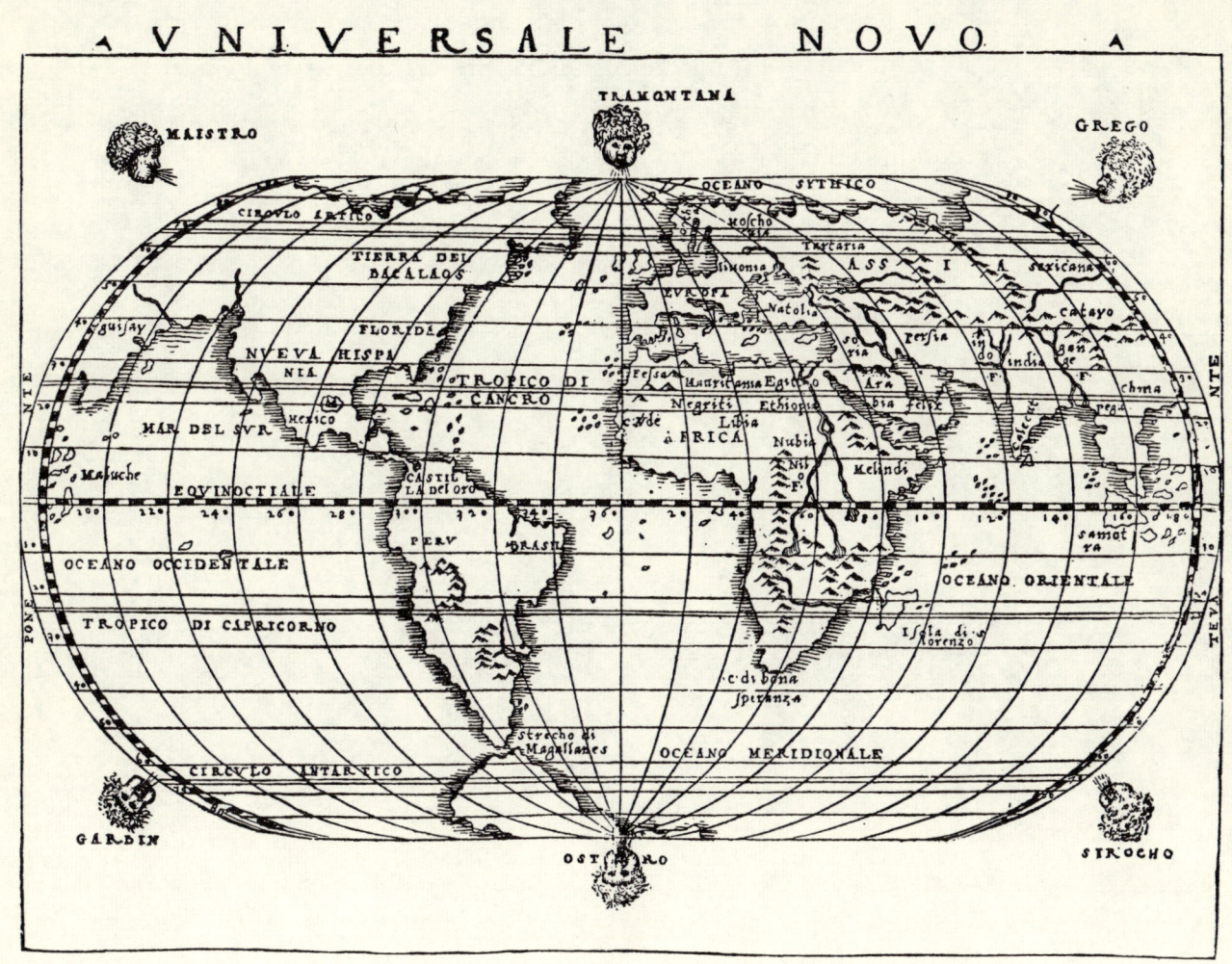

MAP OF THE NEW WORLD, BY GASTALDI.

FROM THE FIRST ITALIAN EDITION OF PTOLEMY'S GEOGRAPHY OF 1548.

MAP FROM THE MUNSTER EDITION OF PTOLEMY'S GEOGRAPHY PRINTED AT BASLE IN 1540.

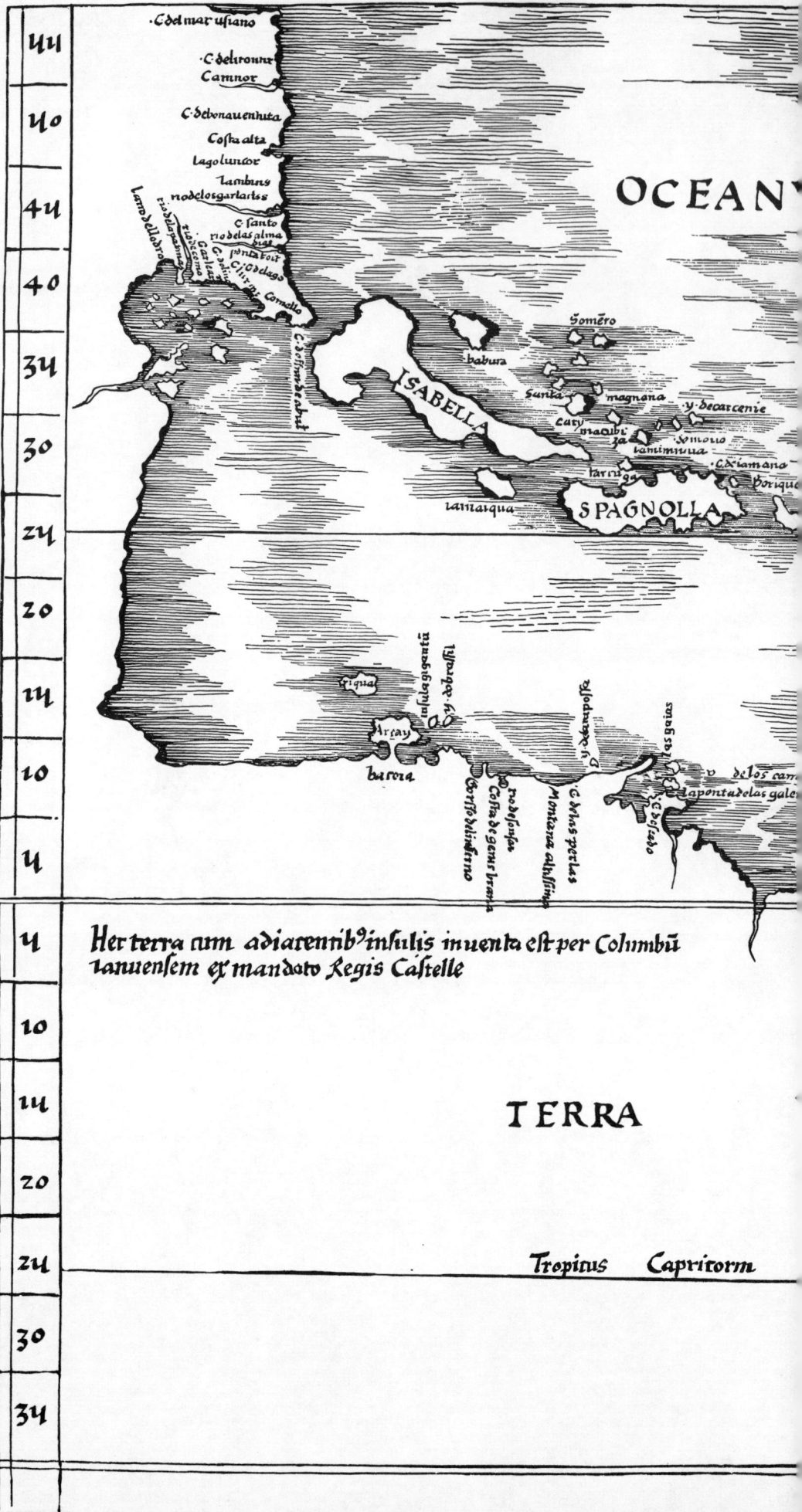

TABULA TER

Hec terra cum adiacentib⁹ insulis inuenta est per Columbū Ianuensem ex mandato Regis Castelle

TERRA

Tropicus Capricorni

MAP FROM THE PTOLEMY GEOG
THIS MAP WAS MADE BY WALDSEEMÜLLER AB

RE NOVE

...D AT STRASBURG IN 1513.
...SHOWS THE DISCOVERIES OF VESPUCIUS.

CHAPTER XIII

The Statue of America

IN the history of chartography Italy furnished the discoverers and Germany the map-makers. It is true that the first edition of Ptolemy ever printed, and the first edition with engraved maps, and the first edition to represent the New World, were all from Italian presses, but forty years had passed since the Ruysch Ptolemy was printed when Jacobus Gastaldi issued at Venice his beautifully printed edition filled with copper engraved maps to the number of sixty. German printing was not as pleasing to the eye as that of the Italian presses. The engraving for the most part was done on wood and executed in poorer drawing than that of the Roman artists. This 1548 edition is small octavo in form and begins with the title

PTOLEMEO
LA GEOGRAFIA
DI CLAUDIO PTOLEMEO
ALESSANDRINO.

On the second folio, marked †*ii*, is a woodcut figure representing Ptolemy taking observations — as in the early editions of the "Margarita Philosophica." After the letter of Gastaldi there is a chapter giving such things as Sebastian Munster thought advisable for the student of geography to know. The folios and not the pages are numbered throughout the book. The colophon tells us that the printer was Nicolo Bascarini; but the bookseller, Giovanni Battista Pedrezano, whose shop was at the foot of the bridge of the Rialto, introduces his peculiar book plate — two infant angels bearing the glorified head of John the Baptist on a charger — several times in the volume. The maps of interest to us are seen in number as follows:

No. 54 — Della Terra Nuova,
No. 55 — Della Nova Hispania,
No. 56 — Della Terra Nova del Bacalaos,
No. 57 — Dell' Isola Cuba Nuova,

No. 58 — Dell' Isola Spagnolla Nuova,
No. 59 — Dell' Universale Nuovo,
No. 60 — Della Carta Marina Universale.

The special interest in these maps is the detail found in the contour of the south part of the New World, but it is worthy of notice that here as elsewhere on the maps the name of Americus is not found. There is no reference to him or his discoveries in the text. But, alas! the northern country is again represented as running into Asia, and in the "Universale Nuovo" one may travel along the west coast of Mexico until he shall rest at Guisay and bathe in the Ganges. Compare the shape of South America as we know it to-day with the drawing of the fifty-ninth map of the Gastaldi Ptolemy, and behold the resemblance.

The most sumptuous map-bearing book of the sixteenth century is the

THEATRUM ORBIS TERRARUM

of Ortelius, printed at Antwerp in 1570. It has been called the first Atlas in distinction from the usual form of cosmographies as at first published. Abraham Ortelius, the author, was a native of Antwerp, where he was born in 1527 and in which city he died in 1598. The story is told of Mercator that so great was his friendship for Ortelius that, notwithstanding his own great work was ready for the press, he kept it back until his friend's Atlas might first be issued. This story appears apocryphal, since Ortelius's work was not printed until 1570, while Mercator's "Nova et Aucta Orbis Terræ Descriptio" was printed at Duysburg in August, 1569. Then, too, Mercator had ready only the first part of his work in 1569, and if any inference is to be drawn from dates it is that he hurried out of the press an incomplete book before Ortelius should send forth his. The holograph letter of Mercator which we have published from our collection may perhaps refer to a continuation of his work. This 1569 edition of Mercator is so rare that we nurse but feebly a hope of some day obtaining a copy.

The title-page of the Ortelius is a work of art. It is a copper-plate engraving 14¾ inches high by 9 1-16 inches wide measured within the border. There are four female figures, representing the four divisions of the world, and thus in this book we have America for the first time admitted into the realm of symbolism as the equal of the other three parts of the globe. Europe with her left hand upon the cross is seated upon a throne above the arch. It is she who is carrying the comfort and the civilizing influences of religion. In the right hand is the scepter of power, while upon her head is worn a royal crown. The figure on the left of the arch is Asia. Her person is richly ornamented with jewels and precious stones. She proffers a box of frankincense diffusing fragrance to the world. The Æthiopian nymph opposite is Africa,

WESTERN HALF OF WORLD—MAP FROM THE ATLAS OF ORTELIUS, 1570.

TITLE-PAGE OF THE ORTELIUS OF 1570,

IN WHICH FOR THE FIRST TIME THE CONTINENT OF AMERICA WAS SYMBOLIZED BY A HUMAN FIGURE.

THE MERCATOR MAP OF 1538, THE FIRST TO APPL

AMERICA TO THE ENTIRE WESTERN CONTINENT.

naked of limb and with rays of fire above her head intended to scantily suggest the heat of that sunburnt land. The balsam branch in her right hand may speak balm and healing. Between these two figures of Asia and Africa is a tablet upon which in large letters is inscribed the title of the book. Reclining in the space between the bases of the two columns is the figure of America. On the verso of the second folio is an explanation of the frontispiece written in verse by Adolph van Meetkercke, a Flemish philologist. It is in his remarks on the fourth figure that we are more interested, and we accordingly herewith give an English translation:

> She whom you see below is called America; a nymph whom lately bold Vespucius, wafted on the open sea, took by force and embraced with tender love. Unconscious of herself, and unmindful of chaste modesty, she sits wholly nude, except for the fillet of feathers which confines her locks, the jewel which marks her forehead, and the tinkling bells which encircle her shapely limbs. A wooden staff is in her right hand, with which she slays men fattened for food. Sometimes she roasts over slow flames the bodies of captives taken in war and cut into quivering pieces; or she boils them in a brazen cauldron; or sometimes, when the fury of hunger overtakes her, she devours their limbs freshly cut and raw, all dripping with the dark gore. The limbs yet warm quiver under her teeth, while she feeds upon the flesh and black blood of the wretched men. A deed horrible to see and horrible to tell. What savage wickedness it denotes! What contempt of the Gods above!
>
> You behold in her left hand a human head defiled with fresh blood. You see the bow and swift arrows with which, when she stretches the tightened thong, she is wont to inflict sure wounds and certain death upon men. When after that she wishes to refresh with sleep her limbs worn out in the chase of men, she mounts up into a bed woven like unto a net, swung by each end from two poles, and reclines her head and form within the woven fabric.

To the left of the figure is the head of a female mounted upon a short pedestal. This represents, we are told, the fifth part of the globe, which is to be called Magellana after him who opened the way to the land of spices; and because this new region, Terra del Fuego, is imperfectly known, she is pictured devoid of hands and feet.

Then follows on the recto of folio Aiiii an epistle to the readers by the author, after which he proceeds to give a catalogue of modern geographers and is able to enumerate ninety-one. A table of index begins on *Avii* and finishes on the recto *Aviii*. The work then begins on the double folio *i*, and the first map, entitled "Typus Orbis Terrarum," is described on the recto, while the verso of the second leaf composing the double folio is blank. This relationship of text and map exists throughout the book. There are fifty-three of these great double-folio maps, far superior in artistic presentation to any before issued. In our copy maps 41, 42, 43, and 44 are placed after 36, and maps 37, 38, 39, and 40 are inserted between 44 and 45. After the maps there are three leaves of an article on the Isle of Man written by Humphry Lhuyd, a Welsh antiquarian who died the same year this book was printed. Then follow twenty-seven leaves of ancient names of regions, islands, cities, mountains, and the like, together with their modern appellations. The first two maps are interesting to us in our study. The first map is entitled "Typus Orbis Terrarum," and, as its subject implies, the entire earth is here depicted. It measures 19½ inches in length and 13⅜ inches in height. The second map is entitled "Americæ Sive Novi Orbis Nova Descriptio," and is devoted entirely to a detailed description. In general outline all that concerns our subject is contained in the first map, and it is because these general outlines enable us to better determine certain geographical facts that we have chosen it for reproduction in this work.

The Western Hemisphere is here represented as a land entirely surrounded by water. It extends from the seventy-fifth degree of north latitude to below the fiftieth degree south of the equator. As the Solinus-Apianus map of 1520 was the first authentic instance of the application of the name of America to the south part of the Western Hemisphere, and as the Mercator map of 1538 was the first to spread the name over both the northern and southern portions, so here we believe is the first time it has rested upon a map only upon the upper or northern half. However, since the entire continent is treated as one land, it is evident the name is to be extended over the whole. Stretching across the northwest country we read:

America sive India Nova. A° 1492 *a Christophoro Columbo nomine regis Castellę primum detecta.* This ought to satisfy any one that there was no desire to ignore the right of the Genoese to be known as the discoverer of the New World. The western coast of North America is dotted with settlements where missions had been established, and a vessel is sailing toward those shores from out the southern seas. Far to the north, beyond the Terra de Baccalaos, is a new named region called Estotilant, which is another name for Labrador. It is here the northern limit of the continent, and straits near the Rio Nevado separate it from Groenlant, which belongs to Europe. Ortelius has brought out of the darkness of uncertainty the Munster belief, and it is now, by its adoption into his accepted Atlas, fixed and sure. The New World is a continent entirely independent of Europe and Asia. Its southern part is joined by a narrow neck of land to its northern portion, and the whole is called henceforth and forever *America.*

And now we leave the reader at the door of the temple in which, close to the statue of Columbus, we have seen that of Vespucius firmly established. We have accompanied the Florentine upon his four voyages. We have gone with him more than five and thirty degrees beyond the equator toward the north under the flag of Spain, and we have been with him under the banner of Portugal as the winds drove his ships two and fifty degrees south of the equatorial line. We have counted with him the fourth part of a great circle in the boundaries of his explorations. Under our eyes the story of his travels has come to the little mountain town in Lorraine, and we have heard in that quiet spot the solemn words of baptism with which the *novus mundus* was given his name. We have traced the first introduction of the New World on the maps of the sixteenth century and its gradual enlargement as the truth broke in upon the minds of men. We have seen in this book of Ortelius the acceptance of the New World into the sisterhood of four continents, a co-heiress to the glory of the earth. Not in all these things have we had one unworthy thought of Americus Vespucius. Having followed him not afar off, but hand in hand, we feel we know something of him and of his work, and as Columbus, his friend, commended him to his son Diego, so we can confidently and with honest praise commend him to you, O reader, and to the world.

INDEX

INDEX

Abbatia omnium sanctorum, *see* Abbey of All Saints.
Abbey of All Saints, harbor named by Vespucius, 219, 234.
Admiral, *see* Columbus, Christopher.
"Admiral's map," importance of, 235, 237, 238. *See also* Charta Marina.
Aezler, Jacob, patron of Ringmann and Waldseemüller, 127; editor of Waldseemüller map, 230.
Afer, derivation of name Africa, 18.
Africa, called Libya, 15; derivation of name, 16, 18; symbolic figure, 254–255.
Agathodæmon, early maps of, 174.
Agisinba, named for Roman general, 220.
Aguado, Juan, commander of Spanish fleet, 63.
Alaminos, Antonio de, pilot of Ponce de Leon, 25.
Alantse, Lucas, published map of Apianus, 239–240.
Alexandrian Library, in charge of Eratosthenes, 13.
Aloe, found by Columbus, 48.
Alpha and Omega, *see* Cape Alpha and Omega.
Aluys, Johann, secretary of Duke René, at St. Dié, 116.
Alvarez, Fernando, royal Spanish secretary, 67, 68.
Amazon river, discovered by Vicente Yañez Pinzon, 72; possibly visited by Vespucius, 79.
Ambrosian Library, in Milan, Spanish edition of Columbus' letter to Santangel, 27.
Amerbach, Johannes, letter from Martin Waldseemüller, 127–128.
America, baptism of, 115, 125, 160; discovery, 21–58; announced by Vespucius, 82; discovery due to Strabo, 14; first recognition of equality with other continents, 254.
America, name of, 3–4, 6–7, 15, 16, 82–83, 115–121, 146; applied to entire continent, 190, 250, 255; first used, 72, 115, 118, 121, 142; first use in Ptolemy, 244; first appearance on map, 241, 242; other names suggested, 159–160; translation of passage naming, 159.
Anaximander, made first map, 11.
Andalucia, climate of Lucayos Islands, similar to, 46, 48.
Anthony, Duke, Waldseemüller's book dedicated to, 152–153.
Antiglia, *see* Hispaniola.
Antilia, legend on Ruysch map, 214.
Anville, on continental appellations, 17.

Aphar, derivation of name Africa, 18.
Apianus, Petrus; map of Solinus, location of Lariab, 72; map of the world, 239–240; description, 241–243; importance, 243; belief in continental discovery, 243.
Aprica, derivation of name Africa, 18.
Aquævivus, letter from Bernardus Sylvanus, 220.
Arcay, on Waldseemüller map, 233.
Archives de Indias in Seville, decree registered in, 67.
Arena, *see* Las Islas de Arena.
Aristotle, on sphericity of the earth, 169–170.
Aryan language, source of Asiatic and European names, 8.
Ash-Kenaz, name Asia derived from, 16.
Asia, daughter of Oceanus and Tethys, mentioned by Hesiod, 17.
Asia, derivation of name, 16–17; boundary on Eratosthenes' map, 13, 15; on Strabo's map, 14; symbolic figure, 254.
Asia Minor, first continental divisions, 18–19.
Asias, King of Lydia, referred to by Homer, 9; Asia not named for, 16.
Astrolabe, early use, 186, 187, 188.
Atlantic Ocean, called River Oceanus, 8–9.
Atlas, of Ortelius, 254–256. *See also* Geography; Maps; Chartography.
Atwood Cay, *see* Samana.
Aucuparius, Thomas, praises Vespucius, 244.
Augerellus, Antonius, printer of the "Novus Orbis," 247.
Avezac, M. d', on Waldseemüller's wrongs, 139; reference to "Cosmographiæ Introductio," 143; interpretation of *Vastum Regnum* on Waldseemüller map, 238.
Aztecs, civilization, 76, 81; not mentioned by Vespucius, 73, 76.
Azzoguidi, Balthazar, first Bolognese printer, 175.

Baculus, early use, 186–187.
Bahia de Todos os Santos, visited by Vespucius, 81, 83.
Balboa, discovery of Pacific ocean, 243.
Bancroft, George, Indian villages upon the water, 75.
Bandini, on life of Vespucius, 61–62; printed letter of Vespucius, 63.
Baracoa, location, 56.

Barnett, Captain E., identification of Guanahani, 26.
Bartholomeo, Giuliano di, bears message from Don Manuel to Vespucius, 81.
Bascarini, Nicolo, printer of Ptolemy, *1548*, 253.
Basin, Jean, de Sendacour, at St. Dié, 116; his "Novus Tractatus" published at St. Dié, 120–121.
Bay of All Saints, erroneously called Abbey of All Saints, 219, 234.
Bay of Todos os Santos, *see* Bahia de Todos os Santos.
Becher, Captain A. B., identification of Guanahani, 26.
Beimeni, early designation of Florida, 225.
Beneventanus, Marcus, editor of Ptolemy, 209.
Benvenuti, Benvenuto, bearer of Vespucius' letter to King René, 88.
Berardi, Juanoto, equipped vessels, 63; death of, 64.
Bermuda Islands, the "hostile isles" of Vespucius, 78; believed to be Iti, 109–110.
Bernaldez, his "Cronica de los Reyes Catolicos," quoted by Harrisse, 65.
Beroaldus, Philippus, alleged editor of Ptolemy, 174.
Bessel, Friedrich Wilhelm, geographic measurements, 183.
Biblioteca Estense, Cantino map in, 205.
Bird Rock, *see* Cape of the Islet.
Blarru, Pierre de, at St. Dié, 116; "La Nancéide," 116.
Bochart, derivation of name Asia, 17; of Africa, 18.
"Booby Cay," hill on Concepcion Island, 55; arguments against identity with Concepcion Island of Columbus, 55.
Boscovich, Roger Joseph, geographic measurements, 182–183.
Bosio, Columbus determines to visit, 48.
Braun, Jacob, letter from Mathias Ringmann, 126–127.
Bread, made by Indians, 104.
Brevoort, James, found map of Mercator, 250.
Buckinck, Arnold, copperplate map, 11.
Burgos, Vespucius called to, 84.

Cabo de St. Augustine, on Waldseemüller map, 235.
Cabo del Isleo, *see* Cape of the Islet.
Cabot, John, first voyage, *1497*, 70, 200; northern limit of discoveries, 201–202; second voyage, 200–201.
Cabral, Pedro Alvarez de, Portuguese discoverer, 81; voyage to New World, 201; possible author of the "Admiral's map," 236.
Cadiz, port from which expeditions to America must start, 66; visited by Vespucius, 78; course of Vespucius to Cape Verd Islands, 79.
Calcographus, pseudonym of Singrenius, 240.
Caminha, Pedro Vaz de, early manuscript, 73.
Campanile, alluded to, 76.
Campeche Bay, visited by Vespucius, 71.
Canary Islands, unknown to Homer, 10; visited by Vespucius, 70, 90–91.
Cancellieri, alluded to, 143.
Canibales, site of battle with the Indians, 79.
Cantino, Alberto, his map, 205–206.
Cape Alpha and Omega, significance of name, 56, 217, 233.
Cape Beautiful, description, 47; named by Columbus, 47.
Cape Cameron, visited by Vespucius, 71.
Cape Cañaveral, possible limit of Vespucius' first voyage, 78.
Cape of the End of April, probably Cape Sable, 233.
Cape Frio, landing of Vespucius at, 83.
Cape Gracias á Dios, landfall of Vespucius, 71; course of Vespucius to Lariab, 71.
Cape Hatteras, course of Vespucius from Lariab, 77–78; possible limit of Vespucius' first voyage, 78.
Cape Hermosa, location, 53.
Cape of the Islet; named by Columbus, 48, 53; location, 49; landing-point of Columbus on Isabella Island, 53.
Cape Laguma, location, 53.
Cape of the Lake, named by Columbus, 47.
Cape Maysi, *see* Cape Alpha and Omega.
Cape Non, doubled by Gil Eannes, 236.
Cape St. Augustine, doubled by Vespucius, 81.
Cape San Roque, seen by Vespucius, 79.
Cape Verd Islands, course of Vespucius from Cadiz, 79.
Cape Verde, on Fernandina, 49, 54; location fixed, 52.
Caput Sanctæ Crucis, on Waldseemüller map, 235.
Carabi, Vespucius and his company called, 108.
Carnesecchi, Father, bears letter to Vespucius, 63.
Casas, Las, *see* Las Casas.
Casimir III., founded university at Cracow, 226.
Cat Island, the Guanahani of Irving, 23–24; the Guanahani of Humboldt, 24; area of, 26; identity with Guanahani denied by Captain Becher, 26; distance from Gomera, 51.
Cathay, on Ruysch map, 216.
Catholic faith, conversion of Indians desired, 66.
Caycos, visited by Ponce de Leon, 24.
Cazabi, native food-word, 72–73, 99.
Cerezo, Maria, wife of Vespucius, 84.
Champier, Symphorien, physician and author, at St. Dié, 116.
Charles the Bold, Battle of Nancy, 116.
Charta, first appearance of word in print, 231.
Charta Marina, map in Ptolemy of *1513*, 231. *See also* "Admiral's map."
Chartography, of the Old World, 8–15; of the New World, 193–257. *See also* Atlas; Geography; Maps.
Chesapeake Bay, possible limit of Vespucius' first voyage, 78.
"Chronicon Nurembergense," strange figures in, 199.
Circumference of earth, estimates, 169–170, 172–173, 179.
Clarence Harbor, anchorage of Columbus in, 54.
Clarke, A. R., geographic measurements, 183–184.

INDEX

Cleomedes, geographic estimates, 170.
Cockburn Town, landfall of Columbus, 56-57; chief town of Watling Island, 58.
Coelho, Gonçalo, commander of Vespucius' fleet, 81, 83.
Colba, *see* Cuba.
Colon, Don Cristobal, *see* Columbus, Christopher.
Columbian Library of Seville, 6.
Columbus, Bartholomew, brother of Christopher, 28.
Columbus, Christopher, relations with Vespucius, 3-5, 6-7, 72, 235; letter to Diego Columbus, 4-5, 61, 84; cipher signature, 4-6; his Ptolemy, *1478*, 11; landfall, 21-26, 51-58; description of Guanahani, 26, 29, 43; letters describing his voyage, 27; his study of the sciences, 28; papers, books, and maps preserved by his son, 29; his plan in naming the islands, 30; belief that his fleet came from heaven, 43, 48; description of harbor of Guanahani, 43, 57; description of Fernandina, 45-46, 53-54; methods of reckoning, 51; declination of magnetic needle noted, 51, 212-213; never visited Grand Exuma, 52; anchored off Riding Rocks, 56-57; exact site of landfall near Cockburn Town, 56-57; complaint to Ferdinand, 65, 67; privileges granted to, 67-68; relations with La Cosa, 68-69; description of Paria, 72; credit of discovery given by Vespucius, 80; influence of discoveries on Vosgian Gymnase, 125-126; his alleged allegorical sketch, 195; knowledge of continental discovery, 208; first biographical sketch, 209; referred to in Ptolemy, *1507*, 211; mentioned on Waldseemüller map, 234; possible author of the "Admiral's map," 236.
Columbus, Christopher, journal of, lost, 27; records kept in, 28, 31; abridged by Las Casas, original Spanish, 32-40; translation, 41-50.
Columbus, Christopher, first voyage of, false reckonings, 41; discontent of crew, 41; signs of land, 41; light seen on Guanahani, 24, 41; takes possession of Guanahani, 42; course from Guanahani to Concepcion, 29, 43-44, 55; lands at Concepcion, 29, 44; course from Concepcion to Fernandina, 29-30, 44-46, 54-55; course about Fernandina, 45-46, 53-54; course from Fernandina to Isabella, 30, 47-49; course from Isabella to Cuba, 30, 49-50, 52; landing at Cuba, 50.
Columbus, Christopher, results of first voyage of, 199-200; of second voyage, 200; of third voyage, 201.
Columbus, Diego, letter from Christopher Columbus, 61, 84.
Columbus, Ferdinand, son of Christopher Columbus, character, 6-7; presented library to cathedral of Seville, 6; his "Historie," 6, 212; title-page of the "Historie," 28; had possession of his father's papers, books, and maps, 29; description of Fernandina, 53-54; on Cape Alpha and Omega, 56, 217.
Compass, variations noted, 51, 212-213; early use, 186.
Concepcion, Santa Maria de la, the second island of Columbus, 29; course of Columbus from Guanahani, 43-44; course to Fernandina, 44-46; named by Columbus, 44; identified with Rum Cay, 54-55.
Concepcion Island, wreck of British ship "Southampton" on, 55; arguments against identity with second island of Columbus, 55.
Continents, naming of, 1-19; early designation, 11, 15; origin of names, 16-19. *See also* Africa; America; Asia; Europe.
Cook, Captain, alluded to, 81.
Corte-Real, Gaspar, Portuguese navigator, 205.
Cortés, alluded to, 77.
Corumberger, *see* Cromberger.
Cosa, Juan de la, companion of Columbus, 24; in Ferdinand's expedition to America, 68; relations with Columbus, 68-69; companion of Vespucius, 79, 84; separated from Vespucius, 80.
Cosa, Juan de la, first map of New World, cited by Humboldt, 24; description, 197-204; changes in, 209.
"Cosmographiæ Introductio," 123-165; advertisement of map of world, 149; authorship, 125, 132, 143; bibliographical description, 129-131, 140-150, 159-165; colophon, 120; countries designated by standards of rulers, 232; dedication, 131, 132, 140-141, 165; error in translation, 234-235; facsimile pages, 134-137, 147, 148, 164; facsimiles of pages which named America, 158; found by Humboldt, 3; four distinct types, 129-131; Latin translation, 87-111; in Library of Seville, 6; publication of, 117, 118, 125, 129; quoted in Stobnicza's Ptolemy, 227; translation of decastich, 165; voyages of Vespucius in, 145; water-marks, 129.
"Cosmographiæ Introductio," alleged first edition, 132-139; corrections made in, 141-152; translation of dedication, 138-139; translation of title-page, 138; transference of leaves, 142.
"Cosmographiæ Introductio," true first edition, 140-144; Vosgian Gymnase's dedication to Maximilian, 140-141; copies extant, 143.
Cosmography, 1-19.
Cotta, John, editor of Ptolemy, *1507*, 209.
Cracow, university at, 226.
Cromberger, Jacobus, printed "First Decade" of Peter Martyr, 223-224.
Cromberger, Juan, first printing-press in America, 224.
Crooked Island, a part of Saomete, 53.
Cuba, Columbus' voyage to, 29-30; course of Columbus from Isabella, 49, 50, 52; course from Las Islas de Arena, 49; described by Columbus, 50; distance from Las Islas de Arena, 52; named by Columbus, 30; omitted on Ruysch map, 217; supposed to be Japan, 48, 49.
Curaçao, *see* Isle of Giants.

Dante, alluded to, 90.
D'Anville, *see* Anville.

Darien, gold from, 84.
D'Avezac, see Avezac.
Decrees, of Ferdinand and Isabella, concerning expeditions to America, 65–68.
Delarapossa, see Margarita.
D'Este, Hercules, patron of Alberto Cantino, 205.
Diaz, Dr. Francisco, registered royal decree, 67, 68.
Diaz, Juan de Solís, visits Honduras, 72; pilot of Vespucius' fleet, 83.
Diodorus, story of Europa, 17.
Distribution of human race, 8.
Dixon Hill, lighthouse on, 58.
Dixon, Jeremiah, geographic measurements in America, 183.
Dommartin, Louisde, member of Vosgian Gymnase, 116.
Drawing of St. Christopher, 197.

Eames, Wilberforce, courtesy extended by, 130.
Eannes, Gil, doubled Cape Non, 236.
El Asi, river Orontes called, 17.
El Viejo, visited by Ponce de Leon, 24.
Enriquez, Beatrix, mother of Ferdinand Columbus, 6.
"Epistola," Vespucius' letter to Lorenzo de' Medici, 82. See also Mundus Novus.
Eratosthenes, his map, B. C. *276-194*, 12; first cosmographer, 13; geographic estimates, 170; errors in estimates, 172.
Escovedo, Rodrigo, secretary of Columbus' fleet, 42.
Etesian winds, suggested name Asia, 17.
Eur-op, "serpent of the sun," name of continent derived from, 17.
Europa, fable concerning name Europe, 17; mentioned by Hesiod, 17.
Europe, derivation of name, 16, 17–18; symbolic figure, 254.
Euros, derivation of name Europe, 17.
"Examen Critique . . ." published by Humboldt, 3.
Expeditions, conditions governing Spanish, 66–67. See also Voyages.
Exuma, Grand, not visited by Columbus, 52, 54.
Eyb, Albertus, his "Margarita Poetica," 117.
Eyries, Jean-Baptiste, purchased "Cosmographiæ Introductio," 130.

Ferdinand, King of Spain, expedition to America determined, 65, 68; selects Vespucius to aid in discovery, 69, 90; employs Vespucius, 84.
Ferdinand and Isabella, issued royal decrees concerning expeditions to America, 65–68; privileges granted to Columbus, 67–68.
Ferdinand Island, see Fernandina.
Fernandina, located by La Cosa, 24; the third island of Columbus, 29, 53; course of Columbus from Concepcion, 44–46; described by Columbus, 44–46, 53–54; named by Columbus, 45; harbor of, 46; Cape Verde located, 52; description suited to Long Island, 53–54.

Fernando Noronha, wreck of Vespucius' ship on, 83.
Fernel, Jean, geographic measurements, 181.
Ferrando, see Ferdinand.
Ficinus, Marsilius, translated Plato into Latin, 13.
Finæus, Orontius, map in "Novus Orbis," 245; description of map, 247–248; life and work, 248–249; charged with plagiarizing new geographical tricks, 249.
Fonseca, Juan Rodriquez de, possessed first map of New World, 197.
Fortunate Isles, see Canary Islands.
Fortune Island, a part of Saomete, 53.
Foscarini, alluded to, 143.
Fox, Capt. G. V., value of his "Methods and Results," 25; identifies Guanahani with Samana, 25; identifies Las Islas de Arena with the Sandy Islands, 52.
Fragrant Isles, identified with Isabella Island, 53.
Francisca, on Ptolemy map of *1540*, 251.
Frisius, Laurentius, editor of Ptolemy, *1522*, 244.
Furak, derivation of Africa from, 18.

Gallois, L., finds map of Canerio, 206.
Garden of the Bahamas, Watling Island called, 56.
Gastaldi, Jacobus, editor of Ptolemy, *1548*, 253.
Geographic divisions, origin of names, 8; development, 8–15.
Geography, among the ancients, 8–10, 169–180; unit of measure, 178–179; accurate methods of reckoning, 177; estimates of earth's dimensions, 169–173, 179, 181–185, 188; government measurements, 184–185; first use of gnomon, 170; early instruments, 186–188; difficulty of mapping, 189; modern methods, 181–185; work of French Academy, 182; work of Ptolemy, 174–177; atlas of Ortelius, 254–256. See also Chartography; Globes; Maps.
Gibraltar, straits, 11.
Gigantum, see Isle of Giants.
Giocondo, Fra Giovanni del, translated Vespucius' letter to Lorenzo de Medici, 127.
Gioja, Flavio, improvement of compass, 186.
Giotto, contemporary with Aztec architect, 76.
Giustiniani, note in Polyglot Psalter, 6.
Globes, 241–242.
Gnomon, explanation of, 170–172.
Gog, in La Cosa's map, 199.
Gold, at Saomete, 45, 47; sought by Columbus, 29, 43, 44, 47; lettered, 46.
Gómara, Lopez de, accusation against Vespucius, 235; authority for expeditions to the Moluccas, 251; on Vespucius' early voyages, 63–64; on early voyages to Honduras, 72.
Gomera, distance from neighboring islands, 51.
Gorée, visited by Vespucius, 81.
Grand Exuma, see Exuma.
Grand Kahn, letters from Ferdinand to, 48; his ships visit Cuba, 50.
Grand Turk's Island, see Turk's Island.

Gravier, historian of St. Dié, 119.
Great Bahama Bank, Las Islas de Arena a part of, 52.
Green Cape, *see* Cape Verde.
Grieninger, Joannes, printer of Ptolemy, *1522*, 245.
Griswold, Almon W., purchased the "Cosmographiæ Introductio," 130.
Grynæus, Simon, his "Novus Orbis," 245–249; letter in "Novus Orbis," 246.
Guanahani, course of Columbus to Concepcion, 43–44; described by Columbus, 26, 29, 43; distance to Gomera, 51; identification of, 23–26, 51–58; first method, 56–58; second method, 51–55; third method unsatisfactory, 51; landfall of Columbus, 41; parallel with Hierro, 42; possession taken by Columbus, 42; Ribero's map of, *1529*, 56; voyage of Ponce de Leon, 25.
Guisay, Columbus determines to visit, 48.
Gunnbjörn, burned island discovered by, 214.
Gutierrez, Pedro, light on Guanahani first seen by, 24, 41.

Halys River, influenced continental divisions, 18.
Harbor of Fernandina, 46, 54.
Harbor of Guanahani, 29, 43; description, 57; identified with harbor of Watling Island, 58.
Harbor of Pamlico Sound, 78, 108.
Harrisse, Henry, translation of Columbus' letter to his son, 4; on relations of La Cosa and Columbus, 24; on Columbus' attitude toward expeditions to America, 65; on continental discoveries, 70; on Waldseemüller's letter to Amerbach, 127; note from H. C. Murphy, 143–144; on Waldseemüller's lost map, 157; on name of America, 159–160; on nomenclature of New World, 202–203, 218–219; history of Cantino map, 205–206; on Portuguese maps, 207; classification of early maps, 223.
Hauslab, General von, his globe, 241–242.
Hazards, Hugues des, at Vosgian Gymnase, 116.
Hecatæus, copperplate map, 10; early map of, 11; name Asia first used by, 16.
Heidenberg, John, letter to William de Velde, 151–152.
Henry, Prince, the Navigator; influence on Vosgian Gymnase, 125.
Herodotus, mentions copperplate map, 10; his map, 11; on contour of earth, 12; on continental appellations, 12, 16; his Asia, 16.
Herrera, on voyage of Ponce de Leon, 24–25.
Hesiod, Europa and Asia mentioned by, 17.
Hierro, parallel with Guanahani, 42.
Hipparchus, on circumference of earth, 172.
Hispaniola, royal decree concerning, 65, 66; visited by Vespucius, 80.
"Historie," by Ferdinand Columbus, 6; facsimile of title-page, 28; account of landfall of Columbus, 29.
Holbein, Hans, work on Ptolemy of *1522*, 244.
Homeric poems, geography in, 8–10; designation of continents, 9–10, 16, 17–18.

Honduras, landing of Vespucius, 70–71; visited by Pinzon and Solís, 72. *See also* Cape Gracias á Dios.
Humboldt, Alexander von, his "Examen Critique," 3; finds the "Cosmographiæ Introductio," 3; finds first map of New World, 196; identifies Guanahani with Cat Island, 24; maintained Vespucius' ignorance of continental discovery, 82; misinterprets Waldseemüller, 238; nomenclature of La Cosa map not completed, 203; on Vespucius' connection with Columbus' third voyage, 64.
Huttich, Johannes, work on the "Novus Orbis," 246.
Hylacomylus, Greek translation of Waldseemüller, *see* Waldseemüller.

Ibarra, Bernardo de, quoted, 68–69.
Iceland, the Thule of Eratosthenes, 13.
Ignami, native food-word, 72–73, 99.
Iguana, roasted by Indians, 103.
Ilacomilus, *see* Waldseemüller.
Immigration to America, conditions of, 66–67.
Inagua, *see* Little Inagua.
Indians, befriended by Las Casas, 31; belief that Spaniards came from heaven, 43, 48, 107–108; villages built upon the water, 71, 75–76, 100–101; huts in trees, 75; killed one of Vespucius' crew, 81; of Guanahani, described by Columbus, 29, 42–43; captives taken by Columbus, 43; escape of captives of Columbus, 44; of Fernandina, description, 45, 46; direct the course of Columbus, 46, 54; of Saomete, description, 48; befriended by Columbus, 48; of Mexico and Texas, characteristics, 73; of Lariab, description, 72–73, 91–100; depilation practised, 73, 93; battle with Spaniards on Iti, 78, 109–110; slaves taken by Vespucius, 78, 111; battle with Spaniards at Canibales, 79; weapons, 93; warfare, 93–94; language, 94–95; family relations, 94; use of hammocks or nettings, 95; customs, 95–96; no religious rites, 97; dwellings, 97; form of their riches, 97–98; burial rites, 98; treatment of the sick, 98–99; cannibalism practised, 81, 99; roasting iguana, 103; method of making bread, 104; of Iti, characteristics, 109–111. *See also* Aztecs.
Inhame, see Ignami.
Innocent VIII., Pope, favors granted to Gualtier Lud, 116.
Insula Gigantum, *see* Isle of Giants.
Iphric, derivation of name Africa, 18.
Irving, Washington, on landfall of Columbus, 23; called Grand Exuma the third island of Columbus, 52; identifies Guanahani with Cat Island, 23–24.
Isabella, *see* Ferdinand and Isabella.
Isabella, the fourth island of Columbus, 30; course of Columbus from Fernandina, 46–49; named by Columbus, 47; course to Cuba, 49–50, 52; identified with Crooked or Fortune Island, 53; topography, 53. *See also* Saomete.
Islas de Arena, *see* Las Islas de Arena.

Isle of Giants, visited by Vespucius, 80, 204.
Isleo, Cabo del, *see* Cape of the Islet.
Iti, fight between Spanish and natives, 78, 109-110; believed to be Bermuda Islands, 109-110; visited by Vespucius, 109, 110.
Iuca, *see* Yuca.

Jal, M., interpretation of Columbus' sketch, 195.
Japan, Cuba supposed to be, 48, 49.
Japheth, son of Noah, early continental divisions, 16, 18.
Java Major, legend on Ruysch map, 215.
Java Minor, legend on Ruysch map, 215.
Josephus, on naming of Africa, 18.
"Journal, of Columbus," Las Casas' abridgment, original Spanish, 32-40; translation, 41-50; description of Fernandina, 53-54; quoted, 57.
Journal of Vespucius, publication intended, 76-77, 100, 107. *See also* "Quatuor Navigationes."
Juan, *see* Cuba.

Kettel, Samuel, translated into English Navarrete's work on Columbus, 32.
Kohl, Dr., criticism of La Cosa's map, 203-204.
Krämer, Gerard, *see* Mercator.
Kunstmann No. 3, map called, *1505*, 234.

La Cosa, *see* Cosa, Juan de la.
La Fernandina, *see* Fernandina.
La Navidad, *see* Navidad.
Lambert, Jehan, published first edition of Vespucius' letter to Lorenzo de Medici, 71.
Landfall; of Columbus, 21-26, 51-58; of Vespucius, on the continent, 70-74.
"Landfall of Columbus," Captain Becher's identification of Guanahani, 26.
Language, origin of races traced by, 8.
La Rábida, death of Pinzon in, 68; land named for, 68.
Lariab, comparison with Parias, 72; course of Vespucius from Cape Gracias á Dios, 71; to Cape Hatteras, 77-78; derivation of names, 73; erroneously translated "Parias," 71, 72, 107; identified with Tampico, 74; on Solinus' map, 72.
Las Casas, Bishop of Chiapa, 31; abridgment of Columbus' journal, 31-50; his "Historia de las Indias," 32; on Cape Alpha and Omega, 56.
Las Islas de Arena, course of Columbus from Isabella, 49; to Cuba, 52; visited by Columbus, 52.
Latitude, how found, 171-172.
Leagues, English equivalent, 51.
Ledesma, Pedro de, visits Honduras, 72.
Lefebvre, Jacques, d'Etaples, instructor of Ringmann, 117.
Lelewel, Joachim, criticizes Sylvanus the geographer, 221; his geography, 231-232.
Lemos, Gaspar de, reported voyage of Cabral, 201.
Lenox, James, found map of Mercator, 250.
Lenox Library, Spanish edition of Columbus' letter to Santangel in, 27; "Cosmographiæ Introductio" in, 130.
Leo, Africanus, derivation of name Africa, 18.
Leonardo da Vinci, manuscript gores, 242.
Lepe, Diego de, voyage to Brazil, 201.
"Lettera di Amerigo Vespucci," original Italian text, 87-111.
Letters: "Bank of St. George letter," 195-196; Columbus to Diego Columbus, 4-5, 84; John Heidenberg to William de Velde, 151-152; Gerardus Mercator to Paulus, 191-192; Ringmann to Jacob Braun, 126-127; Ringmann to Waldseemüller, 154-155; Sylvanus to Aquævivus, 220; Vespucius to Lorenzo de Medici, referred to, 71, 82, 127, 218; Vespucius to his father, 61-62; Vespucius to King René, 87-111; Waldseemüller to Johannes Amerbach, 127-128; Waldseemüller to Ringmann, 133. *See also* "Epistola."
Levilapis, Hermanus, printed Ptolemy, *1475*, 176.
Lhuyd, Humphry, work in Ortelius' atlas, 255.
Libraries; Ambrosian, at Milan, 27; Columbian, at Seville, 6; Lenox, valuable books in, 27, 130; Vienna Imperial, Stobnicza's Ptolemy in, 227.
Libya, in Homeric poems, 9; boundary on Eratosthenes' map, 13, 15; on Strabo's map, 14; Africa called, 15.
License, granted by Ferdinand to visit America, 65-67.
Little Inagua, identified with Yaguna, 25.
Little Venice, *see* Veneziola.
Long Island, the Fernandina of Columbus, *see* Fernandina.
Lopez de Gómara, *see* Gómara.
Lorraine, on map of Waldseemüller Ptolemy, 237-238.
Lucayos Islands, visited by Ponce de Leon, 24; first seen by Columbus, 41.
Lud, Gualtier, allusion to Waldseemüller map, 150-151; death of, 121; injustice toward Waldseemüller, 133, 138; printing-press at St. Dié, 119-121; publication of "Cosmographiæ Introductio," 125; publication of Ptolemy intended, 127, 128; riddle of name, 120; secretary of Duke René, at St. Dié, 116.
Lud, Jean de Pfaffenhoven, head of family, 117.
Lud, Nicolas, Châtelain de Morsperg, brother of Jean Lud, 117.
Lud, Nicolas, son of Jean Lud, secretary of Duke René, *1490*, 117; at St. Dié, 116; injustice toward Waldseemüller, 133, 138.
Lud, Nicolas, secretary of René II, *1477*, 117.

Mackenzie, Commander Alexander Slidell, information given to Irving, 24.
Madrid, map of La Cosa in Naval Museum, 24.
Maestrale, difficulty in translating, 74, 77-78; direction of wind, 108.
Magellan, Ferdinand, Portuguese discoverer, 82; discoveries first mapped, 248.
Magog, in La Cosa's map, 199.

Malacca, sought by Vespucius, 83.
Malchus, Cleodemus, quoted by Polyhistor, 18.
Malte-Brun, on name of Asia, 16–17.
Mannega, voyage of Ponce de Leon, 25.
Manoel, Don Nuño, commander of Vespucius' fleet, 81.
Manuel, King of Portugal, proposition to Vespucius, 81.
"Mappemundi," of La Cosa, 72, 193–203.
Maps, classification of early, 223; fraudulent, 195; locations of important measurements, opposite 184; on metal, 10, 11; probably made by Columbus, 28; of Apianus, description, 241–243; of Canerio, description, 206–207; of Cantino, description and history, 205–206; of Dionysius Periegetes, B. C. 30–A. D. *150*, 15; of Eratosthenes, B. C. *276–194*, 12; of Hecatæus, B. C. *550–480*, 10; of Herodotus, B. C. *484–406*, 11; of Homeric world, B. C. *962–927*, 9; of La Cosa, cited by Humboldt, 24; changes in, 209; of Mauro, *1457*, 216; of Munster, in "Novus Orbis," 245.
Maps, first of New World, 195–204; discovery of, 196; description of, 197–199; ornamentations on, 199; embodying results of early voyages, 199–201; names copied by Harrisse, 202–203.
Maps, of the "Novus Orbis," 245–249; in Ortelius' atlas, 256; of Peter Martyr, 224–225; of Pomponius Mela, A. D. *50*, 14; of Ptolemy, *1478*, 11; of Ptolemy, *1511*, 220–223; errors, 221; of Stobnicza's Ptolemy, *1512*, 227–228; of *1513*, 68, 231–237; of world, by Johannes Ruysch, description, 210; legends on, 212–215; nomenclature, 216–219; of St. Dié, opposite 115; of Solinus, location of Lariab, 72; of Strabo, B. C. *54*–A. D. *24*, 13; "Tabula Terre Nove," 233–237; Waldseemüller's of the world, date published, 152, 153, 154; lost, 150–152, 157. *See also* Atlas; Globes.
Maracaybo, Gulf of, visited by Vespucius, 71, 80.
Maracaybo, Lake, Veneziola near, 75.
Marajo, possibly seen by Vespucius, 79.
Marañon, *see* Amazon.
Mare Pacificum, name first used in Ptolemy of *1540*, 252.
Mare Sugenum, derivation of name, 213.
Margarita, island visited by Vespucius, 79.
Margry, M., interpretation of Columbus' sketch, 195.
Mariguana, Varnhagen's Guanahani, 25; area of, 26; distance to Gomera, 51.
Marinus, geographic estimates, 17
Marlier, Jacques, printing-press of, 121.
Martyr, Peter, on Cape Alpha and Omega, 56; on continental discovery, 72; reference to first map of New World, 197; his "First Decade," description, 224; title and colophon, 224.
Mason, Charles, geographic measurements in America, 183.
Mauro, Fra, his map of *1457*, 216.
Maximilian, Emperor, "Cosmographiæ Introductio" dedicated to, 131, 132.

Medici, House of, Vespucius employed as clerk, 63, 69.
Medici, Lorenzo di Pier Francesco de', letter from Vespucius, 71, 82, 127, 218.
Meetkercke, Adolph van, explanation of frontispiece of Ortelius' atlas, 255.
Mela, Pomponius, earliest Roman geographer, 15; his map, A. D. *50*, 14; on continental appellations, 17.
Mercator, Gerard, his projections, 189–192; holograph letter, 191–192; map of, 250.
Mercator, Sebastian, publication of his map, 254.
Merchants at Cuba, 48.
"Methods and Results," Captain Fox's identification of Guanahani, 25.
Mexico, civilization of Aztecs, 76; Aztec city, 77.
Migrations of the ancients, 8.
Milan, Ambrosian Library, 27.
Mini, Lisabetta, mother of Vespucius, 61.
Moreau, Pierre Louis de Maupertuis, geographic measurements, 182.
Mugello, Vespucius goes to, 62.
Müller, Frederick, & Co., facsimiles of Stobnicza map, 228.
"Mundus Novus," containing account of third voyage of Vespucius, 72, 82, 218, 219.
Muñoz, Juan Bautista, identifies Guanahani with Watling Island, 23; discovers documents, 64.
Munster, Sebastian, map in "Novus Orbis," 245, 246; editor of Ptolemy of *1540*, 250–251.
Murner, Thomas, his "Chartiludium ... memorativa" published at St. Dié, 121.
Murphy, Henry C., note to Harrisse, 143, 144.
Museum, Naval, in Madrid, 24.

Nancy, battle of, celebrated in verse by Blarru, 116.
Napione, alluded to, 143.
Naval Museum at Madrid, map of La Cosa in, 24.
Navarrete, Don Martin Fernandez de, on entail of Columbus, 5; on Columbus and La Cosa, 24; identifies Guanahani with Turk's Island, 25; his "Coleccion de los Viages y Descubrimientos," 31; access to documents, 32; his "Journal of Columbus," 32–50, 53; royal decree concerning expeditions to America, 65; on wreck of the Santa Maria, 69.
Navidad, La, first settlement, 69.
Nevers, St. Deodatus, bishop of, 115.
New World, first map of, 195–204.
Newton, Isaac, geographic measurements, 182.
Niccolini, Donato, fellow-employee with Vespucius, 63.
Nicholas de Linna, his "Inventio Fortunata," 213.
Nilus River, separates Asia from Libya, 13–15.
Niña, ship of Columbus' fleet; signs of land seen from, 41; commanded by Vicente Yañez Pinzon, 68.
Noah, founder of human races, 8, 18–19.
Nomenclature, of the continents, 16–19; of islands, by Columbus, 30; of the Ruysch map, 216–219; of New World, 218–219.

North Star, variations of compass, 51.
"Novus Orbis," maps of, 245-249; title, 246.

Ocampo, Sebastian de, explorations of, 206.
Oceanus River, in Homeric poems, 8-9.
Ojeda, Alonso de, commander of fleet in Vespucius' second voyage, 71, 79; separated from Vespucius, 80.
Ophren, naming of Africa for, 18.
Oreb, Phœnician root of name Europe, 18.
Origin, of peoples, traced by language, 8; of continental names, 16-19.
Orontes River, called El Asi, 17.
Ortelius, Abraham, naming of America, 118; his "Theatrum Orbis Terrarum," 117, 254; his atlas, 254-256.
Oviedo, on early voyages to Honduras, 72.

Pacific Ocean, name first used in Ptolemy of *1540*, 252.
Padre, Puerto del, *see* Puerto del Padre.
Palos, home of the Pinzons, 68.
Pamlico Sound, harbor of Vespucius, 78.
Paria, Gulf of, discovered by Columbus, 71; possibly visited by Vespucius, 79, 80.
Parias, erroneously printed for Lariab, 71, 72, 107; comparison with Lariab, 72.
Paul II, Pope, bull instituting fête, 119.
Paulus, letter from Mercator, 191-192.
Pedrezano, Giovanni Battista, book-plate of Ptolemy of *1548*, 253.
Peninsula, on Watling Island, 43, 57-58.
Pentius, Jacobus, de Leucho, printed Sylvanus edition of Ptolemy, 223.
Perez, Alonzo, registered royal decree, 68.
Periegetes, Dionysius, his map, B. C. *50* – A. D. *150*, 15.
Peter Martyr, *see* Martyr, Peter.
Petit, Jean, printer of the "Novus Orbis," 245, 247.
Philesius, pseudonym of Mathias Ringmann, 117.
Philip the First, inquiries about ships for expedition, 84.
Phœnicians, derivation of name Asia, 17.
Phrisius, Laurentius, editor of Ptolemy, *1522*, 118.
Picard, Jean, geographic measurements, 181-182.
Picus, Joannes Franciscus, of Mirandula, his letter in Ptolemy of *1513*, 230.
Pinelo, the treasurer, paid Vespucius, 64.
Pinta, ship of Columbus' fleet, sighted land, 41; commanded by Martin Alonzo Pinzon, 49, 68.
Pinzon, Martin Alonzo, captain of the Pinta, landed with Columbus, 41-42; directs course of Columbus, 46, 54; alluded to, 49; in Ferdinand's expedition to America, 68; treachery to Columbus, 68; voyage to Brazil, 201.
Pinzon, Vicente Yañez, captain of the Niña, landed with Columbus, 41-42; commander of Ferdinand's fleet, 68; visits Honduras, 72.
Pires, Christovam, Portuguese commander, 83.
Plato, on sphericity of earth, 12-13, 169.

Pliny, on name Asia, 17; on circumference of earth, 172.
Plisacus Sinus, on the Ruysch map, 209, 216.
Polo, Marco, early geographer, 180.
Polyglot Psalter, note on Columbus, 6.
Polyhistor, Alexander, quoted by Josephus, 18.
"Polyhistor," publication of, 239-240; facsimile title, 240.
Ponce de Leon, Juan, expedition to Lucayos Islands and Florida, 24; expedition to Florida made after publication of Peter Martyr's map, 225.
Port, *see* Harbor.
Posidonius, estimates circumference of earth, 172, 179.
Prato, Galeoti à, printed the "Novus Orbis," 247.
Psalter, *see* Polyglot Psalter.
Ptolemæus, Claudius, *see* Ptolemy.
Ptolemy, Claudius, founder of modern geography, 15; portrait of, 175; his geographic work, 174-177; his "Geography" the accepted text-book, 125; publication at St. Dié intended, 126-128, 129; first printed edition, *1475*, 174-176; Rome edition, *1478*, 176; maps on copper, 11; Bologna edition, *1482*, 175; Ulm editions, *1482* and *1486*, 176; edition of *1507*, 209-211; description, 210; Sylvanus edition, *1511*, 220-223; colophon, 222; description, 221-223; errors, 221; title, 222; Stobnicza edition, *1512*, 226-228; description, 226-227; title and colophon, 227; Waldseemüller edition, *1513*, 118, 128, 229-238; address to reader, 156; "Admiral's map," 235-237; colophon, 230; editors, 127; error in translation, 234-235; "Santa Maria de la Rábida" in, 68; title, 229-230; various maps, 237-238; edition of *1522*, 156-157, 244-245; Greek edition, *1533*, 177; edition of *1540*, 250-252; Gastaldi edition, *1548*, 253-254.
Puerto del Padre, Columbus landed at, 52.
Pythagoras, on sphericity of the earth, 169.
Pytheas, geography of, 170.

Quadrant, early use, 186.
Quaritch, Bernard, English translation of Vespucius' letter, 87-111.
"Quattro Giornate," *see* Journal of Vespucius.
"Quatuor Navigationes," publication of, 129; printed with "Cosmographiæ Introductio," 161-165.
Quetzalcohuatl, divinity of Aztecs, 76.

Rábida, *see* La Rábida.
Ragged Islands, *see* Las Islas de Arena.
Regio lucis, on Homeric map, 9.
Regio noctis, on Homeric map, 9, 18.
René, King, letter from Vespucius, 87-111.
René II, Duke, Battle of Nancy, 116.
Ribero, Diego, cosmographer of Charles V, map of *1529*, 56.
Richer, Jean, experiments with pendulum, 182.
Riddle, name Walterus (Gualtier) Lud, 120.

INDEX

Riding Rocks, first anchorage of Columbus, 56–57.

Ringmann, Mathias, at St. Dié, 116; account of his life, 117–118; publication of "Cosmographiæ Introductio," 125; letter to Jacob Braun, 126–127; poem on America, 127; publication of Ptolemy intended, 127–128; dedication of "Cosmographiæ Introductio," 131, 132; his "Margarita Philosophica," 132; letter from Waldseemüller, 133; letter to Waldseemüller, 154–155; verses in the "Cosmographiæ Introductio," 162–163.

Rio de Janeiro, Vespucius' third voyage, 81.

Rio de la Plata, Vespucius' third voyage, 81.

Rio de St. Augustine, identified with Cabo de St. Augustine, 235.

Rodericus, Doctor, witnessed royal decree, 67, 68.

Roquette, De la, translated Navarrete's work on Columbus into French, 31.

Rum Cay, the Concepcion of Columbus, 54–55.

Ruysch, Johannes, referred to in Ptolemy, *1507*, 211; map of world, 209–211; map of the world, nomenclature, 216–219; geographical conclusions from map, 219.

St. Benoit, monastery of St. Deodatus dedicated to, 115.

St. Christopher, drawing of, 197.

St. Colomban, monastery of St. Deodatus dedicated to, 115.

St. Deodatus, St. Dié named for, 115.

St. Dié, founding of town, 115; map of, opposite 115; college organized, 115–116; manuscripts preserved in library of, 116; printing-press of, 119–121; publications issued, 120–121, 125.

Samana, Captain Fox's Guanahani, 25; distance to Gomera, 51.

San Salvador, bay and harbor named by Columbus, 50.

San Salvador, first island of Columbus, *see* Cat Island; Guanahani; Watling Island.

Sanches, Gabriel, Columbus' letter to, 27.

Sanchez, Rodrigo, inspector of Columbus' fleet, 41, 42.

Sandy Isles, *see* Las Islas de Arena.

Santa Maria, flag-ship of Columbus' fleet, 24, 68; owned by Juan de la Cosa, 68; wrecked off Hispaniola, 68, 69.

Santa Maria de la Concepcion, second island of Columbus, *see* Concepcion.

Santa Maria de la Rábida, named by Pinzon, 68; on Waldseemüller map, 234.

Santangel, Luis de, Columbus' letter to, 27.

Saomete, gold at, 45, 47; larger than Fernandina, 46; named Isabella by Columbus, 47; description, 47–48; landing of Columbus on, 48. *See also* Isabella Island.

Scarlatti, Abbé, discovers letter of Vespucius, 63.

Schmidt, Dr. Charles, his "Mémoires ... Lorraine," 127.

Schöner, Johann, his globes, 242.

Schöpflin, possessed copy of Basin's "Tractatus," 121.

Schott, Johannes, printing-press of St. Dié transferred to, 121.

Servetus, Michael, accusation against Vespucius, 235; copied passage in Ptolemy, 245.

Seville, Columbian library of, 6; royal decree registered in Archives de Indias, 67.

Sicily, Cuban mountains like, 50.

Sieber, Louis, discovered Waldseemüller's letter to Amerbach, 127.

Sierra Leone, Vespucius' third voyage, 82; Vespucius' fourth voyage, 83.

Signatures, of Columbus, significance, 4–6; first used in *1468*, 175.

Singrenius, Joannes, publisher of Solinus' "Polyhistor," 239.

Sinus Arabicus, separates Libya from Asia, 14.

Smith, Sir William, on continental appellations, 16.

Snell, Willebroard van Royen, geodetic measurements, 181.

Soderini, Pier, schoolmate of Vespucius, 62.

Solinus, Caius Julius, his "Polyhistor," 239.

South America, legend on Ruysch map, 214.

South Georgia, island seen by Vespucius, 81.

Southampton, British ship, wreck of, 55.

Standard, royal, of Spain, raised by Columbus on Guanahani, 42.

Stadium, unit of measure, 178–179.

Stobnicza, Johannes de, edited Ptolemy, *1512*, 226.

Stobnicza map, facsimiles published, 228.

Strabo, on sphericity of earth, 12, 14; his map, B. C. *54*–A. D. *24*, 13; on circumference of earth, 173.

Strasburg, Ptolemy, *1513*, printed at, 127, 156.

Sweynheym, copperplate maps, 175.

Sylvanus, Bernardus, editor of Ptolemy, 220; letter to Aquævivus, 220.

Tabasco, visited by Vespucius, 71; river in Yucatan, 75.

"Tabula Terre Nove," description, 233–237.

Tampico, the true Lariab, 74, 77. *See also* Lariab.

Tenochtitlan, capital of Anahuac, 76.

Terra Incognita, on Waldseemüller map, 234.

Thule, location of, 13; on Eratosthenes' map, 13.

Tilliard, ——, purchased the "Cosmographiæ Introductio," 130.

Toscanelli, alluded to, 12.

Triana, Rodrigo de, land first seen by, 41.

Trinidad, possibly seen by Vespucius, 79.

Turk's Island, area of, 26; distance to Gomera, 51.

Uebelin, George, patron of Ringmann and Waldseemüller, 127; editor of Waldseemüller map, 230.

United States Coast and Geodetic Survey measurements, 184–185.

Usumasinta, river in Yucatan, 75.

Varnhagen, Francisco Adolpho de, identifies Guanahani with Mariguana, 25; on derivation of name Lariab, 73; on northern limit of Vespucius' first voyage, 78.

Varro, Marcus Terentius, on name Asia, 16.

Velde, William de, letter from John Heidenberg, 151–152.

Venetus, Bernardinus, first biographical sketch of Columbus, 209.

Veneziola, described by Vespucius, 75; identification, 75–76.

Venice, villages on water like, 71, 75, 100–101.

Veraguas, Duke of, possesses original decrees concerning expeditions to America, 65.

Verneuil, Chalumeau de, translated into French Navarrete's work on Columbus, 31.

Vespucci, Giovanni, nephew of Americus, his heir, 84.

Vespucius, Americus, naming of America for, 3–4, 6–7, 15, 72, 82–83; relations with Columbus, 3–5, 6–7, 72, 235; studies with Georgius Antonius Vespucius, 13, 61; autograph signature, 61; holograph letter to his father, 61–62; goes to Mugello, 62; clerk in House of the Medici, 63, 69; paid for loss of ships, 64; in Ferdinand's expedition to America, 69, 90; his education of value, 69; letter to Lorenzo de Medici, 71, 82, 127, 218; Aztecs unknown to, 73, 76; weak points in his narrative, 75–78; failure to identify Veneziola, 75–76; his journal, 76–77, 100, 107; pearls found by, 80; discovery of Hispaniola by Columbus admitted, 80; enters Portuguese service, 81; knowledge of continental discovery, 82, 208; return to Spanish service, 84; attends cortes at Toro, 84; married to Maria Cerezo, 84; made *vecino* of Seville, 84; appointed *piloto mayor* of Spain, 84; death of, 84; his "Lettera," Italian, Latin, and English texts, 87–111; anachronism in letter to King René, 89; varying fortunes, 89; belief that Spaniards came from heaven, 107–108; and his men called Carabi, 108; letters translated by Ringmann, 117–118; the four voyages of, printed with "Cosmographiæ Introductio," 145, 162–165; proof of voyage around Florida, 206, 225; northern limit of discoveries, 233; possible author of the "Admiral's map," 236; his fame established, 256.

Vespucius, Americus, first voyage, 65, 69, 70–78, 85–111; course, from Cadiz to Canary Islands, 70, 79, 90; from Canary Islands to Cape Gracias á Dios, 70, 91–92; from Cape Gracias á Dios to Lariab, 71; finds village built on the water, 71, 75, 100–101; carries home captives, 101; battle with Indians, 101–102; goes inland, 104–105; course from Lariab, 77–78, 108; repairs ships, 108; fight with natives on Iti, 109–110; return to Spain, 78; result of first voyage, 200.

Vespucius, Americus, later voyages; second with Alonso de Ojeda, 71, 79; result, 201; third voyage, course, 81–83; importance, 82; legend on Ruysch map, 215; fourth voyage, 83.

Vespucius, Anastasio, father of Americus, 61.

Vespucius, Antonio, brother of Americus, 63.

Vespucius, Georgius Antonius, uncle of Americus, edited Plato, 13; a Dominican friar, 61; teacher of Americus, 88.

Vespucius, Jerome, brother of Americus, 63.

Vienna Imperial Library, Stobnicza's Ptolemy in, 227.

Villages built on the water, 75, 100–101.

Vosgian Gymnase, students suggest name America, 15, 72, 82; famous members, 116; coterie of three, 117–118; publication of Ptolemy intended, 126, 129; dedication of "Cosmographiæ Introductio," 140–141.

Vosgian Mountains, called baptismal font of America, 115; printing-press, 119.

Voyages: of Cabot, first, 70, 200; second, 200–201; of Cabral, 201; of Columbus, first, 24–30, 41–55, 199, 200; second, 200; third, 201; of Diego de Lepe, 201; of Pinzon, 201; of Ponce de Leon, 24, 225; of Vespucius, first, 65, 69, 70–78, 85–111, 200; second, 71, 79, 201; third, 81–83, 215; fourth, 83.

Walckenaer, Baron, map of La Cosa owned by, 24; first map of New World owned by, 196.

Waldseemüller, Conrad, father of Martin, 118.

Waldseemüller, Martin, at St. Dié, 116; account of his life, 118; relations with Vosgian Gymnase, 125, 133, 138, 140, 151; his "Architecturæ ... Rudimenta," 132–133; letter to Amerbach, 127–128; letter to Ringmann, 133; letter from Ringmann, 154, 155; publication of "Cosmographiæ Introductio," 125; translation of dedication of "Cosmographiæ Introductio," 138–139; publication of Ptolemy intended, 127–128; edition of Ptolemy, *1513*, 229–238; constructed maps of Ptolemy, *1522*, 244; his map, Canibales located, 79; Gulf of Paria, 80; his map of Europe, 156; his lost map, 149–157; approximate reproduction of lost map, 232.

Watling, Captain George, island named for, 56.

Watling Island, the true Guanahani, 23, 26, 55, 56–58; area, 26, 56; distance from Gomera, 51; location, 56; name, 56; called the Garden of the Bahamas, 56; political existence, 58.

Wimpfeling, Jacques, instructor of Ringmann, 117.

Ximenes, Cardinal, Peter Martyr's "First Decade" dedicated to, 224.

Yaguna, identified with Little Inagua, 25; visited by Ponce de Leon, 25.

Yéméniz, Nicolas, purchased the "Cosmographiæ Introductio," 130.

Yuca, native food-word, 72–73, 99.

Yucatan, topography, 75.

Yumey, *see* Fernandina.

Zapeda, Padre, describes Indian huts in trees, 75.